Traitors

Chapman Pincher

TRAITORS
THE
ANATOMY
OF
TREASON

ST. MARTIN'S PRESS
NEW YORK

Library of Congress Cataloging-in-Publication Data

Pincher, Chapman.
Traitors.

1. Spies.   2. Espionage—History—20th century.
1. Title.
UB250.P56   1987   327.1′2   87-4378
ISBN 0-312-00696-9

First published in Great Britain by Sidgwick & Jackson Limited.

First U.S. Edition

10 9 8 7 6 5 4 3 2 1

To Billee – for unswerving loyalty

Contents

Introduction

Treason is loved of many, but the traitor is hated of all.

Robert Greene

In 1986 an American traitor, John Walker, was sentenced to spend the rest of his life in jail for running a Soviet spy ring which had supplied the Kremlin with US naval secrets over a period of seventeen years. His brother, Arthur, received an even more massive sentence, while John's 22-year-old son Michael was jailed for twenty-five years. The fourth member of the ring, a friend called Jerry Whitworth, was given the heaviest sentence of all.

The confessions of all four men showed that their sentences were well merited. Between them the traitors had supplied secrets literally by the sackful; in return for large amounts of cash they had dropped documents in bags for Soviet intelligence officers posing as diplomats to pick up. The secrets included information about American and NATO defences against submarine attack, and provided continuing information about the codes used by US warships. Had there been a war during the time that the Walker ring was active, the US Navy would almost certainly have suffered heavy losses in life and ships. If peace continues, the cost of repairing the damage caused by this treachery will still be enormous; and some of it may be impossible to rectify.

The Walker ring case shattered the complacency of Congress and the American public, who had tended to regard treachery in peacetime as largely a British and European phenomenon. In his testimony, Walker revealed that he had simply gone into the Soviet Embassy in Washington by the front door and offered to sell top-secret codes. Most Americans believed that the embassy was under constant surveillance. But if it was, no effective notice had been taken of Walker.

There had been justifiable American pride in the absence of any proven traitors inside the Federal Bureau of Investigation (FBI) and the Central Intelligence Agency (CIA), while their British counterparts, the Security Service (MI5) and the Secret Intelligence Service (MI6), seemed to have been riddled with them. That myth was demolished in the 1980s, which bid fair to become known as the Decade of Deceivers.

In July 1986 Richard Miller, who had been an FBI agent for twenty years, was sentenced to two life-terms plus fifty years, and fined $60,000, such was the sensitivity of the secrets he sold to the KGB. Described as a 'bumbling Inspector Clouseau-like figure', he passed documents about the FBI's efforts to counter Soviet agents to Svetlana Ogorodnikova, a Soviet immigrant infiltrated by the KGB.

The injury inflicted by Edward Lee Howard, formerly of the CIA, was more disastrously in line with the treachery of British traitors like Kim Philby and George Blake, who both betrayed colleagues to their deaths. Howard, who had joined the CIA in 1981 aged twenty-eight, was being briefed for a field officer's post in Moscow, under the cover of being a junior diplomat, when he failed a final loyalty test involving the polygraph lie detector. The test revealed that he used drugs and had other personality defects making him unsuitable for any kind of CIA work.

Howard was fired in 1983. Out of resentment and in order to make money he decided to contact the KGB and tell what he knew, which included information about a Russian traitor based in Moscow who had been supplying the CIA with Soviet aviation secrets. The KGB quickly identified the traitor, one Adolf Tolkachev, an engineer in an aeronautics institute, and executed him. Other CIA activities involving certain valuable sources inside the Soviet Union were also nullified.

As the FBI moved to arrest Howard he escaped. He eventually surfaced in Moscow in September 1986, when he was pressed into appearing on Soviet television to support the false KGB claim that an American journalist, Nicholas Daniloff, who had been seized as a hostage, was a CIA agent.

These were by no means the only American traitors to come to light in the 1980s. There were others, catastrophically damaging in their way, as will be detailed later. Yet the British security chiefs had no cause for any smug satisfaction at their chief ally's discomfiture; for treachery continued in their own ranks and elsewhere in the British nation.

In 1984 an MI5 officer, Michael Bettaney, was jailed for passing secrets to the KGB and for attempting to pass many more. Two years earlier a much more damaging traitor had been discovered in the shape of Geoffrey Prime – a signals expert who had worked in GCHQ, the electronic interception agency which works in close collaboration with its American counterpart, sharing its secrets. The Pentagon estimate of the cost of the damage inflicted by Prime was $1,000 million.

These and other security disasters appeared to be countered to some extent by the defection to Britain in July 1985 of Oleg Gordievsky, then the head of the KGB mission in London. In a superb undercover operation he was spirited out of the Soviet Union, where he was on summer leave with his family, when it became apparent that the KGB was about to arrest him. With some panache and unusual luck, Gordievsky was smuggled to safety in a van fitted with a false compartment. He had to leave his family behind, however – the alternative being certain death.

The end of Gordievsky as a source of KGB secrets meant that information he had already supplied could be utilized without danger to him. Thirty-six Russians, previously confirmed by him as KGB officers, were expelled, and a list of British citizens known to Gordievsky as traitors or fringe traitors was updated for possible action. Some of these, who are still unnamed, managed to escape abroad, having been alerted by the KGB. Others remain, wondering whether action will be taken against them.

In Europe, and in West Germany in particular, treachery was just as rampant. In 1985 a senior West German counter-intelligence officer, Hans Joachim Tiedge, defected to East Germany. He had a domino effect on a score of other traitors and spies in various parts of the world: men and women who had been serving treacherously in different government and political posts fled to safety, some eastwards, some westwards, causing consternation and disbelief among those who had trusted them.

The 1980s also produced an unprecedented spate of new information from official sources about previous known traitors, both in Britain and America, showing that their treachery had been far more serious than had been publicly admitted. The sources, which included the dissident MI5 officer Peter Wright, whose attempt to publish his memoirs caused an international furore in 1986, also revealed the names of others who had secretly confessed to treason and some who remain highly suspect, including a former Director-General of MI5, Sir Roger Hollis. New evidence even suggests that Commander Lionel Crabb, the courageous frogman who disappeared while surreptitiously examining the hull of a Soviet cruiser visiting Portsmouth Harbour in 1956, may have been betrayed to his death by a traitor.

The official explanation of the Crabb episode put forward by officers of MI6 involved in it claimed that the frogman, who was forty-six and unfit, was accidentally drowned. But documents recently made available show that Sir Anthony Eden (later Lord Avon), who was Prime Minister at the time, believed that he had been killed by the

Russians. Eden, who had forbidden any intelligence operations against the warship because of the political risk, demanded a full investigation of the incident, and must have based his belief on the results, which are still secret.

Crabb had been warned that the Soviet warship the *Ordzonikidze* had a 'wet compartment' – an underwater chamber from which armed frogmen could emerge and hold on to jackstay wires while waiting for any intruder. Nevertheless, Crabb volunteered to measure the pitch of the screws and examine other external features. When the KGB defector Anatoly Golitsin was interrogated by the MI5 officer Peter Wright in 1963 he said that Soviet naval intelligence had known in advance about Crabb's mission, and that frogmen were probably waiting for him. He could have been accidentally drowned in a struggle, or murdered.

If Crabb was betrayed, who was the traitor? While advance knowledge of the operation was supposed to be limited to very few because of the Prime Minister's ban, which is fully confirmed in his personal papers, several people in the Security Service, MI5, knew about it, as did the MI6 team involved. One of them has recently told me how an MI5 officer, Malcolm Cumming, gleefully whispered on the night before the attempted espionage: 'Crabb is going under those ships tomorrow.' Cumming was completely cleared of suspicion of being a Soviet agent when he was investigated as a possible source of an MI5 leak to the KGB agent Kim Philby in 1963. The MI5 man who knew of the Crabb affair and was not cleared of the Philby leak was Roger Hollis, then the Deputy Director-General.

After Crabb's death the Russians exploited their claim, which may have been false, that they had seen a frogman swimming on the surface near their cruiser. Crabb's headless body was washed up months later and the Russians may have dumped it in the open sea when they left Portsmouth.

For the rest of his lifetime Eden was anxious to avoid any suggestion that the Russians had killed Crabb; Anglo-Soviet relations had already been soured by the affair. His belief that they had killed him was not revealed until 1986, when his official biography was published.[1]

This brief preliminary survey of recent events in the dark labyrinths of treason is proof enough that treachery is a growth industry with no shortage of traitors to commit it. In fact, with up-to-date intelligence at such a premium in the nuclear missile age and the ever-urgent Soviet requirement to acquire the West's technological secrets, there has never been treachery on such a scale in the world-wide context, even in wartime. The scope of espionage and the temptation has been expanded due to literally millions of people – in government departments, the armed forces, and the defence industries – now having access to valuable secrets. All major nations – the Soviets in particular – are making unremitting efforts to secure traitor agents among them. In Britain, and in parts of Europe, with the mushrooming of so many left-extremist organizations intent on revolution, there have never been so many potential subversives.

The few cases already mentioned are sufficient also to dispel the common misbelief that, since the advent of the 'spy-in-the-sky' satellite and advances in the interception of secret radio messages resulting from computer technology, the human spy on the ground, who is so often a traitor, has become obsolete. In fact, human spies have never been more necessary. For effective planning when preparations for a nuclear missile attack may not be visually discernible, for the exercise of political judgement in the choice of actions and especially for crisis management, it is essential to know the adversary's *intentions*; and these cannot be gauged from information gathered by robots, however sophisticated. It is the traitor inside the Kremlin, the White House, No. 10 Downing Street, or the various Foreign Offices who is most likely to deliver the crucial information about high-level policy decisions and plans.

Recently Gordievsky, the former 'mole' working inside the KGB for the West, gave invaluable advice, personally, to Margaret Thatcher and to President Reagan, prior to their meetings with Mikhail Gorbachov, providing reliable intelligence about the Soviet leader's true intentions and likely ploys.

Concurrent with the surge in treachery is a growing awareness among academic historians of the impact which traitors have exerted on the course of history.[2] There is now little doubt, for example, that the secret assurance that Japan would not attack the Soviet Union, given to Stalin by the Soviet agent Richard Sorge in 1941, changed the course of the Second World War by enabling Red Army reserves to be withdrawn from the East for the defence of Moscow. Stalin enjoyed a further huge advantage at the Yalta conference, which changed post-war history, in knowing from American and British traitors the bargaining positions of Roosevelt and Churchill and how far they could be pushed. The atomic weapons information supplied by the traitor-scientist Klaus Fuchs saved the Soviets valuable time in their bid to become a nuclear power.

Documentary proof of Soviet duplicity supplied by the Soviet defector Igor Gouzenko was a major factor in the rapid development of the 'cold war' and the Western realization of the Kremlin's global intentions.[3] The much more recent treachery of Geoffrey Prime and Christopher Boyce, an American traitor, greatly assisted the Soviet Union to secure an ascendancy in nuclear missiles, which has dominated super-power politics for the last decade.[4] The treachery of the

American Walker family in the very important field of anti-submarine warfare has tilted the balance further in the Soviet favour.

The growing seriousness attached to treachery is mirrored in the very heavy sentences now being imposed on traitors throughout the West. They are intended as a deterrent yet traitors continue to abound. When there is almost universal condemnation of traitors, why are so many still prepared to strike at their own countries and compatriots in the interests of alien powers, knowing that exposure would brand them and put them in prison or, in the Soviet bloc, probably commit them to execution?

If the motivations of traitors and what I call 'fringe traitors' – those who act within the law – could be more deeply understood, would it be possible to take more active counter-measures to thwart them? In seeking to analyse the motivations of traitors, their behaviour and what treachery does to them, which has not been attempted in such depth before, I could have taken the easy way out and limited this book to detailed studies of a few well-known examples, but that would have been too selective and would have contributed little, if anything, that is new. The motivational factors need to be isolated and dealt with separately, with the evidence speaking for itself, and for that a survey of the whole field up to the present time is necessary to see what can be extracted from the details in the way of generalities, and what lessons might be learned to prevent and counter treachery and subversion.

This has meant a daunting effort, but since I have been engaged in this area almost exclusively for the last eight years, with considerable previous experience and ongoing access to prime sources, which have continued to provide new material, it has not proved too onerous. The only limitation I have imposed on this study is on time-scale. Treachery has featured prominently in the human story down the recorded ages, during which human nature has changed little, but this book concentrates mainly on the last half-century and especially on the current situation.

Since most traitors are influenced by more than one motive, some repetition has proved necessary for the benefit of the general reader, so I make no apology for it. To assist those unfamiliar with some of the traitors mentioned brief biographical sketches are appended.

At this stage it can be said with certainty that the *MICE* concept – that traitors are motivated by *M*oney or *I*deology or *C*ompromise or *E*go – is too simplistic, the motivations of almost all of them being much more complex. Individual traitors may be affected by all four of these factors operating in various degrees. Many other factors have influenced traitors in the past, and there are some relatively new ones which merit consideration, such as the flouting of authority and disrespect for the law, which have arisen out of the 'permissiveness' encouraged in the 1960s by those who felt it to be 'progressive'. There is such general disrespect for the Official Secrets Acts, which authority never imagined would occur, that it has become almost impossible for governments to secure convictions for activities which most people would formerly have considered treacherous.[5] Permissiveness has also encouraged civil libertarians to try to undermine the authority and powers of the secret services and in Australia, for instance, they have had success, with the powers of the Security Intelligence Organization there being curbed in the trend.

Another current factor in Western societies may be the enhanced aura of uncertainty and insecurity, especially among the young, created by the disturbing pace of economic, social, and environmental change and exacerbated by nuclear fears. This could conceivably impel some to favour the regimented life of a totalitarian regime, as so many Germans were prepared to surrender hard-won freedoms to Nazism.

To avoid loose interpretation, it is necessary to establish a few definitions. *Treason* can generally be defined as an attempt to overturn the government established by law, including the activities connected with such an attempt, such as the assassination of leaders. In Britain, according to the Lord Chancellor, Lord Hailsham, levying any form of war against the Queen in her realm is treason and this includes terrorism, which will be dealt with separately in Chapter 19. The term *high treason* which in British law applies to those who surreptitiously assist an enemy in war, by spying, for example, would presumably be resuscitated in the eventuality of war and would certainly apply to those who gave any assistance to invading Soviet *Spetsnaz* – SAS-type – forces, as described in Chapter 18.

In 1964 the distinguished writer Rebecca West produced a book called *The New Meaning of Treason*; but the case records show that there is no new meaning. The several meanings, like the incidence of treason, are as old as man himself.[6]

Those consciously involved in treasonable acts are termed *traitors*, and in British law any conscious accessory to treason is also a traitor. Again according to Lord Hailsham, the miscreant does not have to be a British subject to be guilty of treason. 'Any alien within the Realm owes a local and temporary allegiance to the local sovereign so long as the alien is there.'[7] The same would seem to apply in republics, where allegiance is to the state or government of the day. A similar ruling has recently been applied in South Africa, for example, where it was held that a duty of allegiance extended to residents as well as citizens.

The force of treason as a legal concept was exemplified by the case of William Joyce ('Lord Haw Haw'), the Fascist who broadcast anti-British radio propaganda from Nazi Germany. He was an American citizen by birth who considered Ireland to be his motherland, and had properly acquired German citizenship in September 1940. Yet he was adjudged a traitor by a British court because, by virtue of having a valid British passport during part of the war, he owed local allegiance to Britain and had placed himself under the protection of the Crown. He was, in fact, hanged as a traitor as a result of a legal technicality.

In the Soviet Union a traitor was anybody accused of treason by Stalin or his associates, and thousands met their end, with or without trial, on that score. While the worst excesses there have been halted, any activity deemed to be against the interests of the State – which in practice means the Politburo – can be judged treasonable. Dissidents like Anatoly Shcharansky are imprisoned for 'treason', while traitors in the secret services are executed, usually with no public trial and little public announcement beyond a bare statement to discourage others. No country despises the traitor more or treats him more severely than the Soviet Union, and no country puts so much effort into inducing other nationals to become traitors on its behalf.

Curiously, while treason may be regarded by the offended country as perhaps the worst of all crimes, it is not subject to extradition, being regarded as a non-violent political offence, and therefore qualifying as a just reason for 'political asylum'. It is odd that a murderer who kills one person can be extradited, while a traitor who may have sent many to their death and in a nuclear age may threaten millions, is protected.

In the defence of traitors, and especially when they attempt to justify their behaviour, treason and treachery tend to be examined as moral issues – questions of right or wrong – rather than in the purely legal terms in which trials are usually conducted. This is also the attitude of ordinary people concerning some aspects of treachery such as attempts by well-meaning Germans to assassinate Hitler. Under German law they were certainly traitors and were treated as such but, in view of the millions of lives lost as a result of their failure and the enslavement of much of Eastern Europe, which might have been prevented had the war been ended earlier, it would seem that a majority would regard them as German patriots.

Historically, whether a person who commits legal treason is adjudged a traitor or not may rest on a majority view, the case of the Irishman Sir Roger Casement being what may be called, to borrow a biological term, the 'type specimen' of the genre. Before entangling himself with the Germans in the interests of Irish independence during the First World War, Casement had expressed his allegiance to Britain by accepting honours, like the CMG and a knighthood, having said in a letter, read out at his trial: 'I find it very hard to choose the words in which to make acknowledgement of the honour done to me by the King.'[8] He was executed as a traitor but is now regarded in Eire as a martyred patriot. At some stage most traitors have their supporters and, to some, are heroes.

Treason and treachery, then, are to some extent concepts in the mind of the beholder and there is much in the epigram of Sir John Harington: 'Treason doth never prosper, what's the reason? For if it prosper none dare call it Treason.'[9] It also follows that in the circumstances of a political revolution or a military defeat, many former patriots may suddenly be branded as traitors. In the event of a successful Communist revolution in Britain, for example, there can be little doubt that thousands of true patriots would be consigned to prison or worse as 'traitors to the working class'.

Treachery, which springs from the same word as *traitor* (Old French *trecheur*), is simply an act contributing to treason, while offences against the State regarded as falling short of treason are termed *sedition*. *Subversion* was redefined in 1984 by the then Home Secretary,[10] as 'activities which threaten the safety or well-being of the State and which are intended to undermine or overthrow Parliamentary democracy by political, industrial or violent means'. Clearly it is intended to include any undermining of the infrastructure of democracy and is not limited to criminal acts, because in a free society it is easy to inflict damage within the existing law. Politically motivated strikes and sit-ins may be as effective as explosives in wrecking a factory. The main purpose of widening the definition was to legitimize clandestine counter-measures against those planning or taking part in acts to destabilize the government by the means described. When such activities, usually claimed as 'legitimate dissent', are proved to be responses to the requirements of the Soviet Union or any other foreign power intent on promoting disorder, instability and chaos, then subversives qualify as traitors.

With the growing interest in the serious study of treachery and its emergence as a branch of history there may be need for a name for it. Greek is normally used as the source for the various -ologies, but no term of Greek origin comes trippingly off the tongue or seems likely to be adopted. I am indebted to Professor Peter Levi of Oxford for *catascopology*, from *kataskopos*, meaning a spy, but it is a clumsy word, and not all traitors are spies. Oddly, all the relevant terms in common use – treason, treachery, traitor, disloyalty, perfidy, deception, defection, sedition, subversion – derive from Latin. The best I can suggest, therefore, based on the root *tradere*, meaning to betray, is *traditics*.

Before proceeding to a detailed consideration of those inhabiting the labyrinths of treachery it is necessary first to examine the positive aspects of loyalty which has labyrinths of its own.

xvii

Traitors

CHAPTER ONE

The Concept of Loyalty

Loyalty is the holiest good in the human heart.

Seneca

Loyalty – constancy in a trust or obligation – can be so strong as to lead men and women to prefer death to the traitor's tag or so weak that it can be overwhelmed by a bribe, a threat or a sexual impulse. Lying at the root of treachery, it can be interpreted in many ways – and it is, in fact, easier to define disloyalty, as I learned when taking part in a radio discussion, where it became clear that the attitudes to the issue of some highly intelligent people are vague. Clearly, meaningful standards for loyalty, acceptable to the majority in a society, are essential in the uncertain circumstances in which most people live. In the real world the faithfulness has to apply to some tangible entity and not to woolly internationalist concepts like 'humanity' or 'mankind as a whole', as suggested by two of the participants in the radio discussion.[1] Just as there has to be the concept of evil for the concept of good to mean anything, there has to be some other entity, such as another country or society, to which the transfer of allegiance can result in disloyalty.

It seems to be agreed, except by the few genuine internationalists, that loyalty is owed to one's *country*, and this is universally required by law, *loyalty* being derived from the Latin for 'legal' (*legalis*). But what is meant by 'country', as expressed, for instance, by the recent American traitor, Christopher Boyce, in his vivid statement 'I fucked my country'?[2] A country, meaning a state, is a complex of the territory and the society it supports: the people and their institutions, including their system of government. Boyce's Freudian remark was a remorseful admission that he had betrayed the complex which had succoured and protected him and to which, legally and morally, he owed allegiance.

The legal and moral requirement of loyalty to country is linked with the concept of *patriotism*, love of one's country, which can be very powerful as a corporate force politically and militarily. Though many

1

of the left despise it, or affect to do so, patriotism – sheer devotion to the motherland – was at the root of the successful defence of the Soviet Union against the German onslaught in 1941, as it was at the root of that against Napoleon. Stalin was astute enough to realize that loyalty to the Communist Party and its leaders was unlikely to mobilize the necessary determination and will. So out went the pictures of Lenin, Marx, and Engels, and in came those of Peter the Great, Suvorov, Kutusov, and other Russian heroes. Since that war, which is now always referred to in the Soviet Union as the Great Patriotic War, loyalty to the Communist State, with which the party is synonymous, is officially the accepted loyalty in the USSR, any 'misalignment' with the goals of the state or party being regarded as disloyal and therefore punishable. Nevertheless, affinity to the motherland probably remains a stronger force, as was demonstrated by the reaction of the Soviet traitor Colonel Pyotr Popov when the CIA, for which he had been working, suggested that it was time for him to defect: 'I'm a Russian and it's my country, my land. I'll die a Russian, in Russia. I don't give a damn what they do to me.'[3] And die he did. As the American Eleanor Philby found when she joined her British traitor husband in the Soviet Union, loyalty means a great deal to most Russians.

The intensity of such feeling, which has been mirrored by others of many nationalities, demonstrates the shallowness of Bertrand Russell's definition of patriotism as 'the willingness to kill or be killed for trivial reasons', a remark as superficial as Dr Johnson's 'patriotism is the last refuge of the scoundrel'. Britain's spirited and lonely stand in 1940 and the Germans' fanatical defence of their country against the Red Army's onslaught owed much to patriotism. Hitler capitalized on the innate strength of German nationalism, and those who were not pro-Nazi fought tenaciously on the principle of 'my country right or wrong'; this latter concept has become untenable among the so-called intelligentsia, who are prepared to subordinate their national loyalty to the greater cause of internationalism. In May 1964, for example, the American politician Dean Rusk declared national sovereignty to be outmoded while Walt Rostow, National Security Advisor to President Johnson, called for 'an end of nationhood'.[4] Left-wing extremists now tend to regard patriotism almost as a form of racism. The British novelist Graham Greene, for instance, in a brief apologia for the treachery of his friend Harold (Kim) Philby, published in 1968, asked: 'Who among us has not committed treason to something or someone more important than a country?'[5] Greene was a wartime member of MI6, and if such a view was common there it is not surprising that Philby and others in it behaved as they did. Happily, there are still civilian Britons prepared to put their freedom and even their lives at risk for patriotic motives in peacetime, as Greville Wynne did in his abortive attempt to bring out the Soviet traitor Colonel Penkovsky.

Those making legitimate complaint against their own country are not necessarily unpatriotic – 'We do not accuse Isaiah of being unpatriotic because he thunders against Israel'[6] – but the left-wing contempt for patriotism happens to be in line with the Soviets' requirements of killing national pride in every country except their own, so that they can 'realign' the loyalties of people in countries targeted for subversion or takeover – what they call 'the non-armed conquest of an enemy'.[7]

While patriotism is in some disrepute in Britain, as demonstrated by the attitude towards it of the media, and especially TV, there has been a *pro patria* surge in the USA which seems to have originated during the Los Angeles Olympic Games, has been fostered by the Reagan administration and has uplifted the spirit of the nation, especially among the young.

Examination of the meaning of loyalty to country shows that among many, perhaps most, there is deep attachment to the actual territory as expressed by Walter Scott: 'Breathes there the man, with soul so dead, Who never to himself hath said, This is my own, my native land!'[8] This is shown by the longings of expatriates and the need for some of them, even the British traitor Guy Burgess who took refuge in Stalin's Russia, to be buried or to have their ashes scattered in their motherland. Visiting friends had reported Burgess's attitude to Britain as being 'very patriotic', and the request in his will that his ashes be scattered in an English garden was duly observed by his brother.[9] Among the highly nationalistic pavilions in the Florida Disneyland, where various countries have choice about how best to project themselves to an international audience, those of Communist China, France, and Canada proudly concentrate, with great effect, on the splendours of their respective territories rather than on their culture or peoples. Loyalty to territory regularly extends to a county or state, and deep feelings may be aroused when boundaries are changed. The common loyalty to home towns is a world-wide phenomenon.

Implicit in loyalty to territory is loyalty to compatriots, the others who inhabit it, and this displays itself most obviously during war when common danger makes people more aware of the significance and value of kinship and nationhood. In many countries loyalty to a tribe may be more pressing than loyalty to a nation. A kind of tribal loyalty exists in the United Kingdom, because of its origin from the once separate countries of England, Scotland, Wales and Northern Ireland, and has, on occasion, been responsible for acts of treachery. Arthur George Owens, for instance, was a rabid Welsh nationalist who hated the English and, while ostensibly working for Britain through MI5 before and during the Second World War, consistently betrayed British

3

secrets to the German Secret Service, the Abwehr, as captured German documents have proved.[10] The Irishman Sir Roger Casement is an earlier example from the time when the whole of Ireland was subservient to Britain. According to the German diplomat Franz von Papen who met him in New York in the first weeks of the First World War, Casement was 'fanatically opposed to everything English and was prepared to consider every means to attain Ireland's independence'.[11] Casement believed that a German victory over Britain was the most direct method and went to Berlin to discuss his possible assistance through acts of sabotage, finally landing back in Ireland from a German U-boat at Easter 1916, when he was arrested for treason. It is understandable that the Irish should now consider him a fearless and honest patriot, as von Papen did, but it is equally understandable why, when Britain had its back to the wall, he was hanged as a traitor in war.

The post-war partition of Germany into the true democracy of West Germany, a willing NATO ally, and the pseudo-democracy of East Germany, an enforced satellite of the Soviet Union, created an ambivalent situation as regards loyalty to both territory and compatriots for the German people. Because of their cultural history and linguistic identity, and the sad fact that many Germans have relatives and friends on both sides of the East–West border, feeling in favour of reunifying the two territories one day is strong in both. Successive West German governments have raised no barriers to the movement of East Germans into their territory and huge numbers have emigrated there, mostly as refugees from the Communist regime. Inevitably this situation has been continuously exploited by Soviet-bloc intelligence to insert spies and subversive agents into West Germany and its administration, as will be described later. It is significant that when these East Germans are caught they are often prepared to be 'turned' and work for West Germany with less personal conflict of loyalty than might beset someone from another country.

Zionist Jews in the diaspora experience a dual loyalty to territory now that a homeland exists, and this can lead to conflict, as shown by the recent case of Jonathan Pollard, an American Jewish naval counter-intelligence analyst who spied for Israel. He was recruited to the service of an offshoot of Israeli intelligence while on a kibbutz in Israel and was arrested in the autumn of 1985 when two Israeli 'diplomats', listed as scientific attachés, hurriedly returned home. As with most cases of treachery, other factors were involved. Pollard had a grievance against his American employers and the Israelis had planned to deposit $300,000 in a Swiss bank for his services.

Historically there have been many examples of intelligent people, and their less thinking followers, who placed loyalty to an individual, usually a monarch, above loyalty to territory, often following a deposed or banished leader into exile, though usually with the hope of eventual return. There are few areas left where loyalty to a monarch presents a choice. The United Kingdom is one of them, and it is doubtful that many would follow the Royal Family into exile if it were deposed by an extreme left-wing government, though many might leave for other reasons. Nevertheless, consciously committed loyalty to the monarch, who is also titular Commander-in-Chief of the nation's armed forces, remains a powerful if dwindling factor. In the First World War men fought for 'King and Country', and recruiting posters made much of this inducement. Patriotic loyalty to the individual monarch surfaced only to a slight extent in the constitutional crisis over the abdication of Edward VIII – somewhat to the surprise of the politicians – but then the monarchy as such was not a risk. Loyalty to the monarch was played down in the Second World War but was still a factor for many soldiers, as my own Army experience showed me, and I suspect that it could be again because no monarch has been held in greater genuine esteem than the present Queen. While Presidents, including those of the United States, who are also Commanders-in-Chief of their forces, may be held in high regard, they suffer from the disadvantage of belonging to a political faction and are therefore opposed by a large section of the nation, though this tends to be of less consequence in war.

In almost all countries today the prime loyalty required of their citizens is to the existing *political system*, rather than to any individual. Only a small minority in this century, in either the UK or USA, would disclaim loyalty to true democracy and the freedoms which it has provided, a true democracy being a system in which any government can be rejected at a general election by secret ballot, as compared to the pseudo-democracies, like those of the Soviet bloc, where this can never happen. The Second World War was fought to preserve it by all the Allies save the Soviet Union. It is now probably the most important loyalty in realistic terms, as was implicit in the Government's recent redefinition of subversion which laid special stress on the undermining of parliamentary democracy by the anti-democratic minority.

In war it would be considered disloyal or even treasonable for a person to try to undermine the interests of a close ally when that activity might increase the chances of defeat by a common enemy. Any Britons who had behaved treacherously to Commonwealth countries such as Canada, Australia, and even India, when they were assisting in the joint struggle for survival against Germany and Japan, would almost certainly have been considered traitorous. The same could have applied to any Britons who sought to weaken the American effort

5

once the USA had entered the war. Such strictures do not apply in cold war, though traitors to NATO – of whom several have been convicted of spying for the Soviet Union, like the Frenchman Georges Pâques and the Canadian Hugh Hambleton – are regarded as traitors to all members of the alliance. They inflicted great damage but that was minute compared with the devastation to NATO which would happen if the USA was forced out of the alliance. Could the many thousands of activists and agents of influence who are trying to secure this by promoting anti-Americanism, by almost any means, be rightly regarded as subversive? The answer would seem to depend on their private intentions and connections. If their purpose is to force the USA to withdraw from Europe to 'Fortress America' to improve the Soviet Union's chance of intimidating or defeating the remaining NATO countries, as it unquestionably would, then they could reasonably be regarded as treacherous. If, on the other hand, they wish to end the American connection for other political reasons and genuinely believe that Europe's freedom would not be at risk, then clearly no such stigma could apply, though there can be no doubt that the withdrawal of US forces would be greatly to Moscow's advantage. The situation, which many professional strategists regard as extremely frightening, illustrates the difficulties of defining loyalty.

In a true democracy there are many who might regard their prime loyalty as being to their political party, and when circumstances force a change of party loyalty it is usually a deeply traumatic experience for them. Some Britons remained loyal to the Fascist cause, led by Sir Oswald Mosley, even when the German and Italian Fascists were Britain's mortal enemies. But the party demanding and receiving the most fervent loyalty has been the Communist Party, which is the only one pervading all aspects of its members' lives. Until relatively recently loyalty to the Communist Party in any country has been unique in that it also demanded loyalty to the Communist Party of another country – the Soviet Union, where the 'state' is no more than a collection of the instruments by which the party, with a membership representing no more than 10 per cent of the people, maintains itself in power. British Communists, for example, convinced themselves, as some still do, that by assisting Russia 'with all the means at their disposal and at any price' they were working for a better Britain.[12] In the early stages of the Second World War, when Stalin was still tied to Hitler by the Nazi–Soviet Pact, this assistance consciously extended to working for Britain's defeat by the Germans, by exploiting industrial disputes and every kind of grievance and by spreading disaffection in the armed forces.[13] This was treachery by any standard, but the cult of the Party was so cunningly developed that it was the fount of all truth; it could never be wrong, and to question it savoured of sacrilege.

6

Even when its rulings proved catastrophic they were still judged 'correct'. A German Communist, Richard Krebs, wrote in his memoirs: 'When a man belonged to the Party he really belonged to it. Body and spirit without reserve. . . . We loved our Party and we were proud of its power, proud of our own serfdom because we had given it all our youth, all our hopes, all the enthusiasm and selflessness which we had once possessed.'[14] The British Soviet agent Alexander Foote wrote: 'The loyalty of a Party member lies primarily with the Party and secondarily with his country. It is impossible to have a better recruit for espionage.'[15]

Even though Communism is as much a religion as a political creed, it is an extraordinary commentary on human behaviour that Communists can remain loyal to a system which, in all countries where it is established, and in the Soviet Union in particular, uses repressive police, military forces, and a punitive legal system to wage perpetual war against its own people. The fanaticism of their loyalty was demonstrated by Maria Poliakova, the highly intelligent Russian Jewess who headed the GRU intelligence network in Switzerland in 1936 and 1937 before being promoted to an important desk post in Moscow. She remained devoted to the Communist Party although her brother, father and husband were all executed in Communist purges.[16] As one of her GRU superiors, Ismail Akhmedov, sat at his new desk she told him: 'Comrade, in their own time other chiefs of this division have sat behind this desk, plotting many operations, working day and night for the glory of our Party and country. They were all shot or sent to concentration camps. That was their reward. I sincerely hope that you will not share their unhappy fate.'[17] Among Americans, the journalist Agnes Smedley was described by a colleague as 'completely dedicated to the Communist cause and intolerant of all others'. The Englishman Ormond Uren who was recruited to Soviet espionage by the traitor Douglas Springhall explained: 'I wanted to show Springhall that I had complete faith in him and that he could have complete trust in me as a sincere believer in Communism.'

For the truly committed Communist, loyalty to the party must override all other loyalties; the worst kind of traitor is a traitor to the party. Whittaker Chambers, the American journalist and Communist agent, who quit the party in disgust, was so conditioned by his former loyalty, and so afraid of physical retribution, that it was ten years before he decided to make a public confession. Elizabeth Bentley, another American who left the party, disillusioned, in 1945, also suffered withdrawal symptoms; it was almost a year before she felt she could report to the FBI.

Communists seem to have been appalled when they were instructed to give up their membership and to cease to consort with other party members in order to engage in undercover subversion. The German GRU agent Ursula Beurton, better known as 'Sonia', has recorded how she felt completely lost outside the party and broke the conspiratorial rules by meeting other Communists in Britain.[18] When Tom Driberg, the future chairman of the Labour Party, was expelled from the Communist Party after his work against it for MI5 had been betrayed to the Russians, he was shattered when another Fleet Street comrade conveyed the news to him.[19]

It has been argued that there was some 'climate of treason' in the 1930s which induced undergraduates at Cambridge University to become spies for the Soviet Union, but the real reason they became spies was through unflinching loyalty to the Communist Party. The political climate alienated many young people at various universities against their *government* but only a few against their *country*. The case records show that those few who became traitors were already Communists and did so for the party and the Communist cause world-wide. When publicly exposed in 1979, Anthony Blunt, the art expert who had worked inside MI5 during the war, tried to excuse his espionage for the Soviet Union by claiming that his friend Guy Burgess had persuaded him to serve the cause of anti-Fascism by joining him in his work for the Russians. 'This was a case of political conscience against loyalty to country: I chose conscience,' he said. In fact, at the time of his recruitment, Blunt, who was no fool, was twenty-nine, and his statement meant that he had carefully weighed up the rights and wrongs of the conflicting interests and had deliberately chosen to undermine his own country's security to the advantage of a repressive regime personally controlled by Stalin, the most ruthless and absolute dictator in history. After entering MI5 in 1940, this Englishman who cared so much about conscience, was able to inflict massive damage on his country which was in peril of invasion by Stalin's ally, the other vicious dictator, Adolf Hitler. According to those who interrogated Blunt, there is no evidence that his conscience was pricked at all by the Soviet supplies of petrol, grain, and other strategic materials which enabled the Germans to bomb London, overrun Poland, France and the Low Countries, and round up countless more Jews for concentration camps.

There is, of course, no organization comparable to the foreign Communist parties which can be exploited in Western interests behind the Iron Curtain. So the permitted existence of Communist parties in the true democracies gives the Soviet bloc a huge advantage in its 'struggle' to subvert them.

A member of any political party who uses his membership to spy on his party and report to its opponents is surely a traitor to that party, even though there may be nothing illegal about his activities.

The type specimen here is Arthur Bax, who had been head of the Labour Party's press department for sixteen years when a defector revealed to MI5 that he was receiving regular payments from the Czech Embassy. Surveillance showed him to be visiting a dead letter box which was serviced by a Czech intelligence officer while examination of his bank account proved the payments. Bax was supplying information mainly about Labour Party policy and personalities, but had he still been in control when Labour achieved office three years later he could have been in touch with much more sensitive material. The manner of his confession is described in Chapter 24. To avoid political embarrassment to the Labour Party he was allowed to resign on grounds of ill health.[20]

Tom Driberg was a spy inside the Labour Party and took particular pleasure in lending his flat to colleagues, some of them Labour MPs, for the entertainment of lady friends and then reporting the details to both MI5 and the KGB. Within the Conservative Party the most similar known example was the Tory MP Henry Kerby, who regularly supplied the Labour leader Harold Wilson with inside information, some of it censorious, about Tory affairs and personalities. His motive seems to have been the hope of a peerage or knighthood from a Wilson government plus resentment at getting no such honour from his own side.[21] This might be considered a relatively innocuous degree of treachery, but Kerby's colleagues did not think so when his activities were exposed.

Lord Mayhew has told me how in 1961, when he was a Labour MP in opposition, MI5 endeavoured to recruit him, having induced him to a meeting on a subterfuge. They were disarmingly honest in asking him to spy for them on his Parliamentary colleagues and their policies. He declined, but there is reason to believe that others have accepted and that all the parliamentary parties are currently penetrated by MI5.

Conflict between loyalty to party and country is a constant situation with Communists but it can occur, on occasion, in other parties. An example in which I had personal involvement followed the arrest in 1961 of George Blake, the KGB spy inside MI6, the secret intelligence service responsible for espionage operations abroad, as I have related in detail elsewhere.[22] Briefly what happened was that the Labour Party leadership, headed by Hugh Gaitskell, persisted in demanding more information about Blake's treachery through Parliament. The reigning Prime Minister, Harold Macmillan, who was anxious to preserve as much of the secrecy of the case as possible, offered to give the facts, in strict confidence, to three Privy Councillors, one of whom was the late Lord George Brown. Like the others, Brown was bound by his Privy Councillor's oath, which was then supposed to be proof

9

against possible leakage but, with minimal delay, he gave all the information to me for publication. Brown's explanation to me was that his loyalty to his party, which stood to gain from discrediting the Macmillan administration by exposure of the Blake débâcle, overrode any loyalty to his country required by the circumstances and his Privy Councillor's oath. He tried to justify his action by claiming that Macmillan's offer had been an attempted cover-up, which it had been – but, having accepted it, his disloyalty was indisputable. His hunger for personal power also contributed to his action.

Associated with loyalty to political party, especially in Britain, is loyalty to a trade union as manifested by the coal-miners' strike of 1984–5 when, in the interests of 'solidarity', implying mutual loyalty and loyalty to the union leadership, many thousands of miners suffered great personal hardship and loss with no ultimate benefit whatever. Those who were judged disloyal and worked were castigated as 'scabs' – vocational traitors.

The loyalty to a profession, which, especially in the case of science, can conflict with loyalty to country is dealt with in Chapters 13 and 14. Suffice it to mention here the disturbing new conflict of loyalties demonstrated by the cases of two British civil servants, Sarah Tisdall and Clive Ponting, who leaked information surreptitiously, claiming that loyalty to Parliament or to their interpretation of the public good should override loyalty to their employer or to any individual minister. Their behaviour had been preceded in the USA by the case of Daniel Ellsberg, a government employee in the Defense Department, who leaked the so-called Pentagon Papers to the *New York Times* as a protest against continuation of the Vietnam War.[23] Ellsberg's behaviour contrasted sharply with that of another American, Otto Otepka, who was executive head of the loyalty programme in the State Department. When under pressure from the highest political levels to clear individuals whom he believed to be untrustworthy he put his department and his country above all else. This included his personal career, the ensuing hounding of Otepka for failing to yield to the pressure being shameful in the extreme.[24]

In the past, loyalty to a religion has been a powerful factor in the history of nations and has often been a cause of treason. But in most countries of the Western world it does not figure in the current equation of treachery. Northern Ireland offers an exception, but the religious factor there is more a pawn exploited by political extremists than a force in its own right. In the Islamic world, however, burning loyalty to religion is a burgeoning force which has already had serious impact on the West.

Whether it is felt that prime loyalty should be to territory, leaders, system of government or anything else, the conflicts which it can generate have been forcefully expressed by the behaviour of some exiles in the countries which have given them refuge. Acting under various pressures, some self-generated, they have often been treacherous and returned a country's hospitality by exploiting its freedoms in the interest of its enemy. A straightforward case, and one which arouses some sympathy for the miscreant, is that of Julius Silber, who had been born in Germany but lived almost all his adult life abroad, in South Africa and India, before finally emigrating to the USA. In 1914 deep fatherland feelings for Germany, of which he had hardly been aware, generated bitter hostility to Britain, and he decided to go there to do what he could to supply Germany with intelligence, though he had never had any training as a spy. On his own initiative he contacted the German Embassy in Washington, receiving an address in New York to which he could safely send information so long as the USA remained neutral. He managed to enter the British postal censorship service without proper background inquiries which would have revealed his German nationality, and worked in London and Liverpool throughout the war, using great ingenuity to photograph revealing documents and to post his material to New York and also directly to Germany. After moving surreptitiously to Germany in 1925 he published memoirs showing the extent to which valuable intelligence had come his way and how he had been able to get some of it to the fatherland.[25] As a later biographer has confirmed, his motives appear to have been entirely patriotic towards the country of his birth and he received no monetary reward.[26] Had he been caught he would assuredly have been executed for treason.

Just as Silber insinuated himself into Britain for treacherous purposes, so did the professional Soviet agent Ursula Beurton, known by her code-name 'Sonia', who had been born in Germany as Ursula Kuczynski. She was the daughter of a Communist Jewish economist who eventually took political refuge in Britain, working at the London School of Economics. After operating as a spy in Switzerland, she secured British nationality by marrying one of her fellow spies, an Englishman called Len Beurton, and entered Britain in 1941 on a successful espionage mission which lasted nine years. In her memoirs published in East Germany, to which she defected in 1950, 'Sonia' records with much delight some of the lesser ways in which she exploited the freedoms provided by her British nationality which, of course, required her allegiance, and in a recent interview on Soviet television she has admitted being aware that she faced death had she been caught, implying that she knew that, in legal terms, she was a traitor.[27] She remains silent on her major successes – her work as a courier and radio operator for Klaus Fuchs, the atomic spy, and for a major Soviet agent inside MI5.[28]

11

'Sonia' clearly felt no loyalty towards the country which gave her and her family, as Jews, safety from Hitler. Her total loyalty was to the political system of the Soviet Union, which she wanted imposed on the whole of Germany, if possible. The same applied to her distinguished brother, Jurgen Kuczynski, who also accepted British hospitality and repaid it with base treachery, recruiting Fuchs, a fellow German who, though naturalized British in 1941, felt no loyalty to his adopted country. Sonia's British-born husband, Len, who assisted her and defected with her, was a traitor to his country by any standard.

Flora Solomon, a Russian Jewish immigrant to Britain who enjoyed a long and highly successful career with a chain-store group, expressed her loyalty in a highly selective way. She knew that her friend Philby was a Soviet agent but told nobody, allowing him to continue to damage her adopted country, until he attacked Israel in his newspaper articles. Then, in a fit of fury, she denounced him.[29]

European Communists also took refuge in the USA and repaid their debt in similar fashion. The Austrian KGB agent, Hede Massing, a former actress, has recorded her treachery, with apparent regret, and that of her husband Paul; both recruited American traitors to the Soviet cause.[30] Many of the American citizens who betrayed their country by spying for the Soviet Union either were of direct Russian origin or were born of formerly Russian parents. Jacob Golos, for instance, the KGB agent who ran the American-born spy, Elizabeth Bentley, had been born and reared in Russia. Though a naturalized American, he put his allegiance to his native country first. The same applied to two Soviet spies in Canada, Sam Carr and Fred Rose, who had both been born in pre-revolutionary Russia, Carr having graduated from the Lenin School in Moscow. Victor Norris Hamilton, an American traitor who defected to Russia from the National Security Agency in 1959, was of Arab origin, being born Hindali. Because of his fluent Arabic he was employed in the section dealing with intercepts from Arab countries but was required to leave because of mental instability. His response was to appear in Moscow, where he made damaging statements in *Izvestia* and presumably told all he knew.[31] Larry Wu-tai Chin, a CIA translator convicted of conspiracy and espionage in 1986, had been born in Peking, to which he passed many stolen documents.

More examples of the conflicts of loyalty which exiles face will be given in later chapters. Enough evidence has been provided to show that many lack any basic feeling of loyalty to their new country and continue to remain attached, emotionally and sometimes politically, to their country of origin.

Though all countries attach great importance to allegiance and have strict requirements for loyalty in all major aspects, the true democracies – though not the Communist pseudo-democracies – also accept that, save in time of war, a person may legally switch his or her allegiance by emigrating to another country and taking up nationality there. Outside the Communist world this facility is regarded as a human right, and its widespread use has been essential in the growth of nations like the American, Canadian, and Australian.

The acquisition of a new nationality usually involves an oath of loyalty to the new country. This raises an intriguing conflict for those who have previously worked in secret organizations and carry valuable information in their memories. Such a person may remain bound to silence by contract and by oath of secrecy, but when he acquires a new nationality he may regard his former legal responsibilities as no longer binding. Does he therefore have the right, or even perhaps the duty, to help his new country by imparting any secrets of special interest to it or assisting its defence in other ways? The legal niceties of such a situation were demonstrated, rather sensationally, by the case of Norman Baillie-Stewart, a former British Army officer who had served a five-year sentence for spying for the Germans. He went to Germany, via Belgium and Austria, and applied for naturalization, this being granted in 1940. He then assisted the war effort of his new country against Britain by broadcasting propaganda aimed mainly at British troops, preceding William Joyce in that capacity. Like Joyce, he was charged after the war with high treason on the flimsy fact that his voice had been recognized in broadcasts made in 1939, before his German naturalization had been granted. When he pleaded that the naturalization had been held up only by slow German legal procedures, the prosecution wisely dropped the treason charge and he was sentenced to five years' jail on a lesser charge under British Defence Regulations. He later took legal action on two occasions to prove that he had not been found guilty of treason and, so far as his war service was concerned, he was not a traitor.

What would Philby's position have been if he had announced, in Beirut in 1963, that he intended to renounce his British citizenship and emigrate to the Soviet Union? Once he had been granted Soviet citizenship might he not have regarded it as his duty to his new country to make all his information available to its government? Something similar happened in 1956 to Anthony Wraight, a 22-year-old RAF flying officer who had been questioned about his suspicious relationship with a GRU man working under cover at the Soviet Embassy in London. Quite openly he flew to Berlin, took the underground there to the Eastern sector and after making a pro-Communist broadcast was flown to Moscow. There, as a defector who had switched his loyalty, he provided secret information about aircraft, weapons, navi-

13

gational aids, contingency mobilization plans and American bases in Britain.

In Philby's case his previous treachery had already made him a traitor to his motherland, but if some other MI6 man, who had told the Russians nothing until he openly emigrated to the USSR, renounced his British citizenship and was granted Soviet citizenship, could the word *traitor* legitimately be applied if he then told all? Though his old colleagues would consider him a traitor he could not legally be prevented from emigrating to the USSR in peacetime. It is the surreptitious nature of most defections and the intention of defectors to tell what they know against the interest of their motherland which makes them traitors.

CHAPTER TWO

The Minor Loyalties

The loyalty well held to fools does make our faith mere folly.
Shakespeare, *Antony and Cleopatra*

In addition to the major loyalties to territory, leaders, and political systems, there are lesser and more localized loyalties which, in certain circumstances, can outweigh all others. In Britain one of the strongest of these is loyalty to class. Class feeling has always been strong there and people still tend to identify as either upper, middle, or working class, the latter referring essentially to manual workers. Douglas Hyde, the former British Communist, put the feeling succinctly when he wrote: 'God, for me, had to be in a workman's jacket, not in a boiled shirt and tails.'[1] Highly political leaders, like Arthur Scargill of the National Union of Mineworkers, concentrate on drumming up class loyalty to their objectives, claiming that there are only two classes – the working class and the ruling class – and that any worker who is not in revolt against the latter is a traitor to his class. The Soviet leader Nikita Khrushchev is reported as having said of Hugh Gaitskell, the Labour Party leader who was not left enough for his taste: 'If Communism were to triumph in Britain tomorrow, Gaitskell would be the first to be shot outside the Houses of Parliament, as a traitor to the working class.'[2] It is the current attitude of the many British 'Militants' that if Labour politicians are not of the 'hard left' they, too, are traitors to the working class.

Michael Bettaney, the MI5 officer who switched his allegiance to the KGB in 1983, expressed a strong dislike for the 'upper classes', particularly undergraduates who hailed from public schools. This sense of working-class origin and resentment of lack of privilege may also have been involved in the motives which made some other British intelligence officers become traitors, like John Cairncross and Leo Long, whose cases will be considered later. The late Lord Wigg, a Labour minister who exaggerated the effects of the class system in my opinion, believed that the treachery of many others derived from the class system, which causes deep resentments. When the KGB agent and overt Communist James Klugmann died in 1977 his obituary in *The Times* recorded that 'his commitment was to the international working-class movement and the Communist Party'.

Klugmann and most of the other Cambridge spies who came from reasonably well-to-do homes have been referred to as 'class traitors', as have many terrorists who hailed from prosperous families, the suggestion being that they betrayed their class as a revulsion against it. Alexander Orlov, a Soviet diplomat who defected in 1938, recorded that the Soviet recruiters directed their appeal 'to young men who were tired of a tedious life in the stifling atmosphere of their privileged class'. During the economic depression of the 1930s some sensitive souls who remained privileged may have experienced guilt feelings, but it seems more likely that the class aspect of their treachery derived mainly from the fact that the KGB and GRU talent-spotters were looking for undergraduates likely to achieve important positions and that they would be found among those who had come from the better-known public schools. John Cairncross, a Cambridge KGB recruit from a more modest home, eventually told MI5 that his Soviet controller was concerned because, not having been to a public school, he had a strong Scottish accent which could be a handicap in his Foreign Office career. Snobbery was still an important career factor in Britain and some of the 'class traitors', like Blunt, who affected to embrace the alleged classlessness of Communism remained snobs.[3] What is perhaps more certain is that social snobbery at Cambridge and elsewhere generated resentful inferiority feelings among some of those from less privileged backgrounds, the first known Cambridge recruit to Comintern espionage, Philip Spratt, having sought solace from isolation by joining the Communist Party in the early 1920s.[4]

The treachery of upper-middle-class people like Klugmann, Philby, Donald Maclean, of the Foreign Office, and Sir Anthony Blunt, who had a Royal appointment, caused great disbelief when it was exposed. The reaction to the evidence of treachery against Sir Roger Hollis, the former Director-General of MI5, who was the son of a bishop, was typical: 'He was an English gentleman: he could not possibly be a spy' – the implication being that he could have been a traitor neither to his class nor to his country. The former FBI officer Robert Lamphere, who had to deal with the American end of much of this treachery, was correct when he wrote that the lack of any sense of outrage in Britain at the behaviour of the ring of spies recruited at Cambridge University was related to 'the inability of the British upper classes to believe ill of one of their own'.[5] Incidentally, when I was young there would have been equal resentment among the working class that one of theirs would stoop to treachery against their country.

Class feeling is supposed hardly to exist in the USA but, referring to what he called 'the American middle class', the self-confessed traitor Whittaker Chambers wrote of Marxism–Leninism that the very vigour of the project appealed to 'the more or less sheltered middle-class intellectuals' who felt that the context of their lives had kept them away from the world of reality.[6] When efforts were being made to recruit the young American Harry Gold, the son of a manual worker who became a courier for Fuchs, he was assured by a Communist that 'the only country to which the working man owed allegiance was the Soviet Union'.[7] The wealth of the American Michael Straight, who was briefly recruited to the Soviet cause at Cambridge, seems to have been a factor in turning him to Communism as a counter to his exceptional privilege.[8]

A loyalty which might be expected, on occasion, to be the strongest of all is loyalty to family, the tie implied in the statement that blood is thicker than water. The effect of such a tie in the field of treachery was highlighted recently by the exhumation in Holland of Christiaan Lindemanns, a Dutch member of the resistance movement against the Germans run by the British Special Operations Executive (SOE) during the Second World War. A man so huge and brave that he was nicknamed 'King Kong', Lindemans switched sides to save the life of his brother, who had been captured by the Gestapo. In the process he betrayed more than 200 resistance workers, many to their death. On the other hand, when the Comintern agent Gerhart Eisler was on trial in the USA in 1947, and claimed that he was not even a Communist, both his sister and his former wife testified to his long history as a Communist and Comintern man.

There must have been many wives who, on becoming aware that their husbands were traitors, have had to make a choice between family loyalty and national loyalty. One such recently was the wife of John Walker, the leader of the US Navy ring already described. During his trial in 1986, Mrs Barbara Walker told the court that she had almost contacted the FBI on four previous occasions but was worried about her children's welfare. When she finally exposed her husband, after they had parted, she learned that he had recruited their son; and she said that had she known this she would have remained silent.[9] Walker showed some family loyalty by agreeing to plead guilty in the hope of securing a lighter sentence for his son, who was nevertheless jailed for twenty-five years.

Family loyalties were deeply divided over the plight of Ethel Rosenberg, the wife of Julius Rosenberg, who had been responsible for running a major spy ring in the USA. Though the FBI had been seeking the KGB agent known as 'Julius' for several years, it was the evidence of her brother, David Greenglass, which led to his arrest and

17

subsequent conviction. Greenglass, who was himself convicted of passing atomic bomb secrets to the Russians via Julius, betrayed both his sister and brother-in-law to the electric chair but saved his own wife, who was also involved in the family treachery. There was the additional motive that Greenglass had a grudge against Rosenberg over a past business deal but it seems likely that he would have argued that, if faced with the charge of perjury, he put loyalty to the truth before loyalty to family.[10]

Rhona, the wife of Geoffrey Prime, the spy inside GCHQ, remained devoted to him in spite of her knowledge of his deviant sexual activities with small girls, and pondered agonizingly before deciding that her loyalty to her country took precedence over her loyalty to her husband. According to the Security Commission's report on the Prime case, his previous wife confessed that she had known that he was a spy since 1973 but had avoided denouncing him.

There were no conflicts of loyalty in the extraordinary Kuczynski family to which 'Sonia' belonged, because her father, brother and a sister were also Soviet agents. 'Sonia' was however endangered by a peculiar conflict which beset her old German nanny, Olga Muth, who was regarded as part of the family. When she learned that she would not be accompanying 'Sonia' and her children in her GRU posting from Switzerland to Britain in 1940, she made a desperate effort to ensure that the children would remain in Switzerland by denouncing 'Sonia' and her husband as spies to the British consular representative in Montreux, but no notice was taken of her.[11]

A most grievous clash of loyalties faces defectors who have to flee without their families when the alternative is exposure, arrest and possible execution. The true democracies eventually allow wives and children to join men who have defected but those fleeing from the Soviet Union and its satellites know that they are never likely to see their loved ones again. Some seem to have rated their hatred of the Soviet system greater than loyalty to their families. Others have found defection a means of getting rid of family ties and responsibilities, while a few have avoided the conflict through being able to defect with their immediate families.

Some 'intellectuals' have rated loyalty to friends as the highest of all. The writer E. M. Forster, for example, held that if he had to choose between betraying his country and betraying his friend he hoped he would have the guts to betray his country; but this may have been coloured by the fact that he was a homosexual, for whom friendship meant rather more than it does for most. When Anthony Blunt, also a homosexual, was publicly exposed in 1979 as having been a Soviet agent inside MI5, he claimed that after he had realized the true facts about Russia he could not confess his treachery to the security authorities because it would have meant denouncing friends who had also been involved. 'I was prevented from taking any action by my personal loyalty,' he said. If he was telling the truth it meant that, like Forster, he placed loyalty to a few intimates above loyalty to the whole of society. He then indicated that following an event in 1963, which he was not prepared to reveal, this restraint ceased to exist and in return for immunity from prosecution he had been able to give a full account of his misdeeds to MI5. In fact, this inveterate cheat was still trying to justify his treason, and at that stage the MI5 officers, who had eventually interrogated him and knew that he was lying, were helping him to do so in the interest of preserving the anonymity of Blunt's friends. The only reason that Blunt confessed was because he had been 'blown' to the FBI, and thence to MI5, by one of his Cambridge recruits, Michael Straight.[12] His alleged sensitivity to his friends did not extend to the Soviet people whom he professed to admire and against whom, as he well knew, Stalin was perpetrating the most horrific crimes.

Blunt's real loyalty to his friends was highly selective. Once his treachery was known to MI5 he had no compunction about exposing former friends like Leo Long, the Cambridge traitor, for whom he had acted as spy-master, but he continued to lie about what MI5 came to call his 'fine friends' and about those whose exposure would still damage the Soviet Union. The 'fine friends' were traitorous associates who had achieved high rank and some of whom were still in office and have not yet been exposed because of libel problems, though their names are known to me. The others, whom he considered expendable, included people like Alister Watson, who became an important scientist in submarine research and was probably the elusive 'fifth man' of the Cambridge Ring.

Since my disclosure of Michael Straight's role in the exposure of Blunt, he has put on record a detailed account of how an intimate friendship, with the Communist poet John Cornford, was instrumental in securing his recruitment to the Soviet cause. Cornford was killed in the Spanish Civil War, and under the emotional impact of this event Straight agreed to Blunt's insistence that he should work for the Comintern in America as a pledge of loyalty to his dead friend. Later, until his visit to the FBI in 1963, Straight demonstrated his loyalty to Blunt and Guy Burgess by failing to report their treachery even when he realized that Burgess's activities could have caused the deaths of American soldiers in the Korean War. While he struggled with his conscience about 'turning them in' he did no more than warn Burgess that he would do so unless he ceased to spy. Had he firmly put his country's interests first on his last encounter with Burgess in Washington early in 1950, as he now admits he should have done, he might have prevented the defections of Burgess, Maclean, and Philby and all the unfortunate consequences to the Anglo-American alliance, which he held dear.[13]

Friendship appears to have been the prime reason why the American code-breaker Joseph Sidney Petersen became a traitor to the USA and earned a seven-year prison sentence in 1954. During the war he had worked on Japanese codes alongside a Dutch cryptanalyst with whom he developed a close friendship. When the Dutchman returned home, Petersen began to send him ideas for setting up a new cryptology department in Holland and followed this up with copies of highly secret documents, which he removed from the Armed Forces Security Agency, passing them to an intermediary in the Dutch Embassy in Washington. Security men found a large cache of these documents in Petersen's apartment; he pleaded guilty though there was no evidence that he had received any payment for his services.[14]

I have personal experience of the problem of loyalty to a friend conflicting with what I considered to be duty to national security. When invited to give evidence to the security inquiry chaired by Lord Radcliffe in 1961 I felt it necessary to reveal my knowledge that Stanley Mayne, the likeable and distinguished Secretary of the Institution of Professional Civil Servants, was a secret Communist and, on his imminent retirement, had ensured that a man of similar persuasion would replace him. Though the loyalty of neither was in doubt, the situation was potentially dangerous because the Institution was the union of the most senior civil servants and included many scientists at the secret defence establishments. My point was that if Communists were barred from serving in such establishments it made no security sense to have Communist or pro-Communist union officials with regular access to those working there. The committee took the point, and as a result of its report the government declined to negotiate with such officials. My decision had not been made any easier by the fact that Mayne had been a most valuable source of information but it did not put his job in jeopardy because he was retiring anyway.[15]

While many friends of traitors feel appalled at what they conceive as a personal breach of loyalty when they learn of it, some are able to forgive them. This seems to apply particularly to intelligence officers, perhaps because they appreciate the pitfalls which beset them. The former MI6 chief Sir Maurice Oldfield was so forgiving towards his MI6 colleague Charles 'Dick' Ellis, after the latter's confession that he had spied for the Nazis, that some of Ellis's friends seized on this as evidence of innocence. Oldfield persisted in being friendly towards Ellis even when other colleagues admonished him for it. As a staunch Christian, Oldfield was forgiving by nature and in addition was aware of a serious weakness of his own which made him vulnerable to treachery as I describe in Chapter 10.

Loyalty to family and friends is not approved of by Moscow, which regards such 'misalignments' as bourgeois and dangerous since they could dilute loyalty to state and party. When Eleanor Philby asked her husband: 'What is more important in your life, me and the children or the Communist Party?' he answered firmly and without hesitation: 'The Party, of course.'[16] Presumably his attitude to party loyalty was similar to Richard Lovelace's to his country when he explained to his lady, on going to war: 'I could not love thee (Dear) so much, Lov'd I not honour more.'

There are instances, however, where devoted Communists have put loyalty to friends before loyalty to party. The early Soviet defector Walter Krivitsky claimed in 1937 that he finally broke with Stalin's rule because, as a senior intelligence agent in Western Europe, he was required to deliver for execution one of his closest friends, fellow Soviet agent Ignace Reiss. Told to demonstrate his loyalty by betraying Reiss, who could no longer stomach Stalin's excesses, he chose loyalty to his friend and tried to warn him, realizing that he too would then have to defect to avoid his own execution as a traitor. Again, however, the motivation was more complex. Krivitsky, who was Polish, knew that Stalin was recalling any agent who knew too much about the murderous methods by which he held on to power, and particularly those who were not Russians. So he needed to defect anyway.

Is there one overriding loyalty which, if discharged, preserves the other major and the lesser loyalties? It would seem that there is only one. The most realistic concept of loyalty for the present and forseeable future would seem to be to true democracy, as opposed to any form of totalitarianism, which is pseudo-democracy. Loyalty to a true democracy subsumes the other major loyalties, like loyalty to the land, to its society, to religion, to the government, and to the head of state, whether a monarch or president. It is also, unquestionably, the safest choice for maintenance of the lesser loyalties such as those to family, friends, political party, trade union, and profession.

The obverse of loyalty is treachery, and consideration of the many factors in what might be called the 'equations of treachery' will take us through the gamut of human frailties.

CHAPTER THREE

Types of Traitor

So long as we live in a world divided by profound ideological differences of outlook, there will be those on both sides who will decide at some stage in their careers to switch their allegiance.

The Security Commission

A traitor's basic role is to betray trust, and it is the nature of the trust as much as the nature of the traitor which conditions the extent of the treachery. As with other forms of crime, there are degrees of treachery. A person legally convicted of treachery may have inflicted some damage on the system without putting his compatriots at risk, while a traitor with access to atomic weapons information can endanger the lives of millions.

The severity of a traitor's treachery also depends on how long it continues. To describe those who have unquestionably inflicted massive damage, the term *arch-traitor*, as used in the accompanying list, is useful. Inevitably, the longest-lasting and the most damaging are those who have been professionally trained. Even amateurs, however, are usually given some ongoing training by their masters. During the week when a security team was carrying out positive vetting inquiries on Geoffrey Prime, the agent inside GCHQ, he was undergoing training in KGB espionage techniques in a flat in East Berlin. Even minor traitors, who have had no training, can bring about disaster because of the 'jigsaw effect'. A tiny piece of information which an agent considers relatively harmless can complete a jigsaw which leads to an intelligence or security catastrophe or even the deaths of other agents, this being especially true in war.

It is generally accepted that treachery is more heinous during war than during peace, because it is immediately so dangerous to so many people. There was little sympathy, for instance, for the British merchant seamen, George Armstrong and Duncan Scott-Ford, who were executed in 1941 and 1942 respectively for agreeing to give

ARCH-TRAITORS (Based on damage and active years)

Name	Nationality	Recruited by	When aged	Active years
Blake	Dutch–British	USSR (KGB)	31(?)	7(?)
Blunt	British	USSR (KGB)	28	10(?)
Boyce	American	USSR (KGB)	22	2
Burgess	British	USSR (KGB)	23	17
Felfe	West German	East Germany	33	10
Fuchs	German–British	USSR (GRU)	30	8
Gerhardt	South African	USSR (GRU)	27	22
Goleniewski	Polish–American	USA (CIA)	34(?)	2
Gordievsky	Russian	Denmark–UK	27(?)	19(?)
Guillaume	German E–W	East Germany	26	18
Klugmann	British	USSR (KGB)	22	11
Maclean	British	USSR (KGB)	21	15
Pâques	French	USSR (KGB)	30	19
Philby	British	USSR (KGB)	21	11
Prime	British	USSR (KGB)	30	10
Rosenberg	American	USSR (KGB)	25	7
'Sonia'	German–British	USSR (GRU)	23	20
Sorge	German	USSR (GRU)	34(?)	24
Walker	American	USSR (KGB)	29	17
Wennerstrom	Swedish	USSR (GRU)	42	15

NOTE (?) implies uncertainty. Hollis is not included because his case is not proven. If he was a Soviet agent he was probably active inside MI5 for twenty-seven years, which would be a record period.

For defectors who had not previously been agents-in-place see Chart No. 2, page 201.

convoy information to German agents.[1] The American seaman, William Colepaugh, who had been enrolled into the German secret service and was sent back to the USA as a spy, was detested by the FBI, to which he confessed, as the worst kind of traitor.[2] Similar feelings were aroused by the treachery of 'King Kong' Lindemanns, the giant Dutch resistance worker who began to spy for the British in Rotterdam in 1939, relaying shipping movements to London. At British suggestion he offered his services to the Germans in 1940 and operated as a double, mainly in Britain's interests until 1944 when his brother was captured by the Gestapo. He then confessed his duplicity to the Abwehr, offered to work in the German interest, and began transmitting disinformation to the British. The Germans deliberately left him behind when the Allies occupied Brussels, and his general double-dealing with the Dutch underground in still-occupied Holland is said to have led to the deaths of more than 200 of them.[3] The French resistance agent Henri Déricourt, dealt with in Chapter 8, appears to have behaved in a similar manner.

For a traitor to send others to their death in peacetime used to be an unlikely eventuality, but in the conditions of cold war with the Soviet Union this has frequently occurred. In 1950 about 500 Albanian *émigrés* living in Greece were armed by the Western allies and sent back across the border into their home country in an effort to overthrow the harsh Stalinist dictatorship there. As the whole operation had been betrayed to the Russians by the British MI6 traitor Philby, who was on the organizing committee, they were ambushed by heavily armed Albanian troops, some 200 being killed and a further 120 captured and executed. Philby repeated this murderous treachery by betraying teams of parachutists dropped into the Ukraine and eastern Poland on MI6 missions.[4] The other MI6 spy, George Blake, betrayed more than forty British agents to torture and many to their death. More recently the former CIA officer, Edward Howard, expressed his resentment at being dismissed by betraying the Soviet aerospace specialist, Tolkachev, who had been supplying the Americans with secret information for several years.

Treachery offers the most slippery of all tempting slopes, on which many start out in a tentative way but quickly become more and more irrevocably committed. Many who were confident that they could limit their treachery to minor matters found that they could not, once thoroughly enmeshed, or did not even wish to do so when the habit took hold of them. Some do manage to remain 'fringe traitors', while others, because of the nature of their access to secrets, are major traitors from the start. The slippery slope concept is of major importance in understanding how some traitors have come to remain firmly trapped for so long. It is a factor which recruiters for Soviet intelligence traditionally exploit. Anthony Blunt, for instance, described to his MI5 interrogators how he was recruited by his friend Guy Burgess, who was already knowingly with the KGB, to 'work for peace'. Only later was he told, after being introduced to a Soviet controller, that he would be operating through the Comintern, the organization said to be working for world revolution to defeat Fascism by installing Communism. Later still, when it was too late had he wished to withdraw, he discovered that he was working exclusively for the KGB. Many who have eventually found themselves in full-scale espionage began by providing the Soviets with nothing more than confidential manuals or even commercial catalogues and were then induced to widen the scope of the documents they could provide.

The best-known and perhaps most straightforward form of traitor is the *spy*. 'Spy', as used by the media, is a portmanteau word covering many different kinds of operative, and there is a misleading tendency for the public to assume that anyone called a spy has been involved in pilfering secrets. In fact, clandestine operators do many other things and the term *espionage* is widely used to cover any intelligence activity against another nation to inflict damage by surreptitious means.

It is essential to appreciate the difference between spies who are career *officers* of organizations like MI6, the KGB, and the CIA, and who are mainly planners and administrators of espionage operations, and *agents* who are hired by officers and do the actual spying in the sense of securing information and documents, planting microphones, and so on. For reasons of language and facility of access, agents, sometimes called 'Joes', are usually nationals of the country in which they act. This means that they are working against their own country and so are automatically traitors, while officers, who are working in the interests of their own country, are not.

Officers are regularly sent abroad, usually in the guise of diplomats, to control espionage operations and to recruit agents, but they rarely serve as active spies there. The few who may do so are planted as deep-cover agents with false identities and a careful build-up of what is called a *legend*, a fictitious story to account for every aspect of previous existence. Such deep-cover agents, who are called *illegals*, to distinguish them from *legals* – officers using their own identities and with an official position – can reasonably be held to be guilty of treason against the target country if caught. They are usually men but some women, like 'Sonia', have been highly successful illegals in the past. More recently there has been a spate of them in West Germany, where they have secured work as secretaries in sensitive departments. One such was 'Frau Ursula Richter', a false identity assumed by an East German agent in Canada in the build-up of her legend. Until she defected eastwards in August 1985 she is believed to have been running a substantial network of spies in West Germany while working in a political organization attached to the Christian Democratic Party.

Officers, and even agents, who are operating in the interests of the country to which they legally and morally owe allegiance against a nation which is a potential enemy are not dishonourable. Their methods may be questionable but their motivation is not, and if their exploits become known, which is unusual, they are deemed to be patriotic and often heroic. Dishonourable spies are those who, while pretending to be loyal citizens, surreptitiously and traitorously work against the interest of their own society – even to its destruction – in the interests of an alien nation.

An example of a spy generally considered to be honourable is the Soviet illegal agent Colonel Rudolph Abel, who operated in the USA under the deep cover of being a photographer and artist until he was betrayed by a defector; he then behaved like a good soldier and declined to give any information about himself or his activities, being prepared to serve out his thirty-year sentence. It is an intriguing aspect of attitude to loyalty that spies who decline assistance and take their punishment manfully are admired, in both peace and war. Though Abel was born and had spent his childhood in Scotland – he still spoke English with a Scottish accent – he had been a Soviet citizen for so long that he could not conceivably count as a traitor. That description certainly applied, however, to the Soviet colleague who betrayed him.[5] The Jewish German exile known by her GRU code-name 'Sonia' was held in such Soviet esteem that she received two Orders of the Red Banner for her espionage activities but, being a British citizen by marriage, she behaved in a thoroughly dishonourable manner while taking political refuge in the UK. Her service as a courier to Klaus Fuchs alone made her an arch-traitor to Britain.

Any spy deliberately infiltrated into a country as a political refugee seeking asylum can hardly be considered honourable. Among the worst of these cases was Israel Beer, a Soviet deep-cover agent infiltrated into the Israeli defence establishment as a genuine Jewish immigrant and who provided a vast amount of military information to Moscow which presumably fed it to Israel's Arab enemies.[6] Among the many East German spies who have insinuated themselves, despicably, into the caring West German community as refugees, the most damaging so far exposed has been Gunther Guillaume, who was so successful that he became a close confidant of Willy Brandt, the West German Chancellor. Brandt had to resign when the treason of Guillaume and his wife, who had become West German citizens, was revealed in 1974, but the traitors probably still regarded themselves as honourable spies doing their dangerous duty to Communism.

Count von Stauffenberg, the German officer who tried to assassinate Hitler with a bomb left in a briefcase, is now usually regarded as a patriot, but to many Germans he was a traitor. The brave young German diplomat Baron Wolfgang Zu Putlitz, who served as an agent-in-place for MI6, professed to be an anti-Nazi patriot, but his motives now seem to have been pro-Soviet. After being given a British passport for services rendered, he defected to East Germany.

There were several other instances in the Second World War when German citizens took it upon themselves to betray secrets to their country's enemies essentially because of their opposition to the Nazi regime. Seen in retrospect their behaviour could be regarded as laudable and certainly courageous, but they were traitors by any definition of the word, especially as most of them remained in Germany, continuing with their normal work. The type specimen of such a volunteer is Fritz Kolbe, an otherwise unimpressive man who never rose above the rank of clerk in the German Foreign Office but was a resolute anti-Nazi with the perception to realize, towards the end of 1943, that only military defeat could remove Hitler from power. With great courage he journeyed from Berlin to Berne in neutral Switzerland with a bundle of diplomatic cables of the greatest value to Allied intelligence and made his way to the office of the British military attaché, Brigadier Cartwright.

Angered by what he saw as a miserable German trying to ingratiate himself because his country was losing the war, Cartwright dismissed him without a proper hearing. Kolbe then persuaded a Swiss friend to arrange a meeting with the American intelligence chief in Berne, Allen Dulles, who immediately saw that the sixteen cables in the German's hand were so revealing as almost certainly to be authentic. A check with the British interception centre, which had already deciphered some of the cables when the Germans had first transmitted them in code by radio, showed that they were genuine.

The documents revealed that there was a very productive German spy in the British Embassy in Ankara who had the code-name 'Cicero' and who was quickly tracked down, as described in Chapter 8. Dulles, who was further impressed because Kolbe never asked for money, gave him the code-name 'George Wood' and arranged for further supplies of documents. In five further visits to Berne, Kolbe supplied copies or photographs of over 1500 cables, becoming what Dulles called 'the intelligence officer's dream'. His cables were most valuable in enabling the British to check and to improve the decoding of their intercepted radio traffic – an achievement generally rated as crucial in the defeat of Germany.[7]

A long-standing mystery, which now appears to have been resolved, centres on a similar German traitor who had access to highly secret weapons work which he imparted, voluntarily, to the British in the early weeks of the Second World War. His information in the shape of a small parcel containing seven typewritten pages and a device which was part of a new fuse for shells, was pushed through the letter box of the British naval attaché in Oslo. The document revealed the existence of a secret rocket range at Peenemunde and details of new torpedoes and other weapons.[8] Professor R. V. Jones, who dealt with the report, has tried to discover its author, as others have. I understand that he was definitely a German and that his surviving relatives are opposed to his identification because, even so long after the event, they might be ostracized by friends and neighbours because of the man's treachery.

As the attitude of defectors shows, the question of honour and dishonour among traitors is often a matter of standpoint. Oleg Gordievsky, who was briefly head of the KGB mission in London and had previously worked for MI6 for several years before physically defecting in 1985, considers himself to have been treacherous only to the Soviet system, which he despised, and that the real traitors are the Politburo chiefs who keep the Soviet people in subjection. Viktor Suvorov, who deserted to the British from the GRU, takes a similar view, as do many other defectors. But the Politburo, understandably, does not share it, and most of them have been condemned to death. The British defector Philby makes the same claim in reverse, throwing in the additional justification that to betray one has first to belong. His argument that he never 'belonged' to Britain and therefore owed no allegiance is specious on both legal and moral grounds. He changed his allegiance to a country he had never visited in a clandestine way which was treacherous to his colleagues, friends, and family as well as to the country which had given him education, career and protection.

Among traitors, as among thieves, there are degrees of dishonour. Those pretending to serve their country and taking their salaries, as Philby and Maclean were while seizing every opportunity to betray it, must rank among the most despicable. But in the true democracies treacherous politicians put themselves among the lowest because they persistently present themselves to the voters as people of integrity. Among British Members of Parliament the former Labour MP Will Owen serves as a type specimen because he came to trial. A despicable man who, according to his Parliamentary colleague Leo Abse, 'could be bought for a trifle', Owen served on important committees and received large sums from Czech intelligence in return for secrets and other services. Another Labour MP exposed as having been recruited to Soviet-bloc intelligence was Bernard Floud, and there are others among the 'false flag' crypto-communists who are escaping public censure, if temporarily. Even more dishonourable was the German politician and Soviet spy Alfred Frenzel, whose case is described in Chapter 14.[9]

While most officers of intelligence organizations remain honourable they can become traitors by being recruited by adversary services, for which they act as agents of a special kind known in the 'trade' as *penetration agents* and in the media as 'moles'. Such traitors are the most damaging of all because they not only can secure the most secret of all information but can disrupt the organization's counter-intelligence work, influence policy, talent-spot others for recruitment and facilitate their entry. All countries therefore strive hard to secure penetration agents; and they constitute the counter-intelligence officer's worst nightmare.

Penetration agents, such as Philby or Gordievsky, who appear to be working for one country but are really working for another are commonly referred to as *double agents*, but this is a misuse of the term, which really means a person working for both sides with no prime loyalty to either and almost always for money. Neither side has full control of him, while Philby was controlled by the KGB and Gordievsky by MI6.

Spies who acquire secret information, preferably in the form of documents, are known in the trade as *collectors*. The most productive of these are the penetration agents, like Philby and Blake in MI6, Blunt and, as I believe, Hollis in MI5, Maclean in the Foreign Office, Alger Hiss in the US State Department, Judith Coplon in the US Justice Department, the Canadian diplomat Herbert Norman in the Canadian Foreign Office, and Gordievsky in the KGB. Collectors now include those who acquire actual equipment, such as fuses or military computers, by illegal means. Those who knowingly and illegally assist collectors of such hardware for the USSR are guilty of a form of treachery, because the transfer of goods which the Soviets urgently need for military purposes can be more dangerous than the transfer of information. The position of those who just keep within the technicalities of the law, but know for what purpose the banned equipment is really required, is a matter for legal quibbling, but to those who might suffer from the eventual military use of the equipment they would seem to be fringe traitors at least.

All collectors, especially those who are penetration agents, work under close supervision of *case-officers* or *controllers* who tend to be located in the embassies of the country concerned and, if detected, can claim immunity to prosecution, though illegals are still sometimes used. The recruited spy is not left to his own devices to secure what information he can and then pass it on. The case-officer is in regular contact with his intelligence centre and is instructed at regular intervals about what it requires from the collectors. When Fuchs, the atomic

29

traitor, was seen by his couriers, for example, he was presented with questions from Soviet scientists working on nuclear bombs. Philby took no action of consequence without consulting his controller and Gordievsky must have been in regular touch with MI6.

An experienced case-officer is often required to run several agents, referred to as a *ring*, and is then referred to colloquially as a *spy-master*, as Julius Rosenberg was in the USA and Gordon Lonsdale, a Soviet illegal living under an assumed name, was in Britain. There have also been successful *spy-mistresses* like 'Sonia', who helped to run Fuchs and probably Hollis in Britain, and Hede Massing, a Vienna-born, professional recruiter for Soviet intelligence working in the USA.

Most major spies need regular assistance from *auxiliary agents* whose contribution may seem to be modest, but who are, nevertheless, guilty of various degrees of treachery. These include *cut-outs*, people who serve as intermediaries, say between a spy and his controller to reduce the risk that they might be observed at a clandestine meeting. Such a cut-out may also be a courier, and the type specimen about whom most is known is Harry Gold, the American chemist who serviced Klaus Fuchs in the United States, passing on his written information to a KGB agent based at the Soviet consulate in New York. Auxiliaries also service dead-letter boxes – hiding places for secret messages – find and prepare accommodation for spies and sabotage agents, allow their homes to be used as accommodation addresses and serve as talent-spotters.

Some traitors operate almost exclusively as recruiters of others such as agents and subversive fifth columnists. A growing number of fringe traitors function mainly as promoters of 'active measures'. This is a Soviet term for the use of sophisticated techniques of deception intended to deceive governments, important individuals or mass audiences. The deception is accomplished through forgeries, through the planting of misleading information, through penetration and manipulation of the Western media, and through the dissemination of anti-Americanism and pro-Soviet 'peace' ploys. Active measures operators work through politicians, trade union leaders and journalists, some of whom are unwitting while others are fully aware of what they are doing.

All spy centres, and the Soviets' in particular, put great emphasis on the importance of 'feedback', and some of their spies specialize as *feedback agents*, sending to Moscow a running commentary on the effects of the various operations so that these can be modified to improve their effectiveness. Thus, while the GCHQ spy Geoffrey Prime served mainly as a supplier of secrets, he also performed a valuable service for the KGB by informing them of the effects of a crucial deception concerning the true Soviet strength in nuclear missiles.[10] Any disinformation campaign is likely to succeed only if those running it in Moscow know what effects it is having in the target country and especially on the government there. The proven Soviet ability to react quickly to new situations and handle their secret agents accordingly is an expression of meticulously organized feedback arrangements. Feedback specialists depend on having agents inside the government departments in which they are particularly interested, and those agents who knowingly provide the information which is helping to destabilize their country are traitors of a kind.

Feedback agents achieve their highest utility in time of war, when each side needs to know the effects of its military efforts with minimum delay. For this purpose they are often left in areas which have been evacuated by retreating troops, when they are known as *stay-behinds*. The most successful stay-behind is likely to be a resident of the area and, if this belongs to a country which has been invaded, as France was during the war, then he is usually a traitor. In the Second World War feedback agents who had been captured, as several were in Britain, were often induced to become turncoats and feed back false information, as happened in the brilliant Double X operation used to deceive the Germans on many issues but especially about the forthcoming invasion of Europe.[11] Conversely, the Germans deceived the British through a similar operation, called North Pole, using resistance workers who had been captured and turned under threat of execution.

A further type of subversive, who can inflict enormous damage on his own country and whose effect tends to be grossly underestimated, is the *agent of influence*, whom I rate as so important as to warrant special treatment – in Chapter 4.

Most of the types of traitors and subversives mentioned so far operate in secret and have to hide their true allegiance, but there are also *overt* traitors, like the Australian journalist Wilfred Burchett whose activities are described later, and the British Soviet agent and open Communist James Klugmann, whose treachery, if fully known, would probably put him among the arch-traitors.

Not all traitors are spies. There are many who are *quislings*, a term now in common usage for those who openly side with the enemy in war, or even with a potential enemy in peace, exhorting others to do the same. The term derives from Vidkun Quisling, the Norwegian politician who allied himself with the Nazis and tried to take his country into the Fascist fold. He denied that he had committed treason but was eventually executed for that crime after the German defeat.[12] The British wartime traitors William Joyce and John Amery were quislings, as was Casement in the First World War. Another tragic example was Lieutenant-General Andrei Vlasov, a Soviet general captured by the Germans in July 1942 after he had distinguished himself in the battles for Moscow and Kiev. Regarding Stalin and his clique as traitors to the Russian people, he agreed to form a Russian National Committee and a National Army of Liberation from captured Soviet troops to fight alongside the Germans. He put his name to leaflets showered on the Soviet lines to urge Red Army officers and men to desert. From deserters and Russian prisoners of war he formed a large army; but Hitler and the German General Staff did not trust them, and until the last days of the war the Vlasov Army was restricted to propaganda functions.[13] A portion of it was deployed in the last-ditch fighting in Austria but its full potential was wasted probably because it was undermined by ingenious Soviet counter-intelligence. A White Russian double agent called Turkul convinced the Germans that Vlasov and his troops would suddenly switch sides and fight with the Russians if they were allowed on the Eastern front.[14] Under Soviet law, to which he had certainly held allegiance, Vlasov was a traitor of the worst kind because he and his followers fought against their own compatriots on behalf of an invader in search of territory and intent on making parts of the Soviet Union into a vassal state. Another Soviet general, Rokossovsky, remained loyal to Stalin but earned the title 'the Polish quisling'. He was a Pole who had joined the Red Army and, when in command of troops advancing on Warsaw, deliberately halted them to give the occupying Germans time to destroy the Polish resistance fighters because Polish nationals would have opposed Stalin's plan to clamp Communist control on the country.

General Draja Mihailovitch, the Yugoslav guerrilla leader during the Second World War who was executed as a traitor in 1946, was accused of being a quisling by his Communist political opponents. He led a force of about 150,000 royalist resistance fighters known as Chetniks, many of them Yugoslav Army troops, against the German occupation forces, inflicting heavy losses on them, rescuing hundreds of American airmen, and working closely with British intelligence and sabotage officers. Communists led by Josip Broz, who called himself Tito and had been trained in Russia, were also opposing the Germans but, when the defeat of the Axis became inevitable, they were more concerned to defeat the Chetniks so that they would be the dominant military force in Yugoslavia and be able to impose a peacetime Communist regime with Tito as dictator.

The British were mainly responsible for air-dropping supplies to both the Chetniks and the Partisans, but Winston Churchill and the other British war leaders were induced to abandon Mihailovitch and support Tito only, though this meant that Yugoslavia would inevitably become a Communist country. The insidious way in which this was achieved by British Communist agents of influence is described in

Chapter 4. After his capture by a Communist unit in March 1946, Mihailovitch was brought to trial on charges of treason in a Communist court where a claque was encouraged to shout 'Traitor!' at his defence counsel, who was later imprisoned. He was executed in spite of international efforts to secure justice for him. The substantial documentary evidence that Mihailovitch was a Yugoslav patriot branded a traitor for political spite and to ensure his liquidation has been presented in a scholarly study by the American author David Martin.[15] Most of the Chetniks were summarily shot and the British responsibility in handing over some 26,000 of them to Tito, one of the most dishonourable episodes in Britain's military history, has been described by Nikolai Tolstoy.[16]

Among the cold-war quislings there figure, with the deepest dishonour, subversive agents who would once have been called *fifth columnists* and whose treachery is so heinous that many people are disinclined to believe it. These are the *Spetsnaz auxiliaries*, traitors who would assist the military overthrow of their own country by helping Soviet SAS-type (*Spetsnaz*) troops invading it. Such people exist in substantial numbers in Britain, West Germany, and other countries, as described in Chapter 18. Many have been identified, but no action can be taken against them, outside an emergency, until they commit an offence, which they are careful to avoid.

A further form of traitor who is not a spy or a quisling is the home-grown *terrorist*, like those of the IRA. These are now such a serious and peculiar threat that they too require treatment in a separate chapter – 19.

As already mentioned, the British government's recent definition of subversion has extended the boundaries of treachery. Whether those who seek to overthrow the rule of law and the parliamentary system by organizing 'racial' riots, hostile 'peace' demonstrations, and violent picketing and by inciting industrial strife for political motives qualify as fringe traitors is now a matter for legal argument.

CHAPTER FOUR

Agents of Influence

A university professor who, without being a Party member, supports the interests of the Soviet Union, is of more value than 1000 people with a membership card.

Georgi Dimitroff, Bulgarian Communist

An agent of influence is a person who uses his or her position, influence, power, and credibility to promote the objectives of an alien power, usually the Soviet Union, in ways unattributable to that power. Such agents may operate openly or surreptitiously, and their effectiveness depends on their position and the extent to which they are prepared to misuse it, but any degree of deliberate support for an adversary power, especially if applied in an underhand way, savours of treachery. In fact, the Soviet term applied to all Soviet-born agents of influence operating against the USSR, translates as *traitors of influence*.

These hidden persuaders include politicians, diplomats, civil servants, trade union leaders, members of think-tanks, which are specifically designed to influence government policy, academics, journalists, and churchmen. Their widespread use is part of the Communists' 'long march through the institutions' – democratic Parliaments, political parties, Western government administrative machines, educational and legal systems, trade unions, media, and churches.

Some agents of influence are targeted and secretly agree to be recruited, often for money, as the former Labour MP Will Owen was. They are under some degree of control and are usually required to perform specific tasks. Others act on their own initiative to ally themselves with another country, usually the Soviet Union, and promote its interests without admitting their alliance, as several prominent trade union leaders have done. They include some individuals who know that they have been compromised and believe that the KGB is aware of the fact and may act unless they conform to requirements spontaneously. Some politicians appear to have fallen into this cate-

34

gory. A few take the stance of overt ideological propagandists and usually claim to be pursuing an independent line. In addition there are many unwitting agents, known in the tradecraft as 'willies', who assist the adversary through naïvety, a prime example being the late Olof Palme, the Swedish statesman who exerted great influence, particularly on American 'liberal' politicians. Provided they really are unwitting then their ignorance clearly mitigates their culpability.

The witting agents of the USSR are controlled, directly or more often indirectly, by a large and heavily endowed department of state called the International Department, run for many years by the former Comintern official Boris Ponomarev, and now in the hands of Anatoly Dobrynin, previously the Soviet Ambassador to the USA.

Whether agents of influence are witting or unwitting, their effect, over their years of effort, is to destabilize their own country in the interests of an alien nation and against the security requirements of the majority of their compatriots. It is therefore reasonable to include those who are witting among the effectively treacherous, and there is case-evidence to warrant describing some of them as traitors.

Most agents of influence are usually recognizable because they consistently take a line so advantageous to an adversary country that their reaction to almost any controversial situation is predictable. Currently this is most obvious in the East–West nuclear arms debates, but there are many other instances. When discussing the treachery of Soviet agents like Maclean, Blunt, Philby, and the American State Department official Harry Dexter White, for example, the typical agent of influence will insist that they were helping the Soviet Union because it was an ally, when, in fact, as they usually know, such agents were recruited long before Russia was forced into the war and continued to commit treason against their own countries when Russia was allied with Nazi Germany.

A few are in positions to pursue their objectives so covertly and insidiously that their efforts are never apparent. A high-level official, for instance, may try to wean his Minister towards a pro-Soviet stance on a particular issue, such as arms control, by suggesting that it would be more in keeping with current public opinion and therefore popular in securing support in a forthcoming election. A senior civil servant who is a conscious Soviet agent of influence might sway a crucial decision in the management of a crisis.

The importance attached to such agents was stressed by Whittaker Chambers, a senior editor of *Time* magazine and a former Soviet agent with the KGB code-name 'Karl', who explained that the aim of the Communist group which had infiltrated the American government was not espionage but policy-making – 'something very much more important than spying'. The extraordinary effectiveness of this Sovietorientated policy-making network was summarized by the Senate Subcommittee on Internal Security in April 1953:

> They colonized key committees of Congress. They helped write laws, conduct congressional hearings and write congressional reports. They advised cabinet members, wrote speeches for them and represented them at intergovernmental conferences. They staffed inter-departmental committees which prepared basic American and world policy. They travelled to every continent as emissaries and representatives of the American people. They attended virtually every international conference where statesmen met to shape the future.
>
> They used each other's names for reference on applications for federal employment. They hired each other. They promoted each other. They raised each other's salaries. They transferred each other from bureau to bureau, from department to department, from congressional committee to congressional committee. They assigned each other to international missions. They vouched for each other's loyalty and protected each other when exposure threatened.[1]

The best-known of these clandestine Soviet agents of influence was Alger Hiss, an Assistant Secretary of State for International Organization Affairs, who had been a major American adviser at the fateful Yalta conference in February 1945 and had been in charge of assembling the background papers to be used. He helped to draft the UN Charter, and such was his prestige with both the Americans and Russians that Gromyko suggested to the US Secretary of State, Stettinius, that he should be appointed temporary Secretary-General of the new United Nations![2] His policy, continued by others, encouraged the hiring of Americans for UN posts without any security investigations.

In August 1948 Whittaker Chambers testified before the US House Un-American Activities Committee that Hiss had been an underground member of the Communist Party. As evidence he later produced microfilm, typescripts, and other material which was mainly copies or summaries of State Department documents, some of them in Hiss's handwriting. Chambers insisted that Hiss had given him the material for transmission to Moscow. When Hiss denied this in court he was tried for perjury and convicted on a second trial in 1950, being sentenced to five years' imprisonment. Chambers' testimony was secretly supported by evidence provided by the Soviet GRU defector

Igor Gouzenko.[3] Hiss's treachery was also separately identified from the decipherment of Soviet secret service traffic and was confirmed by the confession of Hede Massing.[4] While still a Congressman Richard Nixon commented in 1950:

> The great lesson which should be learned from the Alger Hiss case is that we are not just dealing with espionage agents who get thirty pieces of silver to obtain the blueprint of a new weapon: this is a far more sinister type of activity, because it permits the enemy to guide and shape our policy; it disarms and dooms our diplomats to defeat in advance before they go to conferences; traitors in the high councils of our own Government make sure that the deck is stacked on the Soviet side of the diplomatic table.

The Hiss case is the best remembered, but there was another American agent of influence with even more impressive qualifications warranting his selection as the type specimen of this genre – Harry Dexter White, Assistant to the Secretary of the US Treasury and later US Executive Director of the International Monetary Fund and largely its architect. White had been born in the USA but both his parents were Russian Jewish immigrants. He was one of a group of young 'flyers' – men destined for high rank in the government bureaucracy – targeted by the GRU. By the late 1930s he was a member of a ring providing secret information to the GRU through a professional case officer.[5] A prodigious worker, he quickly rose to eminence in the Treasury, a department order of December 1941 stating: 'Harry D. White . . . will assume full responsibility for all matters with which the Treasury has to deal bearing on foreign relations.' He played an important role in negotiations with Nationalist China, and had a major hand in formulating the way in which the USA planned to treat Germany after an Allied victory.

White's political chief was Henry Morgenthau, and he was the architect of the Morgenthau plan which called for the de-industrialization of post-war Germany, which was to be transformed into a country 'primarily agricultural and pastoral in character'. The policing of Germany was to be left to the Russians, Poles, Czechs, French, and smaller European neighbours, with all American and British troops withdrawn. Whether by accident or by White's design, this crackpot plan suited Stalin perfectly. Its announcement was used by Hitler and others to urge the German people to fight on to destruction rather than submit to it. It undermined those influential Germans anxious to make peace in 1944, and as a result Soviet forces advanced hundreds of miles further into Europe than could otherwise have been possible.

After the war White put together the plan which became the basis of the International Monetary Fund (IMF) and was appointed to its board. He was also a major influence in securing appointments for other secret Communists, of whom forty-three were named by the defecting Soviet agent, Elizabeth Bentley. Among these were Lauchlin Currie, Executive Secretary to President Roosevelt; Larry Duggan, head of the State Department's Latin American Division and a political adviser to the Secretary of State; Frank Coe, a senior Treasury official; and others of similar eminence and influence.[6] Hede Massing confessed how, after she was sent to the USA to exploit Roosevelt's decision to establish diplomatic relations with the USSR in 1934, she had recruited Duggan. She claimed that she secured Duggan's commitment to provide all available material of interest to the Russians while visiting him in his room in the State Department!

When some of the wartime KGB radio-traffic between Moscow and the USA was later decoded there were sixteen code-names of Soviet agents – most of them still unidentified – inside the Office of Strategic Services (OSS), the predecessor of the CIA. This evidence, which is still classified, indicates that these people, most of whom remain unidentified, were informing the Soviets of OSS activities and influencing them where they could in the Soviet interest. As most of the senior members of the early post-war CIA were ex-OSS, and the Russians could have pressured some of them to remain, it led to a major 'mole-hunt' in the CIA in the 1960s and early 1970s after a KGB defector, Anatoly Golitsin, gave leads to their possible identities.

The pre-war and wartime infiltration of the British departments of state was comparable with that in the USA, if not worse. There were full-blooded spies like Donald Maclean, John King, and others in the Foreign Office; Philby and Charles Ellis in MI6; Blunt in MI5; and others in the wartime subversion organization called Special Operations Executive (SOE). As already indicated, British Communist agents of influence sealed the fate of the Chetniks, the loyal troops of the Yugoslav Army and their leader Mihailovitch and ensured that Yugoslavia would become a Communist dictatorship, then thought likely to remain under Soviet domination. These agents were based in SOE, in MI6, and in the BBC, the best-known proven traitor among them being Major James Klugmann, a desk officer in the Yugoslav section of Cairo headquarters, which controlled not only communications with the resistance movements but supplies as well. As will be seen, Klugmann was a lifelong Communist and had been an important recruiter of spies for the KGB at both Cambridge and Oxford universities. He and others ensured that Mihailovitch was starved of supplies. Urgent messages from British officers with Mihailovitch's forces, which should have reached London, were stifled; and false messages, concocted to prejudice Mihailovitch's position, were sent to London and even to Churchill himself. Both SOE (Cairo) and MI6 falsely slanted their intelligence reports to convince London that Mihailovitch was collaborating with the Germans instead of fighting them, while promoting all the Partisans claims as true, which often they were not. At the same time the Yugoslav section of the BBC angled its broadcasts to give major credit to Tito, deliberately playing down the substantial achievements of the Chetniks. British officers in Yugoslavia complained to the BBC that Tito was being falsely credited with attacks which had been made by the Chetniks, but with no result.

Klugmann and other agents of influence carry a heavy responsibility for the Communization of Yugoslavia, of which they presumably were proud, and for the deaths of thousands of Chetniks, massacred by Tito's command.[7]

Frank Soviet agents like Klugmann were supplemented by Communist sympathizers in many other departments of state. Among those who have been named as agents of influence are Communists like Professor J. D. Bernal, and fellow travellers like Professor Patrick Blackett, who advised on the war effort, and Sir Dennis Proctor, who served as assistant private secretary to the Prime Minister, Stanley Baldwin, and then as principal private secretary to the wartime Chancellor of the Exchequer. Among several who cannot yet be named for libel reasons were men in the Cabinet Office, the Treasury, the Ministry of Economic Warfare and Home Office.

In Canada, Soviet agents of influence have been equally active, the type specimen there being Herbert Norman, a Canadian who, according to his friend, Anthony Blunt, was recruited by the Soviets at Cambridge University and who penetrated the Canadian External Affairs Department and foreign service with great success. Canadian documents recently released show that in August 1942 Norman became chief of a special Canadian intelligence organization concerned with the decoding of intercepted Japanese and French messages, and that for the rest of the war he had access 'to all sources of secret information available to the Department of External Affairs'.[8] Not only would this have been of the greatest interest to Moscow, which was not at war with Japan, but through his post Norman was in close connection with the US and British interception agencies, with American and British military and naval intelligence and with British Security Co-ordination in New York.[9]

After the war Norman became Ambassador to Japan, High Commissioner to New Zealand, and Ambassador to Egypt. Throughout his career, which ended with his suicide in 1957 when he knew he was under deep suspicion, Norman was ideally placed to function as an agent of influence on Canadian policy through his close association with Lester Pearson, who served as Foreign Secretary and then became Prime Minister. Norman's activities have recently been investigated by Professor James Barros of Toronto University and his findings will be referred to in more detail in later chapters.[10]

All penetration agents inserted into senior positions inside secret departments can perform the additional function of being agents of influence because there is often an intelligence input into government policy and they may be the advisers supplying it. Burgess and the arch-traitor Philby had both been advisers to the Foreign Office's post-war Russia Committee which sought ways of enabling Soviet satellite countries to regain their independence. With such traitorous advisers and informers it could never have succeeded.[11] The diaries of Sir Alexander Cadogan, head of the Foreign Office, mention a meeting with Blunt, when he was in MI5, which indicates the level at which such traitors can exert influence.[12] The influence of Sir Roger Hollis, who served in MI5 for twenty-seven years, nine of them as Director-General, was so enormous on many aspects of intelligence as well as security that nobody in authority wants to face up to a study of its effects, especially as these had impact on the USA, Canada, Australia, and New Zealand.[13]

When Philby was in Washington he had become close friends with senior CIA officers like James Angleton, William Harvey and Frank Wisner, on whom he presumably exerted some influence. On previous assignments he had been able to affect the operations of MI6 adversely in many ways. In 1948 when he had headed the MI6 mission in Istanbul he had debriefed the exceptionally valuable GRU defector, Ismail Akhmedov, over several weeks, securing a mass of information about Soviet intelligence operations, coupled with invaluable insight into the way the GRU and KGB were constructed and manned. In a much later debriefing of Akhmedov by the MI5 officer Peter Wright it was realized that Philby had submitted only a tiny fraction of the information to MI6 headquarters but had, no doubt, given a full account to his masters in Moscow.[14] Philby was also able to suppress a lead from the FBI about the Communist affiliations of the atomic scientist Bruno Pontecorvo, who later defected, and another pointing to the MI6 traitor Charles Ellis, who was not unmasked for many years.

Inside the Foreign Office and in diplomatic posts abroad Donald Maclean was an adviser on policy such as nuclear relations with the

USA, and on the British attitude to the Korean War. The value of his eventual co-defector, Burgess, was greatly enhanced when he was made an assistant to Hector McNeil, the Minister in the Foreign Office, the number-two politician there.

Soviet agents of influence are still operating extensively in the USA and in Britain, as shown by the lists provided by the recent defectors, Vitaly Yurchenko and Oleg Gordievsky respectively. William Casey, the CIA chief, is known to have commented that there was nobody on the American list whose name was a surprise, and an almost identical remark was made by a senior MI6 officer concerning the British list.

Some of those on the British list are members of Parliament. The Communist infiltration of that institution began in earnest in 1945, when at least eight or nine 'crypto-Communists', such as Konni Zilliacus, were elected on a Labour ticket.[15] This practice of 'entryism' -- securing election under a false flag – has steadily increased. Peter Wright has revealed on British television how in 1955 MI5 surreptitiously secured the Communist Party's official list of its 'underground' membership, which included thirty-one MPs serving under the guise of Labour Party membership.[16] There are several former ministers of Labour governments who were regarded as Soviet agents of influence by MI5, one of them being paid for the service. There is no reason to believe that the list is any smaller now and, in addition, the Labour Party has been heavily penetrated by the New Left, militant Trotskyites posing as democratic socialists, in order to influence Labour policy in the revolutionary, totalitarian direction. Several British Soviet agents of influence have also been appointed life peers by Labour Prime Ministers and have pursued their purpose in the House of Lords.

Such MPs not only serve on parliamentary committees, where they can exert influence, but are able to put over their views in speeches both inside and outside Parliament and ask loaded parliamentary questions intended to embarrass the government on the Soviet bloc's behalf. They can also serve as feedback agents.

A rare first-hand account of a highly successful political influence operation in a Western Parliament on behalf of the Soviet bloc has been given by Ion Pacepa, the former deputy director of Romanian foreign intelligence who defected to the USA in 1978. It suited Romania to keep the West German Chancellor, Willy Brandt, in office, because of his foreign policy towards the Soviet bloc; in an operation called 'Horizon' certain West German MPs were bribed to vote for him when he faced defeat on votes of no confidence.[17]

Closely associated with parliamentary agents of influence are those trade union leaders who try to slant the policy of their own union in

Moscow's interests and, more importantly, affect the policy of socialist parties with a view to making them anti-American and pro-Soviet in the event of their accession to power. Two Soviet-bloc defectors in particular have given details of how they were required to concentrate on British trade union leaders to serve as paid agents of influence, especially in exerting political leverage on Labour Party policy. They were Josef Frolik and Frantisek August, both professional Czech intelligence officers whose evidence is on record in memoirs and statements to US committees.[18] I also possess tape-recordings of private interviews in which Frolik names various trade union leaders known to him as witting Soviet agents of influence during his service in London. The late Ted Hill, leader of the Boilermakers' Union, was named as a secret Communist agent, but the libel laws prevented those living from being identified, except to the American committees, which withheld them from their published reports.

Other agents of influence named by Gordievsky and other defectors are in a position to exert direct pressure on politicians through service as advisers. The influence of a 'mandarin' – a senior government official – in either Whitehall or Washington can be enormous because a minister's first reaction to any problem is likely to be: 'What is the departmental advice?' and his second is to accept it. Such officials not only can influence policy on a daily basis but can undermine the influence of those whose activities are inimical to the Soviet Union. I know of one recent instance of such a vicious attempt at the character assassination of a leading Whitehall figure that it is hard to believe the person responsible for initiating it did not have more than personal or professional animosity as motive. This person, who did not entirely succeed, was operating at a very high level and remains there. Had the character assassination succeeded, the KGB and the Politburo generally would have been very pleased.

The Soviet bloc has been very successful in placing agents of influence in highly sensitive places in European countries. The modern type specimen is Gunther Guillaume, the professional intelligence agent planted by the East Germans in the office of the West German Chancellor, Willy Brandt. More recently, Herta-Astrid Willner, a secretary in the West German Chancellery with top-security clearance, defected to East Germany along with her husband, Herbert. He was a defence-policy analyst in a Bonn think-tank, with close connections with the Free Democratic Party, a minority party in Chancellor Kohl's coalition government targeted for influence by the Soviets.[19]

In Norway the recent traitor Arne Treholt, in addition to providing the KGB with secrets, served as its influence agent, helping to ensure the Norwegian government's rejection of any proposal to place NATO nuclear weapons in Norway. He also influenced the negotiations about how the Barents Sea, which may have large oil and gas reserves, should be shared between Norway and the Soviet Union.

The Kremlin sets such store by agents of influence that it is prepared to detach an important KGB agent from other work for that purpose, as happened to the Canadian traitor Professor Hugh Hambleton, who was sent to Peru to advise the 'progressive' regime there. During his six months sojourn he helped to push the regime even more to the left. He was also sent by the KGB to Israel in 1970 to advise on economics and he asked so many sensitive questions that Israeli intelligence became suspicious. Later he was required by the KGB to try to enter the Canadian Parliament in the Soviet interest under the usual fraudulent cover of being a 'peace-loving liberal'.

The United Nations and its various offshoots have been penetrated to a contemptuous extent. Most of the 800 Soviet delegates and staff at the United Nations in New York are acting primarily as Soviet agents of influence, according to the chief defector from that organization, Arkady Shevchenko, who has described the UN building in New York as the KGB's tallest observation tower.[20]

The British legal system, which can exert profound influence, has been penetrated by Soviet agents of influence ever since the days of D. N. Pritt, a crypto-Communist barrister posing as a democratic socialist who was instrumental in protecting Soviet agents, such as the German Jurgen Kuczynski. Currently there are open and covert Communist lawyers, both solicitors and barristers. In the USA there has never been any shortage of lawyers anxious to defend those accused of pro-Soviet treachery and prepared to use transparently specious evidence and argument, as the recent book, *The FBI–KGB War*, by the former FBI officer Robert Lamphere demonstrates in detail.

It is the educational system, however, which is penetrated comprehensively. Whenever the Cambridge University spy ring of the 1930s is being discussed, great play is usually made of the influence exerted by a few left-wing dons, but there are now many more Marxist revolutionary lecturers and professors in British universities and in the institutes of education charged with providing teachers for schools. In turn, the schools, right down to primary level, are being penetrated by Marxist agents of influence, as a long-term investment in the revolutionary process.[21]

The area in which the most continuous effort is made to plant agents of influence is the media, and those journalists and radio and television producers who promote a political line surreptitiously are treacherous, at least, to their readers, listeners, and viewers. The extent to which journalists are utilized, both knowingly and unwittingly, to promote

43

Soviet active measures tailored to distort Western perceptions of the Kremlin's real intentions has been revealed in first-hand detail by the KGB officer Stanislav Levchenko, who was controlled by the International Department during his years in Japan. Using bribery, blackmail, and less obvious methods he induced Japanese journalists to plant pro-Soviet propaganda into TV programmes, newspapers with huge circulations and a news agency which served them. Another KGB defector, Ilya Dzhirkvelov, has independently confirmed the importance which the Soviet leaders attach to securing the services of foreign journalists, TV producers, and other media figures as agents of influence.[22]

Many need no stimulation to provide this service, for in all the true democracies the freedom of the press is continuously exploited by politically motivated individuals projecting their own extremist views either openly or in surreptitious ways. The type specimen of the journalist hired for surreptitious influence operations has to be the French writer Pierre-Charles Pathé, the son of the cinema pioneer who was convicted in 1980 after serving the Kremlin for twenty years. Writing under his own name as well as under pseudonyms, he published Soviet propaganda in French newspapers, and circulated a newsletter among politicians and diplomats consistently defending the Soviet position and attacking the USA. Pathé was a paid agent and when caught handing over documents to a KGB agent showed no remorse.[23] The KGB had similar success with a Danish journalist, Arne Herlov Petersen, who published scurrilous pamphlets attacking Western leaders, purveyed forgeries supplied by the Soviets, and provided other services. While ideologically committed, he took money and gifts from the KGB as well as fringe benefits such as free travel facilities.[24]

Currently, the prime media-influence operation is the dissemination of the view that the USA is militarily aggressive, unstable and likely to start a nuclear war in contrast to the dependable, peace-loving Soviet Union. Journalists and other psychological warriors are encouraged to engender the unfounded fear that a nuclear war is imminent and to concentrate on describing its appalling effects, while suggesting that the only way to prevent it is for the West to accept whatever Soviet arms deal may be on offer. The Kremlin requires that any American initiative like the so-called 'Star Wars' strategic defence shall be ridiculed; and in every country journalists, who tend to be ignorant of the technology, oblige, usually by projecting the views of some left-wing scientist. Even newspaper advertisements are being used in the anti-American media offensive. When President Reagan was due to visit Britain in 1984, for example, a large group of Labour MPs joined overt Communists and Trotskyists in sponsoring large advertisements which urged people to picket the American Embassy on his arrival.[25]

Anti-Americanism is also being regularly reinforced by journalists whose dislike of the USA and its ways seems to be born of envy of its material and technological success rather than of politics. One senses it among the TV commentators in the *schadenfreude* when anything goes wrong with American ventures, such as the Space Shuttle disaster of 1986.

The influence of such a relentless media campaign on a free society was demonstrated by the result of the treatment of the Vietnam War in the USA. The American press, radio, and television, with their horrific pictures of casualties, were to a large extent responsible for the American defeat by undermining public support.[26] Many prominent Americans contributed, regularly giving aid and comfort to the enemy through their actions and statements to the media. They would, no doubt, argue that defeat was in the long-term interest of their country, as did some prominent Germans, such as Admiral Canaris, chief of the Abwehr (secret service) in the Second World War.

Contributing to the defeat of one's own country in war must be treasonable, and that was the enterprise of the Australian-born journalist Wilfred Burchett. As the type specimen of the agent of influence able to operate quite openly most of the time, Burchett merits detailed description, especially as I have no doubt that he was a paid KGB agent, having known him and read widely on his history.[27] The son of a 'progressive' lay preacher committed to left-wing politics in Australia, Burchett moved to London and secured a job with the Soviet travel agency, Intourist, in 1936, after being rejected by the British Communist Party as a volunteer for the Spanish Civil War. From then onwards, his dedication to revolutionary Communism continued undiminished to his death in Bulgaria in 1983, at the age of seventy-two, and he descended the slippery slope of treachery with professionalism and relish. His success as a Second World War foreign correspondent for the *Daily Express* and other newspapers gave him scope for making contacts, though he did not become an open Communist until the advent of the cold war in 1946. He consistently showed himself as a Stalinist, castigating the true democracies and falsely portraying Russia as the fount of all progress and peace. An excellent linguist – he had taught himself French, Spanish, Italian, German, and Russian – he covered the trial of Cardinal Mindszenty in Budapest, indicating his guilt of conspiracy against the Hungarian Republic with glee.[28]

After working in Australia for Communist front organizations, Burchett moved to China, where he was financed by the Chinese

Communist Party, his main motive for going there being ideological. In 1951 he began journalistic coverage of the Korean War, in which Australian troops were involved, and fearlessly followed the Chinese 'volunteers' across the Yalu River. His slanted reports there for the French Communist newspaper *L'Humanité* and his other activities over the next two and a half years made him a traitor in the eyes of the Australian government and of many others who knew him. Among a great deal of disinformation which he deliberately purveyed was the totally false claim that the Americans were using germ warfare in both North Korea and northern China.[29] Burchett also fabricated reports of atrocities by American troops against Korean civilians.

He appeared in North Korean prisoner-of-war camps, falsely claiming that American and British prisoners there were almost enjoying themselves in 'holiday-resort' conditions when, in fact, they were being grossly maltreated, with regular attempts at so-called 'brainwashing'. Exceeding his professional functions as a journalist, he harshly interrogated prisoners, extracting 'confessions' to prove the germ-warfare lie. One prisoner later testified that Burchett, wearing a Chinese uniform, warned him that he could have him shot and that it would be a 'good thing' if he were shot.[30] There can be no doubt that he committed treason in the legal sense by giving aid and comfort to the enemies of his country in time of war, as William Joyce had done in Germany, and he was awarded war medals by the North Koreans.

In September 1953 Burchett attempted to supply intelligence to the US military command if they could arrange an amnesty for him from the Australian government, which hoped to charge Burchett with treason because he owed allegiance to the Queen.[31] When the Australian government refused, Burchett moved to North Vietnam, where he became friendly with Ho Chi Minh and supported him in his war against the French and, later, throughout the war with the USA. In the interim, however, Burchett visited Moscow, renewing a relationship with a KGB officer, Yuri Krotkov, who had recruited him in 1947. He made arrangements for Burchett to live in Moscow with his Bulgarian wife, the KGB providing a five-room apartment and other amenities including a car.[32] Burchett returned to Hanoi in 1962 to propagandize for the North Vietnamese until the fall of Saigon. During his 'journalistic' travels he was provided with a sizeable armed guard. His dispatches were widely used by the Western media and he greatly influenced other journalists, such as Harrison Salisbury of the *New York Times*, in ways which helped to swing American opinion against the war.

Once the Labour government achieved power in Australia in 1972 under Gough Whitlam, Burchett was free to return home without fear of prosecution and did so, being imprudent enough to sue for libel on the grounds that a statement that he had been in the pay of the KGB was false. Burchett lost and left Australia to be based behind the Iron Curtain.

The former CIA officer Philip Agee is another blatantly overt agent of influence. Since defecting from the CIA in 1969, when he claimed to be 'disillusioned' but was also in financial and woman trouble, he has become a full-time disseminator of disinformation in the Soviet interest, being extremely adept at exploiting the Western freedom to express his views and the right of residence which would be barred to him under similar circumstances in the Soviet Union.

Over the last seventy years the Soviet Union has striven with great success to bend entire free-world organizations to its purposes as *agencies of influence*. It has set up many to serve as Communist 'fronts': – organizations which do not appear to be Soviet-controlled and can be disclaimed as such, the World Peace Council, with its multifarious offshoots, being currently among the most effective. As the Czech defector Frantisek August has recorded, a major purpose of Soviet-bloc agents of influence in the West is to encourage a climate of defeatism, and the 'peace' movements are bent on convincing the West that it cannot defend itself and may as well put itself at the mercy of Soviet 'goodwill' or depend on the United Nations, which is packed with Soviet client states. 'Peace workers' also function as agents of influence, some deliberate, others unwitting, in that area of operation so dear to the Politburo – the sowing of dissension and distrust between the USA and its NATO allies and particularly between the USA and Britain.

With its current policy of unilateral nuclear disarmament, the British Labour Party also happens to be serving as an extremely promising Soviet agency of influence; whatever the arguments behind the policy, it is exactly what the Soviet Union has been striving for since it is calculated to end the Anglo-American special relationship, fostered over forty years, and to induce the Americans to withdraw not only from Britain but from Europe.[33]

Organizations which provide financial support for revolutionary activities can also fairly be described as agencies of influence. These include the former Greater London Council, trade unions which divert funds to extremist causes, and student unions which channel much of the £30 million of government aid granted to them to Marxist causes and revolutionary propaganda.

So far as influence operations are concerned the East–West balance is hard down on the Soviet side, which, of course, is one of the reasons why the Soviets continue to put such emphasis on agents of influence for the exertion of active measures. Apart from a few dissidents, who are dealt with summarily and severely, there are no overt 'traitors of

47

influence' inside the Soviet Union, and few are able to operate in secrecy, though from time to time it has suited Soviet leaders to claim that they did exist, in the form of Red Army generals or even Politburo members, when they needed an excuse to liquidate them. Western societies, on the other hand, have found it difficult to take any action against agents of influence unless they extend their activities to actual transgression of the law, which the clever ones rarely do. The long lists of KGB agents of influence in Britain and the USA, provided by Gordievsky and Yurchenko have produced no action against any of those named.

The many and varied motivational factors which beckon agents of influence and all other potential traitors towards the slippery slope and then propel them down it will now be considered.

CHAPTER FIVE

The Lure of Adventure and Excitement

The thirst for adventure is the vent which destiny offers.

Emerson

One does not have to be a Walter Mitty to appreciate that treachery in its various forms must have its exciting moments, if only because of the danger of discovery and its consequences. Several subversive agents who have written memoirs or otherwise put their experiences on record have listed excitement at the prospect of being involved in clandestine work as a major reason for their willingness to be recruited. Alexander Foote, the Briton who worked for the GRU in Switzerland, recalled that, as a young man with service in the Spanish Civil War, he was looking for something new and preferably exciting.[1] When Hede Massing met the pro-Soviet German spy Richard Sorge, he convinced her that espionage was both heroic and glamorous before introducing her to her first spy-master.[2] The former German cabaret artiste Maria Knuth, who became an important Soviet-bloc spy shortly after the end of the Second World War, was attracted by the excitement provided by her work as a secret courier, and later in more exacting roles which enabled her to utilize her acting talents. This became particularly important to her when she realized that she had incurable cancer, with only two or three years of life left.[3]

'Sonia', in her memoirs, indicates that she enjoyed her twenty years of GRU service when, according to Soviet TV recently, she was 'exposed daily to mortal danger'.[4] When the Swedish traitor Colonel Stig Wennerstrom ventured into Soviet territory from Latvia and was in some danger of being arrested, the experience had an 'adventurously seductive' effect on his whole attitude to intelligence work.[5] Harry Houghton, the British Soviet spy at the Portland Underwater Research Centre, recorded in his memoirs how he experienced 'sheer exhilaration at getting a scarifying job done in the face of awful risks'. Though he was aware that he was working for the 'wrong side', he recalled, when in the company of his Soviet contacts, the 'feeling of comradeship, of being in a tense situation and enjoying even the riskiest moments together'.[6] Even the shy and sensitive John Vassall, who was black-mailed into spying, found it exciting; he had realized, before the KGB ever approached him, that his posting to Moscow offered a 'new world of excitement and danger.'[7]

The need to live a double life with an ingenious cover for all nefarious activities, the so-called 'legend', adds to the sense of adventure for some recruits to treachery and would seem to be linked with the pleasure of acting a role, for the successful traitor is permanently on stage. It would be instructive to know whether true double agents, who have to lead a double double life through serving two secret masters, experience a double dose of excitement.

The feeling of excitement derives not only from the danger but from the purpose and the circumstances in which treachery is pursued. Sidney Reilly, the born adventurer employed by MI6 in 1918 to undermine the Bolshevik regime was fascinated by the thrill of taking part in the power struggle.[8] A few peculiar personalities among pro-Soviet traitors appear to have been specially attracted by the opportunity for intrigue and the sheer delight in deceiving others. Guy Burgess and Tom Driberg were type specimens. They loved playing off one person against another and there is no field comparable with espionage where this can be done more damagingly and to the secret enjoyment of the perpetrator. To quote Leo Abse, the Labour MP who has studied psychology and knew Driberg well:

> Driberg walked all his life on a tightrope and gained his thrills in public and private by a never-ending series of adventures, courageously and foolhardily oscillating from one role to another almost every day. . . . If the officers of MI5 were inept enough to have attempted to recruit him, then, in turn, Driberg would have gained especial pleasure in fooling and betraying them – the attraction of the sheer villainy of it to the evil intellect.[9]

The same applied to Donald Maclean. When Blunt was questioned in 1963 about the reasons for Maclean's defection he said the Russians were afraid that, if interrogated, he would confess everything for the sheer enjoyment of letting his former colleagues know the extent to which he had duped them, those who had trusted him being idiots in Maclean's view.

The aura of conspiracy and secrecy is an important component of the adventure/excitement factor, and Soviet recruiters, in particular, have always laid great stress on what they call the conspiratorial rules, essentially as a means of survival but also to intensify the inducement. Anthony Blunt was older than the other members of the Cambridge Ring when recruited, but nevertheless stated in his confession to MI5 that he had been attracted by the element of secrecy. Colonel Stig Wennerstrom, the most damaging Swedish traitor, referred in his confessions to the 'deep inner satisfaction' which he derived from knowing that the people around him were unaware of his treachery. As his biographer put it: 'It was as though, for him, secrecy became almost an end in itself. He seemed proud to know things that others didn't.'[10]

Wennerstrom was not peculiar in that respect. Secret knowledge provides a feeling of power and superiority over the herd which many relish. Several senior civil servants and Ministers have told me that what they miss most on being retired is the pleasure of being in the know, the whole atmosphere of a government department involved with secrets being somewhat 'conspiratorial'. Those Cambridge undergraduates and dons, like Blunt, who had already been invited to join the exclusive society called the Apostles, were attracted not only by the honour but by the secrecy required. Since all members had to swear a fearful oath pledging that they would never disclose the name of any of the members, save when recruiting others, and would never reveal anything about the proceedings, the atmosphere was conducive to conspiracy. In the 1930s the club became a haunt of both homosexuals and Communists and a fertile ground for recruiters to the Soviet cause.

Whether traitors derive satisfaction from their efforts, through excitement or anything else, greatly depends on the skill with which they are handled by their case officers. A competent case officer will do what he can to ensure that a valuable source who sets store by excitement continues to experience it by such devices as being told that he has been given officer rank in the KGB; but all recruits are quickly made to understand that the work is extremely serious, demanding absolute obedience to rules and commands, any 'fun' being incidental. Professor G. M. Wickens, now of Toronto University, was not recruited either to the Communist Party or to Soviet espionage when he was at Cambridge, but he was involved in various Marxist discussion groups where he 'quickly became aware of the difference between Communism's then quite genial public face and the grim self-image reserved for the inner circle'.[11]

While the cult of the spy novel was not as strong in the past as it is now, many of these young people who became enmeshed in espionage were romancing to some extent. Clandestine work has always held special appeal for an inveterate romancer – the 'Walter Mitty' – like the Welshman Arthur George Owens, who volunteered his services to the Abwehr in 1936 and became one of its most important wartime agents, being so addicted to the excitement that spying became compulsive.[12] The same applied to the Canadian professor Hugh Hambleton, who enjoyed the conspiratorial life so much, and particularly the gadgetry of espionage, that it became like a drug to him. He claimed that he had been a traitor primarily 'for kicks', not being ideologically committed to Communism, and having received money only for expenses. Indeed, he seems to have become so 'hooked' on espionage, as Wennerstrom also was, that he suffered from withdrawal symptoms when not active. Leo Heaps, a former Canadian friend of Hambleton who interviewed him in prison, told me that the traitor found it difficult to distinguish between his romantic fantasies and what had really occurred; his story of having dined with the KGB chief, Andropov, in Moscow may have been such a figment.

In the so-called cloak and dagger business of espionage the dagger rarely figures, except to the extent that traitors can be responsible for plunging it into the backs of colleagues, but some have been influenced by the action and excitement of war. Philby's experience in Vienna, where he witnessed the killing of 'workers' in an abortive uprising in 1934 seems to have intensified his commitment. He saw action in the Spanish Civil War, as did Foote, Len Beurton, 'Sonia's' English husband, and other young men who became Soviet agents. Involvement in military action reinforced the dedication of the American Communist agent Agnes Smedley to the cause of the Red Chinese, and the military turmoil in China in the 1930s may have been a factor in the recruitment of Roger Hollis by the Soviets in Shanghai. During the Korean and Vietnamese wars, close contact with Communist troops was to cement the conversion of Wilfred Burchett from an extreme left-wing journalist to a KGB agent.

The factor of adventure and excitement in the context of war is, presumably, significant in the recruitment of traitorous agents to assist invading Soviet *Spetsnaz* forces. For those seeking more immediate excitement through action, terrorism clearly has special attraction. Judges who have tried IRA bombers have taken the view that some of them, at least, enjoy their murderous terrorism, and this would seem to be true of members of other organizations dedicated primarily to violence. Agca, the Turk who attempted to assassinate the present Pope, has insisted that he is neither of the right nor of the left but 'just a terrorist'.

There are cases where individuals have joined an intelligence agency in the hope of finding excitement and when this did not materialize have sought it by indulging in freelance active espionage. William Kampiles, a 23-year-old American, secured employment with the CIA in March 1977 and was soon assigned to the operations centre at the Langley headquarters, near Washington, continuously monitoring intelligence around the world received from satellites and other sources. This meant routine and often boring work, and Kampiles, who had expected excitement, was soon agitating for transfer to espionage operations, saying that he had always wanted to be a case officer. When this was not forthcoming he resigned after arguments with his supervisors. He took with him a copy of a manual describing the advanced technology photographic satellite system called the KH–11 or 'Keyhole' satellite – the first 'real-time' system capable of transmitting pictures from space instantaneously – and sold it to an agent of the GRU for $3,000, going to Athens for that purpose. The trip, and the money, no doubt provided the required excitement. To secure a repeat performance, the traitor had also taken with him a blank CIA identification card, to which he had applied a photograph and a forged signature identifying him as a current CIA employee. This enabled him to convince his Soviet contact that he could continue to deliver secrets and to make a deal to return to Athens every three months with a further batch at $10,000 a time. When Kampiles was caught, it was found that he had enabled the Russians to deceive or nullify the KH–11 system; the damage to the US ability to monitor Soviet military preparedness was so great that he was jailed for forty years.[13]

Anyone who joins an intelligence or security agency in search of excitement and adventure is likely to be disappointed, for the work is based on the laborious analysis of reports from agents and tedious research into old files, while the whole organization tends to be run on restrictive bureaucratic lines. On a working day an officer is much more likely to have a date with a desk than with a spy or a blonde. Several senior members of MI6, the secret intelligence service, and MI5, the counter-spy agency, including Sir Dick White who headed both agencies, have complained to me about the false impression given by spy thrillers. The reaction to the disappointment could, conceivably, be a factor in the motivation of officers like Michael Bettaney who introduced an element of intrigue and danger by working for the 'opposition'.

The two young American traitors, Christopher Boyce and Daulton Lee, who inflicted even greater damage than Kampiles through selling satellite secrets, achieved some excitement from their treachery, especially during visits to the Soviet Embassy in Mexico. Boyce, in particular, seemed to enjoy risk of any sort and his espionage certainly provided it. Later, however, when committed to prison for sixty-eight years he confessed that any excitement had been short-lived and quickly neutralized by the fear generated by his guilt.[14]

53

How long the pleasurable feeling of excitement lasts depends on the temperament of the traitor, a factor to be discussed in Chapter 15, on the degree to which fear erodes it and the general satisfaction generated by the treacherous efforts. Some traitors, like Hambleton, continued to enjoy the conspiratorial life over many years, but for others it proved superficial and quickly palled and became drudgery. Whittaker Chambers, who probably lacked the temperament to secure enjoyment from his treachery, described it succinctly in his book *Witness*:

> Its mysteries quickly become a bore, its secrecy a burden, and its involved way of doing things a nuisance. Its object is never to provide excitement but to avoid it. Thrills mean that something has gone wrong. The mysterious character of underground work is merely a tedious daily labour to keep thrills from happening. I have never known a good conspirator who enjoyed conspiracy.

Harry Gold, the American courier who serviced Fuchs in the USA, agreed that the excitement of clandestine work quickly turned to drudgery, which he hated, while Elizabeth Bentley, another Soviet courier in America, referred to it as her 'bondage'.

Both Chambers and Bentley managed to extricate themselves from the labyrinth of treason, but most Soviet agents find themselves trapped by the *realpolitik* of the situation and the ruthlessness of their masters. They then take what comfort they can in their confidence that exposure could not happen to them or, as certainly happened in the past, in the touching belief that if they were caught and heavily sentenced their country would soon be 'Sovietized' anyway, and they would be released as heroes before they had served many years.[15]

A traitor who knows or thinks that he is under suspicion and perhaps under surveillance, as Donald Maclean did, will no longer derive much pleasure from his treachery, particularly if his masters require him to continue with it, in spite of the danger. On the other hand Anthony Blunt, who had never been suspect during his five wartime years inside MI5, remarked to a colleague that it had given him great pleasure to give the Russians the names of every MI5 officer. Later he must have derived particular satisfaction from his continued pro-Soviet activities from his base in Buckingham Palace, even if this was reduced to emptying dead letter boxes for Burgess, as he later told MI5. Blunt seems to have been more immune to fear than most, perhaps because of a well-based conviction that, if detected, the establishment would protect him, but he described Burgess as being 'almost round the bend' with worry.[16]

To summarize, it would seem that the prospect of excitement and adventure is a factor in the recruitment of traitors, especially when they are young and immature, and in the continuing treachery of a few who remain immature, but it is of variable importance because of personality differences.

There is nothing like a major power struggle for providing the arena for conspiratorial adventure and excitement and the factor of power as a motivation will be considered next.

CHAPTER SIX

Power-Lust

It is a strange desire to seek power and to lose liberty.

Francis Bacon

The type specimen of a traitor tempted into treachery by the prospect of personal power has to be that enigmatic character, Vidkun Quisling, the Norwegian politician already mentioned in Chapter 3. There can be no doubt that Quisling, who was intellectually gifted, was passionately devoted to his country. Like Hitler he was fascinated by the sagas and legends of his native land, and this may have been crucial in his support for the Nazi concept of a Nordic race with a special destiny. In his search for service to his country he joined the army and was soon attached to the General Staff but, after a sojourn in Russia as military attaché in 1918 he became politicized. Originally in favour of the Communist system, he turned against it, left the army, and entered politics as a right-winger with a burning sense of mission, convinced that he had been born to lead his nation. He became Defence Minister and, after contact with the German Nazis, soon saw himself as dictator of a Fascist Norway, with anti-Semitism and the sequestration of Jewish property as an inevitable consequence. To further his political power he began negotiations with Germany in 1939, fully convinced of a Nazi victory and the need to tie Norway's fate to the Greater Germany. The German invasion of Norway put him in charge of the government where he met with stout political opposition. After the German defeat in May 1945, he was arrested, charged with high treason, tried, and shot. Whatever his original patriotic purpose, Quisling became totally corrupted by the quest for power; and while there have been more cynical traitors he will assuredly remain the archetype of the genre.[1]

In the Soviet Union Quisling's place is taken by Andrei Vlasov, the renegade Red Army general whose offer to raise an Army of National Liberation to fight alongside the Germans was partly motivated by his power dream of marching into Russia as a heroic leader after the

56

defeat of Stalin, as de Gaulle eventually did into France. De Gaulle may well have suffered the same fate as Vlasov, at the hands of Vichy France, had the Germans won the war. Such is the razor edge on which the politically ambitious walk and from which they can fall into accusation of gross treachery or step up into glorious acclaim.

A psychologist might argue, with some justification, that the traitor in Soviet service enjoys vicarious pleasure through a sense of power filtering down from the Politburo – which, as he knows, wields absolute power in the USSR and ceaselessly endeavours to extend it elsewhere. A study of the Politburo's thinking and behaviour suggests that many of its members have been so imbued with the conviction that the spread of Soviet-dominated Communism is inevitable that they regard any resistance to it as immoral and difficult to understand. Their indignation may even be genuine when action is taken against their espionage and subversion officers serving abroad. So it may be this, as much as vindictiveness, which led them to arrest the American journalist Nicholas Daniloff in August 1986 following the exposure and apprehension in New York of a KGB agent Gennadi Zakharov in a blatant act of subversion.[2] Perhaps the Politburo members really do believe that they have a unique right to spy and subvert wherever they feel it necessary to preserve the Soviet state and their own position and to retaliate, however ruthlessly, when there is interference with this 'right'.

Those in Soviet service are certainly encouraged by their case officers to take a similar view about the historical rightness of their cause. This attitude affects the faithful foreign Communist when he is asked to increase his commitment by taking a more purposeful part, as a secret agent, in the 'struggle', which can never end until the world is communized.

This feeling of taking an active and positive part in a power struggle is particularly attractive in an era when, because of the complications of life, many people, and especially the young, have a sense of impotence. It was a major factor in the recruitment of young men and women to the Soviet cause in the 1930s, when governments seemed impotent against the march of Nazism. Many of them were convinced that capitalism really was in its final stages and that they could actively contribute to its abolition. The American KGB courier Harry Gold, for instance, confessed to the satisfaction he had achieved through being active in a power struggle aimed at changing society, while Blunt expressed his hope of sharing in the acquisition of power by revolution when he said that he fully expected to be the British Commissar for the Arts.[3]

Other traitors may well have agreed to accept the risks of treachery because they believed revolution in their own country – and their personal reward – to be only a few years away. Those like the American Harry Dexter White, who revelled in the wielding of power provided by their positions presumably looked forward to a day when their contribution to the replacement of true democracy by a Soviet-style dictatorship would give them more. As White's chief, Morgenthau, recalled when trying to explain his chief henchman's treachery, White 'wished to remake the world'.[4] Philby, who had soundly based hopes of promotion to the top management of MI6, and Maclean, who could have gone much higher in the Foreign Office, may have entertained even higher ambitions under a revolutionary regime.

The sense of sharing in a power struggle is basic today to the appeal of the campaigns for nuclear disarmament by providing people, young and old, with a feeling, however speciously based, that they are *doing* something positive, even if it is no more than causing a public nuisance by damaging the fences round nuclear bases. This feeling has been intensified by the wide coverage of the activities of the 'peace' campaigners by the media and especially by television. The power of the authorities in the true democracies to counter such agitation has been shown to be very limited and leaders of the 'peace' movement, who would otherwise be nonentities, are elevated to public figures appearing to command authority.

The power factor would seem to be important in the recruitment of fifth columnists to assist invading Soviet *Spetsnaz* forces. Those revolutionaries who hanker after action could be tempted by the possibility of making a physical contribution to their cause, as were British Catholic plotters who were prepared to assist a Spanish invasion in the interests of their faith in Elizabethan times.

In all government administrations the power of patronage – the power to place others in important positions and to promote and even honour them – is rated as a major perquisite of office. Dexter White and others like him used it to introduce other Soviet agents into sensitive positions in the United States administration and to promote them. There can be little doubt that British traitors and agents of influence have behaved in similar fashion.

When a young person is appointed to an official post with access to valuable secrets, the security authorities warn him that he is in such a special position of trust that there are grave penalties for breaching it. It is not difficult therefore to imagine that some of those who are poorly qualified might come to view the opportunity for committing damaging treachery as an expression of power, which is otherwise likely to be denied them because of their career limitations. This may rarely be a sufficiently strong factor to drive a person into treachery but coupled with another, such as resentment or some other 'chip on the shoulder', it might do so.

Defectors must surely experience a sense of power when they are revealing what they know about their old allegiance to their newly adopted side particularly when, as so often happens, they realize that it is all excitingly new to their interrogators. This must be particularly true when they were relatively small cogs in their parent machine. The KGB defector Anatoly Golitsin, for example, had held only the rank of major but was in urgent demand by every Western intelligence agency because of his peculiar and extensive knowledge about KGB agents operating in many countries. Having deliberately memorized as much information as possible from KGB files before defecting, he was fully aware of his power and of his value in money terms. At a stroke, his defection converted him from an unknown, middle-rank official in a secret agency to an international figure.

Those Soviet agents embedded in important positions in security and intelligence services, such as Philby, Blake, and, I believe, Hollis, must have experienced a gratifying feeling of personal power when they were able to influence secret affairs and policy in the direction they favoured. Hollis, with his wartime responsibility for Communist counter-espionage, was able to clear Fuchs time and again on his own initiative for continued work on atomic weapons which enabled that traitor to betray crucial secrets to the Soviets for eight years. Through his membership of secret policy committees Hollis's potential influence was so great over so many years that any retrospective examination of it has been ruled out as impracticable.

One can sense the feeling of secret power which Philby experienced during his treacherous career inside MI6 through the glee with which he retold some of his past successes in his book, *My Silent War*, the grandiose title indicating his satisfaction at undermining his own country. His third wife, Eleanor, recorded how, once Philby had defected, he missed the opportunity for treacherous action and had to rely for satisfaction, rather pathetically, on praise for his past or for his occasional retrospective reports.[5] If the loyal civil servant or intelligence officer greatly misses the component of power provided by his privileged access to secrets once he retires, how much more deprived must the dedicated spy feel once his access has ended.

While Philby told all with relish, a defector can, of course, express his power by withholding information when it suits. Some, like the German KGB agent Paul Massing and the senior KGB officer Alexander Orlov, have certainly done so. Blunt seems to have enjoyed a cynical sense of power, or, at least, his interrogators' impotence, by declining to provide information about his close friends, a ludicrous privilege made possible by the circumstances of his immunity to prosecution.

The power wielded by agents of influence, great and small, has been considered in Chapter 4. I know from interviewing some of them or meeting them socially that those in senior positions find the situation attractively heady, and derive personal, as well as political, satisfaction from exploiting it, especially when they have brought off a subtle manoeuvre. This applies particularly to politicians when they have intervened in some debate in the Soviet interest or damaged British security by using their parliamentary privilege.

Communist and pro-Communist trade union leaders have no doubts about the power they can wield if they so desire. This was brought home to me by the coalminers' leader, Arthur Scargill, during a lunch together some years before his accession to the national leadership, when he explained that he had no intention of entering Parliament because the real seat of power was with the unions, as indeed it was then. 'It is with the unions that the action lies, and action is what interests me,' Scargill said.[6] Communist shop stewards who could never achieve authority any other way, like Derek Robinson in the motor industry, can wield local power with such effect that they can initiate major strikes and bring big capitalist enterprises to their knees, to the satisfaction of Moscow and Communists everywhere. They can also enhance their sense of power and indulge their vanity by guaranteed appearances on television. The extent to which Soviet active measures are directed to securing some control of Western trade unions is evidence enough of their power.

There can be little doubt that the feeling of personal power and the playing of a regular active role appeal to many pro-Communist journalists, of whom perhaps the best example who can be named without libel problems is Wilfred Burchett. Their sense of power is intensified when they are involved in action, as Burchett was in Korea and Vietnam, though he regarded himself as continuously 'at the barricades'. William Joyce offers an example of a radio propagandist who clearly revelled in the sense of power given to him through his regular wartime radio broadcasts from Germany to Britain. As someone unlikely to achieve distinction or influence in any other sphere, the opportunity to make an international impact, in which he certainly succeeded, gave him particular satisfaction.

To those prone to violence and for whom power over life and death is attractive the cult of terrorism clearly exerts near-irresistible appeal. It has all the attributes for the ignorant who could never achieve anything constructive – the appeal of conspiratorial action, the excitement of dealing with dangerous devices, and the clandestine thrill of success, as measured by carnage and destruction, with the additional vicarious bonus of the inevitable publicity, intensifying a feeling of power about which the security authorities can so often do so little. The reaction of the IRA bombers who came so near to assassinating the Prime Minister in Brighton in 1984, especially when they believed they had escaped, can be imagined. Having planted the murderous device so successfully, how they must have been gloating while waiting for the long-term time fuse to detonate it. Success in killing off the Prime Minister and several of her Cabinet would have been a very real expression of power.

It would seem, then, that in many instances, perhaps most, the attraction of power plays some part in the recruitment of people to treachery and in keeping them committed to it.

CHAPTER SEVEN

The Pull of Ideology

Between craft and credulity the voice of reason is stifled.
                                                    Edmund Burke

An *ideologue* can be defined as a person committed to a particular political doctrine – an ideology – and who approaches political and social problems from an unshakably dogmatic standpoint. Case records show that the ideological traitor is usually the most deeply and permanently committed, the most effective, and the most difficult to 'turn', though he may 'turn' himself through personal revulsion against his former beliefs.

Communism, and particularly the Soviet version, Marxism–Leninism, is the most dogmatic ideology of all because of the absolute belief in its inevitability, which means that those who profess it are convinced that they cannot possibly be wrong, whatever they are required to do in its service. In practice it also implies a naïve willingness to accept as holy writ all the sacred texts and slogans devised by the Soviet hierarchy to swamp logical argument; as, for example, the use of 'peace' to disguise massive armaments, 'democracy' to cover tyranny, and other instances of what I call the 'upside-down ploy' – inverting reality as free society sees it. When it suited the Soviet government to declare that British Communists should not support the declaration of war against Hitler because it was an imperialists' war, most of them obeyed the instruction. The Soviet purpose was to expedite the defeat of Britain and its Empire because Stalin had allied himself, most cynically and expediently, with Hitler. Then, when Germany attacked the Soviet Union, Moscow immediately declared the war against Hitler to be just, and British Communists dutifully followed that instruction. Most Communists did not find this difficult because Moscow has always taken the line that ideology can be modified at any time by the Party chiefs to serve the Soviet purpose – the so-called 'zig-zag' approach to objectives.

Soviet-style Communism is, for all practical purposes, a religion, which is why other religions are anathema in the Soviet Union. There can be no higher authority than the 'church' of Marxism–Leninism, which is the Communist Party.

The degree of commitment to the party, with all the demands required of its members, is total. As the KGB defector, Peter Deriabin, expressed the Soviet situation, which has been the template for other Communist parties: 'The Communist is not supposed to have a private life outside his organization. Everything he has and does – family, profession, hobbies, friends – is subordinated to the fact of his Communism. He is a Communist not only when he is at Party meetings but is a Communist everywhere and at all times.'[1] The renegade British Communist Douglas Hyde similarly observed: 'The Party is so organized as to make Communism the whole life of its members.'[2] This, of course, makes it relatively easy for the Soviet Union to recruit agents from among the members of foreign Communist parties, provided these are subservient to Moscow's. So ideology has been a major factor in the pro-Soviet treason committed over the years by Western traitors.

The insidious way in which ideological recruits have been obtained was described in detail by the Canadian Royal Commission which examined the circumstances surrounding the many Canadian traitors revealed by the defection of Igor Gouzenko in 1945, and there is no reason to suppose that such an effective procedure has been radically changed. Promising subjects were first induced to join 'study groups' to develop an interest in Communism and a sense of belonging. Each group, or 'cell', was limited to about five so that the person in control could study each potential recruit carefully, the cells being linked through their controllers. Much was made of secrecy as an inducement to join a cell, and deliberate effort was made to accustom the members to an atmosphere of conspiracy and the 'psychology of a double life'. This was aimed at the gradual erosion of normal moral standards such as frankness, honesty, integrity, and respect for the sanctity of oaths and the induction of a state of mind capable of discarding moral obligations which would previously have been fulfilled as a matter of course.[3] The process closely followed that leading to drug addiction – beginning with soft drugs soon followed by total addiction to something stronger.

The thoroughly indoctrinated Communist ended up hardly speaking the same language as true democrats because of a tortuous understanding of so many terms like 'truth', 'peace', 'democracy', 'freedom', 'human rights', 'imperialism', and 'progressive'. The Communist mind was, and remains, closed to events and circumstances which challenge the ideology, enabling them to be dismissed as 'irrelevancies'.

Once a recruit had been admitted to membership of the party, absolute obedience to Party officials was demanded and, with integrity destroyed, service in some form of treachery could then be required. Again this was usually achieved in insidious stages. Kathleen Willsher, a British girl working in the High Commission in Ottawa, joined a secret cell and was ordered to provide secret information for the Communist Party of Canada when it really went straight to Moscow. When apprehended, after seven years of what amounted to espionage, she said that while she had struggled with her conscience for a few weeks she had felt she had to comply because it was her duty to the party which overrode other duties.[4]

Soviet intelligence has always exploited this willingness of the naïve to commit themselves to espionage, so that by the time the recruits realized who their masters were it was too late for them to withdraw. When Alexander Foote agreed to become a spy against the Nazis he did not know for six months for whom he was working, save that it was for the Communist ideal as a whole. 'I knew I was a spy and knew against whom I was spying but, at first, I had no idea of the why and wherefore or of the directing hand,' he recalled.[5] The same applied to 'Sonia', as she records in her memoirs.[6] When Michael Straight, the American who had been recruited by Blunt at Cambridge, objected to the order that he should return to the USA and use his wealth and social position to service the Soviet interest in Wall Street, Blunt went through the motions, probably spurious, of reporting his reluctance to a 'higher authority'. Straight went to the USA, as ordered, after Blunt told him that his objection had been overruled.[7] Naïvety concerning the Soviet Union's true intentions was certainly a factor in the conversion of Communists into traitors and their continuation in the Soviet service. The irresistibly insidious way in which many of them were induced on to the slippery slope by asking them if they would 'work for peace', as described by Blunt in his confession, was a master-stroke of recruitment psychology.

Recent case histories show that the same appeals to young people to commit treachery through ideology are being made today. When the KGB officer Gennadi Zakharov was trying to intensify the espionage of a young jet-engine technician, a foreigner resident in New York, in 1986 he told him that he should not be motivated solely by money but should feel rewarded when he was able to hurt the United States.[8]

There is a current tendency to regard ideology as being much less potent than it was; but while there are fewer overt Communists and actual Party members in the West than previously, there remain many who are covert Communists or deep sympathizers and certainly enough to provide a dangerous reservoir of potential recruits. There is a further reservoir of potential traitors in the steadily increasing ranks of the splinter groups of Communists: Trotskyists, Socialist

Militants, Workers Revolutionaries, and suchlike. While squabbling bitterly over matters of ideological detail, they all remain dedicated to hatred of a genuinely free society and to overthrowing capitalism by force and establishing some kind of 'dictatorship of the proletariat'. This, as in the Soviet Union, really means dictatorship *over* the proletariat, who would have far less influence on government and on their own lives than in a true democracy. Force is now deemed necessary since, contrary to what Lenin taught, capitalism has not proved to contain the seeds of its own destruction, but has proved to be the most effective system for improving the common lot.

The common communist ground, shared by all branches of what is often described as the 'hard left', is insufficiently appreciated, as shown by the fact that whenever revolutionary candidates stand as representatives of their parties they are rejected with derisory support, whereas if they stand under some other guise, particularly as Labour candidates, they often win. Journalists would serve their readers with greater accuracy if such people were called communists, with a small 'c', which can hardly be held to be libellous, though 'Communist', implying membership of that party, might be. This practice would also do much to correct the misleading view that with the decline of Communist Party memberships ideology can no longer be a powerful factor in the recruitment of traitors. There are more revolutionaries in Britain, and perhaps in other European countries, than ever before and, therefore, more potential traitors.

As recently as 1982, in defending the weird, sex-deviationist traitor, Geoffrey Prime, the Soviet spy inside Britain's GCHQ, his defence counsel observed: 'It is the misfits of society that provide the fertile breeding ground for the ruthless propaganda of the Soviet system and its capacity to foster treachery under the guise of idealism.' Prime, who is believed to have been essentially ideological, said that he greatly admired what he had read and been told about the Russian system and felt 'they ought to know what was being done to their communications'.[9] From their appearance and behaviour, many of those more overt revolutionaries of the 'hard left' who show themselves in public would seem to qualify as misfits. There are, of course, no figures of the numbers of misfits in modern society, and accurate comparisons with the past cannot be made. But to most people of my age, walking about big cities or watching television, there would seem to be more social misfits than ever before. In May 1986 the KGB chief warned that it was the 'misfits' who were susceptible to treachery in the Soviet Union.

Another British misfit who managed to gain entry to a highly secret service was Michael Bettaney, the young MI5 officer, whose confession not only proved that ideology is still a factor to be reckoned with but raised the possibility of self-recruitment to treachery, which must be rare. He is believed to have recruited himself to Communism through reading, convincing himself that in the East–West conflict of ideologies the Russians had a preponderance of right and justice on their side. This is not uncommon among young people, as expressed by the aphorism: 'He who has not been a Communist by the time he is twenty has no heart, while he who is still a Communist after thirty has no brains.' According to the Security Commission, however, Bettaney argued himself into a more desperate step. 'By the summer of 1982 he had come to the conclusion that he must do all in his power to assist the Soviet Union. This meant spying for the Russians while continuing as an officer in the Security Service.'[10] Bettaney was detected soon after he approached the KGB in London, almost certainly because he was betrayed by the MI6 mole inside the KGB, Oleg Gordievsky, who has since defected.

The much more successful traitor George Blake may also have recruited himself, for, according to Kenneth de Courcy who was in prison with him, Blake said that though he did not entirely approve of the Communist system he felt compelled to go along with it because he was convinced of its inevitability.[11]

It may, of course, transpire that in reality both Blake and Bettaney had been indoctrinated by others whom they wished to protect and had then been actively recruited. In that event the Bettaney case would be evidence that Moscow's requirements to secure ideological traitors in Britain, the USA and elsewhere remain as pressing as ever, as witnessed also by the recent flight of ideologues planted in West Germany.

My type specimen of the perfect product of the system for developing ideological traitors is James Klugmann, whose wartime activities as an agent of influence have already been described. He seems to have been motivated from an early age by undiluted dedication to pro-Soviet Communism and became a bigoted 'Moscow right or wrong' Communist. He was born in 1912 of a well-off Jewish family and was educated at Gresham's Holt public school, where he was friendly with Donald Maclean and influenced him politically. At Cambridge University he helped to build the student branch of the Communist Party, which he had joined in 1933, influencing others like Blunt – who, when interrogated by the MI5 officer Peter Wright specifically mentioned Klugmann and Burgess as having influenced him. Blunt claimed that he became a Communist and Marxist in 1935 when, after a sabbatical year, he returned to Cambridge and found that 'all my friends . . . had suddenly become Marxists under the impact of Hitler coming to power'.[12]

Klugmann was among the earliest to be recruited to the Soviet intelligence service. He recruited others, like John Cairncross, at

Cambridge, introducing him to a Soviet controller; he also operated at Oxford, which he visited frequently and where, among others, he recruited the future Labour MP Bernard Floud.[13] After securing a double first in modern languages, he travelled widely on Communist and KGB business, serving as secretary of the World Student Movement, a Communist front in Paris, and leading a student delegation to China to meet Chinese Communist leaders in 1938.

After the war, in which he played such a crucial role in the Communization of Yugoslavia, he was a Communist journalist and indoctrinator, becoming editor of *Marxism Today*, and headed the Propaganda and Education Department of the Communist Party. He was the party's official historian until his death in 1977. All who remember him recall his kindness and charm which concealed a ruthless political will. Though he had a lively intelligence, he produced books which a former Cambridge friend, Harry Ferns, has described as 'distorted garbage', and it is one of the paradoxes of such Communists that they find no difficulty in prostituting their intellectual capabilities for party purposes. When, in 1948, Klugmann was faced with a break between Stalin and Tito, whom he had supported so strenuously, he slavishly followed the Moscow line and remained a faithful and dogmatic party member until he died. Good Communists are required to excuse every kind of excess if it is ordered by the party. Whatever monstrosities are perpetrated, they are 'correct' if the party says so. Accordingly, Klugmann shrugged off Communism's manifest failures as temporary and dismissed the terror and atrocities of Stalin as irrelevant aberrations.[14]

The uncritical ease with which many other otherwise intelligent and academically distinguished young men and women accepted the slogans and the touching belief in the ability of the 'working class' to solve all economic ills was astonishing in retrospect. They could not wait to surrender freedoms for which their ancestors had fought and died and to submit to an infallible authority – the party – when it offered what appeared to them to be the certainty of a solution to all social problems, including employment, and an ordered life demanding no personal enterprise from the cradle to the grave. The prevailing uncertainty of the period, especially to those on the brink of having to earn a living at a time of mass unemployment, may have been a factor in the attraction of Communism, but it is still extraordinary that such faith should be placed in the edicts of a group of hostile foreigners operating in Moscow, a place as alien then to most Britons as the moon. Curiously, this blind belief continues, even when it should have become obvious that Communism as an economic system is unsuccessful and is incapable of competing with capitalism in producing food, raising living standards and providing 'human rights'. The reason must lie in the extent to which the whole-hearted adoption of Communism as a creed and way of life has such profound effects on the personality that it can change the perception of everything, as many Communists and ex-Communists, such as Arthur Koestler, have testified.

Appreciation of this warping effect of Communist ideology is essential to an understanding of the ease with which likeable and intelligent people can so easily bring themselves to betray their country and their kinsfolk.

While Soviet ideology has seduced many intellectuals it has had more success among the ignorant. Ideological Communists of long standing are often highly persuasive when inducing the young and the naïve into becoming traitors. Douglas Springhall, the British Communist Party's one-time national organizer, had little difficulty in convincing Olive Sheehan, a lonely junior employee of the Air Ministry, that she should provide the Russians with secret information on jet aircraft because 'British capitalists' were withholding it from them so that they could compete more easily with the Soviet Union after the war. The Soviet agent Hede Massing confessed to the FBI officer Robert Lamphere that she had never properly understood the Marxist doctrine but assumed that it must be humanitarian, and that since the Soviet government was Marxist she ought to support it, even to the extent of becoming a professional agent. This degree of ignorance probably applied to many others, such as Alexander Foote, who embraced the Soviet cause with a superficial and misleading knowledge of it.

Such naïvety is by no means confined to the young, being displayed to a frightening degree by some politicians. The Canadian Prime Minister, MacKenzie King, experienced great difficulty in believing that Stalin could be party to the espionage network in Canada exposed by the GRU defector Igor Gouzenko.[15] Today many politicians, editors, and others are just as naïve in their willingness to accept Mikhail Gorbachov as a benign hope for a world in which the ideological thrust of the Soviet Union will at least be blunted, ignoring the fact that he has been put where he is because he is dedicated to the system which produced him and which depends for its continuity on that very thrust for world domination and iron control over the Soviet peoples.

The sheer attraction of Communist ideology – what Michael Straight described as 'the pull of the left' – was intensified in the 1930s by other factors like the Spanish Civil War, the imminence of war with Nazi Germany, and German anti-Semitism. Of these the Spanish Civil War was the most immediately compelling for many ideologues in the last years of the 1930s. As Alexander Foote, who served in the Spanish Civil War, recorded: 'It was the bounden duty of anyone who valued democracy to do his best to support the existing government in Spain.'[16] Straight has described how the death of his friend John Cornford in Spain induced him to agree to work for the Soviet cause.[17]

Harry Pollitt, Secretary of the British Communist Party, openly called for volunteers in December 1936; and while enlistment was declared illegal the following month, about 2,200 volunteers, complete with political commissars to enforce party discipline, went from the UK. Late in the war, when the Communists were obviously losing it, the Russians used the fighting to liquidate volunteers, including some Americans, who were considered unreliable, by shooting them in the back, as part of Stalin's lunatic purges. Others, who were rated loyal, like Foote, Len Beurton, and Douglas Springhall, were later to become Soviet agents, while Philby, who had been intruded as a war correspondent to spy on the anti-Communists, was already a full-blooded recruit.

The force of anti-Semitism and its use by the Nazis and exploitation by the Soviets has so many facets that it will be dealt with in Chapter 12.

Some of the Communists who became traitors were to lay stress on the exacerbating factors of anti-Semitism and the Spanish Civil War when trying to explain their treachery, but in nearly all the cases the fundamental factor had been ideological devotion to the Soviet Union. Most of them continued their spying while the Soviet Union was virtually an ally of Hitler under the Nazi–Soviet pact. They seemed unimpressed by the fact that Stalin's assistance helped Hitler to put millions more Jews into extermination camps. According to Blunt's confession he and similar traitors 'simply felt better about things' after the Soviet Union was forced into the war. Nunn May, the atom scientist, gave secrets to Russia after VE day, as did Fuchs.

I experienced the attraction of the Communist ideology and the seductive pleasure of listening to some of its impressive evangelists when I was a student at London University in the 1930s. It was fun to relax in someone's bed-sitter in our Oxford bags and Fair Isle sweaters (now overtaken by jeans and bomber jackets), smoking over-large pipes, to be harangued by some eloquent, American postgraduate Communist determined to convince us that we were all dialectical materialists, whether we understood it or not, and that it was our duty to change society. Some of these indoctrinators were charismatic, as were the open Cambridge Communists, such as Klugmann and Cornford, who convinced intelligent people like Straight and Leo Long that the class struggle was the 'central reality of life'. In America future traitors like Harry Gold and David Greenglass were being drawn into the Communist fold through their admiration for the Soviet experiment. The Rosenbergs were total ideologues, distorting every aspect of life to illustrate the 'dialectical struggle', as their letters from 'death row' show.[18] In both countries it was almost fashionable to be associated with Communists, to be able to trot out the jargon, to reject traditions, conventions, and good manners as 'bourgeois', and to feel a sense of superiority in belonging among the enlightened. For most of us it was intellectual skylarking, but a few of my acquaintances underwent a conversion from which they never freed themselves, and a tiny proportion became secret Communists for clandestine purposes.

Because of the enormous weight of publicity given to the early ideological traitors, to those from Cambridge University in particular, it is necessary to appreciate that they were few in number. Thousands of young people were alienated by the policy of the pre-war British government in appeasing Hitler, but only a minute fraction were sufficiently disgusted to become traitors; any attempt to recruit the others would have been met with angry contempt. Most students, even at Cambridge, remained aloof from left-wing politics, and the only reason that Cambridge has been so strongly identified with the so-called 'climate of treason' is because of the defection of Maclean and Burgess, who were undergraduates there. Without that event the Cambridge ring might never have come to light, and it is my firm belief that small groups of Communists who became traitors existed at Oxford and other universities. Some of the Oxford culprits, like Driberg, Hollis and Bernard Floud, are already known publicly, and there are others known to MI5.

Unfortunately those who were recruited as ideologues and became operational agents – like Philby, Fuchs, the Kuczynskis, Hiss, Dexter White, and the rest who 'never doubted, never wavered' – were hugely effective. Other ideologues became subversives of lesser degree, and intriguing insight into their activities in the past has been provided recently by a veteran British Communist, Richard Kisch.[19] Communists serving in the British forces during the Second World War were required not only to help defeat the Fascists but to prepare for an 'anti-Fascist' post-war world in which the armed forces would be expected to play their part. In 1940 Communists and their sympathizers had taken part in setting up the Army Bureau of Current Affairs (ABCA) on the initiative of Thomas Hodgkin, a Communist Oxford lecturer, and A. D. Lindsay, the Marxist Master of Balliol College, with active support from the left-biased Workers Educational Association. Their main intention was to foment discontent and convert enough Service personnel to vote for a left-wing government in the first election after the war – and in this they succeeded, the Service vote being crucial in ousting Churchill as leader. A group of ABCA

Communists in Cairo, including James Klugmann and Bert Ramelson, were particularly effective, working in collaboration with the Egyptian Communist Henri Curiel, the KGB agent and relative of the spy George Blake.[20] They were assisted in this endeavour by Tom Driberg, the Labour politician and double agent. On his way back from seeing Ho Chi Minh, to whom he promised full Labour support, Driberg returned via India and stayed in Army camps, where he brought about strikes against the slowness of demobilization.

Communists in the RAF succeeded in preventing the dropping of Allied leaflets over Greece warning Communist military mutineers there to desist. Surreptitiously, they were able to switch the leaflets so that the mutineers received messages, drafted by a Communist specialist in psychological warfare, urging them to press on with the intention of staging a Communist coup in Greece. All delivered, unknowingly, by loyal pilots and planes of the RAF!

While many Communists may object to the contention that there is a peculiar relationship between treachery and Communism, it is now supported by the evidence of numerous case records, which have become available under the Freedom of Information Act in the USA and through the revelations of former intelligence officers in the USA and in Britain. They show that while Fascism was characterized primarily by violence, Communism was, and remains, characterized primarily by deception and subversion. In resorting to 'all sorts of tricks, slyness, illegal methods, evasion and conceal-ment of truth', Communists are simply following Lenin's instruc-tions. As Jean-François Revel has put it: 'To the honourable a word is a bond but to the Communist a bond is nothing but words'; this can apply to any bond of loyalty if a Communist feels dedicated enough.

Active Communism trains for duplicity, and covert Communists develop a talent for it, as Philby did. The British Communist Party historian, Noreen Branson, has written with respect to the recruitment of the volunteers to fight in Spain: 'illegal activity was not something to which the Communist Party was unaccustomed'. So it should surprise nobody that there has been a continuously firm link between committed Communists and treachery. Communism also trains, de-liberately, for self-deception, so that disciples will have no difficulty in explaining away, to themselves or to others, what would appear to any objective person to be serious anomalies. Traitorous acts, along with all the Soviet horrors, are explicable as 'historical necessities'. Typical of this 'double-think' was the statement by Jacques Duclos, the Stalinist Chairman of the French Communist Party, in 1952 that while the execution of the Rosenbergs in America was anti-Semitic, the execution of eight Jews in the appallingly rigged trial of Slansky and others in Czechoslovakia was 'correct'.[21] A mind moulded to be so treacherous to itself should have little difficulty in accepting the 'necessity' of treachery to others.

Through its active measures offensive, the Kremlin is pursuing its ideological warfare on a global scale, and the requirement for 'good' Communists to play their part has never been greater. The recruitment of ideological agents therefore continues to be important. While the attraction of the Soviet ideology for foreigners may have waned, so that fewer people are prepared to become traitors for it, this may have been largely countered by the greatly increased Soviet effort to secure recruits. Circumstances comparable to those which bolstered the pro-Soviet ideology in the 1930s exist today in Britain and many other countries. There is mass unemployment, many of the young feel alienated, ignored, and impotent; while the long-continuing cold war and the exaggerated fear of nuclear war may be even more telling than the fear of war with Hitler. While anti-Semitism, except among terrorist sympathizers, may not be so exploitable, the anti-nuclear factor has provided a more potent means of strengthening existing commitment and securing new sympathizers and is being exploited most ingeniously.

The commitment to 'peace', while not new for pro-Soviet Communists, has become something of an ideology and faith in itself for millions of others, in that campaigners are prepared to make great personal sacrifices and are deaf to all opposing arguments. Though the peace movements have been penetrated by Communists for their purposes – sabotaging nuclear weapons before they can be used is a prime *Spetsnaz* requirement – the majority of members would, understandably, deny that their efforts are subversive. However, so long as they continue to interfere with the nation's capabilities and plans to defend itself against Soviet military threat through deterrence, which is the sole purpose of Western nuclear weapons, they will qualify to be considered as subversive. Many 'peace' protestors appear to be prepared even to interfere with the deployment of nuclear weapons in an actual military emergency, and some would rather see their country overrun by an alien invader than see nuclear missiles deployed. Whatever their motives, this would be considered treasonable by any government, and any action to counter it would be legally justifiable.

Ideology is certainly a powerful motivating force in the recruitment of terrorists, 'freedom fighters' and subversives to assist *Spetsnaz* forces. Most of the fifth columnists in Britain and Europe, where they are known to number many hundreds, are probably ideological.[22]

To summarize, the evidence indicates that ideology remains an important factor in the recruitment of traitors and that security authorities are imprudent to regard it as outdated. In Britain the

Bettaney case has delayed any relaxation of the rules against employing Communists or other professed revolutionaries for a long time. But in the USA the belief that ideology is no longer a major recruitment factor has led, under 'liberal' pressure, to a situation where straightforward membership of the Communist Party is not an automatic bar to employment even in sensitive Government departments. I suspect, however, that it will need only one really bad new spy case of proven ideological attachment to cast grave doubt on the wisdom of that.

Though some of the many Soviet-bloc defectors who flee to the West do so primarily for ideological motives, as will be described in Chapter 20, the balance of advantage regarding ideological traitors in the intelligence and subversion fields is clearly with the Soviets and likely to remain so because of their ruthlessly repressive system which makes treachery to it so difficult. While a few defectors of immense value, like Oleg Gordievsky, have been secured, the experience of the CIA officer Robert Chapman, who recruited many agents when he was a station chief in several places between 1949 and 1979, would seem to be significant. He managed to recruit only one who was ideologically motivated towards the West.[23] There may be millions behind the Iron Curtain whose secret loyalty is to true democracy, but relatively few of them have dared to express it in words and still fewer in deeds.

CHAPTER EIGHT

Money and Other Material Inducements

Spies, being human, often invent a better-sounding motive
if their sole reason for betraying their country is money.

General Frantisek Moravec,
former head of Czech military intelligence

While an ideology of deep commitment is always welcome to those
who are talent-spotting for potential traitors, it carries the inherent
danger that revulsion to it may also be so deep that it leads to a
reaction, which can be catastrophic. Such revulsion most commonly
occurs when a Soviet citizen experiences life in a true democracy and
realizes its superiority in terms of freedom and material advantages.
The type specimen of a committed ideologue who betrayed the interests
of the country to which he legally owed allegiance to secure a freer
and more rewarding life elsewhere has to be Igor Gouzenko, the GRU
lieutenant and cipher clerk who defected from the Russian Embassy
in Ottawa in September 1945 and exposed the duplicity of the Soviets
in a way which was truly sensational.

The Gouzenko case is the most thoroughly documented in the annals
of treachery. The Canadian government set up a Royal Commission to
investigate his revelations and published a detailed report in 1946,
since when many of the transcripts of Gouzenko's evidence have been
published.[1] Canadian, American, and British traitors exposed by
Gouzenko have been tried with many of them convicted. Before his
death in 1982 he wrote books and appeared many times on television.

I had the privilege of speaking and corresponding with Gouzenko
and have remained in contact with his widow. I am in no doubt about
his motives for defection, which are not in dispute. Two years in the
freedom of Canada had convinced him and his wife that he and all
his compatriots had been grossly deceived by the Soviet government

about life in a true democracy and that the Soviet system deplored material rewards for the 'masses' only because it was incapable of providing them, except for the corrupt officials who used force to keep themselves in power. When the time came for his recall to Moscow he realized that he might never again be allowed out of the Soviet Union, particularly as he was in some disfavour because of an error he had made in his work. Aware of the danger if detected, Gouzenko and his wife decided to try to seek asylum in Canada for the benefits of a better and freer life for themselves and their children. To establish his bona fides and reasons for defecting, he abstracted extremely incriminating documents from the secret GRU office and, after some frightening hours, handed them to the Royal Canadian Mounted Police, who were quickly convinced of the truth of his claim that the Soviets were busy undermining Canada and their other former allies with a view to possible military action against them.[2]

Gouzenko was only twenty-six when he made his decision. He and his wife had no idea what the future would hold financially and he did not ask for money when he handed over his documents; but the material advantages of life in Canada compared with the grim austerity of the Soviet Union were a major factor. Not only did the Gouzenkos never come to regret their action, but for the rest of his life he did what he could to expose the continuing duplicitous nature of the Soviet regime and its depressing effects on the living standards of the Russian people.

Another Russian, brought up, like Gouzenko, as a good Soviet citizen, believing all he was told, and who fought valiantly at Stalingrad, was Peter Deriabin, whose experience of life in Vienna destroyed his faith in the Soviet system. After defecting, again at great personal danger, in 1954 and without thought of financial gain, though with the surprising prosperity of the West an obvious factor, Deriabin wrote: 'A poison of doubt began to work in my soul. What had looked so shining and wonderful on the outside looked very grey now. It grew greyer and greyer. . . . An idea took hold of my mind that the very few were dictators and the many forced to live under their oppression.'[3] He defected to the USA in search of a better all-round life, and many more Soviet citizens have taken the same path for the same reasons, as will be described more fully in Chapter 20. The most important of recent years has been the senior KGB officer Oleg Gordievsky, one of the new-style sophisticated men promoted by Yuri Andropov when he was KGB chief. From information available so far, Gordievsky was not a true double but essentially a Western penetration agent inside the KGB for many years, and the chief motives for his treachery were revulsion against the Soviet system and preference for the Western way of life and all it has to offer. The KGB may find more of its new-style, better educated officers to be susceptible to the freedom and material attractions of the West, even though they belong to the privileged élite in the Soviet Union.

Whatever their prime motive, most defectors eventually have to take money to survive, at least until they can establish themselves professionally in their new country. Their knowledge and any documents are their only immediately negotiable assets.

Many hundreds of Germans have risked their lives to defect from the Communist regime of East Germany to what they see as a freer and more rewarding life in the West. The Communist authorities regard such behaviour as so traitorous that it is considered legitimate to shoot escapees. Many have been murdered in the attempt to switch their loyalty.

Among the very few who have defected from true democracy to the East because they believed life to be preferable there was Bruno Pontecorvo, the former Italian scientist who fled surreptitiously while on holiday from England. His motives are not yet entirely understood, but one of them seems to have been the promise of exceptional atomic research facilities, which were fulfilled. This was a material factor of a sort. Two young American members of the very secret National Security Agency, Bernon Mitchell and William Martin, who became disenchanted with the American way of life, defected to the USSR in 1960, taking many secrets with them in the hope of finding a more acceptable milieu. Unlike Pontecorvo, they were disappointed.

While the ideological aspects of life behind the Iron Curtain have been attractive to many enthusiastic Communists on paper, some of those given the opportunity to embrace it have declined when faced with the reality of a regimented existence and the poor living standards. The American atomic spy David Greenglass was given the money to defect to escape arrest but could not bring himself to do so. When ordered to flee to Russia to avoid interrogation, Anthony Blunt firmly declined. So did Professor Hugh Hambleton.

Few modern traitors have been rich. One such was Dr Raymond Boyer, the millionaire Canadian scientist and Communist supporter, who gave the Russians the secrets of the explosive RDX during the Second World War. There have also been millionaires who have been treacherous to their countries and fellow-citizens in other ways, like Giangiacomo Feltrinelli, the Italian publisher who founded and funded the savage Red Brigades terrorists.[4] The great majority of traitors, however, have been sufficiently in need of extra money to be susceptible to the mercenary motive – what has been called the Judas syndrome – which they have often cloaked with some alleged political morality, though it is always possible that, once money becomes available, greed ensures that it overwhelms an original, less deplorable drive. John

Amery, the Englishman who volunteered his services to Germany during the war in 1942, gave the impression of being an ideological anti-Bolshevik who tried to recruit a force of British prisoners of war to fight alongside German troops; but as a former bankrupt he was more interested in money and the luxurious life provided by the Nazis in return for his traitorous broadcasts to Britain. Larry Wu-tai Chin, the Peking-born CIA translator convicted in 1986 of passing secret information to Red China, claimed he had been motivated only by a desire to improve Sino-American relations, but he had received large payments, including lump sums ranging up to $150,000.[5]

Of those traitors entirely motivated by sheer greed the type specimen must now be the American naval chief warrant officer John Walker, the founder and runner of a ring of Soviet spies drawn from his own family and friends, as already described. Walker is believed to have been recruited by the Russians when serving on the nuclear submarine *Simon Bolivar* in 1968 when he was thirty. After leaving the Navy he ran a detective agency in Norfolk, Virginia – an excellent cover for peculiar activities – and induced his son, Michael, to join the Navy so that the lucrative access to submarine warfare secrets could continue. John Walker used Russian money to recruit at least two others, one being his brother, Arthur, a former lieutenant-commander and instructor in anti-submarine warfare, employed by a defence contractor concerned with carriers and amphibious ships. The other was a friend, Jerry Whitworth, a retired US Navy signals petty officer who had served on the carrier *Enterprise*.

Walker Senior, who was enjoying a flamboyant life-style, was arrested after dumping a bag containing secret documents in a wood near Washington, as he had been doing regularly for fifteen years in exchange for dollars left by the Russians when they picked up the bags. The Russians secured a good bargain. The bags are believed to have included details of underwater listening devices planted on the ocean floor to detect the movements of Soviet submarines.[6] His last batch had been supplied by his son, who was arrested on the nuclear aircraft-carrier *Nimitz*. Whitworth's services for the Soviets between 1974 and 1983 earned him £225,000 ($332,000) on which, naturally, he failed to pay any tax.

Even the most truly ideological have almost all been forced into accepting some money, whether in need of it or not. Elizabeth Bentley, for example, revealed when confessing her treachery how her Soviet controller, the senior KGB agent Anatoli Gromov, had forced her to accept $2,000 in default of which she would be considered a traitor in Moscow.[7] Fuchs and Nunn May, the atomic spies, were induced to accept small bribes, £100 in the case of Fuchs, while Nunn May took two bottles of whisky and $200. Later Fuchs was to insist to a fellow prisoner that he took money only once 'as a symbol of allegiance' and then repeatedly refused it to show that he could not be bribed into betraying secrets. He also spurned a lucrative offer while in prison for assistance with a film about his life.[8] Others, like Cairncross, took money for expenses.

The recruiters took care not to introduce the money factor in the early stages if they felt that a target might take offence but they almost always managed to secure acceptance eventually and with some it was on offer from the first approach. The major Soviet purpose was to secure handwritten receipts which could later be used for blackmail, if necessary, but the taking of Soviet money was also something of a ritual acceptance of service to Moscow, rather like the old 'King's shilling' paid to British Army recruits. The Soviet reasoning appeared to be that once a spy was on the payroll he was under firmer control, and money also furthered the moral corruption. As Professor Hambleton put it at his trial: 'Once you start accepting payment, they've got you.'

Alexander Foote, who first became a Soviet agent essentially for adventure and the Communist ideal, admitted in his memoirs that there was a mercenary motive, but it was 'subsidiary'. Harry Gold insisted, when confessing, that he had not betrayed his country for the money but for the cause, though he had taken $200 to cover the expenses of each of his journeys.[9] Guy Burgess, who was essentially ideological but led an expensive life, was regularly given wads of banknotes, which he kept in his flat in shoe-boxes. Philby was assuredly ideological but he was paid some money, though the MI6 chief Sir Dick White told Philby's wife, Eleanor, that during his time in Beirut, at least, he was believed to have been working without pay from the Russians.[10] John Vassall, the Admiralty clerk who was homosexually blackmailed into spying for the Soviets, accepted substantial sums which enabled him to enjoy travel and a life-style above his normal means.

Recruiters will always try to secure a traitor's services at minimum cost but are usually prepared to pay well when dealing with a tough negotiator with plenty to offer. The Swedish Air Force colonel, Stig Wennerstrom, began his fifteen years of treachery by offering to give the Soviets the location of an important airfield for 5,000 kronor, then worth about $1,000. The Russians gave him the money in a package, and later he rationalized this action as his way of gaining entry to the Soviet intelligence service. As an advance for further information he received 10,000 roubles, making him a full-blown Soviet agent with pay of 5,000 roubles a month and the promise of bonuses for good results. On his arrest he said, with some pride, that his account in Moscow held 'hundreds of thousands of kronor'; when he was sentenced, the Swedish court ruled that he had received the equivalent of some $100,000, excluding the amounts in his Moscow account, and he was fined that sum.[11] The South African Soviet spy Commodore Dieter Gerhardt, who professed to be ideological, was also paid very large amounts, one Swiss bank account alone containing £85,000; while the French agent of influence Pierre-Charles Pathé received about 100,000 francs.

Human nature being as it is, and being unlikely to change, a policy of paying low salaries to people with access to secret information of obvious value to an adversary is short-sighted economy. This was demonstrated by the case of Captain John King, a cipher clerk in the British Foreign Office on a meagre salary and with no pension rights, during the 1930s. While he was briefly seconded for duty in Geneva, where he had an American lady-friend whom he could not afford to entertain, his plight was spotted by a Soviet agent, a Dutchman called Pieck. In return for 'commercial' Foreign Office information which would be of value to a mythical business friend, Pieck induced King to accept regular payments. It was a high-gradient slippery slope, and King soon found himself handing over top-secret intercepts to the chief Soviet espionage case officer in Britain.[12] Following a lead from the Soviet defector Krivitsky, British security men found that high-denomination banknotes paid into King's account had come from a Russian bank.

Times of uncertainty like the 1930s, and currently when unemployment is rife, intensify the appeal of money whether it is easy or not. Those intelligence officers who believe that Sir Roger Hollis, the former Director-General of MI5, was a long-term Soviet agent suspect that Soviet controllers were able to induce him to enter MI5, when it was looking for staff in 1938, because he was out of work, with no academic qualification and no job prospects.

The evidence of recent cases indicates that the appeal of money is particularly strong today because of the materialism in Western society, with its accent on possessions and consumer goods. Admiral Bobby Inman, a former Deputy Director of the CIA, has recently said that he knew of no American case in the previous fifteen years where ideology had any role at all, money being the prime objective. The Director of the FBI, William Webster, has also stated that almost every US citizen lately recruited to Soviet espionage has been secured with money as the main inducement, though other factors may have been partly responsible. The KGB seemingly agrees; the Soviet defector Stanislav Levchenko claims that there is a statement in a KGB manual to the effect that 'all Americans can be bought'.

The intensified Soviet drive to secure Western technology has greatly increased the search for people prepared to supply it, and because the defence industries of the USA are so extensive and so successful most of the effort and pressure is being applied there. This may account, at least in part, for the exaggerated Soviet claim that all Americans can be bought, since it is particularly easy for the millions working in defence industries to acquire saleable secrets, and on sheer statistical grounds some are likely to succumb to such easy money. There is also the factor that it is perhaps easier for people who betray such secrets to convince themselves that they are 'only commercial'. The Soviet effort has certainly been highly successful. According to an official US report of 1985, about 5,000 Soviet military research projects benefited each year in the 1980s from Western technical documents and acquisitions of hardware. The bulk was acquired illegally in ways too technical to detail here, but in many cases the treachery of supplying equipment illicitly to the Soviet bloc has involved a conspiracy of several people in the firm or organization concerned to evade the security restrictions.[13]

Soviet intelligence has wide experience of the art of bribing an organization rather than an individual and does not always have to use money. For example, in return for special reporting facilities, a Western newspaper may be prepared to run dispatches from the Soviet bloc which it knows to be slanted. A Japanese TV network was induced to air some Soviet propaganda in return for exclusive rights to telecast to Japan the 1980 Moscow Olympic Games.[14]

While the number of cases of treachery which have reached courts or been otherwise exposed has recently reached flood proportions in several Western countries, notably the USA, West Germany, and Britain, the mercenary motive for treachery has long been rooted in man's acquisitive nature. Even Judas was paid, and as Sir Roger Hollis, when Director-General of MI5, remarked to his friend Commander Anthony Courtney in the late 1950s: 'My experience is that every man, without exception, has his price – but mine is a very high one.' Understandably, Courtney, who then had no knowledge of the suspicions which were later to surround Hollis, regarded the remark as odd.[15]

With some the price has been incredibly low. As mentioned previously, the British merchant seamen George Armstrong and Duncan Scott-Ford were prepared to have their comrades torpedoed for a few pounds. Armstrong, a marine engineering officer with no right-wing tendencies and simply interested in easy money, contacted a German consul while in the USA in 1941 and offered to spy for cash. He deserted from his last ship when it was berthed at New York, and it may be no coincidence that it was torpedoed seven weeks later. Scott-Ford, then aged twenty-one, could not resist temptation when approached in Lisbon by German agents seeking information about

Allied convoys. For about £22 he gave them details of convoy routes, knowing they would be passed to U-boat captains.[16] William Kampiles, when aged twenty-three, sold the extremely valuable secrets of the American KH–11 satellite to the Russians for only $3,000. Youth may also have been an additional factor in the case of the 25-year-old American airman Bruce Ott, who was determined to make some quick money to invest and yielded to the temptation of trying to sell documents about the use of the advanced SR-71 'Blackbird' reconnaissance aircraft. Sadly for him the men with whom he was dealing, in 1986, were US government agents posing as Soviet spies, and his case introduces what may be an uncommon factor in the production of a traitor: the use of the *agent provocateur*.

Cold-blooded treachery for pittances is not restricted to the young. In 1986 James Morrison, a long-retired counter-espionage officer of the Royal Canadian Mounted Police, was sent to prison, aged seventy, for betraying an important Russian agent who had been recruited from within the KGB in 1953. He had condemned this Russian to severe punishment, probably execution, for the equivalent of a year's salary, then about $3,500, so that he could indulge his fancy for flash cars, clothes, and cigars.[17]

Most 'Judas syndrome' traitors fall to the temptation of money offered to them by recruiters who have been told by talent-scouts that they are probably susceptible. However, some, especially in recent years, have volunteered their services for money, being known in the 'trade' as 'walk-ins'. A literal 'walk-in' was Ronald William Pelton, a former officer of the US National Security Agency with experience of work in Britain alongside GCHQ, who visited the Soviet Embassy in Washington in 1980 specifically to sell secrets. He had been driven there by bankruptcy, and by the time he was arrested in November 1985 he had been thoroughly 'debriefed' by the Soviets while in the USA and particularly during at least two visits to Vienna.[18]

Usually the 'walking in' is done less obviously and is often accomplished abroad. The recent CIA renegade Edward Howard, for instance, volunteered his store of secret information to the KGB and received money for it while on a visit to Austria for which the Russians paid. The British traitor Geoffrey Prime made his first contact while serving with the RAF in Berlin. He handed a note to a Soviet officer when passing through a checkpoint between East and West Berlin and at subsequent meetings accepted small sums of money; these were followed by large amounts once he started supplying extremely valuable information from GCHQ, to which he subsequently gained entry.

The American counterpart to Prime, the equally damaging Christopher Boyce, used a friend to make the approach and then to serve as a courier. This was Andrew Daulton Lee, who was in debt and needed money to buy drugs for his drug-pushing business. Boyce and Lee took $16,000 from the Russians.

The textbook specimen of the volunteer mercenary spy is always likely to be the Second World War German agent code-named 'Cicero', whose real name was Elyesa Bazna. He was valet to the British Ambassador to Turkey, Sir Hughe Knatchbull-Hugesson, and made imprints of his master's keys, purloined from his trousers when he was pressing them. This enabled him to photograph top-secret telegrams from the Foreign Office and other documents taken from the ambassador's boxes and safe. 'Cicero' spontaneously offered his material to the Germans in Ankara for cash. Though he operated for only a few months – from October 1943 through the spring of 1944 – he received large sums. Hitler and his aides feared that he was a British plant feeding false information, but events confirmed that he was genuine and the Germans were able to make use of many of his disclosures, especially concerning Britain's efforts to bring Turkey into the war, which the Germans were able to foil. They did not, however, secure any information about the Allied invasion of Northern Europe, beyond the fact that it was code-named Overlord and would take place across the English Channel. 'Cicero' escaped retribution by resigning from the Embassy in April 1944, when he realized that investigations into the leakages were in train.[19] There is some doubt about the belief that the Germans tricked 'Cicero' by paying him in counterfeit money but having received in excess of £300,000, a huge amount in those days, he certainly died impoverished. 'Cicero' was massively disloyal to the ambassador, but whether he should count as a traitor is a matter for argument. He seems to have been born in Belgrade, though he had probably acquired Turkish nationality through long residence. Had he been caught, the Turks – who by that time were convinced of ultimate Allied victory – might well have found some legal way of punishing him for his treachery.[20]

No such doubt attached to the treachery of Hans Thilo-Schmidt, a German cipher expert, who offered his information to French intelligence in October 1931 and sold them valuable documents about the Enigma encoding and decoding machine which would later enable the British to decipher so much of the secret German radio traffic during the Second World War. It was said of him: 'He was fond of money; he also needed it because he was fonder still of women.'[21] Another German traitor, Rudolf von Scheliha, a member of a noble family and with no political interest in Communism, sold diplomatic secrets filched from the German Foreign Office to both the Soviets and British before and during the Second World War to finance his expensive life-style and gambling losses.

Equally mercenary and despicable was Paul Thummel, a senior official of the Abwehr, the German secret service. A Nazi from an aristocratic family, he sold detailed information about the German order of battle, plans, and other valuable intelligence first to the Czechs and then to the British before and during the Second World War. He claimed to be opposed to the Nazis, but money seems to have been his major motive until he was caught and executed by the Gestapo.[22] Arthur George Owens, the Welsh nationalist who spied on behalf of the Abwehr exclusively from 1936 until the outbreak of war, later becoming a double agent also working for Britain, was essentially interested in money and the women which it helped to provide during his visits to the Continent.

The wartime spy with the most overblown reputation and who spied essentially for money was the famed 'Lucy', the Swiss Soviet agent whose name was Rudolf Roessler. Originally a German national and of German parents, he moved to Switzerland as a political refugee in 1933 – he was not Jewish – and founded a publishing company. In 1939 he was invited to work for Swiss intelligence and he was paid very substantially by two Swiss intelligence agencies. He was also paid regularly by the Soviet GRU, receiving more than 30,000 Swiss francs and regularly agitating for more.[23] He appeared to have extraordinary sources in Germany, enabling him to supply Moscow with details of German troop movements and intentions but this may have been supplied to him by the Swiss authorities, who perhaps knew of his GRU connection and wanted him to relay the information to Moscow. In his various capacities he operated essentially as a courier or cut-out, and he was not the master-spy some authors have claimed him to be. There is a common belief that he also received information originating in Britain from the Ultra deciphering system to pass on to Moscow but this has been repeatedly denied.[24] No doubt 'Lucy' would have denied that he was a traitor but the Germans would certainly have treated him as one. Unless the Swiss intelligence chiefs really knew what he was doing, he was being massively disloyal to them.

Another 'walk-in' traitor who offered his services to the Soviet bloc, mainly because of his greed for money, though partly through resentment, was Karel Zbytek, a Czech refugee who had been in England during the war with the Free Czech Army, returned to his native land but then defected to Britain while touring with a choir in the early 1950s. He joined the Czech Intelligence Office in London which was run by MI6 and was recruiting Czech exiles in Britain and Europe to work against the illegally established Communist regime in Czechoslovakia. Zbytek contacted the Czech military attaché in London, named several agents operating in Czechoslovakia, and offered more names for payment. In return for about £40,000 this traitor, whose code-name was 'Light', betrayed 120 Czech agents based in Britain and others inside Czechoslovakia, who were arrested, some being executed. By the time his treachery was revealed by other Czech defectors in 1969, Zbytek had died in retirement.[25]

In a reverse situation a would-be KGB defector, Konstantin Volkov, walked into the British Consulate in Istanbul in 1945 with an offer of secrets which might have led to the early arrest of the whole Cambridge ring, among other traitors, had it been properly followed through. He asked for £27,000, which was probably a round sum in roubles and, while large for those days, it did not represent much for a man prepared to plunge into the unknown, to give up his entire career and to risk his life.

Astute recruiters are ever alert for the twin incentives of greed and need. The need may become known if the target is being pressed for money by creditors. The recent and extremely damaging defection of the West German counter-espionage official Hans Joachim Tiedge seems to have been the result of such enterprise. Tiedge, whose brief was to counter East German espionage in West Germany, was in debt and in regular need of extra money for drink, to which he was heavily addicted. In a note from East Germany he explained that he had fled because he was 'in a hopeless situation'.[26]

David Barnett, who had resigned from the CIA in 1970 after twelve years' service because he was not earning enough money, had encountered financial problems in business. To resolve them he offered his services to the Soviets in 1976 and, in return for $92,000 (then about £38,000), he provided technical weapons secrets and the names of CIA officers and agents.

The case of the British naval sub-lieutenant David Bingham, who was jailed for twenty-one years in 1970 for selling submarine warfare secrets to the Russians may be unique in that it was his wife who, needing money to resolve family problems, approached the Soviet Embassy in London to offer her husband's services. Living above their modest means, they had sold their car without informing the hire-purchase company and owed money to many people. He received £3,800 for what his trial judge called a 'monstrous betrayal'.[27]

Matrimonial problems exacerbating need through alimony demands or the extra costs of a mistress are often observable to talent-spotters. Brian Linney, a British electronics engineer, was always short of money and had a weakness for it. His vulnerability, intensified by domestic difficulties, was shrewdly observed by the military attaché at the Czech Embassy, who then proceeded to recruit and run him as a mercenary spy. William Holden Bell, an American radar engineer at Hughes Aircraft, was approaching sixty, heavily in debt, saddled with alimony payments, and under investigation by the tax authorities when he became friendly with a young Polish woman, Marian Zachar-ski, in 1977. She was an 'illegal' agent who had been sent to the USA to recruit technological sources, her cover being a Polish machinery company which she represented. She first recruited Bell as a technical consultant and he was soon handing her classified documents concerning new 'quiet' radar systems, used on fighters and bombers, for extra money. In all he took $110,000, inflicting damage on American defence interests later assessed at hundreds of millions of dollars.[28]

In 1984 the FBI arrested one of its own officers, Richard Miller, a 47-year-old counter-espionage agent, and charged him with espionage, this being the first certain case of FBI penetration by the Soviets. Miller, who had been in the FBI for twenty years, was in touch with Svetlana Ogorodnikova. She and her husband had emigrated to the Soviet Union in 1973. They were deep cover 'illegals'; she worked as a day nurse while he worked in a sausage factory. Both were receiving welfare payments when arrested! Miller, who had eight children and was in financial difficulties, admitted while under the polygraph 'lie detector' to asking for $50,000 in gold and $15,000 in cash from Mrs Ogorodnikova, who is believed to have been a major in the KGB. He gave her secret FBI documents of such great value to the KGB in their espionage operations in the USA that he was sentenced to two life-terms plus another fifty years and a fine of $60,000.[29]

Another whose over-large family may have helped to push him into selling secrets for money was the American staff sergeant Jack Dunlap, who, after serving with distinction in Korea, found himself in a special position of trust. As a clerk-messenger in the National Security Agency he had extraordinary access to particularly precious secrets at a time when he was finding it difficult to keep his seven children on his pay and was also hankering after a lusher life. His estimated payment in his first year of espionage was at least $30,000; during three years of work for the KGB his new life-style included a mistress, fast motor-boats and cars, none of which excited official concern. Whether from guilt, fear, or some other cause he committed suicide in July 1963 and was buried with full military honours, his treachery coming to light only when his widow reported a cache of highly secret documents in their home.

Sailors are especially vulnerable to being targeted by recruiters because they can be approached in the relative safety of foreign ports. Since 1982 at least eight other American sailors, apart from the Walkers, have been court-martialled for selling or attempting to sell secrets, or what they claimed to be secrets, to the Soviets. One of them was found to have accumulated more than 150 secret papers, including code documents, before going absent without leave from his ship in 1984.[30] Others who serve abroad in foreign diplomatic services are not only easier to approach but can be kept under surveillance so that their susceptibilities can be studied. Harry Houghton, who provided secrets from the Admiralty's Underwater Detection Establishment at Portland and was essentially a mercenary spy, was 'talent-spotted' in Warsaw, where he was clerk to the naval attaché in the British Embassy and was making money through black market operations, his love of easy pickings being duly noted.

Among the material factors utilized by Soviet-bloc recruiters when talent-spotting young people in Western embassies in Iron Curtain capitals, especially in Moscow, is the offer of a 'good time', as evidenced by the case of William Marshall, a young radio operator working in the British Embassy there. He was lonely, did not make friends easily, and was left by his superiors too much to his own devices in a grim and forbidding city. The Russians quickly spotted his plight and invited him to parties and dinners, ensuring the company of attractive girls. Sensing his future use, no attempt seems to have been made to compromise him there. Instead the cultivation continued when Marshall was posted back to the Diplomatic Wireless Service in Britain, and Pavel Kuznetsov, a KGB officer posing as a diplomat, continued the warm friendship and free entertainment. Whether through gratitude or blackmail Marshall soon began to pass the Russians secret information which he learned daily from his work.

An earlier and much more important case of recruitment abroad through financial temptation was that of Charles Howard 'Dick' Ellis, a British officer in MI6 who later enjoyed very senior positions. According to close colleagues, Ellis was 'always hard up and living beyond his means'; he was recruited by the German secret service while serving in Europe shortly before the outbreak of the Second World War. He later confessed to having sold the complete order of battle of MI6 – its organization and disposition of its personnel – among other appalling mercenary betrayals. He even used a brother MI6 officer to bring back money, unwittingly, from the Germans after the outbreak of war. There are strong, but unproven, suspicions that Ellis was also a mercenary spy for the Soviets.[31]

Many men who have served abroad and have become accustomed to a high living standard, because of generous foreign allowances, have been reluctant to accept a lower one on their return home. One such was Frank Bossard, who had enjoyed living in Bonn, where he had been attached to the British Embassy. After his return to London, where he worked in the Aviation Ministry, he was approached in a public house by a Soviet recruiter who affected to share his interest in coins. He was soon leaving films of photographed documents in hiding places which Russian agents emptied, leaving sums of up to £2,000 as reward. A study of Bossard's past made after he had been detected showed that he had previously been prepared to break the law for easy money.

Politicians also have occasional reason to visit the Soviet bloc. Among those recruited to service there was the former British parliamentarian Will Owen, Labour MP for Morpeth. Owen acknowledged in court that he had received payments from Czechoslovakia in return for information which he learned through his duties on parliamentary committees but claimed, successfully, that it was not really secret. After his acquittal, however, when he knew he was safe from prison, he was pressured by MI5 for the truth. Owen, a miserable little man, appealed for help to fellow MP Leo Abse, who arranged immunity against any prosecution for what he might tell MI5 and agreed to be present at the interrogations, when Owen confessed to deliberate espionage over several years. Being interested in psychology, Abse believed that Owen's treachery did not spring entirely from avarice but was also rooted in a sexual problem regarding his parents. 'Owen did his puny best to rape his motherland,' he wrote.[32] There may have been such a factor but his Czech controllers were probably nearer the mark when they dubbed him 'the greedy bastard'.[33]

If money is the most despicable motive for treachery, then the double agent who takes it from two opposing sides would seem to be doubly despicable and the least deserving of sympathy when caught. My type specimen of the true double is the Frenchman Henri Déricourt, who served in the French Section of the British SOE – the organization ordered by Churchill to 'set Europe ablaze' – and was also assisting the Germans. Déricourt was of humble origin, a pre-Second World War air pilot, and responsible for arranging the RAF's nightflights ferrying agents in and out of France. He was known to be friendly with German intelligence officers and to be in regular touch with them – a dangerous situation condoned by British intelligence officials as being essential to enable him to move about the Paris area without hindrance. They relied on his greater loyalty to the Allied cause, but mistakenly; for it is certain that he betrayed an entire SOE network, causing the execution of literally hundreds of brave agents, including Britons, and that he took £20,000, then a very large sum, in blood money from the Germans. There has been some suggestion that he did this at the instigation of MI6 for a more important intelligence purpose, but I can find no former MI6 officer who believes it.[34]

Considering the modest rewards made by the West to most defectors, it would seem beyond question that the Soviets have invested far more heavily in Western traitors and agents of influence, especially when the cost of acquiring technological information and equipment surreptitiously is taken into account. The information supplied by defectors like Gordievsky and Gouzenko can hardly be priced too highly; but it is the view of most professionals whom I have consulted that the Soviets have achieved far greater value for their outlay of cash because of the enormous financial damage inflicted by certain traitors, particularly the recent ones like Prime, Boyce, and the Walker ring.

The case records show that in the equation of treachery the factor m, for money, figures to some degree in the great majority. The other ubiquitous factor, according to experienced officers of all intelligence agencies known to me, is factor s: for sex.

CHAPTER NINE

The Hetero-Sex Factor

There is an old adage in the FBI to the effect that there has never been an espionage case in which sex did not play a part.

Robert Lamphere

In the oversimplified mnemonic used by the CIA to summarize the motives for treachery, MICE, the letter *C* stands for Compromise, which can be subdivided into three distinct elements: heterosexual compromise, homosexual compromise, and compromise (usually blackmail or the fear of it) of a non-sexual nature. It is convenient to consider the hetero-sex factor first.

Recruiters of traitors usually exploit human weakness; and none, with the possible exception of greed, has been more productive in that respect than the sex drive. Men are generally more susceptible to irresistible sexual temptation than women, and, sadly perhaps, the compelling force is lust rather than love, though the latter sometimes supervenes. The recruiter starts with two major advantages which apply more generally to men, though there are some female exceptions. The sex drive tends to be compulsive, especially when tempting circumstances exist or can be contrived, and it cuts clean across normal intelligence so that people are often prepared to take sacrificial risks to indulge it. The instances where politicians and other public figures have taken ludicrous risks with their reputation to satisfy a sexual craving – often knowing it to be superficial and temporary – are legion. Such people do not seem to be deterred by the certainty that, if they are exposed, the media publicity will destroy their career. Many of those very private figures, the secret traitors, whose freedom, and sometimes life, depended on avoiding any addition to their burden of risk, were also often unable to resist the dangerous complications of lust.

The medical and psychological literature offers evidence that sex drive is a component of general drive and in men may even be the main fount of it. This is supported by the behaviour of many men of achievement who have been inveterate philanderers with excessive sexual appetites. Traitors who continue to operate over many years in the face of daily danger certainly exhibit drive, and a compulsion for sexual satisfaction may be natural to them. In trying to explain Philby's succession of mistresses, besides his four wives, his third wife, Eleanor, suggested that the 'intensity of his sex-based relationships' was a compensation for all the repression demanded by his secret life.[1] It could also have been due to the fact that he was highly sexed and would probably have displayed that kind of behaviour whatever active profession he had undertaken.[2] The possibility of a connection between frequent disloyalty to a spouse and disloyalty in other directions is well recognized by security authorities, who, in their positive-vetting inquiries, regard promiscuity as a character weakness which needs to be noted. Case histories of known traitors indicate that a totally amoral attitude to sex, expressing itself in abandoned promiscuity – as practised by heterosexuals like Richard Sorge and by homosexuals like Guy Burgess and Tom Driberg – may well be linked with a similar attitude to loyalty.

Sex can be a straightforward reason for joining the Soviet cause, as it can be for joining any other. When the beautiful Viennese actress Hede Massing was seventeen she fell in love with Gerhart Eisler, the professional Soviet agent whom she eventually married. Under his influence, she joined the Communist Party and its espionage arm, the Comintern. In old age she recalled that she had understood nothing about politics and that her original attachment had been entirely emotional. 'I married into the Party,' she wrote.[3]

Sex can also be the major factor in keeping a traitor active. Elizabeth Bentley fell in love with her American controller, Jacob Golos, who was dedicated and held her to the cause. When he died suddenly in 1943 she quickly began to doubt the merits of her treachery and eventually gave herself up to the FBI in 1945, naming more than eighty people linked with the Golos network.[4] It would seem significant that when put in touch with a US Army officer, who was probably working for the FBI, she had a sexual affair with him. The convicted American Soviet agent Judith Coplon claimed to be having a truly romantic love affair with her Soviet controller in an attempt to account for the various clandestine meetings, but this was proved to be false by the fact that she was simultaneously having an affair with another man!

Sex, in the shape of a handsome former German officer, who had been recruited as an agent while in Russian captivity, was the initial means of entrapment into espionage in 1951 for Maria Knuth, a former German cabaret artiste, who was so susceptible that she quickly agreed to assist him. She used her sexual favours to attract British and American officers who might then be blackmailed into providing information about the re-arming of Germany. Ironically, the German counter-intelligence agent later detailed to keep her under surveillance found it easy to do so by replacing her former lover, who had committed suicide.[5]

In evidence given on Canadian television shortly before she died in 1981, Hede Massing, who operated for many years against the country which gave her refuge, explained how she had induced American women to allow their homes to be used for clandestine 'mail drops': 'I would send somebody who was handsome: they generally went to bed and it worked.'[6]

Sex may also have been Kim Philby's mode of entry into a life of treason through Lizi Friedman, the young Austrian Jewess he met in Vienna who was already working for the Comintern. He certainly found her exciting, according to his accounts of their love-making in the snow which he enjoyed recounting to MI6 colleagues; it was Lizi who introduced him to active illegal work in 1933.

Harry Houghton of the Portland spy ring claimed that it was the threat of pressure on his former girl-friend in Poland which forced him into working for Soviet intelligence, though money would seem to have been more potent; the girl-friend was perhaps the excuse for the approach. In his memoirs Houghton records how he was introduced to sex orgies involving girls and young boys while serving in Warsaw. This experience must have given him a taste for them. A former MI5 officer who was involved in the surveillance of Houghton in Britain has told me that the telephone tapping and bugging of his home revealed that he took part in sex orgies which he then discussed with his girl-friend on the telephone, presumably for further thrills.

Blunt was able to recruit one of his Cambridge colleagues partly through the pressure he could apply through his knowledge that the man was having a clandestine affair with the wife of one of his friends. Whether Driberg was an active recruiter for the KGB is unknown, but he was certainly a talent-spotter, being in the habit of loaning his flat to Parliamentary colleagues for illicit sexual purposes and then reporting the names of those concerned to his KGB or Czech controllers, as well as to MI5. One of his reports referred to an occasion when a very senior Labour minister had taken lunch-time advantage of his accommodation. Driberg had found an envelope inadvertently left between the cushions of a sofa by the lady, who proved to be an important Labour figure herself.

The contrived recruitment of an agent to treachery through sex, which usually entails the employment of professional seducers or seductresses, is commonly referred to in the intelligence trade as *entrapment*, and when the victims are men, which is usually the case, the baited situations are called 'honey-traps'. My type specimen of a honey-trap victim is Roy Guindon, a Canadian Royal Mounted Policeman who worked as a security guard, and occasionally as a cipher clerk, in the Canadian Embassy in Moscow in the late 1950s. Guindon was what his colleagues called 'a stud'. When he found little response among the Canadian ladies at the embassy, the KGB, which had the usual Russian talent-spotters working inside the embassy, quickly ensured that a professional temptress was put in his way. A glamorous and lusty lady called Larissa Fedorovna Dubanova was seated next to Guindon when he attended the Bolshoi ballet. She happened to speak excellent English, which ensured their rapid progress to a 'romantic' liaison. Eventually, after Larissa falsely told him that she was pregnant, the KGB arranged a fake secret marriage, which broke Soviet law and Canadian diplomatic practice, thereby providing a blackmail lever on Guindon. Under the threat of never being allowed to see his 'wife' again he was pressurized into disclosing Canadian ciphers. As a night security guard, he could remove them from safes, and he provided a stream of the secret messages that were sent to and from the embassy. Long after Larissa 'miscarried', he was also able to perform services like planting listening devices in sensitive parts of the building.

When Guindon was transferred to the Canadian Embassy in Warsaw, his Russian 'wife' was allowed to visit him. Thus his treachery continued, as it did when he was posted to Israel. He was detected by Israeli counter-intelligence officers when he became careless on the telephone and an MI6 officer from the British Embassy tricked him into visiting London; there he was met by Canadian security officials, who took him to Ottawa. In return for a confession of his activities over the years he was not prosecuted.[7]

Since few men are totally immune to sexual temptation, Soviet intelligence has been no respecter of rank and has often aimed high with its honey-traps. The defector Yuri Krotkov revealed that he had been involved in the successful entrapment of a French Ambassador to Moscow, Maurice Dejean, for whom beautiful women were irresistible. The KGB had organized the ambassador's Soviet servants so that both his chauffeur and his wife's maid were agents, and he was easily set up for the ruse in which the husband returns unexpectedly to find his wife and her lover in intimate embrace. The payment for not revealing a diplomatic scandal was the requirement that Dejean should become a Soviet agent of influence.[8] The British Ambassador to Moscow, Sir Geoffrey Harrison, was similarly set up by his wife's

Russian maid, Galya, an attractive KGB prostitute, who enticed the hapless diplomat into a flat during a visit to Leningrad where, as anyone with security sense might have anticipated, hidden KGB photographers were installed. Unlike Dejean, Harrison had the wit to report his predicament and was extricated from Moscow. When publicly confronted with his behaviour on British television in 1981, the explanation offered by this senior ambassador, who had been in charge of the most besieged of British embassies, was: 'My defences were down.' His claim that 'it could have happened to any of us' angered his former colleagues in the Moscow embassy, who had seen through Galya as a KGB plant so clearly that she was an embassy joke.[9]

An alternative way of countering the photographic compromise, needing supreme confidence, has been described by the KGB defector Major Aleksei Myagkov. In his brief memoirs he decribes how the KGB tried to recruit a foreign diplomat in Moscow in the early 1970s by means of a 'beautiful and clever woman who was prepared for him'. The diplomat was duly hooked, and employees of the KGB's technical section took the usual photographs. One day when he turned up at his mistress's flat, tough KGB officers were waiting for him but were confounded when he said that he was delighted with the photographs as proof of his capabilities and would like several as souvenirs, while the KGB could send the rest wherever it liked, including to his wife. The KGB ruefully attributed this failure to the Western permissive trend in matrimonial relations.[10]

As the Czech defector Josef Frolik stated in his evidence to a US Senate committee: 'Sex exploitation is an important weapon used by the Czech intelligence service in its daily life, as it is with all the Soviet satellite services.' Frolik's former colleague and fellow defector Frantisek August has described how a British diplomat in Prague was deliberately compromised by a woman agent and agreed to hand over the names of British intelligence officers, code-books and ciphers in return for the Czech authorities allowing his mistress to leave Czechoslovakia with him. August identified this man for the British security authorities, who suppressed any publicity about him.[11]

When the Norwegian diplomat and junior minister Arne Treholt was arrested in 1984 he claimed that he had been recruited to KGB service after being shown compromising photographs of a sexual orgy in which he had taken part. He later withdrew the statement, however, alleging that it had been made under pressure.

Women are often supplied to heighten the enthusiasm of a spy and to keep him 'hooked'. This happened with the double agent Arthur George Owens, for whom the Abwehr supplied a stream of women when he visited the Continent to meet his spy-masters.

Soviet-bloc intelligence officers have even been required to use their own wives as bait in honey-traps, as happened to one of my former Fleet Street colleagues, a defence correspondent who had guilelessly accepted several invitations to the Polish Embassy. The wife of one of the so-called attachés there, having indicated her attraction, suggested a visit to her residence; when the journalist found that the husband had been 'called away' they began the intended intimacies. Returning unexpectedly, the husband demanded satisfaction in the form of a flow of information, the alternative being a complaint to the seducer's editor. The attempt failed because the journalist was wise enough to take official advice, and it was the Pole who ended up with a warning that a complaint would be lodged with his ambassador if he persisted.

Setting its traps wide, the Soviet bloc has paid attention to perhaps the softest target of all: the serviceman on duty abroad. In the early 1950s, when British soldiers were stationed in Austria, Czech intelligence made use of a call-girl system to entrap a corporal of the East Yorkshire Regiment. A young Austrian prostitute, deliberately planted, was able to extract seemingly trivial information from him for which he received by court martial eight years' imprisonment in spite of having eventually reported the lady, who received seven years.

Spy-mistresses like 'Sonia' and Hede Massing can be mistresses in more ways than one. Some have been prepared to use sex quite callously to recruit traitors or to keep them going. In her memoirs 'Sonia' hints at this by remarking that the rules of conspiracy may occasionally be broken to permit an intimate association with a fellow agent – of whom Roger Hollis may have been one – though Soviet intelligence has in general frowned on romantic liaisons as being too dangerous.[12] Indeed, Russians living abroad who become entangled with women, unless it be on orders, have always been regarded in Moscow as potential defectors and some have been summarily flown home.

The type specimen of the lady prepared to use her exceptional sexual attraction to create traitors has to be the American known to her Allied intelligence masters during the Second World War as 'Cynthia'. A striking redhead, she began her honey-trap career while married to a British diplomat who was serving in the embassy in Warsaw. She formed liaisons with several high-ranking members of the Polish foreign service, reporting to MI6, and is believed to have helped in providing information about Poland's secret knowledge of the Enigma code-machines used by the German forces. After the fall of France in 1940 'Cynthia' worked for British Security Co-ordination, the special intelligence service based in New York and headed by the Canadian, Sir William Stephenson. Using the name Elizabeth Thorpe, 'Cynthia' was set up in a house in Washington where one of her previous conquests, an Italian naval officer, was serving in the Italian Embassy. The officer, who felt that Italy would not last long in the war and is said to have been 'enfeebled by passion', let her have naval information and documents for copying, an act of gross treachery that is believed to have contributed to Italian naval defeats.

'Cynthia' was then asked to penetrate the embassy of Vichy France, in which she succeeded by seducing the press officer, a former naval captain called Charles Brousse, who assisted her to secure and copy cipher-books from an embassy safe. Again the code-breaking team at Bletchley benefited hugely.[13]

More recently the Israelis succeeded in a spectacular fashion through the wiles of a woman. In August 1966 an Iraqi pilot, Munir Redfa, landed in Israel in his Soviet Mig 21 fighter, one of many which had been supplied to the Iraqis, who were fiercely hostile to Israel. The Israelis had badly needed to know the fullest performance details of the plane, which they expected to encounter in combat, and Redfa's defection was no chance event. He had been set up by an attractive woman agent of Mossad, the Israeli intelligence service, who had an American passport. On a contrived visit to Iraq, she met Redfa, who had been targeted as a possible defector because he was known to be strongly opposed to the war being waged by the Iraq government on its Kurdish tribesmen and disliked the Russian 'advisers' on the Iraqi air bases. The lady's charm proved irresistible.[14]

'Woman trouble' and unhappy marriages have caused several career Soviet intelligence officers, from both the KGB and the GRU, to defect – some with encouragement from the West, others spontaneously. George Agabekov became so enamoured of a British girl, whom he had hired in Tehran as a language teacher, that he defected to marry her. But my type specimen for this motivation has to be Oleg Lyalin, a 34-year-old KGB officer serving in London in 1971 in the branch formerly known as SMERSH. He had been recruited by the British as an agent-in-place early in that year. Lyalin had a wife and a mistress who was also married, a Russian secretary living in London, through whom the recruitment had been achieved. On MI5's promise of an eventual home together in Britain, the girl induced her lover to continue in the very dangerous position of an informer inside the KGB instead of defecting physically at that stage. Lyalin was providing most valuable information when, after a night out in the West End with his girl, he drank too much and was picked up by the police on a driving charge. There is some evidence that he had been told he was being recalled to Moscow and his drinking that evening was a reaction to the fear that he had been rumbled. In any case his misdemeanour and appearance in court – as a 'trade official' he had no diplomatic immunity – meant that he would be recalled anyway, so he and his

95

girl-friend decided to defect physically and have since made a new life in Britain.[15]

In view of the general eroding effects of the need for constant deception on a traitor's character, the additional burden of secrecy imposed by illicit sexual affairs can hardly be helpful. Yet even some of the most professional agents have been unable to resist burdening themselves in that way. Richard Sorge, the German who spied so effectively for the Russians in China and Japan, was an incorrigible womanizer. He broke the conspiratorial rules by having affairs with his own women agents, such as 'Sonia', and patronizing geisha girls in Tokyo, being recklessly indiscreet in their presence, according to some accounts. The GRU traitor Pyotr Popov, who was a highly productive agent-in-place for the CIA in the 1950s, undoubtedly loved his wife and children but took insane risks with his cover through his devotion to his mistress. In spite of repeated warnings from his American controller that the Russians would hear of it and regard it as a severe breach of security discipline, he refused to end the liaison and was eventually detected and executed.[16] The Polish agent Michal Goleniewski arrived with his East German mistress when he suddenly had to flee to the West in 1960. This complicated the escape at a time when the Polish security authorities were actively looking for a traitor in their intelligence service.

Even Fuchs, the so-called ascetic, was shown to be having illicit sex relations with the wife of one of his senior colleagues, who had befriended him, when police inquiries were made into his secret activities. Hollis, regarded by most of his MI5 staff as cold and withdrawn, who repeatedly warned them of the dangers of illicit sex, threw caution to the winds and made his secretary his mistress. He vainly hoped to conceal the relationship, knowing that it would be most unwelcome to his ministerial employers should they hear of it.

Loneliness, which may severely affect the traitor who feels it safer to limit his natural gregariousness, may drive a man to the solution of one mistress or the impersonal use of prostitutes, which has attendant dangers. Criminals are often associated with prostitutes and may see the possibility of blackmail if the identity of a customer becomes known. Sir James Dunnett, a former very senior civil servant in the Defence Ministry, experienced this danger at the hands of a person he believed to be a female prostitute but who was in fact a notorious transvestite who called himself Vikki de Lambray. No attempt was made to blackmail Sir James, but de Lambray, who had a criminal record, subjected him to disrepute by selling the story to a newspaper.

In general, hetero-sex does not present such tempting blackmail opportunities as homo-sex, because of the greater stigma still attaching to the latter, but much depends on the rank of the man concerned. While no treachery was involved in the tragic cases of John Profumo and Lord Lambton they did highlight the danger of public disgrace which association with call-girls can carry.

The extrovert Dusko Popov, MI5's wartime penetration agent, solved his urgent requirements for sex and companionship by insisting on continuing with his inveterate womanizing because it would be out of character not to do so and might arouse suspicion among his German contacts. To the highly disciplined professional head of the FBI, J. Edgar Hoover, however, Popov's behaviour was proof enough that he could not be trusted; as a result, evidence which Popov supplied pointing to the coming attack on Pearl Harbor was ignored.[17]

Probably the most hazardous complication which sex poses for the traitor who fears exposure is the danger of the woman scorned. John Walker, head of the American naval spy ring, treated his former wife so shabbily that, while he enjoyed his illicit wealth, she toiled long hours in a shoe factory. Before they had parted he had been foolish enough to make his treachery obvious by servicing dead letter drops on family outings, and when his wife had argued against his disloyalty he had silenced her with a beating. She eventually exposed him to the FBI out of bitterness.[18]

The British naval spy Houghton was also in serious conflict with his wife, who eventually told his superiors that he was engaged in espionage. Houghton claimed that his wife knew this because he had been in the habit of giving her extra money whenever he was paid by the Russians; he said that she reported him only when a divorce was imminent and he ended the extra payments.[19] The American Soviet agent Sergeant Robert Lee Johnson, who provided secrets by the bagful from the security vault at Orly airport, was 'blown' only when his wife was questioned following his disappearance in 1964 to escape her nagging and threats to reveal his treachery. She told so much that in the end Johnson confessed all.

The KGB could not have been happy when Philby prejudiced his marriage to Eleanor, the American whom they had allowed into Russia, by seducing the wife of Donald Maclean, especially as Maclean was a dependent character who badly needed his wife's support. Philby had used a typical deception, claiming that he was ghosting the memoirs of the Soviet agent Gordon Lonsdale, to cover his long absences with his new mistress. There were obvious intelligence problems when Eleanor finally parted with Philby and returned permanently to the USA where the KGB was sure she would be interrogated at length.

Some highly sexed women spies have also taken risks or otherwise increased their problems by liaisons with men. The highly professional

'Sonia' produced an illegitimate daughter, fathered by a fellow agent while she was still married. Her friend in China, the redoubtable American writer and Communist recruiter Agnes Smedley, was nothing less than promiscuous.

As a recent report by the West German security agency revealed, the Soviets make blackmail use of love as well as of lust. When a West German applies to marry an East German spouse it is the regular practice for Soviet-bloc intelligence to insist on future 'co-operation' in some subversive capacity or other as a condition for allowing the East German to emigrate.[20]

Love rather than lust is the usual motive when women fall victim to sexual entrapment, the type specimen being Barbara Fell, a former senior official in the Central Office of Information in London. Aged fifty-four when arrested, she admitted taking papers classified no higher than 'confidential' to show to her lover, Smiljan Pecjak, the press counsellor at the Yugoslav Embassy. She also told her MI5 interrogator that she might have been compromisingly photographed. Though she helped the court by pleading guilty, had done no real damage to British security and had been motivated by nothing but affection, she was sentenced in 1962 to the maximum term of two years' imprisonment, which was not reduced on appeal and led to her sad circumstances being known in Whitehall as the 'barbarous' Fell case.

Whether Miss Fell's lover had been required to seduce her in order to secure information is unknown, but agents are certainly trained for this purpose. One such was Rafaat El-Ansary, a young Egyptian intelligence officer working in the embassy in Israel, where he managed to seduce a British woman diplomat named Rhona Ritchie. She was indiscreet enough to show her lover diplomatic telegrams. When Israeli intelligence alerted the British Ritchie was charged under the Official Secrets Act, and, though given only a nine-month suspended sentence, her promising career was finished. The East Germans in particular have become adept in the employment of men trained to use sex to attract West German women for recruitment to espionage – in the 'trade' known as 'Romeos'. These men have concentrated on vulnerable secretaries employed in sensitive departments and have been highly successful. At least twenty West German secretaries are known to have been recruited to Soviet-bloc intelligence, and some of them have been required to defect to save themselves from arrest, with the inevitable damaging publicity to the Western intelligence system. One of these 'honey-trapped' women, Ingrid Barbe, was secretary to a West German diplomat attached to NATO. Through her access she managed to supply her 'Romeo' with details of NATO forces' strengths, weapons, and plans for crisis management, all of the greatest intercst to thc Sovict bloc. Shc had operated as a traitor-spy for three years before being jailed for four years in 1980.

Another secretary, who called herself Sonja Luneburg, was infiltrated during the mid-1960s into West Germany's Free Democratic Party, which has always been a Soviet-bloc target for influence. After a succession of posts she was secretary to the politician Martin Bangemann, who became a minister in the Bonn government and a member of its Security Committee. She not only had access to information about defence and foreign policy but was well positioned to talent-spot other secretaries who might be ripe for the attentions of a 'Romeo'. She vanished to East Germany in August 1985.[21]

The length to which Soviet-bloc intelligence services will go to entrap females was dramatically described by Josef Frolik to the US Congressional Committee on the Judiciary. In what Czech intelligence called Operation Rubber Dummy, a woman secretary in the British Embassy in Prague was targeted as someone who enjoyed sex, wine, and 'good times'. A handsome Czech who was a secret agent was put her way, and she succumbed to a 'love affair'. To secure a blackmail hold on her an ingenious rubber dummy of a man, containing a blood-like liquid, was thrown at her car from bushes as she drove back alone to Prague at night, somewhat intoxicated, from a dinner with her lover. She believed she had killed a man, especially when she saw the 'blood' on her car, but Czech intelligence was unable to recruit her because she had failed to stop. Had she done so, 'police' arriving on the scene would have offered her a choice of prosecution, with imprisonment a certainty, or an undertaking to commit treason against her country.[22]

Unrequited love could occasionally be a psychological factor in inducing a man to betray his country by making him into a loner with a chip on his shoulder. This might have happened to Michael Bettaney, who in 1974 wrote to a German girl living in Berlin with whom he seemed to be deeply in love but whom he could not marry, if only because of the geographical difficulties. 'For the first time in my life I cursed the fact that I am an Englishman,' he wrote.[23]

A stable marital relationship welded by love can be an enormous advantage to a traitor when his wife knows of his treachery, supports it, or at least condones it and may even be an active party to it. The type specimen of a man-and-wife team giving mutual support, both emotional and practical, in their dangerous work is the German couple Gunther and Christl Guillaume, whose exploits have already been described. Both professionally trained by East German intelligence, they entered West Germany together, posing as refugees, joined the Social Democratic Party, on instructions, and assisted each other to steady promotion until Gunther became adviser and confidant of

Chancellor Willy Brandt himself. They supported each other in their joint treachery, involving regular communication with their East German controllers, and in their adversity, when caught.

More recently Herta-Astrid Willner, a secretary in the office of West German Chancellor Helmut Kohl, and her husband Herbert, who spied together for the Soviet bloc, defected together in September 1985. Both were traitors because they held West German citizenship.

In the case of Commodore Dieter Gerhardt, the South African who spied for the GRU for more than twenty years, the marital arrangement was even more professionally supportive. Gerhardt, who offered the Soviets his services when he was twenty-five, divorced his English wife and married Ruth Johr, a Swiss woman who was already a Soviet agent, the match having been blessed by the GRU. Dieter rose in the South African naval service, eventually becoming commander of the Simonstown dockyard with access to other defence centres. Ruth acted as courier, taking documents and information to Geneva, ostensibly to visit her mother but also to communicate with a GRU controller, as there were no Soviet-bloc 'diplomats' in South Africa. They were also able to take joint vacations to Vienna, sometimes journeying on to Moscow surreptitiously for further training. With Gerhart never needing to contact any other intermediary, the arrangement worked so well that they committed continuous treason – for which both were eventually convicted in 1983 – and were caught only because a Soviet defector happened to know about them.

In Britain the American traitors Morris and Lona Cohen, using the name Kroger, assisted each other in the 'housekeeping' duties required by the espionage network run by the Soviet controller who called himself Gordon Lonsdale: the transmission of messages by radio, the provision of a safe house for meetings, and other functions, perhaps including being paymasters. The Rosenbergs, Julius and Ethel, likewise supported each other in their widespread espionage operations involving many other American traitors. 'Sonia' was similarly sustained by her British husband, Len Beurton, during the last few years of her traitorous activities in Britain. Eleanor Philby, who saw much of the Macleans in Moscow, is not the only one to believe that Donald's wife, Melinda, had been a long-time accomplice, supporting him through most of his treachery including his secret flight to Moscow, where she eventually joined him by equally clandestine means.[24]

No arrangement in the field of treachery is without its attendant risks. In the case of husband-and-wife teams the main danger is that one may confess and incriminate both. Harro and Libertas Schulze-Boysen were German man-and-wife leaders of a Soviet ring spying on the Nazis and no doubt gave each other valuable support; but, when captured, while the husband held out, Libertas betrayed him and his other collaborators to avoid torture and in a futile attempt to save her own life. There is also the risk that, if caught, a couple can be accused of the more serious offence of conspiracy, as happened with the Rosenbergs and sent them to the electric chair.

Among East–West defectors some of the most knowledgeable have felt able to make the break with country and culture only because they were able to take their wives with them. When Walter Krivitsky had to move fast to save himself from execution in Stalin's paranoid purges, his wife, Tania, who was a dedicated revolutionary from Leningrad, defected with him. When Vladimir Petrov, a KGB officer, defected in Australia in 1954, his wife, who was also a KGB officer, elected to stay with him, achieving this in dramatic circumstances when the Australian police intervened to prevent her forcible removal by KGB guards.

While the inability to take wives and children with them has deterred some from defecting from the Soviet bloc, others have taken the opportunity to rid themselves of entanglements they considered to be burdensome. Others, like Stanislav Levchenko, had to make a choice between family and freedom and chose the latter, their disquiet being compounded when their deserted wives and children were then persecuted.

The companionship and moral and emotional support of a woman seems to be a necessity for many defectors. Most of those who have had to leave wives or mistresses behind in the Soviet-bloc countries, and have been unable to secure their release, have quickly acquired new ones. While some professional intelligence officers believe that the recent KGB defector Vitaly Yurchenko was a deliberate plant with a political mission, fulfilling it by returning to Moscow, as will be explained later, the CIA maintains that he was genuine and that his failure to induce a Russian woman he loved to defect with him contributed to his decision to return home to face an extremely dangerous future. When Yurchenko was taken to see the woman, understood to have been the wife of a Soviet diplomat stationed in Canada, she is said to have declined Yurchenko's advances and to have told him that she had no wish to live with a traitor.[25]

There is a possible negative association between sex and treachery in that impotence may induce some men to feel so deprived that they take revenge on society. However, the only example I can find of a spy affected in that manner was Harry Gold. After falling in love in 1948, he felt driven to end the relationship because of what he described as his 'lack of ardor'. He had committed his major espionage offences by that time, but his problem could have manifested itself earlier.

Deviant heterosexual behaviour is usually an expression of some degree of impotence, sexual satisfaction having become difficult or impossible by means considered normal. This can be very dangerous to a traitor if it is compulsive and of a kind that is criminal, as happened with Prime, the KGB agent inside GCHQ. Security there was so poor that his treachery might never have been discovered but for his compulsive need to masturbate in front of very young girls, for which purpose he had compiled a card-index of possible victims. It was only after the police learned of this depravity that his past espionage came to light. Considering what Prime had to hide, his behaviour offers some indication of the risks which such people are prepared to take to secure sexual satisfaction. Some authorities, both British and American, with whom I have discussed the case think that Prime was first recruited while in Berlin by KGB men who discovered his perversion and threatened to expose it.

Every profession has its quota of men with peculiar sexual requirements needing fulfilment. My inquiries have produced evidence that a few very senior members of the secret services and civil servants involved with secret operations have been subject to heterosexual deviations such as voyeurism. Their activities were potentially blackmailable, but I know of no instance where they were put under any such pressure.

The reader may wonder why I provide no examples of the use of heterosexual blackmail for the recruitment of agents by British intelligence officers. A short-term recruit to MI6 has described to me a sexually compromising film involving a Middle East diplomat, which was shown to him and others on a training course; but officers of both MI6 and MI5 have for many years been forbidden to make any practical use of sexual blackmail of any kind for the recruitment of agents. I understand that the same restriction is applied by the CIA and FBI. Some officers of both the British and American services deplore the restriction, when sexual blackmail is so heavily exploited by the Soviets.

CHAPTER TEN

The Homo-Sex Factor

I sought by love alone to go where God had writ an awful No.
I only know I pay the cost, with heart and soul and honour lost.

Sir Roger Casement

There is a common belief that homosexuality is particularly wide-spread among traitors and that the 'Homintern', the fraternity of homosexuals, was as potent as the Comintern in producing Soviet agents. This is untrue in both respects. The misbelief has arisen because some of the more notorious traitors, whose cases have attracted wide publicity, like Blunt, Burgess, Driberg, and Maclean (when drunk), happened to be 'gay' deceivers, and because of the few cases of homosexual blackmail, like that of John Vassall, who must be the type specimen of a spy compromised by that means.

With homosexuals like Blunt and Burgess who became revolution-ary Communists and traitors, homosexuality may have been a factor in inducing them to rebel against a society which not only disapproved of their habits but regarded them as criminal. As Blunt's brother, Wilfrid, also a self-confessed homosexual, has expressed it, the treat-ment of homosexuals as criminals and degenerates was hardly likely to encourage uncritical devotion to the established regime in which they were growing up and which they would see as inhuman and oppressive.[1] The social and legal condemnation of homosexuals may well have converted some of them into 'outsiders' with a chip on the shoulder, deeply resentful of a society which made a serious offence of the sexual expression which they found natural.

Psychologists suspect that such resentment can create a 'minority complex', with the victim subconsciously or even consciously prepared to hit back at the privileged majority if opportunities offer, treachery being one way of doing so. Realizing, as a boy, that he was homosexual made Vassall lonely and unhappy; in his autobiography he wrote: 'Being a homosexual had given me a dreadful inferiority complex.' A

103

former Conservative politician who had been dangerously involved with Vassall bemoaned his condition sadly to a psychiatrist, declaring that he was 'neither fish nor fowl' – the implication that he was bisexual finding its way to MI5.[2] The notoriously blatant homosexuality of Guy Burgess was not the major cause of his treachery but may have been a factor by warping his character in a general way. It seems to be widely believed by psychologists and psychiatrists that what are referred to as 'disturbed' homosexuals, like Burgess, feel themselves driven to take revenge on authority, of which the state is an obvious embodiment. Freudians further suggest that this is often the result of upbringing by a hostile or uncaring father and that traitors are hitting back at paternalistic authority when they strike at the state. Burgess was often cruelly spiteful, and treachery was a most potent protest. This expression of resentment may also have been true, in part, of the American, Whittaker Chambers, who was bisexual; Chambers called the homosexuality which he did his best to hide his 'darkest personal secret'.[3]

The use of homosexual compromise to obtain recruits for treachery is also referred to as *entrapment*, but there seems to be no male counterpart for 'honey-trap'; perhaps 'drone-trap' would be apt. Without question the most bizarre drone trap ever was that exploited by Chinese intelligence after setting it for the French diplomat Bernard Boursicot, who was sentenced to six years' imprisonment for espionage in May 1986. When Boursicot was posted to Peking as a junior diplomat in 1964 he allegedly fell in love with a celebrated Chinese beauty known as Shi Pei Pu who spoke French, acted classic roles as a singer and dancer in Chinese opera, and was highly regarded by the ruling Communists, including Chairman Mao. Their affair continued by post after Boursicot was transferred to Saudi Arabia, one letter informing him that he had become the father of a boy. By the time he secured a posting back to Peking the opera had been suspended by the 'cultural revolution', but he found Shi Pei Pu and they continued their lovers' meetings. At one of them they were seized by Red Guards. The local political commissar, sensing an opportunity, threatened to send the opera star to agricultural labour unless the Frenchman was prepared to supply copies of dispatches to and from the French Embassy. In this way Boursicot was blackmailed into providing confidential diplomatic information for the Chinese intelligence service, his case officer being a certain 'Mr Kang'. The treachery, which Boursicot claimed to be unimportant, continued after the diplomat left Peking.

In 1982 Boursicot was reunited with his Chinese lover and their child by arranging a lecture tour for Shi Pei Pu in France. They lived in his flat in Paris until the French counter-intelligence service (DST) became suspicious and made inquiries, probably because Chinese intelligence was still doing all it could to blackmail the Frenchman into continuing to supply diplomatic documents.

The most extraordinary aspect of the affair came to light when the two were arrested. Although Boursicot claimed that Shi Pei Pu, with whom he had been intimately associated for twenty years, was a woman, examination showed that the Chinese singer had male sex organs. Boursicot claimed that he and his lover would meet secretly in Peking and have sexual relations in the dark. He entertained no doubts that he was the father of the child, who proved to be an orphan bought by Shi Pei Pu in a Chinese market. In court he admitted passing French Foreign Office documents but insisted that he had done it for love and not for money.

Boursicot was forty-two when convicted. His lover, who was forty-six, also received a six-year jail sentence. Understandably, one of the judges seemed to be less incensed by the treachery, which had not been very serious, than by the inability of a Frenchman to tell the difference between a man and a woman.[4] The likeliest explanation is that Boursicot knew the truth and was hopelessly entangled in a web of lies, begun to hide his homosexuality, which he continued to deny.

I know of no other proven case where both partners in a stable homosexual relationship have been involved in treachery, but such cases may exist. MI5 has evidence of such a bond between a known traitor and a prominent politician who is suspected of having been blackmailed by the KGB.

There appear to be many instances of two homosexuals having a lasting and loving relationship comparable to marriage; and when one partner is a traitor, the same questions arise as with a heterosexual pair. Does the lover discern his partner's treachery? Does he give him emotional support? I can find no case of a homosexual traitor being exposed by his partner. Blunt's live-in lover insists he had no knowledge of his partner's treachery or of his confession.

Most acts of treachery involving homosexuality arise out of promiscuity, the classically straightforward case being that of John Vassall, whom I have interviewed. He is an obvious passive homosexual, and, as he wrote in his autobiography: 'The fact that an obvious homosexual should have been appointed to Moscow and allowed to remain there is a severe indictment of our security services.' A Russian KGB agent on the domestic staff inside the British Embassy in Moscow, where Vassall was working as a clerk to the naval attaché, quickly spotted his sexual abnormality and his loneliness. He was compromised at a drunken homosexual party and, when shown photographs of his involvement in various perversions, was weak enough to agree to spy

105

for Soviet intelligence, which he did successfully for seven years.[5]

The case of another British embassy official compromised in this way, whose name has not been disclosed, was described in the testimony of the Czech defector Josef Frolik to the US Senate's Committee on the Judiciary in 1975. Czech intelligence had discerned that a cipher official in the Prague embassy was homosexual and set him up with a homosexual agent. A film of their activities was taken and shown to the victim. It may well be that he was sensible enough to report what had happened because he was quietly sent home within a month.[6] Not long ago a highly sophisticated American journalist with homosexual tendencies, who was visiting Moscow, was deliberately seated next to a young and handsome Russian officer at an official dinner. They spent the night together and within hours the KGB showed the journalist incriminating photographs and warned him that unless he helped them as an agent of influence his career would be ruined. Wisely, he reported the threat and was advised to play along with the Russians until he was approached by the inevitable Soviet 'diplomat' back in the USA. The 'diplomat' was then told that if he and his colleagues in the Soviet Embassy made anything of the matter they would be quickly expelled from the USA. They took no further action.

Tom Driberg, the Labour MP and MI5 agent, was also compromised in this way while indulging himself in Moscow. He was a much tougher character and claimed to have laughed off the blackmail threat, which was unnecessary because he was prepared to work for the KGB anyway, so long as he was paid. The photographs could, however, have been used damagingly, if widely distributed in Driberg's constituency, where his sexual promiscuity was not widely known. Indeed, this lever is believed by MI5 officers to have been important in inducing Driberg to work primarily for the KGB and only secondarily for them.[7]

A tragic case of Soviet subornment of a high-level homosexual diplomat, of which I have been given first-hand information by officers who investigated it, is that of John Watkins, the Canadian Ambassador to Moscow in the middle 1950s. During a tour of the Soviet Union he was successfully set up for photo-blackmail by the same KGB agent, Yuri Krotkov, who had organized the honey-trap for the French Ambassador, Dejean. Watkins was later called to the presence of a senior Soviet Foreign Ministry official, really a KGB general, who offered to do his best to stop the KGB from making any use of the photographs. All he asked in return was that when Watkins went back to Ottawa, where he was being appointed to a high-level post, he would 'steer things' in the Soviet interest. Watkins was warned that his Soviet friends in Moscow would be 'watching'.[8]

A variant on the homosexual blackmail theme has been reported by the KGB defector Golitsin, who saw it described in a KGB training manual for recruiters. The KGB had learned that the President of a developing country was a homosexual. When he visited Moscow, the KGB warned him about a fictitious 'world-wide criminal organization' which was planning to blackmail him. Claiming to be the only agency powerful enough to silence the 'criminal organization', the KGB offered to do so if the President would co-operate 'against the imperialist powers'. The naïve visitor complied.[9]

It is commonly believed that the legal permissiveness concerning homosexuality between consenting adults has virtually eliminated the blackmail weapon, but this is far from being true. The fear of criminal prosecution may have been removed, but the fear of public exposure persists because homosexuality still carries severe social stigma for most people, including employers. This was tragically demonstrated as recently as 1982 when Commander Michael Trestrail, a senior Scotland Yard detective who served as the Queen's bodyguard, was publicly disgraced. No aspect of treachery on Trestrail's part was involved, but his career was ruined following an attempt by a male prostitute to blackmail him.[10] The continuing danger of the blackmail threat is officially recognized in that homosexuals are still supposed to be barred from the secret services and foreign and diplomatic services, though not from the home Civil Service. Homosexual acts remain an offence in the Armed Forces and the Parliamentary Select Committee on the Armed Forces Bill has recently recommended that the ban should continue, in spite of objections by the National Council for Civil Liberties and other 'progressive' bodies.[11]

The change in the law may have had one important impact on the relationship between homosexuality and treachery, in that, in theory at least, by eliminating its criminal aspects for consenting adults, it should reduce the resentment which homosexuals feel against society. Yet homosexuality among men is still deplored as an unnatural vice by most people in spite of the various movements to make the 'gay' community acceptable, and homosexuals remain aware of this.

If more homosexuals could conceal their tendencies the chance that Soviet recruiters could notice and exploit it through blackmail would be greatly reduced. Regrettably, many – perhaps most – of them find this very difficult and even distasteful. There are several reasons for this. First, homosexuality is often so compulsive that those addicted to it are driven to take fearful risks to find partners. The risks are compounded by the strange need of many homosexuals to indulge themselves with what would in former times have been called guttersnipes – rough young men who may be criminals or associated with them, called in the homosexual fraternity 'rough trade'. This may arise because a homosexual with no steady relationship has need of male prostitutes, who are to be found among such people, but others seek them out because they find promiscuity exciting, as Driberg described with abandon in his book *Ruling Passions*.

Sir Roger Casement was another homosexual traitor who patronized 'rough trade'. He described his sexual encounters in detail in the diaries which fell into the hands of his prosecutors and not only showed him to be a severely warped character but prejudiced his chance of a reprieve from his death sentence.[12]

A further factor increasing the blackmail risk is the compulsive need of many homosexuals to draw attention to their perversion, not just to attract partners but for the pleasure of shocking others. Guy Burgess, for instance, was noted for such remarks as, 'I can never travel comfortably by train because I am always feeling that I ought to be having the engine-driver.' Driberg also revelled in his homosexuality, which he took no pains to hide. While on a visit to the Middle East as an MP, Driberg seduced a soldier and was threatened by the commanding officer with incarceration in the guard-house. Driberg's response was: 'In that case I'll have to seduce the guards.' His parliamentary colleague Woodrow Wyatt has told how, when he upbraided Driberg for being so long in the MPs' lavatory while he waited to take him to lunch, the explanation was that Driberg had been 'having one of the House of Commons chefs'. The astonishing recklessness of Driberg's sordid sex life in public lavatories and back streets, while he was serving as an agent for both MI5 and the KGB, was revealed by himself in his explicit biography, published posthumously, though his worst excesses with guttersnipes and criminals were withheld on the advice of close friends. Driberg claimed that his real reason for joining the Communist Party was to bring him into touch with working-class males.[13]

As noted in Chapter 9, Driberg served as an MI5 and KGB talent-spotter among his Parliamentary colleagues for many years. Among the many whose sexual character weaknesses he reported was a very senior Labour personality, an occasional homosexual who was desperately anxious to keep his lapses secret and was, therefore, potentially blackmailable.

Driberg escaped public censure only because, when caught in various acts by the police, he was able to call on the services of MI5 and also exploit his position as an MP. On one occasion he was saved from prosecution by Lord Beaverbrook, who employed him as a journalist. Others have been less fortunate. The dangers of homosexual promiscuity and especially of patronizing male prostitutes, first thrust into prominence at the trial of Oscar Wilde, were more recently and just as tragically exposed by the enforced resignation of Commander

Trestrail. Another homosexual on the Buckingham Palace staff, Sir Anthony Blunt, was extremely fortunate to have escaped a similar fate during his tenure of office there.

It would have been reasonable to expect Blunt to be discreet, because of his public appointments as Surveyor of the Queen's Pictures, Director of the Courtauld Institute, and Professor of the History of Art at the University of London. On the contrary, as he confessed to the MI5 officer Arthur Martin during his subsequent interrogation, his need for promiscuity had driven him to frequent London's 'gay' bars and public lavatories to pick up sailors and other casual partners, whom he paid, while one of his regular partners served as a procurer for him. He was even indiscreet enough to involve himself with some of his male art students at the Courtauld Institute.

According to Professor G. M. Wickens, who had known Blunt at Cambridge, his homosexuality there when he was a young don had been nothing short of notorious. Professor Wickens has recorded that: 'At one of the left-wing parties in the luxurious suite of rooms rented from the college by the American millionaire Michael Straight, I once caught sight of Blunt in bed with a gifted young scientist.'[14] Evidence originally collected on behalf of the BBC shows that Blunt's promiscuous homosexuality was not only widely known in the large 'gay' community but that other homosexuals knew or suspected that Blunt was a Soviet agent, living in horror of being exposed, and could have betrayed him.[15]

Such behaviour, which most homosexuals would still wish to keep secret from their employers, especially if they are in government service, offers further scope for blackmail and exposes their activities to the ubiquitous Soviet talent-spotters, some of whom are chosen because they are homosexuals themselves.

Homosexuals increase their vulnerability to blackmail through their understandable need to write love letters to their partners. Goronwy Rees has described how Burgess, a close friend, kept hundreds of letters from his many former lovers all separately bundled – as MI5 officers found when they searched his flat after his defection.[16] Burgess tried to recruit anyone he regarded as suitable for the Soviet cause, and such letters offered a powerful weapon to such a pitiless character.

Another friend of Blunt, and also of Burgess, who certainly knew of their flagrant homosexuality and possibly of their treachery was Baron Wolfgang zu Putlitz, a German whom the Nazis would have taken pleasure in executing as a traitor to them. While at the German Embassy in London, between 1934 and 1938, this dedicated anti-Nazi contacted Sir Robert Vansittart of the Foreign Office and bravely offered to supply secret information, including details of Luftwaffe strength, which Winston Churchill was able to use in his parliamentary attempts to secure a stronger RAF. He continued to work as a British spy when posted to Holland. When he fell under suspicion he decided to defect and was rescued by MI6, insisting that he had to bring his valet, Willy, his homosexual partner, with him. Perhaps through ideological conversion by Blunt and Burgess, he became committed to the Communist cause and may have served as a Soviet agent, because in 1952 he became a citizen of East Germany.

Some homosexuals are also prone to involvement in violence, such is the tempestuousness of some relationships. Through his insulting behaviour Burgess was often involved in fights, in one of which he was quite seriously injured, while Blunt inflicted injury on one of his homosexual friends. The additional factor of alcohol is often involved in such circumstances. Maclean, who was physically powerful, was inclined to become violent in drink, and alcohol also weakened the control he could usually keep on his homosexual tendencies.[17] According to the FBI officer Robert Lamphere, who was in charge of the American aspects of the case, Maclean took fright when another Communist, Douglas Springhall, was convicted of espionage in 1943. So Burgess, fearing that he might quit serving the Soviets, 'got Maclean drunk and photographed him nude in another man's arms', making it possible for him to be blackmailed if necessary. The following year Maclean was posted to Washington, where he inflicted his greatest damage.

Wilfred Mann, the British scientist who worked in the British Embassy in Washington when Philby and Burgess were there, has recorded how he called at Philby's house on the morning after a heavy drinking party and found Burgess and Philby in bed together drinking champagne. This may have been of little significance, but Mann reported it to the security authorities.[18]

The sad story of the effects of alcohol on a young British diplomat who was trying to repress his innate homosexuality was told to me by the late Lord Harlech, formerly ambassador to the USA. Foreign Office officials knew that he had been a homosexual but believed that he had conquered the habit before posting him to Washington. This hope seemed to be confirmed when he became engaged to an American girl; but when, in honesty, he told her of his past problem she broke off the engagement. The young man was so shattered that he took to drink and was eventually picked up by the Washington police for soliciting a male. When the FBI reported him, Harlech had no alternative but to send him home because he was regarded as a potential blackmail victim.

The publicly known homosexuals who have worked in or with the British secret services are Blunt, Burgess, Driberg, Zu Putlitz, and Maxwell Knight. The last, whose code-name was 'M', was an important agent-runner for MI5, operating outside headquarters from a flat in Dolphin Square. His former girl-friend, the late Joan Miller, has revealed that Knight was bisexual and had a homosexual 'crush' on Driberg. There is no evidence that his sexual deviation affected his work, which seems to have been highly effective. The same applies to an officer of MI6 who, on his retirement in the 1960s, wrote a letter to his chief, the late Sir Maurice Oldfield, revealing with spiteful glee that he had been a lifelong homosexual and had not declared it on his positive-vetting form as he was required to do. The purpose of this confession has been in doubt, but a possible explanation has recently come to light: Oldfield himself was a practising homosexual and had also omitted to declare it. The letter may have been the retiring officer's way of making Oldfield aware that he had detected his secret.

I have known of Oldfield's staggering duplicity – for that is what it was – for several years and have been diffident about revealing it because he was a friend. But the indisputable facts of the case are being commonly discussed by very senior officials who were involved with it and who have made them known to me in order to have them put on record. In writing a book of this nature, the case must, in honesty, be considered; for if homosexuality is a bar to employment, because of the blackmail danger, then the appointment of a practising homosexual to the highest secret-service position in the land and his continuation in that and in further office is of public concern.

Oldfield, a man of charm and erudition, was a lifelong bachelor. Former close colleagues of his whom I have consulted say they were unaware of his homosexuality, as were their wives, who are usually perceptive in this respect. Some believed that his reason for not marrying was because he suffered from psoriasis, which embarrassed him when it flared. His homosexuality, which was clearly compulsive, came to official notice only following his retirement from MI6 in 1978 and during his appointment a year later to an intelligence post in Northern Ireland, which he took up at the request of the Prime Minister, Mrs Thatcher. Oldfield's new duty was to serve as co-ordinator between the Royal Ulster Constabulary and the Army, which were in conflict. He required rigorous personal protection, not only because his job made him a prime IRA target, but because there had already been an attempt on his life in October 1975 when an IRA assassin hung a 30 lb bomb in a holdall on the railings below his London flat. The bomb was spotted and defused within a few minutes of its set time to explode.

Round-the-clock protection was provided by Scotland Yard, and certain of the detectives concerned became worried by the number and type of men visiting Sir Maurice's London flat so frequently. These callers included waiters of various nationalities and young men who, the detectives deduced, had nothing to do with intelligence. One of them, whom they described as a hobo, had to be barred from the property because he was so persistent at demanding entry. Some of these men were traced, and the detectives' inquiries convinced them that some were homosexual and functioned as male prostitutes.

The police kept closer watch and questioned the porters at the apartment block, who disclosed that the men had been in the habit of visiting the flat over several years, while Oldfield had been chief of MI6, and to such an extent that the porters themselves had become suspicious. They recalled that Sir Maurice had returned one night scratched and bruised, as though he had been in a fight. He told one of the porters that he had fallen, but this was thought to be an unlikely explanation. While in the flat alone one of the detectives found books and magazines about sexual perversions with photographs of nude young men.[19] The policemen put in a report to the head of the Special Branch suggesting that Oldfield might be a security risk. The situation was then reported to the Metropolitan Commissioner, Sir David McNee, who was so perturbed that he called on the Home Secretary, William Whitelaw.

There was concern that Soviet counter-intelligence might be aware of the situation, but there was no evidence that Oldfield had been subjected to any kind of pressure. Because he undoubtedly was the best man available for the Northern Ireland post, he was interviewed on the government's behalf by a senior Minister. In the most direct language he was told that his unfortunate sexual habits were known, but as they appeared to have led to no harm, he could continue with his work in Northern Ireland, provided he gave a solemn promise that he would curb himself throughout his tenure. Oldfield, who made no denials, promised to do so and seemingly caused no trouble before he had to leave on the grounds of serious ill health in 1980. He may have been under some degree of surveillance in Ulster and during his regular visits to the flat in London.

Continuing inquiries produced no evidence that Oldfield had ever been compromised in any way. But it was realized that to have become 'C', as the MI6 chief is called, he must have falsified his positive-vetting form with respect to the homosexuality question at some stage and probably more than once. Anyone who does this normally disqualifies himself on the grounds of being untruthful and unreliable. The retrospective question also arose as to what action Oldfield could have taken, in his position, had he discovered that one of his senior officers was also a surreptitious homosexual. There was also concern about the fact that because of his reputation for integrity Oldfield had been sent to Washington as liaison officer in 1960 to remedy the intelligence mayhem and distrust of British security caused by the Maclean–

Burgess–Philby affair. His smoothing-down operation with the CIA and FBI seemed to have been reasonably successful, even though he was still there in 1963 when Philby defected, after having been publicly cleared of suspicion by Harold Macmillan.

Oldfield's personal secret may explain an aspect of his behaviour which puzzled his colleagues and dismayed some of them. While his sincere Christian charity was a byword he was much too forgiving towards known traitors for some MI6 officers, one of whom, Nicholas Elliott, chided him about it. Though Oldfield knew that his former and much older colleague Colonel 'Dick' Ellis had confessed to spying for the Nazis for money and was strongly suspected by MI5 of being a Soviet agent later, he remained in friendly touch with him. Such magnanimity, which came naturally to Oldfield, may well have been intensified by his knowledge of his own vulnerability.

While senior politicians and civil servants were greatly relieved that Oldfield did not appear to have been suborned and were confident that he would have resisted any attempt by anyone to influence him, there was nevertheless serious concern because his case highlighted the continuing danger of having homosexuals in such sensitive positions. He had not been able to control his compulsion even when he had achieved his ambition of becoming 'C', and his case demonstrates that a man at the summit of a secret service can have a guilty secret and survive there for many years. There can be little doubt that if Oldfield's problem had been discovered while he was still in MI6 he would have been required to resign 'on health grounds', because it was the view of responsible officials that his requirement for 'rough trade' made him blackmailable. Compulsive homosexuality is easily recognized by others of the fraternity, and the danger that some ruthless homosexual of the stamp of Driberg could have sensed Oldfield's was noted.

The discovery of his deviant behaviour and the need to confront him with it was a sorry event in a distinguished career which came to a sudden end when Oldfield was taken mortally ill early in 1981. Whether or not the Prime Minister had been informed of the problem when she visited Sir Maurice in hospital shortly before his death is uncertain, but I have reason to believe that she was. Precautions to prevent the accession of homosexuals to highly sensitive positions have certainly been tightened.

There are, of course, many women in posts involving access to secrets, and one would expect a proportion of them to be homosexual. Lesbianism, however, does not seem to be much of a lever for securing recruits, probably because it does not carry the social censure of male homosexuality and offers negligible opportunity for blackmail. A case of alleged blackmail of a lesbian was reported from Pretoria in

September 1986. Miss Vanessa Twine, a South African citizen employed in the visa section of the Australian Embassy, claimed that a South African security man had threatened to expose her lesbianism, which she admitted and had not revealed, unless she agreed to provide information.[20]

A search of the medical literature, which I made for another purpose, produced little evidence to support the belief that homosexuality or excessive heterosexuality is genetically inherited.[21] Had this been so, it would have merited a place in Chatper 12, which deals with parentage, among other factors, predisposing to the commission of treachery.

CHAPTER ELEVEN

Non-Sexual Blackmail

Blackmail – any payment extorted by intimidation or pressure.

Cassells English Dictionary

While knowledge of illicit sex is the commonest blackmail weapon used to recruit agents, the Soviets are quick to use any other compromising situation which may arise or can be contrived. The KGB and GRU set great store by talent-spotters who submit regular reports on professional colleagues indicating character weaknesses of any description which might be exploited. I have seen some of these reports, prepared by a Communist member of a trade union who had been trained in the Lenin School in Moscow. They dealt with scientists and scientific workers, and the detail was quite remarkable.[1] When the South African traitor Dieter Gerhardt confessed in 1983 he described how, while seeking recruits for the South African Navy in London, he had interviewed many sailors serving with the Royal Navy, including some in Polaris submarines, and had given the Russians a list of those who seemed discontented or might have exploitable character weaknesses.

Driberg did not restrict his derogatory information about his parliamentary colleagues to sex matters. As a former journalist he was a trained observer and as an arch-intriguer was adept at discovering damaging details of MPs' former lives which they had managed to conceal. According to an MI5 source, he wielded a non-sexual blackmail hold over prominent members of the Labour Party and put forward their names to Czech intelligence as possible recruits. According to the Czech defector Josef Frolik, several of them were recruited. All these activities had not gone unnoticed by the Labour leadership. According to Lord Harris of Greenwich, Hugh Gaitskell was intensely suspicious of Driberg as being involved with the KGB and treated him accordingly.[2]

Foreigners working behind the Iron Curtain are frequently induced to take part in black-market deals and are then threatened with exposure to their superiors or with police action unless they agree to collaborate in treachery of some kind. My type specimen is a Canadian corporal who was chauffeur-assistant to the military attaché at the Canadian Embassy in Moscow in the early 1970s. He was caught black-marketing in Moscow and then blackmailed into serving the KGB by planting 'bugs' in the embassy and talent-spotting other Canadians with exploitable weaknesses. In the usual Soviet manner he was rewarded both with money, for which he was required to sign receipts, and with women. He continued to work for the Soviets when posted to Peking and was not caught until transferred to West Germany in 1974.[3]

When Franz Arthur Roski, an official of the West German Interior Ministry, was sentenced to five and a half years' imprisonment for spying for East Germany in September 1985, he claimed that he had given in to the threat of blackmail. He said that he had agreed to spy only after East German officials had threatened to expose him for violating currency regulations while on a trip to their country in 1971.[4] Talent-spotters are required to seek out any criminal offences, however old, committed by individuals who have been targeted and they make use of newspaper-cuttings libraries for this purpose. Once hard evidence is on file and an individual has been warned of it, the Soviets are prepared to wait, for years if necessary, before taking action. One British business man who was recruited through non-sexual blackmail in Bangkok in 1932 was left alone until 1956, when he was seen to be in a position of interest and was sharply reminded of his undertaking twenty-four years previously.

No opportunity to secure what the Moscow centres might regard as potentially useful material is lost, as is illustrated by an extraordinary experience which befell the eminent civil servant Sir Richard Way when he was Permanent Secretary of the Aviation Ministry and Chairman of the D-Notice Committee in the mid-1960s. He was driving down a country lane accompanied by his wife one Sunday afternoon, on his way to see his children at boarding-school, when a car overtook him very slowly and grazed his vehicle. The driver apologized, introduced himself as a colonel in the Soviet Embassy, and offered to pay for the repairs. A bill was sent to the embassy, but the colonel responded by insisting on payment in cash, because he had no bank account, and on giving Way lunch so that he could hand it over personally. Way agreed, after being assured that his security department would give him cover at the lunch, in a restaurant known to be frequented by Soviet-bloc agents.

Instead of handing over the money in an envelope, the colonel, now known to be a GRU officer, counted out the notes at the table in an obvious way that could have been photographed by a concealed camera. Sir Richard could not spot anyone taking photographs but he could not recognize the security surveillance men either. The Russians had chosen the wrong target, and no approach was ever made to Sir Richard, who was anyway in no difficulties because he had immediately reported the circumstances. But MI5 has little doubt that the photograph of a distinguished civil servant receiving money from a Russian remains in the files of the GRU centre.[5]

Most intelligence agencies have no compunction about wielding the blackmail threat to keep a reluctant traitor in line, as was done with John King, the treacherous cipher clerk in the Foreign Office, whose case has already been described. When the American Cambridge graduate Michael Straight, who had been recruited to the clandestine Soviet cause by Blunt, objected to Moscow's requirement that he should leave Britain and work as an economic spy in the USA, he was told that the Russians had rejected his plea in tough terms, which made Straight realize that he had to obey or face exposure. Shortly after the RAF radio technician Douglas Britten decided to cease providing the Soviets with communications information in Cyprus after spying for them for six years, he was shown a photograph of himself receiving money from Russians and was told that a copy would be sent to the British authorities unless he resumed, which he did.[6]

The KGB had no incriminating photographs when they tried to put blackmail pressure on a young American in whom they had invested money by giving him part of his fees for tuition at the Massachusetts Institute of Technology; but when he declined to provide information which he learned in the Institute they produced the receipts he had signed for the money. The blackmail attempt proved futile because the young man, safe in the knowledge that he had committed no offence, simply told them to do their worst.[7]

The unending Soviet search for any kind of incriminating information which can be exploited has been stressed by the KGB defector Peter Deriabin, who has vividly described the Soviet use of German documents captured during the war to compromise influential Germans in West Germany and Austria years later. Selected German war captives were deliberately held in Soviet prison camps for years when they should have been released, and when their spirit was broken they were allowed to return to West Germany – if they had agreed to work as agents and informers. As Deriabin has recorded, the KGB 'took every precaution to see that they kept their promises', the chief weapon being the threat of exposing their 'Nazi crimes' once they had secured jobs. They were warned at intervals that if they failed to produce information, their crimes, real or invented, could suddenly be produced and trial as war criminals demanded.[8]

The pressure was sometimes applied to the relatives of prisoners who were in sensitive posts, with the promise that release of their loved ones would depend on how effectively they were prepared to work as agents. In reality, the more effectively the recruited relatives worked the less likely were the prisoners to be released, and many never were.

Relatives are never spared, however eminent the target. A British Labour minister was forced to resign, quietly and with total suppression of the real reason, when Czech intelligence was found to have a hold over his wife.

The most damaging instance of Soviet-bloc recruitment by the blackmail use of previous Nazi connections seems to be that of Gunther Guillaume, the East German spy inside the office of Chancellor Willy Brandt. Guillaume was born in Berlin in 1927 and had been a young member of the Nazi Party. The threat of exposing this, which could have made employment difficult in any part of Germany, may have been the lever which enabled East German intelligence to force the Guillaumes to flee to West Germany as 'refugees'.

The post-war exploitation of German prisoners mirrored the Soviet treatment of Russian *émigrés* before and during the Second World War, when no effort was spared to threaten any relatives still in the Soviet Union to secure co-operation for espionage and subversion against their newly adopted countries. Penetration of the White Russian populations of Paris and New York by this method was particularly successful. A code-break in the KGB radio traffic – part of the American operation code-named 'Bride' – gave the FBI a lead to a former Russian called Mark Zborowski who eventually confessed that he had worked among the Russian *émigrés* for fifteen years on behalf of the KGB and had been responsible for setting some of them up for execution. He received a sentence of only five years' imprisonment because he betrayed other KGB agents in the White Russian community.[9]

According to the Jewish Soviet *émigré* Cyrille Henkine, some of the Jews who are permitted to leave the Soviet Union have already been recruited and trained as agents to infiltrate the Jewish communities where they are to settle, with the intention of applying pressure on those in interesting occupations. Other Jews who have relatives behind the Iron curtain are being subjected to blackmail pressures, he claims.[10]

There is little doubt that the Polish communities now in many Western countries are being similarly infiltrated. In 1959 I was requested by MI5 to expose a major infiltration mounted by the Polish intelligence service and was provided with all the evidence for doing so. At least a dozen young Poles, who had been specially indoctrinated, had been sent to Britain as students to cultivate expatriate Poles and others, in the hope of finding ways by which they might be blackmailed, the threat of persecution of relatives still in Poland being one weapon. One 22-year-old student at London University, Jerzy Florczykowski, had just been deported, and the publicity was intended to deter others from being sent. He had been recruited by Polish intelligence officers after he had asked permission to visit his sick father, who lived in Britain. They arranged to pay all his expenses as a student for five years if he would send back regular reports on all promising people he met; the illicit communication was to be made by means of microdots – messages reduced by micro-photography to a minute negative which could be disguised as a full stop on a postcard. The operation had been detected because some of the suborned students had sought political asylum.[11]

It is in West Germany that the infiltration by Soviet-bloc agents is currently most severe and most likely to continue because of the case of entry. In 1986 Manfred Rotsch, a 61-year-old West German aerospace engineer, tearfully admitted in a Munich court that he had been passing high-technology secrets to the Soviets for thirty years. He claimed that he had been living in East Germany until 1954 and was permitted to move to the West, where he wanted to live, only after signing a contract to work for Soviet-bloc intelligence.[12] A report published by the West German security agency in 1986 cited the case of a West German civil servant who fell ill while visiting East Germany. While in hospital there he was visited by two East German intelligence officers who warned him that unless he signed a contract to pass on documents which came his way he would be convicted of drunken driving, with unfortunate publicity guaranteed. He signed to secure his release, then reported the facts on his return.[13] The Soviet defector Golitsin has recorded how the KGB uses blackmail to force an adversary agent whom it has detected to become a double and work in its interests. From the KGB's penetration of British intelligence it knew that a senior minister of an African country was a paid British agent and successfully used the information, which could have destroyed him politically at home, to blackmail him.[14]

Levchenko has described how, when working for the KGB in Tokyo, he persuaded Japanese journalists to write harmless articles for payment; then, once handwritten receipts had been obtained, he virtually blackmailed them into writing Soviet-inspired reports for their newspapers.

All blackmail is based on fear, and the Soviets have regularly used the threat of personal violence to keep backsliders in order. When Arthur Koestler rebelled against Communism and made his views known in print, the lifelong Communist Gerhart Eisler warned him:

'When the time comes we will cut your throat in the first five minutes.' A study of Eisler's life suggests that he might even have enjoyed doing so.

A peculiar kind of blackmail leading to gross treachery was practised by an MI6 officer, Major Jack Hooper, who later became a traitor (if he was not already one). In 1936 Hooper's superior in the MI6 mission in The Hague, one Major Dalton, embezzled £2,000 from the 'slush fund' to finance a love affair. Hooper discovered the theft and threatened to expose Dalton unless he received some of the money himself. Dalton then committed suicide, and Hooper's threat was uncovered during the inquiries into Dalton's death. Hooper confessed and was dismissed but was then approached by German intelligence in Holland. Deeply resentful at having being sacked, he told the Germans all he knew about MI6, its officers, and their operations. Among this information was the identity of a highly placed German naval engineer who had been a British agent for twenty years, one Dr Otto Krueger.[15]

Perhaps the most extraordinary case of what amounted to blackmail was the behaviour of Blunt after he had been given immunity from prosecution in 1964. He quickly realized that the Whitehall and Palace authorities were every bit as fearful of a leak leading to public exposure of the immunity deal as he himself was, and he played on this fear to such an extent that Peter Wright and other MI5 officers involved in the case were repeatedly warned not to upset him or press him too hard for fear that he might 'go public'. The Cabinet Office prepared a document to counter any statement he might make or even leave for posthumous publication.

While there must be many more instances of non-sexual blackmail to secure recruits for treacherous purposes, and to keep them active, it is clear that sexual blackmail has been a more potent weapon and will probably remain so.

CHAPTER TWELVE

The Influence of Background

By their roots ye shall know them.

Anonymous

Britain is commonly believed to have had more traitors than other nations. This is almost certainly due to the fact that British writers and journalists have been more active in exposing them. The British media have given great prominence to such cases, believing that they are of wide interest. However, if defectors are to be considered as traitors to their own countries, there have been far more traitors in the Soviet Union and its satellites than anywhere else, most of these receive no publicity when they arrive in the West, especially if they happen to be soldiers, as many are. In the West the Germans are currently the most susceptible to treachery, because of the unnatural East–West political division and border, but all nations have traitors, whose motivations are an expression of human nature common to all.

Nationality can be a potent background factor through what might be called ties of blood. The case of Julius Silber, the exile German who felt a surge of patriotism for the country of his birth and the people in it when they were involved in war, has already been described. The Russian expatriate Flora Solomon who befriended Philby when she knew he was a Soviet agent hostile to Britain, her adopted country, may have felt similar ties with the old country. In this connection a recent discovery of mine about Sir Roger Hollis might be significant. The first probable lead to Hollis, given by the defector Gouzenko, referred to a Soviet agent inside MI5 who 'had something Russian in his background'. As Hollis's elder brother, Christopher, has recorded, the Hollis family had good reason for believing that they were related to the Tsar Peter the Great, a circumstance which fits Gouzenko's statement perfectly.[1] Even if Hollis only referred to this in a jocular way to his several Communist friends in China, they are likely to have reported it to Moscow and Soviet recruiters who may have exploited it.

121

Even some of the White Russians who fled from the Revolution and lost all their property eventually became Soviet agents, apparently out of a feeling of kinship; while others born of exile Russian parents in the USA and Canada, in particular, chose secret loyalty to the Soviet Union. The influence of parents who had been born in Russia and yearned for the motherland was probably a major factor in inducing such people to become traitors.

In general, family background could be expected to play an important formative role in the development of traitorous behaviour, especially when parents or other close relatives hold extreme political views. The type specimen of such a family is that in which 'Sonia' and her brother, Jurgen Kuczynski, were reared. They were children of Dr Robert René Kuczynski, a German-Jewish authority on population studies, who was of Polish origin and became a Communist and a Soviet agent. Both Sonia and Jurgen have written autobiographies which show that they and another sister were so dedicated to Communism at an early age that they all assisted Soviet intelligence, to an extent which made the Kuczynskis almost a family of spies.[2]

Klaus Fuchs declined to give any information about the politics of his parents but admitted that one of his two sisters had been active in the German Communist underground and had married a Communist sympathizer, while the other had married an active Communist. The father also emigrated to East Germany.[3] Professor Hugh Hambleton was influenced by his very dominant pro-Soviet mother, while the father of Wilfrid Burchett was Communist-inclined. Herbert Norman, the Canadian diplomat, had a religious father who believed that Jesus taught Communism and that 'many of the best and noblest of men' had been Communists.[4] A relative of the arch-traitor Blake was Henri Curiel, who had helped to found the Egyptian Communist Party and became one of the KGB's main spy-masters in France, where he was eventually assassinated. Philby's wife Eleanor concluded that the training given to Philby by his father, a distinguished Arabist and Muslim convert, was to some extent responsible for his inclination to question and to flout authority of any kind.[5]

I am not suggesting, however, that family political influence has been a common cause of treachery: in fact, save for defectors from the Soviet bloc, it has probably been the exception. Many traitors, like those of the Cambridge ring, for example, have hailed from conservative families, some having long traditions of military service. The father of Christopher Boyce was a former FBI officer, as was his uncle.

Examined across the board, the case records show that traitors come from all walks of life. Maclean, Blunt, Boyce, and Lee for example came from reasonably affluent homes, though not from rich homes. It is a misbelief that the Cambridge traitors belonged to the *jeunesse dorée*.

They did not. Maclean's father was a former Cardiff solicitor who happened to be knighted for political services later in life but was never well off. Burgess's father was a not very successful naval officer, while Blunt's was a parson. Philby's father was not from the so-called upper class, while others, like Cairncross, were from modest homes. When questioned following his exposure in 1981, Leo Long, one of the Cambridge ring, said: 'I was a working-class boy and had a deep sense of the inequity of society.' Michael Bettaney, the MI5 officer who tried to become a spy for the KGB, was also brought up in a working-class home – a terraced council house in the Potteries – as was Prime.

Most of the known American traitors came from what in Britain would be called middle-class homes – some more privileged than others – but, again, none from what would in Britain be called the upper class. Michael Straight derived from the very rich American upper crust, but while he admits being recruited to the Soviet cause, he denies ever having done anything traitorous.

The wartime German traitors, Schulze-Boysen and von Scheliha came from noble families, but Kolbe and most of the others hailed from modest backgrounds. The Soviet defectors Penkovsky, Suvorov, and Levchenko were from military families, while Pyotr Popov and Major-General Jan Sejna, the Czech defector, were of peasant origin.

Thus, just as traitors come from all nationalities they come from all classes. The former method of recruiting secret service officers from 'good families', based on the belief that 'by their roots ye shall know them' was not trustworthy; but neither is their recruitment from 'redbrick' universities, an expansion of choice made at a time when Oxford and Cambridge tended to be associated with the upper classes.

Psychologists lay great stress on the effects of family strife, and particularly of broken homes, on the generation of character defects of a kind which may produce a traitor. Both Alger Hiss and Whittaker Chambers lacked paternal guidance, and a succession of family suicides affected both when they were boys.[6] Vassall and Prime were the products of unhappy marriages which led to their loneliness. The psychiatrist who examined Prime considered that his sense of inferiority and inadequacy was partly the result of his unhappy childhood; his father had been 'bad-tempered, intolerant and socially withdrawn' while after Prime's birth his mother suffered from constant ill health, for which Prime felt he was to blame.[7]

According to Leo Abse, George Blake had been subjected to peculiar family pressure likely to make him yearn to take revenge on Britain. His father, an Egyptian Jew holding a British passport but living in Holland, was an 'ostentatious British patriot', and his son had been named after King George V. On his father's death, Blake had been sent to an uncle in Egypt, and when he returned to Holland and the Germans occupied it he was arrested because he had a British passport; his Dutch mother managed to escape to Britain. When he finally reached Britain his foreign descent and experience barred him from ever being fully accepted.

Abse has also drawn attention to the love-hate relationship which Philby had with his father: 'The childhood picture of the father as a figure of almost unlimited power can sometimes set a problem in loyalty if the child does not succeed in disposing of the hostility which goes together with his strong feelings of love. . . . Like many spies, Philby found his good father in Russia and the bad father at home.'[8] The pernicious influence of the American naval traitor John Walker on his family has already been described.

It would seem to be no coincidence that several traitors came from strongly ecclesiastical backgrounds. Quisling's father was a Lutheran pastor. Fuchs was the son of a German Quaker preacher who became a professor of theology. Blunt's father was the vicar of St John's, Paddington, while Vassall's father was an Anglican priest. Herbert Norman's father, who saw much good in Communism viewed from a Christian standpoint, was a Methodist missionary to Japan. Wilfred Burchett's father was a 'progressive lay preacher'. Could it be that some of these became susceptible to treachery as a reaction to an excessively religious atmosphere? It would seem to have been so in the case of Fuchs, who made it clear to his fellow-prisoner Donald Hume that he was not a Christian. 'He was contemptuous of religion,' Hume told me, and he was very bitter about the attitude of the Stafford Prison chaplain who was interested only in inmates who were devout Christians. Fuchs told Hume that Christ was 'a quisling because when the Jews were struggling for their freedom from the Romans, he made his remarks about rendering to Caesar what was Caesar's'. Embracing Soviet Communism, as Fuchs had done, involved the rejection of religion and the acceptance of atheism. The Soviet founders resented competing faiths; most dedicated Communists, such as Philby, became dogmatic atheists. Blunt's brother, Wilfrid, has written of the 'pantomime' of the religious ceremony at Anthony's cremation in 1983 when he had been 'openly agnostic and had no belief in an afterlife'.[9]

The impact of Herbert Norman's forceful father, a zealous missionary, is believed to have made his son 'anti-establishment' from an early age and therefore susceptible to the influence of thoroughgoing Communists at Cambridge University. Commenting on Norman's Communism, Professor Viktor Kiernan, the British Marxist historian who knew him at Cambridge, has drawn attention to the close relationship between far-left attitudes and religion. Kiernan, who grew up as a Congregationalist, remained in the Communist Party for twenty-five years. He thinks that the way in which Communists like Norman and himself regarded themselves as committed to the party for life was an inheritance from their religious background. 'Obviously, if you belong to a religion and take it seriously, then you are in it for life,' he argues.[10]

Once committed to the creed, a true Communist should go to any lengths, including treachery to his own country, to serve and protect it. As the Communist Claud Cockburn put it in defence of people like Philby: 'As an English Catholic in the days of Elizabeth I, I would have seen nothing disgraceful in spying against the English in the interests of the Vatican.'

When Sir Roger Hollis was interrogated on suspicion of being a Soviet agent in 1970 he said that he had dropped out of Oxford University and left home for China 'to get away from the Church and from the family'. Hollis's father was Bishop of Taunton, his mother was the daughter of a Canon of Wells Cathedral; and his eldest brother, who married a daughter of the Dean of Salisbury, became Bishop of Madras. His elder brother, Christopher, a Catholic convert, has described the ecclesiastical atmosphere:

> We began the day with family prayers. . . . The maids, in their little white caps, trooped demurely in to hear a collect or two, recite the Lord's Prayer and listen to a passage from the Bible. We were regular attenders at the Cathedral. I, of course, knelt down and said my prayers morning and evening. The atmosphere of one who grew up in a cathedral close was wholly different from that of the average Englishman who casually enters himself as C. of E. on some official form.[11]

Dr Maurice Cowling of Peterhouse, Cambridge, who has made a deep academic study of the attitudes of clergymen to society, has pointed out that 'even when surrounded with landed or aristocratic influences they were a long way from identifying themselves with English political establishments'. In the context of provoking a deliberate breach with what he calls 'the bourgeois, public-school . . . and Kiplingesque varieties of Anglicanism', Dr Cowling has commented: 'it would not be incredible, if it were true, that while one son of an Anglican bishop [Hollis of Taunton] became a Roman Catholic, another son became a successful Russian spy'.[12]

In his teens Bettaney, the MI5 traitor, developed religious fervour and after converting to Roman Catholicism wished to become a priest. For some time he had lived with a parish priest in Germany. One of his Oxford tutors suggested that because he was such a devout Catholic he had none of the common undergraduate worries about the state of the world.[13] He did not achieve his ambition to enter the Church and dedication to Communism may have become something of a mission substitute.

The young American traitor Christopher Boyce and his courier Daulton Lee had been raised as devout Roman Catholics, and Boyce had seriously considered becoming a priest. Vassall was also a Roman Catholic convert and like Boyce and Lee not ideologically committed to Communism; in his memoirs he stated that, when in prison, Blake had told him that he had thought of becoming a Roman Catholic priest (he was only half-Jewish) but decided that the alternative course of Communism was the solution for him. Also speaking in prison, Bettaney told the Security Commissioners that he did not regard his Marxist, and Communist, convictions as inconsistent with his Roman Catholic religion. This, of course, has been the view of many Roman Catholics recently, including priests in Italy, France, and South America. Communism has the Roman Catholic attraction of infallibility, and however erroneous events may prove a doctrinal pronouncement or action to have been, the party invariably claims that its action was 'correct'. It may or may not be significant that Richard Miller, the only FBI officer known to have been a traitor, had been excommunicated from the Mormon Church.

The ease of the switch from Christianity to Communism has been described in detail by Douglas Hyde, who experienced it. He had been a student of theology with a view to becoming a missionary in India but his wide reading engendered severe doubts and, because of his need for some crusading cause, he switched to Communism, which seemed to answer all his questions, though he was later to state that it was 'a gigantic hoax, a deliberate and total deception of the public'. Hyde wrote: 'The majority who come to Communism do so because, in the first instance, they are subconsciously looking for a cause that will fill the void left by the unbelief or, as in my own case, an insecurely held belief which is failing to satisfy them, intellectually and spiritually.[14]

Professor Kiernan agrees. Explaining how he grew up as a Congregationalist with religious parents and was converted to Communism through reading, he wrote: 'I am rather led to think that this feeling of ours that we were committed to the party for life was an inheritance from our religious background.'[15] Significantly, Hyde's eventual disillusion, particularly with Stalin's behaviour and his destructive attitude to the Marshall Plan for rebuilding Europe, drove him to embrace the Roman Catholic faith. In evidence to the FBI, Whittaker Chambers said that he left Communism in disillusion because he realized that it was the absence of God which made it so evil in practice while it appeared so rational in theory. Finding God gave him the strength to make the break and to unmask what he knew of the evil.[16]

Sir Roger Casement had a lengthy problem with religion – he was born a Protestant and for most of his life declared himself to be one, but had himself secretly baptized a Roman Catholic while on holiday in North Wales.

It is beyond dispute that converts to religion often become the most zealous. This would seem to be true also of converts to Communism who express their zeal secretly as treachery on its behalf. If so, it would explain the CIA adage that an agent is always at his most effective when he is working against his own country.

The apparently devout Anglo-Catholicism of Tom Driberg is as mysterious as much else about him. He was a member of the Central Board of Finance of the Church of England and was the first layman chosen to preach the university sermon at Oxford. Yet he seemed to be without scruple of any kind, and betrayed anything and anybody if it suited him. Possibly he used his religion as a part of his cover, as he used his Labour politics. He certainly used it to mount a sustained and virulent attack on a major target of the KGB – the Moral Rearmament Movement – claiming that it was pro-German, which was untrue. MRA, which embraces all religions, seeks to promote moral values in all societies – anathema to the Soviet authorities, who seek to undermine the moral values of the societies which are their targets. When the MRA founder, Dr Frank Buchmann, died and was buried in Allentown, Pennsylvania, many world figures attended the funeral and signed their names in the church book. A week later Driberg appeared and tore out the relevant pages.[17]

Communism has provided an alternative religion for many Jews who rebelled against their orthodox upbringing or ceased to believe for other reasons, and the well-documented experience of Arthur Koestler is instructive in this respect. Koestler's mother came from a family of Czech rabbinical scholars and with particular awareness of his Jewishness he became a dedicated Zionist. After only a few months in Israel, however, with disillusionment on a kibbutz, he turned instead to Communism as a replacement faith and was quickly enmeshed in subversive work for the Comintern.[18]

Jewishness embraces much more than religion. It is also racial and, because the Jews have been scattered throughout the world in minority groups which have tended to remain clannish, they have generated resentment, both genuine and contrived. This has expressed itself in anti-Semitism which proved to be a powerful factor in the past recruitment of Jews as Soviet agents and often as traitors. The father of Harry Gold, who became the American courier for Fuchs, was an

127

immigrant Russian Jew to the USA and was treated abominably by his workmates. Gold himself was warned by a recruiter for the Communist Party to hide his Jewishness in a new job because the superintendent was violently anti-Semitic. Such social injustice could well have been potent in generating a chip-on-the-shoulder mentality, which has been important in turning people towards treachery.

Like many other Jews before and during the Second World War, Harry Gold believed that the USSR was the only country that was not anti-Semitic, and that the only hope of eradicating anti-Semitism was through world Communism. Even while the KGB was liquidating leading Jews in Stalin's great purge, Jews being recruited to serve Soviet intelligence were assured that only by supporting Stalin and Communism could the Jewish demands for a homeland be realized; the extent to which so many of them were misled remains astonishing. Harold Gerson, the Jewish Canadian GRU agent, sentenced to five years' imprisonment after the Gouzenko defection, said that his initial reason for joining the Communist study group, which led to his recruitment as an agent, was to fight anti-Semitism. Several of the other Canadian traitors in the Soviet cause exposed by Gouzenko were Jewish, as were many of the Americans exposed by the decoding of KGB radio traffic – for example, Judith Coplon, the Rosenbergs, and their large ring including Joel Barr, Morton Sobell, William Perl, Alfred Sarant, and Max Elitcher. Jews were generally so clannish in those days that others of their acquaintance whom they might try to recruit would also tend to be Jewish, and the Rosenbergs may not have tried to recruit outside the Jewish community.

Most of these people were already Communists for ideological reasons, but when it became obvious that anti-Semitism was fundamental to the Nazi creed their conviction was intensified. Then when Stalin signed his pact with Hitler, which soon delivered millions more Jews to his savagery, their dedication proved the stronger factor. As the continuing ill-treatment of Jews in the USSR clearly shows, their trust was cynically fostered and was totally misplaced. Douglas Hyde, who was involved in the recruitment of Communists for clandestine work, has described how 'quite deliberately we used the Jewish fear of Fascism and anti-Semitism for our own political ends. . . . Yet nowhere will one find a more cynical anti-Semitism than in the Party itself.'[19]

There were inevitably some traitors who favoured anti-Semitism, believing that the Jews were responsible for various evils. One such was the daughter of a White Russian admiral, Anna Wolkoff. She was secretly in touch with an Italian diplomat in London, passing him copies of highly sensitive cables extracted from the American Embassy through her friendship with a cipher clerk there, called Tyler Kent.

She was a traitor to her adopted country, having been naturalized, and was sentenced in 1940 to ten years' imprisonment.

The case records show that Marxism–Leninism, the ideological basis of Soviet Communism, has a peculiar attraction for Jewish intellectuals, which may surprise those who associate Jews with successful capitalism – though, of course, Marx was himself Jewish. Klugmann and Dexter White were typical examples, and they influenced many of lesser mental calibre. So did Jurgen Kuczynski, 'Sonia's' brother, who was a persuasive speaker. Like other intellectual Marxists, Kuczynski took a ruthlessly pragmatic view of events, as did many of the other German Jewish exiles taking refuge in Britain. He welcomed the Hitler–Stalin pact and stood by that view when the partition of Poland ensured that many thousands of Polish Jews were handed over to the SS for transport to the extermination camps. The same applied when France and the Low Countries were overrun, events which would not have been possible but for the petrol, food, and other war commodities supplied by the Soviet Union which helped the Nazis to withstand the Allied naval blockade and also to send many more Jews to the gas chambers.

It is hard to avoid the conclusion that these Jewish intellectuals, some of whom were Soviet agents and were responsible for recruiting others, supported the Soviet Union not as a protest against anti-Semitism and Fascism, but because they were already totally committed to the Communist ideology. They were pro-Moscow right or wrong and were prepared to accept and excuse any Soviet excesses or atrocities as minor and necessary deviations. The same applies to current Jewish Communists who can see how the present regime expresses its anti-Semitism towards dissidents, like Anatoly Shcharansky, and thousands of others who simply wish to emigrate to Israel. Douglas Hyde explained such behaviour by pointing out that, 'Just as the Catholic turned Communist tends to become the most anti-Catholic, so the man or woman from a religious Jewish home who turns Communist will become anti-Jewish.'[20]

In so far as intellectualism has been a factor in the production of traitors, a university education is obviously a component. A few traitors, like Elizabeth Bentley in America, and the Britons Klugmann, Maclean, Nunn May, and Driberg appear to have been seriously introduced to left-wing extremism at school, and the current deliberate politicizing of school pupils in Britain seems set to produce many more. But for the majority it was enrolment at a university which was the gateway to a career in treachery. Students making the most of a university's corporate life with its various societies and debates are almost expected to be 'progressive' and to sow political wild oats. They can be greatly influenced by charismatic lecturers and dons, especially at universities like Oxford and Cambridge which operate the tutorial system, when the relationship between dons and undergraduates is particularly intimate. The situation at Cambridge University was described by Blunt in an interview in *The Times*: 'I had a sabbatical year from Cambridge and when I came back in 1934 I found that all my friends had suddenly become Marxists under the influence of Hitler coming to power.' There was more to it than Marxism, because professional Soviet recruiters were on hand, the identities of several of them now being known. The same trend was in train at Oxford, at London, especially at the London School of Economics, where one alumnus was Kathleen Willsher, the Soviet agent inside the High Commission in Ottawa, and at other universities.

While university life may have converted many to the Soviet cause and laid them open to the attentions of KGB and GRU recruiters, its most significant influence on the lives of future traitors was providing them with the academic training and degrees which enabled them to obtain posts providing access to secrets and influence. The recruiters showed remarkable acumen in picking those who were likely to succeed professionally; most of the Cambridge ring, for example, were recruited while still undergraduates, as was the American spy Judith Coplon, who joined the Young Communist League while at Barnard College and was soon recruited to KGB service. There have been some traitors who were not graduates, but with few exceptions the arch-traitors on both sides of the Atlantic had high qualifications ensuring their professional success.

For some, attendance at a university laid them open to a psychological factor through the effects of what is now called 'dropping out'. Whittaker Chambers, Hollis, and Boyce all failed to stay the course and take a degree – an experience likely to have given them inferiority feelings. Dropping out can lead to rootlessness, railing against society, and a need to belong to something else. It can also engender wanderlust – a desire to escape parental censure and 'get away from it all', as happened with Chambers and Hollis. As Allen Weinsten states: 'Chambers' precise reasons for becoming a Communist are unknown, but this decision came during a period that included many elements of personal failure.' He was yearning for some credible scheme of values and a sense of purpose, as Hollis may have been.

The chance that a student will be targeted for recruitment to espionage may depend on the subjects being studied. Recruiters, who are still active around the universities, will have obvious interest in a left-wing science student who may gain entry to a defence establishment. Surprisingly, perhaps, they also take note of promising mathematicians. Two of the most damaging traitors in US history were both defectors from the National Security Agency: William Martin and

Bernon Mitchell; it was through their interest in advanced mathematics and its application to code-breaking that they joined the NSA. Many of the code-breakers in the team which devised the famed Ultra system of breaking wartime German Enigma codes at Bletchley Park, the forerunner of GCHQ, were mathematicians, too. The same applies to many of the current staff of GCHQ and the NSA and while there is no insidious connection between mathematics and treachery, Soviet talent-spotters are continuously on the look-out for possible recruits among young mathematicians likely to enter code-breaking and intercept work. They are even more interested in students of the Russian language.

There are still so few Russian-speakers in the West that they easily secure intelligence posts. They are also likely, as part of their studies, to visit Russia where they might be compromised. It seems to have been Judith Coplon's study of the Russian language, while at Barnard College, which raised her interest in the Soviet Union and eventually caused this daughter of an old American family to become a Soviet spy in a government office liaising with the FBI. It is believed that Blake was recruited to active Soviet espionage while taking a Russian course at Downing College, Cambridge. When the Swedish spy Wennerstrom had to choose a language course while briefly in the Navy before transferring to the Air Force, he decided on Russian. Similarly, the traitor Geoffrey Prime, later to end up at GCHQ, studied Russian while in the RAF. MI5 and the FBI have reason to believe that as a result of these and other successes the KGB keeps lists of all known Russian speakers in the West for possible targeting.

Others were recruited to intelligence posts and spied for the Soviets there because of their knowledge of German. John Cairncross, for example, gained entry to the ultra-secret code breaking establishment at Bletchley during the Second World War and betrayed much of interest to the KGB. It was Herbert Norman's knowledge of Japanese which led to the Soviets' special interest in him at Cambridge and to his eventual recruitment. Later his facility with the language and his academic study of Japanese culture led to his senior appointments in Canadian counter-intelligence departments operating against Japan during and immediately after the war. According to Professor Barros this was the Soviets' first intelligence success in penetrating Japan.[21]

The study of a language stimulates interest in the whole culture of the country concerned and this can exert additional attraction, reducing any natural opposition to becoming a traitor on its behalf. The Prime case offers one example: his interest led to what he called a 'misplaced idealistic view of Russian Communism' and resentment against Western capitalist society, which he came to regard as inferior. Anthony Wraight, the RAF officer who defected to the Soviet Union

131

in 1956, offers a further example. Knowing that his RAF career was likely to be limited because of eye trouble, he began to study the cinema industry as an alternative, and his inquiries brought him into contact with the Society for Cultural Relations with the USSR – a Communist front used by the Soviets for talent-spotting and recruitment among other things. He was put in touch with the London embassy representative of the Soviet state cinema organization, who happened to be a GRU officer using that cover. Under his guidance Wraight became attracted to Communism and to the idea of studying at the Soviet State Institute for Cinematography.

While a positive attraction to an Eastern alien culture has been a factor in the psychology of treachery, revulsion to the Western way of life has been perhaps more powerful and is certainly so at the present time. American material success, and the personal rewards deriving from competitive and acquisitive drives, led to profound anti-Americanism on the part of theoretical egalitarians like Blunt, Maclean, and Burgess who, like many of their kind, enjoyed the élite life in practice. Currently, anti-Americanism has never been stronger in Britain and Europe, particularly among students and those calling themselves students, having been whipped up by the anti-nuclear 'peace' movement, which is even more anti-American than it is pro-Russian. As the security authorities are well aware, the 'peace' movements offer a huge pool of potential pro-Soviet recruits, especially as agents of influence.

A further aspect of university life which has exerted positive impact on potential traitors is the way it generates crusading internationalism – a belief that national pride and personal preference for kith and kin are social crimes. Contact with other students of many nations, coupled with 'ivory tower' philosophical reflection remote from reality, can lead to the attitude expressed by the American Walt Rostow, security adviser to President Johnson:

> It is a legitimate American national objective to see removed from all nations – including the United States – the right to use substantial military force to pursue their own interests. Since this residual right is the right of national sovereignty and the basis for the existence of an international arena of power, it is, therefore, an American interest to see an end of nationhood as it has been historically defined.[22]

The cult of internationalism, now more fashionable than ever and stimulated by the post-war waves of immigration from East to West, has eroded national patriotism and made service to an alien country that much easier to justify.

CHAPTER THIRTEEN

Vulnerable Professions: The Impact of Access

Stop up the access and passage to remorse. . . .
Shakespeare, *Macbeth*

The one common factor in the equations of treachery relating to most peacetime traitors is access to secrets. Case histories indicate that once a traitor has decided to provide information he tends to supply everything that comes his way without reserve, save for material which might easily expose him. So the degree of damage inflicted by a traitor depends on the quality of his access and the length of time for which he operates.

Access usually results from employment and some professions are more likely to provide it than others. Some also carry special vulnerability to recruiters. The case records point to seven professions as being more likely than most to provide traitors: security/intelligence services, defence services, defence industries, diplomatic services, civil services, politics, and journalism. There have been many instances where traitors were recruited in anticipation that they would achieve access to these professions, but recruitment after access has been obtained is much commoner. The dangers to those serving in the first five of these professions is real enough for the British security authorities to have circulated booklets warning them of the approaches likely to be made and the best ways of rebutting them. The only reason they have not been issued to the last two is because they are classified.

The greater the number of people who have access to information officially classified as secret, the greater the likelihood that certain of them can be induced to betray some of it. Official secrets are generated by officials, and if there were none treachery would be rare, whereas in fact it seems to be increasing. A brief consideration of secrecy and its part in creating treachery is therefore necessary.

In most countries secrecy has become a cult and a curse. A moat of secrecy, with various other protective devices, is created by bureaucrats partly to preserve secrets the preservation of which is of real advantage to the state, but also to preserve the privilege of their own access. Secrecy is favoured by all politicians, including those who have been critical of it in opposition, because it enables errors of judgement and scandals to be concealed and reduces the risk of political embarrassment. In closed societies like those of the Soviet bloc secrecy is absolute, with grave penalties for any who attempt to breach it; yet in the open societies the extent to which governments are able to operate in secrecy is astonishing.

The unremitting effort made by the Soviet bloc to secure Western secrets is proof enough of the continuing need for the classification of information, but it is freely admitted in Britain, the USA, and Canada that classification is used to excess.[1] Documents are routinely classified by bureaucrats playing safe. In Whitehall the definition of an official secret is any information generated by an official department which has not been officially released. To put 'top secret' on a paper also ensures that it will be dealt with more quickly and be less likely to sit in someone's in-tray. The situation in the USA is less severe, but the cult of secrecy flourishes there, too, and the extent to which secrecy is imposed as a bureaucratic fetish is demonstrated by the recent experience of the former CIA chief Admiral Stansfield Turner. When writing his book *Secrecy and Democracy*, he was forbidden to state that the USA obtains any reconnaissance information from satellites or that Britain has a secret intelligence service still operating in peacetime and commonly known as MI6! It was admitted by the CIA that the existence of both facts was well known, but nobody with such official authority could be permitted to state them.[2] The ludicrous and damaging situation in which the British government found itself when it de-unionized GCHQ arose from the fact that, while it was common knowledge that GCHQ intercepted other nations' private messages and read them if it could, no Foreign Secretary had ever been prepared to admit it.

Nobody can operate in areas of secrecy over many years, as I have, without experiencing the farcical. I was repeatedly threatened with official retribution for printing defence information which, unknown to the British authorities, had been published in the USA.[3] When the Foreign Office official, William Clark, became press attaché at the British Embassy in Washington he was briefed on the Official Secrets Act by Donald Maclean![4] A recent American study showed that there are about 500,000 Americans with 'top-secret' clearance in the Defense Department and defence industry, plus more than 2 million cleared for access to documents stamped 'secret'.[5] It is perhaps surprising that more do not go astray when secrets are so saleable.

There is a backlash effect to secrecy in that when leaks occur the political damage may be greater than if an announcement had been made, because the attempt at concealment compounds the error when it is exposed. Such breaches of the security moat have been central to some of the recent political embarrassments known in Britain as 'banana skins' and provide ammunition for the civil-liberties lobbies opposed to a degree of secrecy which may be justified.

In some minds reaction to excessive secrecy may create its own impetus to breach it, especially as regards merely restricted or confidential information. This factor was a regular source of leaks to me during the thirty-five years when I was active in Fleet Street.

Except for those who deliberately set out to pursue a career in secret establishments like MI5 and the CIA, potential traitors find themselves with access to secrets almost accidentally, perhaps because of a posting or promotion which they never anticipated. The young American Tyler Kent found himself serving as a cipher clerk in the American Embassy in London in 1940 when messages of crucial significance for the conduct of the war were passing between Churchill and Roosevelt. Kent, who is still alive at the time of writing, claimed to be incensed by what he saw as a plot to embroil the USA in the war without the knowledge of the American people. He made copies of the relevant cables and many others, and showed them to various people, including Anna Wolkoff, a naturalized Briton who was spying for the Italians, who passed the information to the Germans.[6] Judith Coplon, who was already committed to the Soviet cause, secured a post as a political analyst in the Justice Department in Washington, headed by the Attorney-General. She could hardly have expected to handle FBI documents dealing with information known about foreign agents operating in the USA but that became her speciality.

Vassall had no conscious expectation of seeing secrets when he entered the Civil Service. His first access, in Moscow, arose because he was keen to travel and applied for the post. David Greenglass, a wartime GI at Los Alamos, was plunged into contact with the most sensitive secrets in history. Without stealing a document or going into a restricted area where he should not have been, he picked up enough gossip, through talks with friends, to draw and give to the Russians a reasonably accurate sketch of how the plutonium atom bomb worked.[7] Christopher Boyce found himself, at twenty-one, with daily access to secrets of incalculable value to the Soviets, but by chance, not design. Prime could have had no idea of the depth of his access when he joined the RAF. Without such accidental access it is unlikely that treachery would have entered the minds of any of them.

Philby is the type specimen of a traitor who contrived his access and the story of how he entered MI6 and secured particular posts there is well recorded.[8] He also had the bonus of additional access which was purely accidental. When the scientist Dr Wilfrid Mann was in a highly sensitive post in the Washington embassy dealing with nuclear matters, he sent all high-classification cables via Philby, who had secure facilities.[9]

The CIA has provided a more recent example of a traitor-spy deliberately infiltrated by an adversary service in the form of Karl Koecher, a Czech who was trained in Prague in the early 1960s and sent as a sleeper to the USA where he managed to become an American citizen. In 1973, following instructions, he secured employment with the CIA and then proceeded to pass secret documents to Prague, using the agency's own copying machines, and with his wife serving as a courier. He was not arrested until 1984.[10]

Cairncross is an example of an already recruited traitor who, on the advice of his controller, managed to move from one government department to another in search of ever more sensitive material.

All these cases illustrate that in the world of treachery it is access not rank that matters. Insignificant people can have remarkable access as did 'Cicero' (a valet), US Army Sergeant Jack Dunlap (a chauffeur at the National Security Agency), and Sergeant Robert Lee Johnson (a guard who systematically looted the secrets held in a vault near Paris).

Officers and ancillary staff inside intelligence and security agencies have the best and most continuous access to secrets of consuming interest to adversaries and are therefore likely to be targets. Their work sometimes brings them into personal contact with foreign agents and double-agents who have the opportunity to try to suborn them. George Blake, for example, was regularly in touch with East Germans in line of duty. The American traitor Lieutenant-Colonel William Whalen succumbed through being in touch with GRU agents in Washington.

Some of the worst known traitors operating inside secret services were recruited before they entered, but others, particularly in the USA, were netted afterwards and sometimes after they had left. So it is reasonable to ask if, because of the nature of the work, the secret services attract a peculiar type of mentality, and whether training for such a shadowy world, and for life in it, makes a person more susceptible to treachery. Is there, in fact, a secret service mentality?

I shall deal with what the cult of secrecy does to the personality in Chapter 21, but a few observations are relevant here. Admiral Stansfield Turner, who was briefly head of the CIA, suggests that a clandestine career, however honourable in intent, may involve the perpetration of 'dirty tricks', subterfuge and deception on a scale which deforms the character. The degree to which secrecy can warp behaviour was shown by the case records of Graham Mitchell, the former Deputy Director-General of MI5, when he was under suspicion of being a spy in the late 1960s. Watchers who were tailing him reported that when he wandered about in parks he would repeatedly turn round as though to check that he was not being followed, while in a street he would peer in shop-windows, looking at the reflections of passers-by. There were other peculiarities which he was later to explain as the normal precautions always to be taken by an intelligence officer. When I discussed this case with Harold Macmillan his view was that over-long service in MI5 had affected Mitchell's mind and that nobody should serve longer than ten years.[11]

Secret service officers should not tell their friends or their children the nature of their occupation and they may therefore appear to be something of a failure, since any promotion has to be concealed. Stansfield Turner concluded that over many years this, too, can warp a man's character.

One peculiarity of secret-service officers which I have noticed is their general dislike of each other, and especially of their superiors. They tend to denigrate their colleagues as 'incompetent', 'useless', 'a disaster', 'everything he touched went sour', etc. Malcolm Muggeridge, who served in the wartime MI6, observed that the officers were 'ferociously disposed to each other'.[12] That has not changed.

The drink problems experienced by secret service officers in general are severe enough to warrant separate treatment, in Chapter 17.

Work inside a secret service not only provides the material to betray but facilitates the act of treachery. When Bettaney decided to spy for the KGB he knew, from his work in MI5 Russian counter-espionage, exactly who to approach and the KGB chief's London address. Such a traitor also has near-perfect cover. Peculiar habits, such as secret trysts with suspicious-looking people, can be explained to friends and relatives, even perhaps to colleagues, as being in line of duty. Driberg escaped prosecution for homosexual extravagances by pleading his MI5 connection. My researches into the Hollis case convince me that if the relationship between him and 'Sonia' could be proved there would be no doubt about his guilt. But some of his supporters are already arguing that if he was seeing her, it was in line of duty.

Mary Trevor, who worked for an intelligence agency in Holland after it had been liberated from the Germans, has told me how she and two officers called at a unit where George Blake worked and found the place in darkness, except for a small light in a garden shed. When they opened the shed door they saw Blake and one of his British colleagues sitting round a radio transmitter and clearly appalled at having been discovered. The officers agreed that they had never seen two people look so guilty but they did nothing because they assumed that the two must have been about their normal secret business.[13]

Such service abroad by intelligence officers of organizations like MI6, the CIA, and the KGB who have to operate in foreign countries in order to recruit and control agents there increases the risk of exposure to recruitment themselves. Indeed the danger of subornment is rated so high that, with only rare exceptions, anybody who has resided in a Soviet-bloc country is ineligible to join MI5.

When some degree of deception is an everyday professional event it may be easier for a man to bring himself to deceive his colleagues. It may also increase the tendency for self-deception so that treachery can be justified. Former employees may justify their treachery to themselves as simply 'selling their knowledge and skills' to another employer, as people in other professions are entitled to do. The danger of this is intensified by the fact that secret-service officers are not well paid considering their responsibility, and have modest pensions, and may sometimes be tempted by money. This has happened recently in the USA. Ronald Pelton, an NSA technician for fourteen years, was accused of inflicting 'exceptionally grave damage' on American security by telling the KGB how the NSA dealt with Soviet codes and revealing the location of listening devices planted inside the USSR. In 1977 Edward Gibbons Moore, a retired CIA employee, was sentenced to life imprisonment on a charge of espionage. Richard Miller, the former FBI agent described as an 'Inspector Clouseau figure', was sentenced to life imprisonment in 1986 for selling secrets to the Soviet bloc.

There is a further way in which an individual who has had access to intelligence secrets may dispose of them in a way which brings money and incidentally draws them to the attention of potential enemies. This is the process whereby a secret-service officer who has retired and is living abroad may pass his information to an investigative writer and agree a deal by which either he shares the proceeds or he writes a book under his own name. The type specimen of such an individual is the retired MI5 officer Peter Wright, whose case caused an international furore in the last months of 1986. As I was so deeply involved in the issue I will describe it in some detail.

On 4 September 1980 I was telephoned by Lord Rothschild, a friend who had also been a distinguished member of MI5, to be told that an interesting person who now lived abroad was visiting Britain and wished to see me. I went to Lord Rothschild's house in Cambridge where I was introduced to the man, who called himself 'Philip' and said that he was a former officer of MI5. His real name turned out to be Peter Wright. Before then I did not know of his existence, but it later transpired that he knew a great deal about me.

Wright was an old friend and colleague of Lord Rothschild who was being subjected to damaging allegations that he had been a Soviet agent – the so-called 'fifth man'. Rothschild had been a friend of both Burgess and Blunt at Cambridge University, and he and his wife had remained friendly with Blunt until the time of the latter's public exposure as a Soviet spy in November 1979. In the event that he might have need to defend his reputation in court, Rothschild wrote to Wright and asked him to prepare an objective statement about the positive contributions which Rothschild had made to British security through work for MI5 and other means. He knew that this, when vouched for by an MI5 officer, would prove that he had not been a spy. So that they could talk about these highly secret matters, Rothschild sent Wright an air ticket and enough money to enable him to visit Britain.

When I met Wright on that late summer's evening he looked much frailer than his sixty-six years, and needed a stick to walk. Rothschild left us together and Wright explained that he was living in Tasmania in straitened circumstances because his MI5 pension was only £2,000 a year, and the small Arab horse stud which he ran for a livelihood was in severe financial difficulty. He said that he had started a book which would contain new revelations about the Soviet penetration of MI5 and MI6. He had written about 10,000 words in eight or nine short chapters but was finding the effort too laborious, as was his overworked wife who had undertaken to type it. He said that he urgently needed £5,000 to save the stud.

I did not know that a few years previously Rothschild had warned the MI5 management twice that Wright was writing a book of memoirs which could be damaging to British security if published under his name. MI5 had taken no action, beyond sending Wright the standard warning that former officers remained bound to secrecy.

Wright proposed that I might like to complete the book using information which he would provide, on the understanding that he would receive half of any proceeds. He declined to let me read the chapters, which he had brought with him and which he had mentioned to Lord Rothschild, but he did have a list of about a dozen proven or alleged traitors, including Sir Roger Hollis, Colonel Dick Ellis, Anthony Blunt, and Tom Driberg. Understandably, I was interested.

I told him that I could not possibly be involved in giving him any money, but that if a book was feasible and a reputable publisher could be found, it would be normal practice for a share of the royalties to be paid to him. I said that nothing could be done until I had seen the material and decided if it could be safely published. Wright insisted that it would be unsafe for him to tell me anything of substance in Britain, and that I would have to spend some time with him in Tasmania where he was out of reach of the Official Secrets Acts.

When we were rejoined by Lord Rothschild I assumed that he was in favour of the book. This surprised me because a few weeks previously he had sent me a letter trying to deter me from continuing with my rather desultory inquiries into the case of Sir Roger Hollis, of which I knew a little but not much. I was to learn later that Wright had made it clear that he intended to publish his book somehow. Perhaps realizing that it was inevitable, Rothschild had suggested me as a collaborator, believing that I could be trusted not to reveal Wright's identity and would do a quick professional job. He feared that if Wright failed to find a collaborator he would eventually publish his knowledge and experiences under his own name from the safety of Tasmania. Such a book, with its enhanced credibility, would do far more damage to MI5 and security in general than a book under my name, with no mention of its sources.

After considerable thought I decided that my wife and I would visit my daughter living in Sydney, so that if the project collapsed the journey would not have been wasted. We arrived early in October and I moved on to Tasmania. I interviewed Wright for about ten days, usually for around ten hours a day. The most exciting information poured from his remarkable memory. Wright had never held high rank in MI5, but because of his unusual qualifications he had enjoyed an unprecedented degree of access to cases. As a scientist he had been involved in technical operations such as the bugging of embassies and the surreptitious entry of other properties. For example, when an opportunity had arisen for 'bugs' to be inserted in a new Soviet Embassy in Ottawa, Wright had been sent out to supervise the work. The years which he had spent as a special assistant to the Director-General of MI5, mainly with Sir Michael Hanley, had made Wright privy to most secret matters concerning intelligence relations between Britain, America, and the 'white' Commonwealth: Canada, Australia, and New Zealand.

As I have written elsewhere, to someone as obsessively curious about the secret services as myself, the experience was like being led into an Aladdin's cave; nuggets and jewels sparkled everywhere. It was clear from Wright's evidence alone that gross incompetence and treachery at a high level inside MI5 and MI6 had been concealed, and that public exposure was probably the only way of securing action to improve their efficiency.

The chapters already written by Wright were largely unusable and the whole book had to be rewritten. I told Wright that he could receive no money until a contract with a publisher had been signed, when he would get his halfshare of the normal advance payment, which I would endeavour to pitch high enough for him to receive the £5,000 he needed with all practicable speed.

I secured a contract with my existing publisher, Sidgwick and Jackson, on 12 December 1980. Wright insisted that, for his own security, he should not be named in the contract. His share of the royalties was sent to him by the publisher, through banking facilities arranged by Lord Rothschild, who is a banker, so that Wright's confidentiality could be preserved.

Once the book was written, under the title of *Their Trade is Treachery*, it was checked by a libel lawyer, who insisted on the removal of many names of spies and suspects as there was no way that Wright could give evidence in the event of a libel action. We then faced the problem of the Official Secrets Act which, although I had omitted all material I felt might be prejudicial to MI5's current or future operations, threatened suppression of the book either before or after publication. Since the all-embracing Official Secrets Act was offended on almost every page, I and the managing director of Sidgwick and Jackson had to take a decision; we decided to go ahead in the belief that if we could get the book out without MI5's advance knowledge they would be unlikely to take any action against it. I believed that if MI5 got hold of it in advance it would have no option but to suppress it.

The serial rights of the book were sold in advance to the *Daily Mail*. When the first instalment, which was the first public exposure of the Hollis case, appeared on Monday, 18 March 1981, the publisher received a telephone call from the Cabinet Secretary, Sir Robert Armstrong, asking for two copies of the book, because the Prime Minister would be sure to be questioned about it in Parliament and she needed time to study it. I was opposed to providing the copies when we had gone to such lengths to keep them secret, so I suggested that they should be provided only if Sir Robert gave an undertaking not to interfere with the book. To our surprise, delight, and mystification he did so in a letter sent round by hand from his office.

Two days later, on the day the book was published, the Prime Minister, Mrs Thatcher, gave what was, in effect, her review of the book from the Dispatch Box. She confirmed that Hollis had been suspect, but seized on some alleged inaccuracies to suggest that the whole book was speculative and ill informed. Then she announced the first independent inquiry for twenty years into the efficiency of the secret services' defences against Soviet penetration, to be carried out by the Security Commission. The media, incensed at being scooped by the *Daily Mail*, joined in 'rubbishing' the book. Despite this it remained on the bestseller lists for several weeks.

Within a month I learned from secret-service friends that our valiant efforts to keep the book from MI5's clutches had failed; either photocopies of the typescript or page proofs had been circulating in the most secret areas of Whitehall including the Cabinet and Prime

Minister's offices. Sir Robert's letter had been a subterfuge to cover the fact that the Prime Minister already had the book, and to make sure that no last-minute changes had been made.

I was astonished that no effort had been made to stop the book. But I was later told that the legal advisers to both MI5 and MI6 had been convinced that the publishers and I would fight any court attempt to have the book suppressed, and that in the process they would have to make too many damaging admissions. The Prime Minister, the Home Secretary, the Cabinet Secretary, and the Director-General of MI5 were all in favour of having the book suppressed, but they were overborne by the advice of the MI5 and MI6 legal advisers. It seems that the source who had provided the page proofs had required anonymity and, to ensure that, a promise was given that no legal action would be taken against myself or the publisher. The Cabinet Office was left with the political problem of reacting to the book once it was published, and decided that the best way out was to give the Prime Minister a brief that would rubbish it; they were confident that I would not respond by naming my sources.

I remained in touch with Wright by letter, gleaning further information for the paperback edition of *Their Trade Is Treachery*, which became a greatly improved and extended version, containing some of the names which had been omitted from the hardback. Though I had warned Wright that it would take time for his royalty payments to reach him, I received frantic cables and letters pleading urgent need to save him from bankruptcy. These continued even after he had received substantial payments, with complaints about the heavy Australian taxes and the poor exchange rate of the Australian dollar.

Wright then suggested a further collaborative book to be called *The Atlantic Connection* for which he would supply information about the intelligence and security connections between Britain, the USA, and Canada. Wright sent a few rather uninteresting items and, since the book was clearly going to take a long time to produce, he suggested that I should write a book entirely on the Hollis case. He could produce no more information about it but clearly wanted half the proceeds. I declined on the grounds that it would be no more than a repeat of *Their Trade is Treachery*. Wright then offered to provide information for newspaper articles which would result in quick sales and I rejected that too. Shortly afterwards, in the spring of 1983, Wright ended the correspondence, and I have not heard from him since.

Wright, in fact, had formed a new and more promising association with a British television company which had offered to pay all legal expenses if the government prosecuted him, and to make up any pension he might lose. As a result, in July 1984 he appeared for an hour on British television restating much that had appeared in my book, and mentioning certain sensitive matters which I had deliberately omitted.

The programme produced no response from the government, and Wright followed it up with a 150-page memorandum entitled 'The Soviet Assault on the Security Services of the West' which reached the Prime Minister. Again, though the existence of the report was given much publicity, there was no official response and no reaction in Parliament.

Meanwhile, I had heard from a television producer that Wright was well advanced with a book to be published under his own name. He had previously told me that he knew that the government would react strongly to such a venture, as I was able to confirm from inquiries I made in Whitehall. In the end he decided to go ahead, and secured a British publisher – Heinemann. The government soon made Heinemann aware that it could face restraint and possible prosecution if it published the book called *Spycatcher* in Britain, since Wright was bound to remain silent by the terms of his contract, as well as by the Official Secrets Act. The publisher's response was to use an Australian subsidiary company to produce the book, and to export copies from Australia to Britain and elsewhere.

Attempts were made by Heinemann's lawyers to have the book vetted by the British security authorities, and a typescript was sent to the Attorney-General. The government took the view that the whole book was so full of official secrets that it should be suppressed, even though the great bulk of the material had already been published by me. This led to court action in Sydney in mid-November 1986 on the grounds that Wright was in breach of his solemn commitments, whatever the content of his book. Meanwhile, the Attorney-General had let it be known that he had decided that Wright should be prosecuted if he ever returned to Britain.

Although Wright received royalties from *Their Trade is Treachery* and stood to make a great deal of money from his own book *Spycatcher*, he claimed that he had been mainly motivated by his desire to reveal incompetence and treachery inside the secret services with a view to improving them. There is, however, another way of looking at his actions from the point of view of this book. If Wright had moved to an Iron Curtain country instead of to Australia, and had published his secret information there, few would have described it as anything else but treachery.

Coinciding with the Wright case was another incident: a 31-year-old Israeli technician called Mordechai Vanunu, who had worked in the very secret Dimona atomic establishment in the Negev desert, visited Britain and sold secrets and photographs said to relate to the production of nuclear explosive and weapons, including neutron bombs,

143

to the *Sunday Times*. Somehow he was spirited back to Israel to face a charge of treason. Vanunu had flown from London to Rome and claimed that he was kidnapped by agents of Mossad. Clearly, in the eyes of the Israeli government, a calculated leak of secret state information to a newspaper which then prints it constitutes treason; presumably they would argue that if a potential enemy reads it in the the paper it does as much damage as if it had been handed to one of its intelligence agents.[14]

So far as professional writers are concerned, such as myself in Wright's case, there are conflicts between the requirements of loyalty and press freedom. The only principle on which an investigative writer can function effectively in a country where there is no censorship is to endeavour to secure as much information as possible, and then to make a value judgment based on experience as to the virtue of publishing it. While a serious view is taken of government staff who break their solemn undertakings, a succession of British Attornies-General have worked on the principle that in a true democracy investigative writers should be as free as reasonably possible to go about their business, the onus being on the authorities to prevent leakages of information. The reaction of the Prime Minister to my exposure of Wright's disclosures was proof enough that they had served a public purpose. Mrs Thatcher set up the first independent enquiry in twenty years to examine the defences against the penetration of secret departments by foreign agents. The Security Commission which carried out the enquiry discovered many weaknesses and made many recommendations which were put into effect.

The most important security lesson to be learned from the Wright affair is the stupidity of allowing anyone with highly saleable secrets to go into retirement on a pension so inadequate that it is likely to produce the dangerous combination of burning resentment and financial pressure.

CHAPTER FOURTEEN

Vulnerable Professions: Defence, Diplomacy, Politics and Science

Travel makes a wise man better but a fool worse.
                                    Thomas Fuller

Until comparatively recently traitors operating inside secret services had a further built-in advantage: they were the least likely to be suspected because treachery there was regarded as unthinkable. It has long been 'thinkable' in the fighting services, which provide perhaps the easiest professional access to high-grade secrets, because of the many historic examples of officers who betrayed their comrades and country. Some have already been mentioned among those who spied for money, but the most memorable in modern times was the young Seaforth Highlander Norman Baillie-Stewart, whose ready access to details about British weapons enabled him to spy for the Germans in what became the treachery case of the 1930s. His prime motive was ideological; for, as he later confessed following his release after serving a five-year sentence, he was an admirer of Hitler and his regime, and he eventually left Britain to belong to it.[1]

Admiral Muselier of the wartime Free French Forces, a friend of de Gaulle, proved to be a Soviet sympathizer. There can be little doubt, in view of evidence provided by the defector Golitsin, that a senior officer in the Royal Navy who eventually reached flag rank served for several years as a Soviet agent, supplying top-secret documents. (MI5 officers who followed up the lead were confident that they had identified him, but their chief, Sir Roger Hollis, would not permit them to interrogate him on the grounds that a prosecution would be too damaging to Navy morale and to Anglo-US relations, and that the man was so near retirement that he could do no further harm.[2]

In the USA the most heinous service offender of recent times was

145

Army Lieutenant-Colonel William Henry Whalen, sentenced to fifteen years' imprisonment in 1966. He had been recruited in the late 1950s when he was serving as a military liaison officer with the intelligence adviser to the Army Chief of Staff. His last appointment had been in the Pentagon with the Joint Chiefs of Staff, a position which enabled him to tap the combined intelligence resources of the CIA, NSA, and other agencies. His profession provided access, and temptation appeared in the form of a Soviet military attaché in Washington, whom he met in 1955. He was recruited as an agent-in-place and gave the Soviets highly secret information about weapons, both atomic and conventional, troop movements, plans for the defence of Europe, plans for retaliation against a Soviet attack and many other items. He also served as a most valuable feedback agent. So great was his service to the Soviets that one of the attachés who ran him is said to have been promoted to GRU two-star general for his handling of the case.[3] He was not detected and arrested until 1966.

In Sweden the very damaging traitor Stig Wennerstrom was an Air Force colonel with wide-ranging professional access, while in South Africa the Soviet spy Dieter Gerhardt held the higher rank of commodore. The record of service traitors, however, provides the best evidence of the general unimportance of rank in the practice of treachery. The case of David Bingham, a naval officer of modest sub-lieutenant rank but with sensitive access to torpedo secrets and methods of submarine detection, has already been mentioned, as have the treacherous exploits of Anthony Wraight, the RAF officer who defected in 1956. He was only a flying officer aged twenty-two, but his air-crew duties gave him access to information and experience of the greatest interest to an adversary power. Nelson C. Drummond, the American sentenced to life imprisonment for espionage in 1963, was just a Navy enlisted man, as was Michael Walker of the Walker family spy ring. The American traitors Robert Lee Johnson and Jack Dunlap and the Britons Nicholas Prager and Douglas Britten were NCOs.

Military service is another profession commonly providing residence overseas, which increases the risk of contact with foreign recruiters. Prime, for example, made his first contact while serving in Berlin with the RAF. British and American servicemen stationed in West Germany are vulnerable to the continuous drive mounted by the Soviet bloc there.

Service in those industries connnected with defence offers similar professional access to secrets of extreme interest to adversaries, the classic instance of recent times being the espionage of Christopher Boyce in the USA. Soviet agents devote much effort to talent-spotting promising targets at technological exhibitions and scientific conferences. Again, rank is not necessarily important; a laboratory assistant may know more of interest than a managing director.

Soviet concern to secure Western technology has intensified in recent years but it dates back to the early days of revolutionary Russia. The Soviet trade organizations, AMTORG in the USA and ARCOS in the UK, were engaged in securing industrial and commercial secrets of every kind and by any means. Communists like Harry Gold began by passing on simple industrial formulae, the argument being that this was simply helping the Soviet economy to 'catch up on capitalism'. They soon found that they were on the slippery slope, and more and more information of a sensitive nature was required. The recruitment by such means of a British electronics engineer by Romanian intelligence in the early 1970s has only recently been revealed by the defector Ion Pacepa, a former deputy director of the Romanian Department of Foreign Intelligence. This man, as yet not publicly identified but code-named 'Armand', had business contacts with a major American company and agreed initially to provide non-classified information for money. He ended up providing a mass of secret NASA documents regarded by the Romanian dictator, Ceauşescu, as of enormous value.[4]

Another profession providing ready access to secret information and with special susceptibility to being targeted is that of the diplomat, a term commonly used to include ancillary foreign-service staff. Donald Maclean's betrayal of the cable traffic between Churchill and both Roosevelt and Truman, which revealed their negotiating positions in advance of the conferences held at Yalta and Potsdam, strengthened Stalin's hand in what is now regarded as having been a political triumph for the Soviet Union. A British ambassador who is still alive and cannot safely be named for libel reasons, was photo-blackmailed homosexually and did enough damage for the Foreign Office, which was anxious to avoid another scandal, to require him to leave the service.

The pro-Soviet activities of the Canadian diplomat Herbert Norman in Tokyo in 1950 have convinced his biographer, James Barros, that his activities 'went far to contribute to Moscow's decision to give the North Koreans the green light to invade South Korea in June 1950'. Barros is satisfied that Norman was deliberately recruited for infiltration into the Canadian foreign service.

The attempt to blackmail the Canadian Ambassador to Moscow, John Watkins, has already been described, as has the case of the French Ambassador, Maurice Dejean. When Orlando Letelier, the former Chilean Ambassador to the USA was murdered in 1976, papers in his briefcase revealed that he was being financed by the KGB, through Cuban intelligence, to install a Communist government in Chile. He had been a successful agent of influence, inducing American newspapers to print many articles about the violation of human rights in Chile.

Such high-level cases show that rank is no bar to Soviet recruiters who will try to target anyone considered vulnerable. Yet in the diplomatic field, as elsewhere, many of lowly rank, like Vassall, Houghton, and Guindon, found themselves with a dangerous degree of access. Cipher clerks, like Tyler Kent, John King, and Gouzenko in daily contact with secret telegrams may know more detail than an ambassador.

Service abroad, which is the essence of diplomacy, greatly increases the exposure to recruiters especially for those diplomats behind the Iron Curtain. Wennerstrom, who was recruited by the GRU while in Moscow for a Russian air show, had previously served there and been targeted. The KGB agent Vladimir Petrov was spotted as a possible defector by a Polish émigré while based at the Soviet Embassy in Canberra and was cultivated for Australian counter-intelligence, which eventually secured his defection. Gordievsky was successfully suborned in Scandinavia and later in London, while Vladimir Kuzichkin, a KGB major, was induced by the British to defect in Tehran while posing as a vice-consul there. The case records presented in other chapters provide many more examples of recruitment while in service abroad.

Vassall and many others who were successfully suborned in Moscow would probably never have transgressed but for their postings there. The KGB enjoys an enormous advantage in having its nationals working in the Western embassies in Moscow as servants, providing opportunities for the infiltration of talent-spotters and provocation agents with so little supervision that until the Vassall case there was no full-time MI5 security officer in the British Embassy there. Vassall blamed loneliness in Moscow for the ease of his recruitment, and so did Mrs Gunvor Haavik, a 64-year-old clerk in the Norwegian Foreign Ministry who had been suborned by the KGB while serving at the embassy in Moscow and handed over secrets, later being paid for them.

As with intelligence officers, diplomats were above suspicion before the defection of Maclean and Burgess. Those who have been traitors have enjoyed other built-in advantages, particularly their reason for foreign travel, which has facilitated their contact with controllers. Even when serving in the home country, in the Foreign Office, a diplomat may be regularly exposed to Soviet recruiters through the necessity of meeting foreign counterparts, socially and in line of duty. The Norwegian diplomat Treholt apparently believed that he could improve East–West relations through 'working meals' with Soviet diplomats, and this was his first step on to the slippery slope. Those who have been recruited have reason for regular and open consort with foreigners whom they know to be agents. Burgess, for example, who did not have a room of his own in the Foreign Office, was always able to borrow a colleague's to brief the TASS correspondent. 'He would go in there alone with him carrying a great sheaf of papers,' one of his former colleagues told me.[5]

The profession affording access to secrets for the largest numbers of people is that of the government-employed bureaucrat, known in Britain as the civil servant and generally on the increase everywhere. The extent to which the Soviets have recruited civilian traitors in government departments in Britain, the USA, West Germany, France, and elsewhere is evidenced by case records at many points in this book. They succeeded in penetrating many departments of interest to them and at almost every level, rank being again of no great consequence. The clerk conveying secret documents between offices or the secretary making photocopies may not understand the contents but may be perfectly placed to betray them, as Vassall demonstrated during his time at the Admiralty.

A relatively new type of government employee whose profession offers automatic access to secrets is the scientific civil servant – the trained scientist employed in defence research establishments or as an analyst or adviser in headquarters. He is a tempting target and may prove to be a 'soft' one because of certain features of the scientific discipline.

Science is essentially international in the sense that scientists of all nations have contributed to its advancement of knowledge. It is fundamental to the work of research scientists that they should have access, through published papers, to the results achieved by others everywhere, and there is such professional objection to secrecy that many scientists decline to work in any area where there is restraint on publication. These attitudes have undoubtedly contributed to the treachery of scientists like Fuchs and Nunn May, who found themselves caught up in secrecy because of war but still maintained that their 'discoveries' belonged to everyone. The attitudes were, however, secondary to their Communism, because they would never have considered revealing their researches to their scientific 'colleagues' in Germany. The crookedness of their reasoning was demonstrated when Fuchs refused to tell his MI5 interrogator the technical details of the atomic bomb which he had betrayed, on the grounds that his security clearance was not high enough, though he believed it right to have given them to Russian 'scientists'! He provided these details in a separate confession to his technical chief.[6] The Canadian scientist Professor Raymond Boyer said that he gave secret information to a Communist friend in breach of his oath of secrecy to his country to 'further international scientific collaboration'. He made no effort to find out what the Russians were supplying in return, which was nil.[7]

Fuchs and others like him not only betrayed information which they regarded as being the results of their own efforts but surreptitiously provided anything that came their way.[8] They used the 'universality of scientific knowledge' – which is not different in kind from any other – as a deliberate or self-deluding cover for treachery.

The internationalism of science even makes some non-political scientists vulnerable to an approach that their knowledge should be universal, and this was basic to the post-war campaigns in the USA and Britain to share atomic bomb secrets with the Soviet Union. It was common after the war for scientists to argue that there should be no secrecy in science and that the locked laboratory kept out more secrets than it preserved. That, however, has never been the view of the Soviets, who have continued to set special store by secrecy to a degree unparalleled in free societies and with the severest penalties for security breaches.

Soviet recruiters also exploit the special appeal which Communism seems to hold for the scientific mind searching for order and explanation and sometimes naïve enough to believe that the scientific method can solve any problem. Marxism–Leninism has proved to be especially attractive to the young scientist enthusiastic for his discipline and with his critical faculty limited by shortage of experience. Fuchs was an active underground Communist operator long before he acquired any secrets. So was Nunn May. In France the atomic scientist Frédéric Joliot-Curie, while something of a Nazi collaborationist during the war, became an ardent Communist after the liberation and is believed to have supplied the Soviets with nuclear information as well as openly supporting their political cause.

The wartime alliance with the USSR enabled many Communist scientists in Britain, the USA, and Canada to infiltrate government departments involved in the war effort, and they were difficult to remove once the Soviet Union became the main adversary. But it was after the war, which science had helped to win, that scientists reached their peak of influence. Because they had been so successful in solving technical problems of war, they rashly and unscientifically assumed that they and their like could solve the problems of peace, which were essentially economic, social, and political. Fuchs, for example, worked in prison on a system of applying mathematics to economics, claiming that booms and depressions could be faithfully plotted.[9]

As a newspaper scientific correspondent for many years after the war I was in regular touch with many scientists and attended their international conferences. I was appalled by their arrogance and their naïvety, which seemed never to be diminished by their catastrophic failures, such as the groundnuts scheme in Tanganyika, or their absolute assurance in the middle 1950s that the manned fighter and the manned bomber had no future. Famous figures of science and mathematics, such as Einstein, Bertrand Russell, and Bernal, displayed profound political naïvety. There was pressure to place scientists in positions of authority in almost every Whitehall ministry, and it succeeded. Many from universities, including some left extremists, were appointed to secret committees or to staff jobs with international organizations like NATO. The fact that their influence has since declined to the reasonable position where they are 'on tap but not on top' is evidence of the failure of the vogue of the scientist as the answer to all ills.[10]

The advent of military and civil nuclear power made scientists particularly aware of the social impact of their researches and led to a further development: the cult of social responsibility among scientists. This concept attracted many who were genuinely concerned but also some who have used it with considerable impact as a left-extremist front, particularly in the Western agitation against nuclear weapons and the generation of nuclear electricity.

The case records show that the Soviet bloc has paid special attention to politicians, recruiting them through ideology when they are young and through money and blackmail when they are established. A former Director-General of MI5, Sir Martin Furnival Jones, put the Soviet attitude succinctly when he told an investigative committee: 'If the Russian Intelligence Service can recruit a back-bench MP and he climbs to a ministerial position, the spy is home and dry.'[11] Some recruits have become ministers and at least one in Britain was required to resign, while pressure was applied to others. But a politician can remain a back-bencher all his life and still gain important access, through select committees on which he may serve or simply through parliamentary gossip.

The treacherous behaviour of Driberg and Owen has already been mentioned. Some MPs, like Konni Zilliacus, who was of Finnish origin, used their parliamentary positions to associate overtly with KGB agents. There are others, including some peers, who have been more discreet and cannot yet be named for libel reasons. The Canadian MP Fred Rose, born Rosenberg in Poland, was one of the full-blown GRU agents exposed by Gouzenko, receiving six years' imprisonment for being a key figure in an extensive spy ring. In France the outstanding Soviet recruit was Pierre Cot, an ardent left-winger who became Minister of Aviation after the war and was awarded the Stalin Prize in 1953.

The type specimen of the traitorous post-war politician, however, has to be Alfred Frenzel, a member of the West German Parliament. Born in Sudeten Czechoslovakia in 1899, he had joined the Communist Party there when he was twenty-one. When Hitler marched in, in 1938, he escaped to England and served with the RAF ground staff until the end of the war, when he returned to Germany posing as a former RAF pilot. He joined the West German Social Democratic Party, became a member of the Bavarian Parliament, and in 1953 was elected to the Federal Parliament in Bonn, becoming a member of parliamentary committees including the Defence Committee, which gave him access to a steady flow of most secret West German and NATO papers. In 1956 he was approached by Czech intelligence which, having induced him to accept 'expenses', recruited him on a regular basis through an implied blackmail threat and more money. Over the next four years he handed over highly secret defence documents for photocopying. Czech intelligence appeared so well informed about West German defence developments that the intelligence service became suspicious and investigated all the Defence Committee members. Frenzel was caught changing briefcases with a courier, arrested, and tried in 1961. Having made a full confession he repeated it in court, claiming that his treachery had been entirely for money, though some innate loyalty to his original homeland and compatriots may have been a factor. He was sentenced to fifteen years' imprisonment. The ultimate confirmation of his guilt was provided by the KGB when, in 1966, he was exchanged for a German woman journalist who had been imprisoned in Moscow.[12]

When politicians cannot be recruited directly, the Soviet bloc attempts to suborn their assistants. There have been Soviet attempts to recruit some of the women secretaries and the many advisers who work for MPs or for organizations with which MPs are closely associated. My type specimen is Arthur Bax, the Englishman whose activities have been described in Chapter 1. The US Congress is a prime Soviet-bloc target, and one way in is to recruit congressional staff, especially those serving the oversight intelligence committees – the parliamentary bodies responsible for supervising the secret services and which have access to much secret information. Two such staff members who had been approached, James Kappus and Keith Tolliver, were 'turned' by the FBI. Kappus, who worked for a member of the House Armed Services Committee, was asked by the KGB to steal confidential files. Tolliver, who was on a Senator's staff, was paid $20,000 for information which the FBI had in fact allowed him to pass. Another, called James Sattler, an East German agent, disappeared before he could penetrate his target.[13]

Another profession with an excessive contribution to the ranks of traitors is journalism. Access is journalists' life-blood, and to acquire it they cultivate sources in sensitive positions. Looking back on my own career as a defence correspondent in Fleet Street my penetration of the Defence Ministry and other secret establishments was deep and wide; though greatly deplored by MI5, nothing effective could be done about it because of the high level of most of the sources and the fact that many were politicians, who are virtually untouchable. Journalists are therefore common targets, and their work also exposes them to expert recruiters, especially if they need to consort with Soviet-bloc diplomats who are so often professional intelligence officers. A serious attempt was made to recruit me, and other former colleagues had similar experiences.[14] Frequent foreign travel increases the exposure of journalists to recruiters. The extent of the efforts to suborn them when they visit Moscow has been described in detail by various defectors.[15]

Journalism also provides excellent cover for the traitor because in the true democracies its practitioners have legitimate reason for asking any question, especially for use as 'background', and to meet anybody surreptitiously, even known KGB agents. They have ample excuses for visiting foreign embassies and for trips abroad where case officers can be contacted. Journalists' wives and families are unlikely to be suspicious of any clandestine activity.

Journalists who were recruited as Soviet agents and made themselves traitors include Chambers, Sorge, Burchett, Pathé, and Peter Smolka, an Austrian who worked in the British information service during the Second World War and afterwards on the *Daily Express*. Roger Hollis also began his career as a journalist in China. There have been others, more recently, who cannot safely be named, including many powerful and deliberate agents of influence. As a result of information from a Soviet-bloc defector in the late 1970s, the proprietor of a leading Fleet Street newspaper was told by MI5 that one of his chief reporters was a secret Communist who took regular payments from Soviet-bloc intelligence in return for information he could supply and influence he could wield. The journalist, who had access to politicians and civil servants of great interest to the Soviets, did not contest the evidence and chose to resign from Fleet Street without fuss, neither MI5 nor the newspaper concerned being keen on publicity. For comparable behaviour in the countries whose interest he was assisting this journalist would have been given a long prison sentence or worse.

When Sir Max Aitken was running Beaverbrook Newspapers he was approached by MI5 to be given the names of journalists on the staff who were suspected of being dangerous. He declined to take any action fearing trouble with the unions and preferring – as he put it – 'a quiet life'.

The Czech defector Josef Frolik, who had served in London, told MI5 that there were several Communist agents in the *Daily Express* and the *Daily Mirror*. Another, who remains active even though exposed by a defector, was denied an important political post only because MI5 declined to give him security clearance.

The US administration experienced a severe shock when it examined some 30,000 pages of documents captured after the successful invasion of Grenada in 1983. They incriminated many prominent Americans, including journalists who clearly had been prepared to write anything which the Cubans and other pro-Communists gave them about the situation in Grenada and other issues.

Only rarely has it proved possible for the West to recruit a Soviet journalist, but West German intelligence managed to do so recently in the shape of a Novosti science editor called Ilya Suslov, who sold scientific and technological information secured through background briefings and private scientific contacts. In 1986 he was jailed for fifteen years because he had been imprudent enough to flaunt his affluence by driving around Moscow in a new Volga car – a 'sign of wealth and privilege' according to the Soviet newspaper *Trud*.[16] While the KGB continues to concentrate with success on journalists, the CIA, under regulations imposed by Admiral Stansfield Turner in 1977, is barred from using journalism as a cover for any CIA officer. Under US law, therefore, journalists can work for the KGB without necessarily committing an offence, but not for the CIA. There is no such ban on British journalists, some of whom are surreptitiously attached to the secret services.

As already pointed out, the staff of information departments of government ministries and international bodies such as NATO have access to much information and many background documents which are classified, and they also attend secret briefings. Not surprisingly the profession of information officer has been the target of Soviet recruitment with some outstanding successes. The most recent case involved Arne Treholt, a section head of the information department in Norway's Foreign Ministry. Before him the type specimen of an information officer abusing his position in Moscow's interest was Georges Pâques, deputy head of the French section of NATO's press and information department. He had supplied the Russians with so much valuable information over twenty years, until exposed by the defector Golitsin, that the KGB was able to supply another NATO agent, the Canadian spy Hambleton, with the file code-numbers of documents in the NATO registry which it wanted him to photocopy.

Apart from those in professions already listed, any Westerner travelling in the Soviet bloc is a possible target. Even lists of tourists are routinely scrutinized by the KGB. Particular attention is paid to trade union leaders, as evidenced by the public disclosure in 1985 by Sam McCluskie, assistant general secretary of the National Union of Seamen, that the Russians had tried to suborn him to spy for them when he was visiting Moscow in 1983. He told them wisely to 'get lost', but the KGB has had more success with others in the trade union movement. They do not have access to official secrets but are always useful as agents of influence on socialist governments and occasionally as wreckers of industry.

Senior business men who may be in positions of influence are also of perennial interest. Hede Massing has recorded that after being recruited to Soviet intelligence she was used to entertain important Americans when they visited Moscow. In that way she made personal connections of use to her when she was posted to the USA to recruit Soviet agents there.[17] The risk is so well appreciated that the security authorities take the initiative in warning business travellers, especially about the danger of sexual blackmail from hotel prostitutes and other women working for the KGB. They also issue indirect warnings, when large numbers of business people are involved, as happens when exhibitions are staged behind the Iron Curtain. In May 1961, shortly before a major commercial exhibition of British electronics in Moscow, I was asked to publish a series of case records showing how men and women had been suborned by Russian agents, as a warning which MI5 felt it could not itself issue.

Subornment of business men travelling abroad is by no means restricted to the Soviets. Western business men occasionally have used their trips and foreign commercial contacts to offer or accept traitorous services. Arthur George Owens would probably never have volunteered to work for the Abwehr had he not been in and out of the Continent so frequently on business trips.

A concomitant of professional foreign travel widely believed to have been a factor in the production of traitors is the process known as *brainwashing* – the political indoctrination and ideological conditioning of people held captive with a view to changing their loyalties – which is relevant here. Brainwashing has been inflicted on imprisoned civilians and captured servicemen in the hope of making them traitors, and has also been applied by the Soviets to their own dissidents as part of the concept of 'psycho-politics' – the practice of asserting and attempting to maintain dominion over the thoughts and loyalties of individuals, masses, organizations, and nations. The first stage of the brainwashing process is to produce chaos, distrust, and turmoil in the individual or corporate mind. The second is to eradicate individualism, self-will, and personal creativeness, using physical ill treatment and other forms of degradation, medical treatment such as electric shock and drugs, and false evidence and disinformation. The final stage is to inculcate Communist beliefs and dogma to 'realign' loyalty for ever.

While supposedly based scientifically, on the work of Pavlov's experiments with dogs, most scientists who have examined the evidence have concluded that the effects of brainwashing on humans are very limited. Like every dog, every man is believed to have his breaking-point, but it does not follow that his real beliefs have changed. In fact the methods of political indoctrination used by Soviet and Chinese interrogators were little more than refinements of methods devised and used by inquisitors down the centuries, including close confinement, isolation, the induction of a state of hopelessness, deprivation of sleep, interminable questioning, fear of physical violence, actual physical violence, and the promise of rewards for collaboration. Such methods can secure confessions and collaboration but rarely, if ever, change a person's private thoughts and beliefs. Once free of the pressures the individual will reject the implanted teaching except in cases where it happened to conform with his previous ideas. This helps to explain why some apparently committed Communists undergo a revulsion if they become free of the regular conditioning by indoctrinators and of the all-important claptrap repetition of mindless slogans – as evidenced by the mass rejection of the stupidities of Chairman Mao, which millions of Chinese had accepted as holy writ.

Similarly, while the haranguing of German crowds by Hitler and Goebbels was underpinned by political conquest or war, what looked like mass brainwashing was achieved in the style of religious conversions, such as those of evangelical preachers exploiting mass hysteria. When the underpinning collapsed, so did the effects on the mass mind.

In the Soviet Union the political authorities, and those prepared to abandon professional ethics and do their bidding, have been driven to the use of strong drugs, electric shocks, and other 'psychiatric' treatments, including brain surgery, to convert some of their courageous dissidents to belief in the Soviet system while the victims are confined in mental institutions. The treatments, called 'stress techniques', seem to be aimed at causing mental confusion and breakdown in the hope of impairing judgement and increasing suggestibility, so that the required ideology can be implanted. They have certainly failed with some dissidents and serve mainly as an appalling commentary on a regime where to deny the dogma is to be considered mad.

It would seem that true conversions through brainwashing techniques are possible only when the new ideology fits in with the temperament and state of mind of the person concerned. An extreme authoritarian type of person who is a Fascist might be converted to Communism, or even vice versa, but the reasonably balanced individual will not be affected, whatever he might say to put an end to the treatment. Much depends on the morale of the subject. While many of the 7,000 American prisoners of war in Korea were 'converted' sufficiently to collaborate with the Communist regime, few British or Turkish prisoners were, and this has been explained as due to poorer American morale. Many of the Americans, however, were really opportunists who took part in broadcasts and other forms of collaboration to ease their lot.

156

On their release, nearly all proved to have feigned conversion to escape from insupportable conditions imposed by cruel captors. The twenty or so who actually accepted Communism were men who in the past had been unable to form strong loyalties of any kind.[18]

The type specimen of the alleged convert to Communism and treason through brainwashing is George Blake, who became a Soviet agent inside Britain's Secret Intelligence Service (MI6) after being brainwashed in a prison camp in Korea. According to Kenneth de Courcy, who spent two years in prison with Blake, often discussing the reasons for his treachery, Blake said that he believed 'individual choice would eventually be mastered by a central Soviet control of thought process'; but this may just have been philosophical dreaming and a cover for the truth. It is now certain that Blake had committed himself to Communism long before the Korean War. He admitted his early Communism to Vassall when they were in prison together, and may have been recruited to the KGB by a recruiter at Downing College, Cambridge, where he took a course in Russian in 1947. I suspect that the prison camp 'brainwashing' was invented by MI6 officers to cover the fact that they had recruited a dedicated Communist to their ranks, a man who also had active Communist relatives, including the notorious KGB agent Henri Curiel, and who had entered Britain on a forged passport. Sir Norman Brook, the Cabinet Secretary who confidentially briefed George Brown and other Labour Privy Councillors on the details of Blake's treachery, specifically stated that there had been no brainwashing.[19] This was also the view of security officials and doctors who questioned Blake. An officially approved East European historical account of the CIA makes no mention of Blake's imprisonment in Korea but claims that he contacted the Soviet authorities after fearing the rebirth of militarism in West Germany.[20] More recently, the seven British servicemen who confessed to passing GCHQ secrets to the Soviets in Cyprus, and then withdrew their statements because they had been obtained under duress, claimed to have been brainwashed by their interrogators, but an independent inquiry concluded that no unlawful techniques had been used.[21]

To summarize, it is clear that if it provides the all-important access to secrets the profession which a young person selects is crucial in determining the risk of being targeted for recruitment or of spontaneously deciding to commit treachery. Those professions which involve foreign travel, particularly inside the Soviet bloc, are likely to increase the exposure to recruiters, who can operate more freely abroad and especially in their own country. Once having achieved access through profession, a person's vulnerability to subornment or temptation will greatly depend on personality traits, which will now be considered.

CHAPTER FIFTEEN

Personality Traits

Character is destiny.

George Eliot

According to Dusko Popov, who would have been considered a traitor by the Abwehr but a hero by MI6, Sir Stewart Menzies, the MI6 chief, listed the following characteristics (which he sensed Popov had) as being valuable for a spy: being ambitious; being ruthless, without scruples, and unbothered by conscience; not being subject to panic when frightened; when in danger being stimulated to clearer thinking and to quick and better decision-making. Menzies added a further requirement which Popov did not then have: being prepared to obey orders.[1] The careers of the most productive traitors show that they had further qualities, and to consider the extent to which general character is a factor in the generation of treachery, it is necessary to examine many more.

Character changes with age, and the great majority of traitors, especially the arch-traitors, began their treachery when they were young. With the exception of Blunt, who was twenty-eight, the Cambridge group were all in their early twenties when recruited. Christopher Boyce was twenty-two when he conceived his joint treachery with Andrew Daulton Lee, who was a year older. William Kampiles, who likewise betrayed satellite secrets, was twenty-three. The Rosenbergs were in their twenties when they began underground Communist work; so was Klaus Fuchs. The British Foreign Office employee William Marshall was only twenty-four when convicted. The American counter-intelligence analyst Jonathan Pollard was in his late twenties when recruited by the Israelis. The US naval spy John Walker was still short of thirty when he began his long and damaging espionage, while his son, Michael, whom he recruited was only twenty-two. Geoffrey Prime made his first approach to the Soviets when he was thirty; Bettaney made his at thirty-three.

These cases, and many others I have listed in my researches, strongly suggest that age is a definite factor in the initiation of the pro-Soviet ideological traitor. He tends to be recruited when young, partly because his judgement is immature, being naïve and enthusiastic, and also because Soviet recruiters specialize in targeting young people. Though there are exceptions, like the NSA Soviet spy Ronald Pelton, who was in his early forties, and the FBI traitor Richard Miller, who was forty-seven, older people seem to be generally too wise to be inveigled by Communism or any other ideology.

The young may also fall prey to the temptation of money, as demonstrated by the case of Lance-Corporal Philip Aldridge, who in 1982 at the age of nineteen abstracted a top-secret document which he was supposed to destroy and tried to sell it to the Russians. Generally, though, the mercenary traitor is likely to be older for several reasons. In early middle age he is more likely to be beset by serious money or marital problems. He is also more prone to bear resentment because of professional failure, especially if he has been required to leave the service which gave him access. Defectors from both sides of the Iron Curtain tend to be middle aged, perhaps because it takes many years before they can convince themselves that they are sufficiently dissatisfied with their system of government or that they have enough 'assets' to offer the country where they propose to seek asylum.

Whether there is a link between age and recruitment through sex is harder to establish. The young, like Guindon and Vassall, are supposed to be more in the grip of desire; but the old may be more grateful for opportunity.

A few years ago there was a vogue among psychologists, particularly in the USA, to link body build with character to a degree suggesting that it could offer some guide to likely behaviour. It was alleged that the proportions of the body offer pointers to personality. Lean folk with stringy muscles, long heads, and long necks, the so-called 'asthenics', were likely to be quiet, shy, self-conscious, over-ambitious, dogmatic, and tight-fisted; while the stocky 'pyknics', with round heads and short necks, were more extrovert, sociable, impulsive, moody, and generous. A brief survey of the physical characteristics of traitors indicates that no such connection exists as far as treachery is concerned.

Anthony Blunt was thin, lanky, and languid; Harry Gold, short, squat, and round-shouldered. Dieter Gerhardt was so huge and ungainly that he was nicknamed Jumbo, while Andrew Daulton Lee was only 5 ft 2 in. tall, although he was broad-shouldered and chunky. Wennerstrom was tall, slim, blond, and blue-eyed, 'a man of unusually handsome appearance', but Fuchs was weedy, stoop-shouldered, and sallow-complexioned, with an over-large head. William 'Lord Haw

Haw' Joyce was short with sloping shoulders and short arms. The 6 ft 3 in. height and 260 lb weight of Christiaan Lindemanns earned him the nickname of 'King Kong'. The KGB defector Golitsin was squat and powerfully built, being only about 5 ft 5 in. tall but weighing 200 lb, while Gouzenko from the GRU, who was about the same height, was slim and weighed 150 lb. The Polish defector Goleniewski was tall, powerfully built, with piercing blue eyes and a commanding presence, while Burgess was described by a friend as 'like a worn-out Pan'.[2] The MI6 traitor Charles Ellis was short – 'a horrible little man', according to one colleague. Donald Maclean was tall, slim, and good-looking. The West German traitor Hans Joachim Tiedge who defected to East Germany in 1985 weighed 19 stone, being grossly obese, as was the FBI traitor Richard Miller, who weighed 17 stone. On the other hand, Vassall was slight and slim. And so the contrasts could be continued.

Women traitors have been similarly diverse in build. 'Sonia' was slim and feminine, but Juliet Poyntz, a well-educated American who joined Soviet intelligence in 1934 and went to Moscow for training before returning to recruit agents in the USA, was somewhat masculine, tall, and heavily built. Hede Massing, a former actress, was also tall but beautiful in a Nordic way. Elizabeth Bentley was plump and sharp-nosed, while Judith Coplon was petite.

It can safely be said, then, that traitors come in all shapes and sizes. Body build would not seem to be a factor in their make-up except perhaps in instances where a physical shortcoming or deformity might contribute to a feeling of resentment against the unfairness of life and an unconscious requirement for some kind of revenge.

The temperaments of traitors seem to be just as variable. Witnesses testify that Klugmann was a most pleasant, kind, and charming person.[3] Herbert Norman was said to have warm humanity, expressed in his sympathy for the underdog.[4] Pontecorvo certainly had charm in abundance, as did Driberg, and not only for other homosexuals. Philby had charm for women; but his one-time colleague, Malcolm Muggeridge, a perceptive observer, considered him unstable and recognized a quality of violence in his character, his stutter and the convulsive clenching and unclenching of his hand being manifestations of it.[5] To the less observant who did not know him so well, Philby appeared 'suave, self-possessed, gracious, charming and erudite, maintaining the strong cloak of secrecy that was appropriate to his position'.[6] The superficiality of Philby's charm was expressed by the joy with which he announced to friends at a cocktail party the demise of his ailing wife, when he had heard of it by telephone: 'You must all drink to my great news. Aileen's dead!'[7] Such ruthlessness was a regular feature of Philby's secret life in which he sent many people to their death – yet, like some murderers, he was squeamish about cruelty to animals.[8]

Several of Blunt's close acquaintances have described him to me as spiteful, vindictive, and with a terrible temper when angered or frustrated. When I alluded publicly to his friend Sir Dennis Proctor, without naming him, as a source of secret information for Guy Burgess, Blunt telephoned him to say he would recognize himself. According to Sir Edward Playfair, a mutual friend who told me that this showed a cruel streak in Blunt's nature, Proctor was not pleased to be reminded of 'his difficulties with the authorities'. It was this vindictive streak which led MI5 and the Cabinet Office to fear, before Blunt's public exposure, that he might leave an unpleasant testament after 1972, when he was diagnosed as having cancer and feared he might be near death. Many have remarked on Blunt's charm, but he displayed it selectively and was a social snob, perhaps because he was a distant relation of the Queen Mother. He was also an intellectual snob and seems to have been widely disliked for his intellectual arrogance, holding those whom he considered lesser mortals in contempt. He is said to have been 'sad' on admitting to a friend that he might have sent 'some – not many' British agents to their death.

Burgess was aggressively uncouth, slovenly, and dirty; he liked to shock with sheer effrontery, to draw attention to himself.[9] He had sufficient self-control, however, to curb his behaviour when he knew he was in danger. An outrageous temperament may enhance a traitor's cover, and Burgess and Driberg both engendered the question, How could a person with such flagrantly dissolute habits possibly have functioned as a spy? Maclean, on the other hand, was reserved and highly professional, when sober, with deep concern for his diplomatic career, though prone to uncontrollable outbursts of violence when drunk, as his friend Cyril Connolly has described.[10] Even after his defection, with his career ruined, so inflated was Maclean's ego that he regarded himself as a 'diplomat and statesman'.[11]

Among more recent traitors, Bettaney of MI5 was described by colleagues as intelligent, articulate, and an agreeable and entertaining companion with a somewhat bizarre sense of humour. His FBI counterpart, Richard Miller, on the other hand, was described as bumbling, slovenly, dangerously absent-minded, and a fantasizer who imagined himself as a James Bond.[12]

The temperament of the women involved in treachery is just as variable. Hede Massing had charm, while Judith Coplon was fiery and unpleasantly aggressive. 'Sonia' had charm for men but was ruthless, curt, and disliked by some of the women who knew her. Maclean's wife, Melinda, who tricked MI5 into accepting her total innocence before she herself defected to Russia, was described to me by an MI5 officer as being 'a breathless, convincing sort of person, with an aura of sincerity. The officers who dealt with her were charmed by her and thought she was a poor betrayed little woman.' This view is supported by Eleanor Philby's account of Melinda's successful efforts to woo Philby away from her: 'She was putting on her brave-little-woman act and I could see that Kim was falling heavily for it.'

Though many more men have had access to secrets, the number of women who have been in a position to betray their country must run into many thousands. There are women officers in all secret services, female civil servants in the secret departments of all governments, and women in almost all secret sections of the armed forces. Yet very few indeed are known to have become traitors. Are they simply more loyal by virtue of their femininity? I would hazard a guess that they are. Those of my acquaintance certainly seem to be more tight-lipped than men when bound by requirements of secrecy. Women who worked in the wartime decoding establishment at Bletchley, for example, still decline to talk about it, even though a great deal has been freely published. Considering the number of women who are personal assistants or secretaries to men dealing with matters of the highest secrecy, it is remarkable how few have been indiscreet. In my long experience men are much likelier sources of 'leaks', if only because it boosts their ego to be seen to be 'in the know' – a peacock vanity which most women seem able to resist.

The records also suggest that women are far less vulnerable to the temptation of money and less susceptible to blackmail. They have the advantage of relative immunity to homosexual blackmail in that little social stigma attaches to lesbianism. Women are not, however, without the quality of ruthlessness, as the behaviour of some women terrorists has demonstrated.

A particular aspect of temperament which may well be of significance for the counter-espionage officer is the 'loner syndrome', the introverted condition expressing itself by social withdrawal and brooding in solitude. Loners who make friends only with difficulty may be both more susceptible to clever recruiters who curry their company and also inclined to do their bidding to retain the association and to become very dependent on their case officers. Harry Gold, the American KGB courier, was such a 'target' with few emotional ties and a total lack of success with women. Professor Hambleton was also of a retiring nature, though with some female conquests. Whittaker Chambers was essentially a loner, while Fuchs was described by a Harwell friend as 'an ascetic theoretic'. The Security Commission described Bettaney's life-style as 'somewhat withdrawn and isolated', and it considered that Prime's general inability to make friends had contributed to his feeling of inadequacy and to his sexual problems.

It is possible that some traitors who are naturally extrovert and gregarious choose to lead a lonely life because they fear that friends might be too perceptive. I regard it as more than coincidental that Hollis was a rowdy, party-going 'bottle-man' at Oxford and a socialite in Shanghai, then became withdrawn and remained that way.

True temperament can, of course, be effectively concealed through acting ability, and there is no doubt that many traitors have had this in extraordinary measure. When Blunt was discussing how he had led a double life with his elder brother, Wilfrid, after his public exposure in 1979, he said: 'You must admit, I'm a very good actor', as indeed he was.[13] Lord Rothschild admits to having been completely hoodwinked by Blunt over many years. He was so sure that Blunt had 'high moral and ethical principles' that he would have 'put his hand in the fire' for him.[14] The unexposed traitor, especially the spy, is an actor who is permanently on stage, except for those occasions when he is with his controller; although he begins as an amateur he needs to become highly professional. Richard Sorge was able to conceal his fanatical dedication to Soviet Communism behind a façade of German and Nazi patriotism. Klaus Fuchs described how, by what he called 'controlled schizophrenia', he developed two sides to his nature: his real personality, dedicated to Marxist philosophy and Communism, which he could display naturally in his underground Communist life, and his 'cover personality', which he presented to non-Communist friends.

When Philby was penetrating the Anglo-German Fellowship, before the Second World War, he convinced friends of his sympathy with Nazism so effectively that some still believe that he was really flirting with it. Later he fooled his colleagues in intelligence, including his chief, even when there was strong evidence against him. His performance at a press conference following his 'clearance' in Parliament was sparkling. The GRU defector Ismail Akhmedov has testified to Philby's mastery of the art of deception, recording that he was debriefed by him over several weeks in Istanbul without sensing anything untoward. Philby was 'all smiles and courtesy' while trying to discover how many Soviet secrets Akhmedov had already betrayed to the Turks and the names of any GRU comrades still in the Soviet Union whose loyalty was in doubt and who might be ripe for liquidation.[15] Even when befuddled with drink Philby never betrayed his secret life.[16] Philby's traitorous associate Charles Ellis fooled his wartime MI6 colleagues so completely that even when he had confessed some of them refused to believe it.[17] Some former MI5 officers still cannot bring themselves to believe that Sir Roger Hollis was a Soviet agent in spite of the weight of evidence against him, though their number is declining.

Some traitors have more natural acting ability than others. Leo Abse MP believed that Driberg could have 'played the part of a spy with superb skill', while George Blake's ability has been put on record by Sean Bourke, the Irishman who 'sprang' him out of prison and organized his escape to Moscow. Bourke joined him there and wrote later: 'I was deeply impressed by Blake's charm, good manners and humanitarian concern for the well-being of his fellow-men. . . . But when we arrived in Moscow, he very quickly began to show himself for what he really was – a ruthless traitor. . . . It had been an elaborate and calculated pose with a long-term objective.'[18] Blake's wife was to claim that she had never really been married to him because he had turned out to be someone quite unknown to her.

A secretary who serves a traitor in his normal job for a long period may be even better placed than a wife to detect suspicious peculiarities of behaviour. A young Canadian woman who was secretary to Maclean in Washington remains astonished by his secret life.[19]

Traitorous women have been equally good at counterfeiting their true nature. Judith Coplon displayed great acting ability in court when concealing her normally abrasive personality to play the demure girl being harassed by the FBI for meeting a Russian, with whom she professed to be deeply in love. When suddenly exposed as a fraud, however, her true self took command.[20] When the normally perceptive diplomat Malcolm MacDonald was told that one of his staff in the British High Commission, Kathleen Willsher, had been working treacherously for the Russians, he declared: 'I'll stake my life on the integrity of that. woman.' The German spy Maria Knuth had a good start because she had been a professional actress, as had Hede Massing. 'Sonia' had only the example of Sorge and the benefit of brief training in Moscow but she was so effective in playing the ordinary housewife and mother that neither her lodgers nor her neighbours saw much amiss.[21]

Acting ability must be bolstered by cunning, which most successful traitors display. Blunt is probably the type specimen of choice because of his cool behaviour during the most critical time for any traitor: his interrogation by counter-intelligence officers when he was under suspicion. On eleven occasions before his final exposure in 1963 he managed to lie his way through questioning and he had been so confident of doing so that he had repudiated a KGB order to defect. Philby was not so effective during his grilling but did well enough to survive. Ellis, on the other hand, was broken.

While acting ability implies a capacity to delude others, it would seem that traitors have a more than usual capability to deceive themselves. Everyone probably has some capacity for self-delusion, which often expresses itself as explanation or justification for rash or reprehensible behaviour, and it is not surprising that pro-Soviet traitors have an above-average share of it. Communism is a system depending on self-delusion; its exponents continue to believe in its efficacy after seventy years have shown it to be a failure for the 'masses', for whom it was allegedly intended, producing neither prosperity nor happiness for them. So those infected with Communism are to a considerable extent conditioned to self-delusion when they become traitors. Georges Pâques, for instance, seems genuinely to have believed that he was acting in France's long-term interests by assisting the KGB. Arne Treholt and others have put forward a similar argument. Hambleton claimed that his motive for helping the KGB was 'to preserve peace', while Richard Miller, the traitorous FBI agent, insisted that he was making a freelance effort to penetrate Russian intelligence. Those Soviet supporters who persist in claiming that wartime spies like the Cambridge ring were only helping an ally are similarly deluding themselves by ignoring the fact that the traitors were recruited and operating before Russia was forced into the conflict.

Some traitors have fantasized – to boost his ego Harry Gold invented a wife and family and described them to friends – but I can find no evidence of pathological delusion or any other serious mental condition as being responsible for treachery. As for normal intelligence, it would seem to be no reliable guide to loyalty, since the brilliant, the stupid, and the in-betweens can all become traitors. The Intelligence Quotients of various traitors are not available but those of Blunt, Klugmann, Burgess, Dexter White, Alger Hiss, and many others were assuredly high and were no deterrent to treachery. Some of those who sold secrets for money, apparently confident that they would not be caught, were far from stupid.

Some people have been trapped into treachery through general weakness of character when threatened with blackmail, which they could have avoided by reporting the circumstances to their superiors; but it has to be admitted that to continue as a traitor, with the possible penalties always looming, requires courage of a kind. Some have displayed it to an extraordinary degree, especially when continuing to operate knowing that they were under suspicion. Others have displayed it after exposure and conviction – William Joyce, for example, being very courageous when sentenced to death.

In sum, it would seem that except for the 'loner syndrome' the general facets of personality offer little reliable guidance to the type of individual likely to be or to become engaged in treachery. There are, however, additional characteristics that most people would reasonably regard as defects of personality, which may be more profitable for study by those in counter-intelligence.

CHAPTER SIXTEEN

Defects of Character

By reason of the frailty of our nature we cannot always stand upright.

The Book of Common Prayer

To perform his task and to survive, the traitor has to be fundamentally dishonest. In addition to being a good actor he must be a consummate liar – a serious defect of character by any standards. Alger Hiss lied so brazenly about his Communist past and his relation with Soviet agents that he was jailed for perjury. Herbert Norman also lied about his Communism, which now has to be admitted even by his most fervent friends. According to Anthony Blunt's brother, Wilfrid: 'One could not believe a word Guy Burgess said.' John Cairncross continued to lie when marginally exposed in 1979 and refused to make any public admission when fully unmasked in 1981.[1] Hambleton lied consistently in court, insisting that he had been a double agent for France and Canada, until dramatically caught out by the Attorney-General, when he suddenly decided to plead guilty.

The life of deception, often including a degree of self-deception, permits the traitor to parade two further character defects which the case records show to be common among traitors: arrogance and vanity.

Arrogance, the making of exalted assumptions, is particularly characteristic of the ideological traitor and is one of his most dangerous traits, both to his country and to himself. It seems to arise, at least partly, from the Soviet attitude that pro-Soviet Communists have an absolute right to do anything that is necessary to further the cause, any interference with that duty being unwarranted and even outrageous. This is built into the indoctrination and training of Soviet agents. Those who are truly ideological also partake of the basic arrogance of all politicians and activists, who believe themselves especially qualified to arrange the lives of other people.

Philby's extreme arrogance was reflected by his many years of cold-blooded treachery, which had the ultimate purpose of subjecting his compatriots to the murderous domination of Stalin – because he, the great Kim, had become convinced that it would be best for them. Similarly Blunt displayed arrogance when he explained privately to his brother, Wilfrid, that 'he betrayed his country because he believed it to be in its best interests' – a remark which Wilfrid interpreted as meaning that his treachery 'would therefore have seemed to him the act of a patriot'.[2] On leaving MI5 Blunt could not resist displaying his arrogance further by stating to his distinguished colleague Colonel 'Tar' Robertson: 'Well, it's given me great pleasure to pass on the names of every MI5 officer to the Russians' – a list which included Robertson's own name.[3]

Klaus Fuchs demonstrated his arrogance by privately taking the decision that all atomic-bomb secrets, British and American, should be given to the Russians and by immediately taking steps to provide all those he could muster. The young American cipher clerk Tyler Kent behaved similarly in deciding to show secret cables to a Fascist spy because he personally disapproved of arrangements that Churchill was making with Roosevelt without the knowledge of Congress or the American people. The CIA renegade Philip Agee decided to expose everything about the CIA because he claimed to disapprove of its methods. Arne Treholt seems to have convinced himself that he was specially equipped to go beyond the usual diplomatic boundaries and consort with the KGB to bring about improvements in East–West relations. The MI5 officer Michael Bettaney was another example of an arrogant young man taking matters into his own hands and deciding to contact the KGB.

John Amery, the pro-Nazi traitor, was so arrogant that, involved in a car accident for which he was responsible, he produced a revolver when the other driver remonstrated with him and announced that nothing could be done if the police came because he was not an ordinary person. It would perhaps be a kindness to attribute to understandable arrogance the attempts by the late Duke of Windsor to promote official British friendship with Hitler and his regime, attempts regarded by some as coming close to treachery, especially after war was in progress.[4]

Like arrogance, vanity is an expression of egotism, the tendency to overvalue personal qualities and achievements. The egotism of Blunt and other members of the Cambridge ring was evident at an early age. Professor G. M. Wickens, who knew several of the Cambridge traitors, wrote to me about Blunt's 'egotism, cleverness and superficiality' and judged that 'Philby, Burgess, Maclean, Hollis and company' must have had 'an almost insane arrogance and an unnatural delight in deception for its own sake, to say nothing of their morbid hatred of their own background while living well on its comforts'.[5] Wickens has recalled hearing Blunt say that 'he fully expected to be Supreme Commissar for Art' after the Communist revolution in Britain. He has also described Leo Long, the traitor recruited by Blunt, as vain and a social climber. 'Blunt played him like a fish, taking advantage of his vanity and his tendency towards social climbing.'[6] In his interview with the *Sunday Times* when publicly exposed, Long explained his treachery as 'the arrogance of a young man. I thought I was helping a wider cause.'[7]

When Fuchs arrived in Wakefield Prison he refused to do the intelligence tests along with the other new prisoners, and made a point of reading everything written about himself in the newspapers. He was convinced that he had prevented a third world war by enabling the Russians to secure atomic bombs quickly and thus create a balance of power. Otherwise, he told fellow prisoner Donald Hume, the Americans would have attacked the Soviet Union.[8] Later, after his arrest while working at the Harwell atomic establishment, he was to claim: 'I was Harwell.'

The high spot in Hambleton's life, if his claim is true, was when he dined with Andropov, then the KGB chief, on a clandestine visit to Moscow. Hambleton was generally so vain that he could not stop boasting about his achievements, a weakness which contributed to his exposure.

It is reasonable to assume that when people agree to become traitors they believe that they are unlikely to be caught, as others before them have been, and this is a further expression of vanity. The sentence of thirty-five years' imprisonment imposed on Geoffrey Prime did not deter Michael Bettaney from contacting the KGB within a few months. Some who have spied for relatively small sums of money, and without any initial blackmail pressure, agreed to do so not long after the forty-two year sentence imposed on George Blake.

Vanity makes anyone more susceptible to flattery, and Soviet re-cruiters and case officers have exploited it, pandering to an agent's self-satisfaction at being chosen for secret work. The type specimen in this respect is the Swedish agent Wennerstrom, who was given the deliberately grandiose code-name 'Eagle'. For many traitors, becoming a spy has been a form of self-aggrandizement. Max Elitcher, a prosecution witness at the Rosenberg trial, said that he had found it immensely flattering when Rosenberg had tried to recruit him. Case officers have exaggerated their own rank – say, from colonel to general – to increase the self-importance of an agent, while inflated honorary ranks in the KGB and GRU have regularly been awarded to agents to keep them keen and active, as happened with Wennerstrom and Philby.

An extreme expression of arrogance is what is commonly called 'brass nerve', which many traitors have displayed. Driberg tried to infiltrate Buckingham Palace, with some success, through his association with Lord Mountbatten and may have exploited his connection with MI5 for this purpose. Blunt showed extraordinary nerve and coolness when stopped by the police during the wartime blackout, carrying a briefcase full of secret documents which he was taking to his Russian masters for photocopying. As he eventually told his interrogators, with some glee, he had managed to bamboozle the policeman, though the encounter had been a close call. Even more insolently bold was Blunt's determination to bring a libel action against anyone who revealed that he had been a Soviet agent. He was fortified in this by his knowledge that MI5 would refuse to provide any witness against him and also by his certainty that no court would disbelieve him because of who he was. He failed because the Attorney-General, Sir Michael Havers, realizing the long-term political implications if he succeeded, induced the Prime Minister to announce Blunt's guilt.

The West German MP and paid Soviet agent Alfred Frenzel was also bold enough to sue and lucky enough to win, after a politician had issued a pamphlet correctly revealing that he had been a Communist with a discreditable past and had never flown with the RAF as he was claiming. After the MI6 officer Colonel Charles Ellis had confessed his espionage for the Nazis to MI5, he had the impudence, in 1976, to write a 'historical note' extolling the virtues of secrecy in the book *A Man Called Intrepid*! Philby's behaviour at the press conference he called after his false clearance in Parliament is a classic instance of brass nerve.

The facility to lie and to deceive is also an attribute of the common criminal, as are ruthlessness and lack of conscience. So it is not unfair to wonder if the individual who is prepared to steal secrets would jib at stealing anything else, and whether the man who knowingly betrays people to their death, aware that he is an accessory to murder, would recoil from other crimes. In short, is there any connection between a general dishonest and criminal streak and the propensity to become a traitor? And does a life of treacherous duplicity lubricate the slope to other forms of criminality, perhaps by coarsening the attitude to lesser crimes?

The person addicted to petty theft when opportunity arises may regard a secret document as just another saleable object. Or he may betray his country and his colleagues in other ways. Scott-Ford, who betrayed convoy secrets to German agents, had previously been discharged from the Royal Navy for forgery. Bossard, who sold aviation secrets, had a petty criminal record, which he did not reveal when recruited for secret work. Houghton, the Portland spy, had developed a taste for easy money through dishonest dealing on the black market in Poland. The American naval spy John Walker had joined the Navy as a teenager because he was given the option of prosecution or national service after being arrested for breaking into an office.

Tom Driberg, later Lord Bradwell, had close association with criminals and was alleged by one of them to have taken a share of £2 million stolen from Heathrow Airport in 1976. Driberg had given alibi evidence, almost certainly false, which had previously cleared a friend called Stephen Raymond of a murder case. Later, after Raymond had masterminded the airport theft, he claimed that Driberg was given £25,000 as a reward for past favours.[9] Driberg also had associations with the murderous gangster twins the Krays, and was involved in other criminal cases.

Andrew Daulton Lee, who was the courier for Christopher Boyce, was a drug-pusher.

Another criminal whose treachery brought him to international notice in a most sensational way was the former Israeli soldier Morde-chai Louk, who defected to the Egyptians in 1961 while on manoeuvres near the Egyptian border. Louk, who had a criminal record, owed money, and had woman trouble, was also unstable; he tried to commit suicide after the Egyptians jailed him as a suspect spy. When the Egyptians offered him his freedom in return for becoming an agent in European countries, he readily accepted. After making anti-Israeli broadcasts he was given a Moroccan identity and, because he spoke several languages, was sent to various European countries to curry favour with Israelis and find out anything of interest to Egyptian intelligence. While based in Italy he began to demand more money from his masters, threatening to sell his knowledge of Egypt's activities unless they increased his pay. The Egyptians responded in November 1974 by kidnapping Louk in Rome, where they put him into a specially constructed crate for air-shipment to Cairo as 'diplomatic luggage'. Italian intelligence had learned what was in progress, and intercepted the crate at Fiumicino Airport. They found Louk jammed in the crate in a jack-knife position, roped to a stool, with his hands tied behind him, gagged, and half-drugged. Examination of the crate showed that it had been used for similar purposes before.

The story made world headlines. Louk offered to confess his trea-chery to the Israelis if the Italians would return him home. They did, and he was sentenced to thirteen years in jail.[10]

Many would find it hard to believe that a 'gentleman' like Blunt would stoop so low as to be an ordinary criminal, but for many there is no crime lower than treason, and Blunt literally stooped low when he left Buckingham Palace to collect Russian money left for Burgess in a hiding-place on a common in the East End of London. There is

Above: Julius and Ethel Rosenberg, separated by the wire screening of the US Marshal's van, following their conviction on charges of transmitting atomic secrets to Russia. They died in the electric chair in 1953 (*UPI/Bettmann Newsphotos*)

Below: Harold ('Kim') Philby (left) was forced to resign from MI6 when his connection with the Burgess and Maclean defection was suspected. George Blake (right), an MI6 officer who betrayed many projects and many agents to their deaths, was sentenced to forty-two years' imprisonment but escaped to Moscow in 1966 (*Mail Newspapers*)

Left: Michael Bettaney on trial in 1984, facing ten charges brought under the Official Secrets Act. He was sentenced to twenty-three years' imprisonment (*Mail Newspapers*)

Right: Geoffrey Prime, a gaunt, broken man, following his arrest in 1982. His treachery at GCHQ was exposed only as a result of his arrest on sex charges (*Press Association*)

Above: A bizarre web of blackmail, exposed by French secret servicemen, left Bernard Boursicot (left) devastated by the discovery that the 'mother' of his child, Shi Pei Pu was actually a man (*Agency France Press*)

Below left: Oleg Gordievsky, a KGB officer recruited as a penetration agent by MI6 and who became KGB chief in London. His defection in 1985 was followed by the expulsion of twenty-five Russian spies from Britain (*Associated Press*)

Below right: The senior KGB officer, Vitaly Yurchenko, at a news conference in 1985. After defecting voluntarily to the CIA he claimed to have been kidnapped and returned to Russia (*UPI/Bettmann Newsphotos*)

The signatures or handwriting of 1) Sir Roger Casement, 2) Klaus Fuchs, 3) Anthony Blunt, 4) Guy Burgess, 5) Kim Philby, 6) Richard Sorge, 7) Leo Long, 8) Igor Gouzenko, 9) Donald Maclean, 10) 'Sonia', 11) Alger Hiss, 12) Jurgen Kuczynski, 13) Lee Harvey Oswald, 14) John Vassall, 15) Michael Bettaney and 16) Whittaker Chambers

While graphologists contend that handwriting offers clues to personality traits, this selection would seem to be too varied to permit any generalizations to be drawn about any connection between handwriting and a tendency to commit treachery

Above: Hans Joachim Tiedge, the West German counter-intelligence officer, seen here in carnival costume. An alcoholic burdened by debt, he defected to East Germany in 1985 (*Stern*)

Below: Christopher Boyce, who betrayed crucial satellite secrets, is led away by federal police to be tried on charges related to his escape from prison in 1980 (*UPI/Bettmann Newsphotos*)

'Sonia' Beurton in old age with her formerly British husband, Len. Both had been professional Soviet agents before defecting to East Germany in 1950

John Walker (left, in handcuffs) was the master of a spy ring which sold naval secrets to the Russians, literally by the sackful. His brother Arthur (below) was a member of the ring along with John's son, Michael. All were convicted and received heavy sentences in 1986 (*UPI/Bettmann Newsphotos/Popperfoto*)

Anthony Blunt claimed to have broken his connection with the KGB when he left MI5 to become Surveyor of the King's pictures in 1945. He remained in occasional contact, however, and was publicly exposed in 1979 having secretly confessed his treachery fifteen years earlier (*UPI/Bettmann Newsphotos*)

also some evidence of behaviour of a kind close to forgery. It has been suggested by the art historian Christopher Wright that Blunt, under whom he studied, may have connived at the authentication of paintings knowing them to be fakes.[11] One of these paintings, a Poussin, belonged to Blunt's MI5 chief, Guy Liddell. In that context the friendship between the art dealer Tomas Harris, who found paintings, and Blunt, who authenticated them, when they were then sold to galleries at high prices, may be significant.[12] Once an individual is committed to treachery, knowing it to be criminal, it may be easier to turn to other crimes – especially when money has been provided, as it usually has. The Cambridge ring traitor John Cairncross, who had fled to Italy after MI5 discovered a minor part of his treachery, was arrested on the Swiss border in June 1982 with a suitcase containing 52 million lire (then £22,000) which he was trying to smuggle into Switzerland. By then aged seventy, he was sentenced to a year in prison and fined £43,000.[13]

Some recent CIA cases have revealed the extent to which secret agencies may attract people with criminal tendencies, and perhaps the extent to which the secret service encourages such inclinations. Two former officers of the CIA, Edwin Wilson and Frank Terpil, had particularly vicious careers after leaving the service; they were responsible for running weapons for terrorist purposes to the Gadafi regime in Libya and its one-time ally, Idi Amin of Uganda. They illegally supplied Libya with more than 20 tons of an American plastic explosive called C4, which has been used and continues to be used in small bombs; a few ounces are sufficient to destroy a large airplane.

Terpil, whom I met once in a different connection, supplied some of the guns found in the Libyan Embassy in London following the shooting of a British policewoman, and is believed to have supplied the timing mechanism for a bomb placed at Amin's behest on a small Kenyan plane parked on Entebbe Airport. The bomb killed all four people aboard, including Bruce McKenzie, a former Kenyan Minister and a personal friend of mine.[14] Both Terpil and Wilson, who are regarded by the CIA as renegades to the service if not as full-blooded traitors to their country, made large fortunes and, while Terpil is still at large after jumping bail, granted all too readily, Wilson is currently serving fifty-two years' imprisonment in the USA. Their training may have induced an element of ruthlessness but any secret service will inevitably attract a few people who are already 'rotten apples'.

While several traitors, such as Philby, Blake, Blunt, and recently the American, Edward Howard, have been accessories to murder, as already described, few have actually committed it. Of those who did, the one likely to be best remembered historically is Lee Harvey Oswald, the assassin of President Kennedy. Apart from this monstrous act of treason, Oswald, a former member of the prestigious Marine Corps, had made himself a traitor by defecting to the Soviet Union, having committed himself to the Communist cause. Following his return to the USA he came to regard assassination as a heroic act.

Psychologists aver that many criminals behave as they do because they have a chip on the shoulder making them resentful of society and driving them to secure revenge on it. Such a 'chip' is certainly characteristic of many traitors, often being associated with inferiority feelings.

The alienation of homosexuals, which has already been discussed, is an example of a 'chip' originating from a psychological problem. 'Chips' can also arise out of physical problems. Andrew Daulton Lee, for example, was deeply concerned about being so short, having severe acne, and being inadequate with girls. The psychiatrist who examined Prime described him as 'an unhappy and unfulfilled man, a sexual and social misfit whose failures left him with a sense of inferiority and insecurity'. This was exacerbated by frustration caused by set-backs to his career and his inability to accept that his qualifications and performance were the cause. He deeply resented the progress made by others and made no secret of his bitterness, rejecting any personal responsibility for his failings. This inner turmoil is believed to have crystallized as resentment against Western capitalist society as a whole.[15]

John Cairncross's chief in MI6, David Footman, told me that Cairncross had a big chip on his shoulder, probably connected with his strong Scottish accent which even his Soviet controller had regarded as a drawback to promotion. Leo Long was unduly aware of his social inferiority at Cambridge, regarding it as grossly unfair. Bettaney was described by the Security Commission in terms suggesting that he suffered from a considerable sense of inferiority and insecurity. Bettaney was 'acting out a role' to impress those he met, and he was motivated 'by the need to embark on a course of action which would enhance his own self-importance and compensate for his sense of failure both socially and in his job'. Gold saw himself as a solitary victim of social injustice with a pressing need for respect.

Mary Trevor, who knew George Blake in Holland, says it was very noticeable that he regarded himself as being socially unacceptable. He seems to have been well aware that his colleagues disliked him. So taking revenge on them may have been a factor in his treachery. A former MI6 colleague has told me that Blake was especially resentful at being posted to Korea when he had hoped to be based in London: 'he arrived in Korea with a chip on his shoulder . . . with a feeling that he had been pitchforked, half-trained into the Korean situation'.[16] His resentment may have been due to the wider opportunities in London for assisting the Soviets.

Farce attended the attempt of Corporal James Wood, a record clerk in a signals unit in Germany, to hand military secrets to the Russians in 1963 as a result of deep resentment at failing to secure a posting he desired. Carrying a bundle of secret documents late at night, he knocked on the door of a house he believed to be occupied by the local Soviet commander. It happened to be the home of the British liaison officer to the Soviet mission, a major, who, dressed in his pyjamas, chased and caught him. Wood was sentenced to twelve years in prison, later reduced because of the circumstances.

The treacherous FBI agent Richard Miller had been the butt of his colleagues' jokes because of his incompetence. Alfred Frenzel, the West German traitor MP, felt so insecure and so in need of praise that he invented false wartime exploits to boost his ego. The KGB defector Vladimir Petrov who had been the victim of petty jealousies in the Soviet Embassy in Canberra, vowed: 'I'll fix them all. I'll write a true story if it's the last thing I do!'[17]

Feelings of inferiority and alienation frequently arise from a sense of failure. Wennerstrom's treachery was linked with his disappointment at lack of promotion. As he explained later: 'I had been passed over in the appointment to wing chief. . . . In such a situation one feels one has been slighted . . . one is out of the game and made an exception of. One no longer has any influence.' Determined to be successful as an agent, he found that 'here was something calculated to increase my prestige'.[18] More recently a Soviet Air Force captain attempted to defect from a station in Siberia, exposing himself to grave danger, purely out of resentment against his commanding officer, who disliked him and had told him he would never be promoted if he could prevent it. Questioning indicated that the officer had no ideological objections to the Soviet regime or any other motives. There have been many instances of successful defections from the Soviet Union by people who resented the behaviour of their superiors and of the privileged bureaucracy there – the *nomenklatura* – as will be described in Chapter 20.

Understandably, the deepest resentment of all is generated by dismissal, and the danger of dismissing secret-service officers or retiring them prematurely has been underlined by some recent American cases. Edward Howard was dismissed from the CIA in June 1983, when a trainee in his early thirties. Fifteen months later he started giving the KGB information stored in his mind, his treachery being exposed by the short-term defector Yurchenko. Howard then escaped arrest and fled to Moscow, where he appeared on television in September 1986 doing his best to denounce the CIA at the time when the

American journalist Nicholas Daniloff was being accused of being a CIA spy.[19]

The resentment danger was very much in the mind of the chief of West German counter-intelligence when wondering what to do about his important subordinate Hans Joachim Tiedge, who was known to be an alcoholic, a depressive, and seriously in debt. When asked to explain why Tiedge had not been removed he argued that it would have created a greater risk. He had a point, but Tiedge defected anyway and his chief was required to resign.[20]

According to relatives, Hollis, the future head of MI5 was deeply disappointed and resentful at being deprived of what looked like a promising career in the British American Tobacco Company when he was dismissed, in his early thirties, after contracting tuberculosis in China. When Philip Agee left the CIA because of personal and financial problems he expressed his admiration for it in his resignation letter but has since voiced his resentment at the failure of his career by doing all in his power to denigrate his old service.[21]

The Israeli nuclear technician Vanunu, who treacherously sold his country's atomic secrets to a British newspaper, was burning with resentment at having been dismissed for instability.

Admiral Stansfield Turner, the former CIA chief, deals with the danger of dismissing intelligence officers in his *Secrecy and Democracy*. He records how he was 'reprimanded' by a 'senior British official' for enforcing the retirement of a large number of CIA officers who in his opinion were below standard. He has responded by criticizing the British secret-service chiefs for failing to 'clean house'.

Those with personalities warped by 'chips' could reasonably be called misfits of society. Their susceptibility to recruitment to treachery has been stressed not only by Western security authorities, like the British Security Commission, but by the KGB. At a major conference of KGB officers attended by Mikhail Gorbachov, in Moscow in May 1986, the KGB chief Viktor Chebrikov specifically warned that Western intelligence services were trying to subvert the state by suborning 'social misfits'.[22]

To summarize, there can be little doubt that any record of criminality, however far back, should be a bar to employment in a secret agency, which should always be given the benefit of any doubt, irrespective of possible unfairness to an applicant. Counter-intelligence officers in search of possible traitors or concerned with preventing the employment of potential traitors would be wise to take note of features like undue arrogance or vanity. More importantly, they should look for evidence of chips on the shoulder, and especially of excessive professional disappointment or smouldering animosity to superiors which can be subsumed under the single factor of resentment.

CHAPTER SEVENTEEN

Drink and Drugs

... to Guy Burgess ... I leave a keg of whiskey, the sweet deceiver.

W. H. Auden and Louis MacNeice,
Last Will and Testament (1937)

Personality defects of almost every kind can be exacerbated by alcohol, and some which may normally be kept in total check can assert themselves to a dangerous extent under the influence of drink. Alcohol is not a stimulant, as commonly believed, but depresses the nervous system, reducing its general efficiency. The first of the human mental faculties to be affected is the power of judgement, and this influence has exerted considerable effect on the recruitment of some traitors and on the exposure of others.

John Vassall is typical of the many who have been recruited by the Soviets under the influence of drink. He was plied with alcohol until he indulged in homosexual activities with KGB male prostitutes and was later faced by the incriminating photographs. While Vassall was easy prey, because such practices were normal for him, alcohol can be instrumental in forcing latent homosexuality to surface and exposing more difficult subjects to sexual blackmail. Donald Maclean exhibited this weakness and is said to have been compromised homosexually by Burgess when drunk.[1] Alcohol has been a regular factor in 'honey-traps', lowering the victim's resistance.

The Soviet agent Reino Hayhanen was an illegal immigrant living in America under a legend requiring self-effacement but he continually drew attention to himself by fighting noisily with his wife when they were drunk, and was eventually arrested for drunken driving. Drink was a major factor in his defection to the USA following news of his recall to Moscow, and he became a traitor, revealing the identity of the important master-spy Rudolph Abel.[2] One well-established feature of alcohol is the way it intensifies a tendency to violence which otherwise can be held in check. Again, Donald Maclean is an excellent

175

example. Cyril Connolly has recorded how, when drunk, he would punch anyone he did not like; and his repeatedly violent behaviour in Cairo, which to most of his Foreign Office colleagues was alien to his real character, could have led to his exposure had the cause of it been properly investigated. Both Burgess and the elegant Blunt were prone to involvement in violence when drunk – again, their escapades should have laid them open to investigation. Malcolm Muggeridge noted that the Philbys' 'explosiveness' was intensified by alcohol.

Drink can also undermine the security of a traitor simply through loosening his tongue. When Maclean was drunk, not long before his defection, he is alleged to have remarked to his former friend Goronwy Rees: 'You used to be one of us but you ratted.'[3] If Rees was telling the truth when he recounted this – long after Maclean had safely defected – he could have reported it earlier, and Maclean might have been investigated rather more thoroughly and more urgently. The honoured Soviet spy Richard Sorge was a heavy drinker prone to giving parties which developed into drunken orgies, hardly conducive to good conspiratorial practice. This habit seems to have been responsible for an uncharacteristic act of carelessness which led to his arrest by Japanese counter-intelligence and to his eventual execution. Aino Kuusinen, who served as a Comintern and GRU agent in Japan, was distressed to find Sorge 'lying on a sofa, half-seas over with the remains of a bottle of whiskey beside him – he had evidently dispensed with a glass'.[4] Sorge came near to killing himself when driving his motorcycle at high speed while intoxicated.[5]

While the ambience of social drinking is often an advantage to recruiters of traitors, the public bar being a regular hunting-ground, alcohol can pose serious danger to the traitor's cover. The type specimen of the traitor exposed through alcohol has to be Oleg Lyalin, the KGB officer who had been recruited by MI5 and was working bravely in London as an agent-in-place, the most difficult type of spy to acquire. He might have continued his operations on his return to Moscow, but this possibility collapsed when he drank too much and was arrested by the police on a drink-driving charge, after an evening in the West End with his girl-friend. MI5 realized that he would be expelled from the KGB after being sent home in disgrace, so he was encouraged to defect physically, and this ended his value as a spy.[6]

Addiction to alcohol may also have contributed to the 'insane risks' taken by the valuable GRU officer Lieutenant-Colonel Pyotr Popov, who spied for the CIA, and to his eventual arrest and execution.[7] Indeed, a study of the general habits of traitors makes one wonder why more of them were not detected earlier in their treacherous careers. Burgess, whose drunkenness had already been put on official record by Lord Selborne to keep him out of the SOE staff in Cairo,

176

would return to duty at the Foreign Office in London 'as tight as a tick'.[8] His appalling drinking habits in Washington have been recorded by Wilfred Mann, who noted that as a result he insulted many influential Americans and made enemies when his function was to make friends.[9] A 'drink problem' is often evidence of an unstable temperament. Burgess was never able to free himself from the addiction, which may have contributed to the diabetes that helped to kill him in Moscow, at the age of fifty-two. The actress Coral Browne recorded that he was drunk when he stumbled into her dressing-room in a Moscow theatre.[10]

There are, on the other hand, instances of traitors who were habitual heavy drinkers and did not seem to be adversely affected. Blunt was a heavy gin drinker and regular party-goer, but Lord Rothschild, a close friend over many years, cannot remember having seen him the worse for it.[11] Alcohol may have been a contributory factor to his dangerous compulsion to go in search of casual homosexual adventures.

Some traitors may not be consciously aware that their drinking is a means of escape from otherwise intolerable pressures, but there can be no doubt from case records that others knowingly resort to alcohol to secure some forgetfulness from their tensions and plight, particularly when they have reason to believe that they have fallen under suspicion. Maclean's appalling behaviour in Cairo, which brought about his recall to London, occurred after he had been warned that his code-name and some of his activities had been deciphered from intercepted KGB messages. After he had allegedly been 'dried out' he was drunk on the night before his return to work at the Foreign Office.[1] Harry Gold sought relief from his double life in 'extended bouts of heavy drinking'.[12] Philby was frequently drunk, as his wife and several friends have testified; when his father died he drank himself senseless, indicating that it was a way of alleviating intolerable pressures.[13]

Regarding secret servicemen who became traitors, there is such a common need among secret service officers for alcohol as a crutch that one is left wondering if the renegades drank to secure relief from anxiety or whether their heavy drinking was symptomatic of an unstable nature which had made them susceptible to treachery. Surely the most outrageous example of peculiar behaviour by a high official in a Western counter-intelligence department is that of Hans Joachim Tiedge, who served in the West German Office for the Protection of the Constitution and defected from Cologne, where he was based, to East German intelligence in August 1985. He was a habitual drunkard, heavily in debt, inflicted by severe depression, and grossly overweight. Yet his department was responsible for countering espionage and subversion from the East, and he also had knowledge of counter-intelligence operations inside East Germany. The facts so far revealed would make it seem that he fled to escape from his debts, his inability to cope with his children after his wife's death, and fear of losing his post through his alcoholism. Whatever the reason for his flight, he has assuredly told Soviet-bloc intelligence officers all he knew, including the names of Western agents. Too little is on public record to form a judgement on how much Tiedge's treachery derived from his innate nature, and how much was the result of the effects of secret-service life upon it.[14]

A history of drunkenness has been no bar to entry into the most secret departments of Whitehall, as evidenced by Maclean and Burgess in the Foreign Office, Philby in MI6, Hollis, Bettaney, and many others in MI5. Yet when consumed in even moderate amounts alcohol can loosen tongues and induce those who are required to keep their profession secret to reveal it and increase the risk of prying and recruitment attempts.

Some of the worst American traitors have been drunkards. Edward Howard was fired from the CIA when it was discovered that he had a drink and drugs problem shortly before he was due to leave for Moscow. Alcohol addiction was a major factor in the defection of Hans Joachim Tiedge, in 1985. My type specimen of a secret service officer with a drink problem, however, has to be the Briton Michael Bettaney. This aspect of his behaviour has been carefully studied by the Security Commission. In its report on Bettaney, the first forthright statement about alcoholism in public servants, the Commission stated that his 'more extravagant idiosyncrasies of behaviour seem only to have been manifested when he was heavily under the influence of drink'. Apparently, when the police found him drunk and incapable in a London street, he cried: 'You can't arrest me, I'm from MI5!' or words to that effect. The fact that he was often drunk and behaved unacceptably at office parties raised little alarm before his conviction on the drink charge, when it was realized that he was vulnerable and could become a security risk, though little effective action was taken even then. The likeliest explanation of his heavy drinking having caused little concern in MI5 is that it was all too common there, as had happened with Philby in MI6 and Maclean at the Foreign Office.

The Security Commission understandably considered that Bettaney's MI5 chiefs paid too little attention to this sign of his instability. 'The ethos of the Security Service in the past has tended to be insufficiently alert to the potential security risks of excessive drinking among members of the Service,' it commented.[15]

MI5 has not been alone among counter-intelligence agencies in this respect. The West German Chancellor, Helmut Kohl, also found it 'completely inexplicable' that Tiedge had been allowed to continue in

178

his highly sensitive counter-intelligence post when he was well known as an alcoholic suffering from depression, who sometimes turned up for work unshaven and smelling of drink. In my experience of Whitehall I have found it equally inexplicable that permanent secretaries in charge of highly secret departments and some chiefs of staff have continued in office when known to be near-alcoholics.

West German intelligence, at least, seems to have learned from its errors. In December 1986 it was announced that a senior civil servant, Jurgen Westphal, had been arrested before he could hand over any important secrets to East German intelligence which had recruited him. He had been put under precautionary surveillance when it had been discovered that he had a serious drink problem, was in debt, and, like Tiedge, was suffering from depression. He was followed to Vienna where he was seen to meet an East German agent who offered him regular payment.[16]

Drink can also be a security problem among civilians with industrial access to secrets, and it was a factor in the espionage activities of the American traitor Christopher Boyce. The ultra-secret area at the satellite-servicing plant – the so-called 'black vault' – in which Boyce and a few others worked was used as a private drinking den. There was even a marijuana plant growing there![17]

Equally incredible is the case of Ruby Louise Schuler, the secretary to the president of an important Californian company involved with the Minuteman ballistic missile nuclear deterrent system. This woman, who was such a serious alcoholic that she died from its complications, was in the habit of taking her friend, James D. Harper, an electronic engineer, into the secret factory at night and during weekends, where they spent profitable hours photographing highly classified documents, which were later sold to Polish intelligence, acting on behalf of the KGB. The damage inflicted on Western defence by affording the Soviets 'a unique look at future ballistic missile defence programmes' was so great that in May 1984 Harper was sentenced to life imprisonment with the recommendation that he should never be paroled.[18]

When the KGB ordered Guy Burgess to defect along with Maclean they feared that if he was interrogated he would break easily because he was not only dependent on alcohol but was taking drugs. Since then drugs have become a much more potent factor in the security equation because of their widespread availability and the tendency of young people to use them, partly to be 'trendy' but also perhaps to escape from current uncertainties. They played a particularly important role in the very serious treachery committed by Boyce and Lee.

Boyce became addicted to marijuana in his teens, while Lee deliberately set out at the age of eighteen to make quick riches by becoming a pedlar of heroin and other hard drugs, to which he himself became strongly addicted. Through their friendship Boyce then became addicted to cocaine. During one of their drug sessions Boyce, who had turned against nationalism and patriotism because of the Vietnam War, suggested that they should sell the secrets to which he had access. Lee scoffed at the proposal at first but, being in trouble with the police over his drug-pushing, he could not resist the easy money. He became Boyce's courier for stolen secret documents and cipher cards which enabled the Russians to unscramble highly secret messages passing between the 'black vault' and the CIA on telephone and teletype machines and to tap into American satellites. In return, Boyce picked up large sums of money from the Soviet Embassy in Mexico City and used much of it to finance his drugs business.[19]

The Soviets are currently very aware of the effect of drugs, on teenagers in particular, in creating 'the necessary attitude of chaos, idleness and worthlessness' which can make people susceptible to re-education by Communism, and on soldiers in reducing their will to fight.[20] While there is no suggestion that the Soviets are supporting the influx of drugs into Western society, they seem to believe that it is assisting their general effort to undermine it.

The British security authorities are equally aware of the additional problem which drugs pose for them. Applicants for the secret services are now required to state that they do not take drugs when they complete their positive vetting forms. One young officer has already been required to leave MI5 for making a false statement in that regard.

If, as the FBI adage runs, sex is usually present somewhere in the equation of treachery, then it would seem that drink is often there too, and the two may be complementary. At long last there is an awareness in the British secret services and, I believe, in the CIA of the importance of heavy drinking as a symptom of secret internal pressures, perhaps with causes in need of investigation, and of possible susceptibility to external pressures which might be applied by an adversary.

CHAPTER EIGHTEEN

Spetsnaz Traitors

... they come not in single spies but in battalions.
Shakespeare

Scores of KGB and GRU agents have been expelled from various Western countries in the last few years. In 1983 forty-seven were expelled from France, eighteen from Bangladesh, and eighteen from Iran; in 1985 thirty-one from the UK; and four more from France in 1986, with many others from several different countries. Twenty-five are under notice of expulsion from the United Nations in New York at the time of writing, plus a further fifty-five from the USA itself. The officially stated reason for these expulsions is that the offenders were engaged in activities not consistent with their diplomatic status. This is generally interpreted by the media and the public as meaning that they had been 'spying' – the clandestine process of obtaining secrets in which all nations indulge, given the opportunity. In fact many of these offenders were engaged in activities of a much more insidious and offensive nature: subversion on behalf of the Soviet commando forces, the so-called *Spetsnaz* troops, which could be used in an invasion of Europe and for attacks on targets in Britain and the USA.[1]

These activities included the regular reconnaissance of key targets earmarked for elimination in advance of a major Soviet assault on NATO, such as command and control posts, nuclear storage depots, power supplies, and communication facilities. *Spetsnaz* targets also include key personnel listed for assassination, such as military and political leaders responsible for taking nuclear decisions; so GRU headquarters responsible for the *Spetsnaz* forces require reconnaissance of the places where such people are likely to be in a military emergency.[2]

Reconnaissance of most targets requires continuous updating, because of unforeseeable changes. There are obvious limitations on the extent to which it can be carried out, even in open societies, by Soviet 'legals', such as so-called diplomats, and 'illegals', sleeper agents living under deep cover. Many of those who have been expelled and many

181

more still in position have therefore been engaged in the recruitment of traitors prepared to assist in this reconnaissance and to give active support to the *Spetsnaz* forces in advance of their assault and during it.

I have secured official information about *Spetsnaz* forces and activities on their behalf, and what I state is not exaggerated. Those who find it difficult to believe that any Briton would be prepared to assist an alien power in taking over his own country should recall that at the beginning of the Second World War hundreds of Fascists and pro-Fascists were taken into custody because there was reason to believe that some of them would assist the Nazis. There are many more pro-Soviets and other revolutionaries now than there were pro-Fascists then.

It should also be remembered that in the early stages of the Second World War, and when Britain was at Hitler's mercy after the débâcle of Dunkirk, thousands of British Communists were slavishly following the party line dictated by Moscow and actively working to secure Britain's defeat by Germany, as a step towards revolution and the ending of 'imperialism'. After Stalin's pact with Hitler the British Communist Party instructed its members to take no part in the war effort, including work in factories, or even in air-raid precautions. Western Communist parties had halted their anti-Nazi campaigns when Stalin signed his friendship pact with Hitler – projected as Stalin's supreme effort to prevent an imperialist war – and actively wanted Hitler to defeat Britain. This would have meant a Nazi occupation of the British Isles with all that meant for the Jews, Communist refugees, and others on the Nazi death lists; but that did not matter if it was the party line ordered by Moscow. Only when Russia was attacked by Germany did the war suddenly became 'just'.

A few centuries previously many prominent Britons had favoured the Spanish conquest of their native land in the interest of preserving their Catholic faith. Devotion to Soviet-style Communism requires similar commitment.

A great deal of information about *Spetsnaz* forces and activities on their behalf has been provided by Soviet defectors. The first to supply details was Oleg Lyalin in 1971, though Gouzenko had provided information about GRU plans for contingency military action in Canada and the USA in 1945. Gouzenko told the Canadian Royal Commission that 'the Soviet government was trying to establish a fifth column in Canada', using a phrase first applied to 'sleeping' traitors in the Spanish Civil War, and the Commission referred to the Canadians involved as 'fifth columnists' in its report.[3] In the course of Operation Foot, the handling of Oleg Lyalin and the subsequent expulsion of 105 Soviet nationals in 1971, the defector produced documentary evidence, including maps, of *Spetsnaz* plans to blow up the ballistic missile warning system at Fylingdales in Yorkshire and bombers on airfields. Many of the 105 'diplomats' and 'trade officials' had been concerned with *Spetsnaz* planning operations. The involvement of British traitors as auxiliaries was not revealed at the time of the Lyalin defection and has rarely been mentioned since, mainly because of MI5 and Foreign Office objections.

Lyalin was a KGB officer and knew nothing about the activities of his GRU colleagues, who, being military, were more closely involved with the *Spetsnaz* forces. Oleg Gordievsky, the KGB mission chief in London who defected in 1985, has provided more up-to-date information about *Spetsnaz* targets in Britain and West Germany, including detailed plans for the assassination of political and military leaders. Much of this remains secret, but among his information was the surprising disclosure that KGB agents kept a round-the-clock watch on Downing Street over a long period between 1981 and 1983 on orders from Andropov. The purpose was to see if American emissaries went there for very late-night secret talks, because the KGB allegedly had some indications that the USA, with Britain's agreement, might be planning to attack the Soviet Union. The KGB had simply misread Reagan's new-look tough stand. While the watch was not necessarily for assassination purposes, it indicated the capability of the KGB to keep surreptitious surveillance on the Prime Minister's residence.[4]

Among the sparse information prised by the CIA from Yurchenko was the fact that his last department had been responsible for planning the deployment of KGB personnel and their agents in the early stages of a war, confirming Lyalin's evidence that the KGB supports the GRU in *Spetsnaz*-type operations.

Much more has been learned from defectors directly from the GRU, like Viktor Suvorov, who are passing on their first-hand knowledge in lectures to NATO forces. In addition to targets already mentioned, the *Spetsnaz* hit-list includes radar warning systems against aircraft and missiles, command and control posts, intelligence centres like those of GCHQ, military headquarters, including those with BBC and Post Office communication facilities, and civilian targets such as the London Underground, which could be flooded to increase the general chaos. A *Spetsnaz* assault on Britain would not necessarily be followed by an invasion by Soviet forces. Its more likely purpose would be the short-term elimination of those British facilities which are essential for the quick reinforcement of American and British forces in Europe, where the main Soviet thrust could be expected.

The Soviet military command must also try to discover how much the British and NATO counter-subversion forces know about Soviet *Spetsnaz* activities and planning. This is a further function of KGB and GRU officers and their agents.

Spetsnaz units practise landing on beaches simulating those of Britain and Western Europe, including Sweden. They are trained in entering a country by parachute or landing-craft and even to jump off fast railway trains safely. They train regularly on large-scale models of their specific targets – said to include Greenham Common – using mock-ups of British, American, and French nuclear weapons, on which they practise planting demolition charges.[5] According to Suvorov, whose statements have been accepted by British defence intelligence, their training includes fights with vicious guard-dogs of the type they might encounter in action against defended targets, while criminals who have been condemned to death are used as 'gladiators' in training fights with *Spetsnaz* personnel selected for specially dangerous missions. Some have had real combat experience in the seizure of Prague's main airport immediately prior to the invasion of Czechoslovakia, and in Afghanistan. They regularly practise operations on neutral Swedish territory. When called out to action stations they never know whether it is for exercise or for real combat.[6]

The Soviet military authorities do not use the term 'subversion' but include it, under the heading 'diversion', along with sabotage and terrorism. So all the information compiled from the study of successful and unsuccessful terrorist assassinations is carefully assessed by *Spetsnaz* instructors, and the lessons are incorporated in training programmes. As Lyalin, Suvorov, and other defectors have confirmed, the assassination of leaders like the US President, the British Prime Minister, and others with personal responsibility for decisions on the use of nuclear weapons is so important in *Spetsnaz* planning that *Spetsnaz* troops have mock-ups of Camp David, 10 Downing Street, and other locations where target leaders might be when an assassination attempt is required, and they practise assaults on them.

It may be difficult for Westerners to believe that in the 1980s the Soviets would stoop to the assassination of key figures in advance of a military assault. However, the routine training of *Spetsnaz* forces and their agents to that murderous end has been fully authenticated by defence intelligence and by military events. *Spetsnaz* forces were involved in the murder of the Afghan leader Hafizullah Amin and of many of his staff in Kabul in December 1979.

The reality of the assassination threat was demonstrated by the immediate reaction to the attempts on the lives of President Reagan and Margaret Thatcher. Chiefs of staff were immediately alerted in case the attempts might be the first moves in a Soviet assault. In the USA, after President Reagan was shot, defensive forces were automatically put on alert. It is a cynical commentary on international diplomacy that, while Western leaders like President Reagan and Margaret Thatcher, have been fully informed that they are top priority targets on the *Spetsnaz* hit-list, they are required to talk with Mikhail Gorbachov, who is party to their predicament.

For many years the GRU has infiltrated *Spetsnaz* officers and NCOs into Britain, Western Europe and the USA in the guise of diplomats, defence attachés, officials of Aeroflot, the various timber, agricultural, and other trade delegations, as seamen and even as athletes. According to Suvorov, some of the Soviet athletes taking part in the recent Olympic Games, including some women, were *Spetsnaz* troops.[7] As all *Spetsnaz* personnel are required to be fluent in the languages of their target countries so that they can pose as nationals there, they are regularly rotated between those countries and their home bases. There is a continuous flow of them in and out – a situation which would be impossible in an Iron Curtain country but is only too easy in the democracies. It is officially estimated, for example, that some 50,000 Soviet seamen come ashore in Britain annually and they can move wherever they like; this privilege is afforded to all foreign merchant seamen, though it is fully appreciated that the Soviet merchant marine (*Morflot*) is virtually part of the Red Navy. Many are believed to have hired cars and driven them to familiarize themselves with routes from what would be their landing points to their targets. The *Spetsnaz* planners have also been taking advantage of a ludicrous situation at Ullapool in Scotland where until mid-1986 there were no officials to check on Soviet fishermen landing or to ensure that they returned to their ships.[8]

The Defence Intelligence department of the Ministry of Defence has established that as a result of these activities, secretly conducted over many years, the Soviets have established a deeply embedded infrastructure in which various legitimate Soviet facilities are closely linked, geographically, with key targets.[9] Nevertheless, while Soviet *Spetsnaz* personnel have been able to exploit British, European, and American freedoms to this extraordinary extent, they remain dependent, like ordinary spies, on locally recruited agents who are more easily able to carry out the regular reconnaissance needed to update information about targets and can provide assistance during an actual assault. This was demonstrated by the extent to which home-grown *Spetsnaz* auxiliaries were in position, with their various tasks fully rehearsed, before the Soviet advances into Hungary, Czechoslovakia, and Afghanistan and were instrumental in the rapid capture of key targets.

The British *Spetsnaz* agents are organized in subversive units of varying sizes, depending on their locality and tasks. They are trained to spring into action, on GRU instructions from Moscow, to serve the regular *Spetsnaz* troops, who would be landed by air or sea, probably from merchant ships, wearing civilian clothes or even British uniforms.

185

They would act as guides and drivers, providing vehicles in some cases, in the way that local people assisted Allied invasion forces in Europe in the Second World War. Some would be required to stage operations to deceive and divert the defences, to create chaos and terror at a time of mounting tension, and to promote mass exodus from cities to block routes required for the movement of British and American reinforcements to Europe. Others would be expected to take part in the assault on certain targets which could be as 'soft' as selected electricity pylons supplying computer centres, for example.

The various installations of GCHQ and its partner the American NSA, which has several facilities in Britain, would be among the prime *Spetsnaz* targets because of the crucial importance of intelligence communications in the run-up to a military emergency. It was the potential influence of left-wing extremists in unions involved with GCHQ staff which was responsible for the British government's decision to de-unionize GCHQ in 1984. Nobody thought that membership of a union increased the possibility that any man or woman might become a traitor, though the unions claimed this to be the implication. What the government feared was that, in the future, control of GCHQ unions might fall into the hands of extremist leaders who would be prepared to serve the general Soviet purpose by disrupting essential communications in an emergency, on instructions from Moscow, or even to secure the infiltration of communications centres to assist *Spetsnaz* operations. There has never been any suggestion that those currently in control of any of the unions concerned would be party to such treachery, but many defectors have stressed the importance which the Soviet military authorities attach to the disruptive capabilities of the British unions.

The value of local agents in providing information about the immediate whereabouts of leaders listed for assassination is obvious. The bombing of the Prime Minister and other government ministers in the hotel in Brighton in 1984 demonstrated the effectiveness of weapons with long-term fuses planted by local agents. According to the Czech defector Major-General Jan Sejna, whose information has been corroborated by later defectors, the Politburo and its satellite counterparts have lists of enemies to be liquidated after a successful invasion or coup, just as Hitler did, and local traitors would be expected to assist in the search for them.[10]

Each subversion unit has a 'squirt' radio transmitter sending messages on punched tape at such speed that its location is difficult to pin-point by the usual methods of radio-goniometry, especially since it tends to be moved about. The set is normally carefully concealed and used only occasionally to ensure that it is in working order. In 1980 such a set was accidentally dug up by a farmer near Llangollen,

North Wales; MI5 is in no doubt that it belonged to a subversion unit, probably centred on Liverpool to deal with the American base at Burtonwood, among other targets. Investigations revealed that some ten years earlier a party of Russians had booked into a nearby hotel, claiming to be part of a trade delegation. They had ventured out only in the dark, and four of them were among the 105 expelled for subversive activities in 1971. The chances of finding such transmitters are remote, but the unearthing of an almost identical set in Austria, after three Russians had been spotted burying it in woodland, has been described by the former CIA officer William Hood.[11] I understand that others have been found, but their discovery is never announced by the security authorities.

This secret burying of transmitting sets has been a regular feature of Soviet subversion for many years, as the GRU defector Ismail Akhmedov has recorded: 'Exact topographical drawings of the selected sites of the buried sets were prepared and kept on file in Moscow against the day they might be needed in uprisings or guerrilla warfare.'[12] Akhmedov also disclosed that GRU officers serving in target countries, as he himself did, are required to recruit local radio 'hams' if possible to operate transmitters.

By any standard such *Spetsnaz* agents who are UK citizens, certainly including some women, qualify as potential traitors of a particularly monstrous kind – though no doubt the Soviets would call them 'partisans' or 'freedom fighters'. Some indication of how they are recruited has been given by the KGB defector Major Stanislav Levchenko, when describing the work of the KGB's Illegal Service to a US Congress Select Committee: 'Its main activity is recruiting foreigners as agents for sabotage, assassinations and all kinds of things. . . . This department sends its own illegals abroad to sit and wait and recruit individuals who would be ready to blow up a certain bridge or telecommunications system.'[13] Levchenko was one of the many professional intelligence officers trained for infiltration into Britain in time of emergency to report on the state of readiness of the nuclear strike forces there. Other Britons are recruited during goodwill visits to Moscow arranged by trade unions and by Soviet friendship and cultural organizations.

Such traitors have been recruited, in varying numbers, in all the front-line European NATO countries, and the odds are that subversion units are now being set up in Spain. More than 400 subversion units in West Germany are known to the Office for the Protection of the Constitution, the West German counter-subversion organization, and to British military security, based at Rhine Army HQ, Rheindahlen, which has close links with MI5.[14] There are believed to be others in West Germany and elsewhere living under deep cover as illegal sleepers maintaining contact with the home-grown subversion units. It is currently believed in the British Defence Ministry that the *Spetsnaz* threat is aimed more at the Continent than at the UK; but even if that were so, Soviet intentions could be quickly changed. There is no doubt about the capability to inflict great damage on key points in the UK.

In June 1982 a Soviet defector, Anton Sabotka, appeared on television in Canada to describe how he had been infiltrated into that country as a deep-cover illegal to plan the destruction of key oil-refining and pumping stations in the event of conflict and to serve as a link with a KGB sabotage network in North America. It would be most surprising if *Spetsnaz* subversion units have not been set up in the USA to deal with key targets there, especially in view of the easy run enjoyed by GRU and KGB agents posing as officials at the UN in New York. In 1983 the FBI had the names of 23,000 potential saboteurs and terrorists on file, and while the number is currently only about 100 that is entirely due to legal restrictions which have since been imposed on the FBI's activities following civil rights agitation.[15]

What are the motives which could induce men and women to assist an enemy attacking their country? The major spur would seem to be ideology, perhaps coupled with a sense of exerting power. For obvious reasons the security authorities in Britain and West Germany remain silent about those *Spetsnaz*-linked traitors whom they have identified, but for Moscow's purposes they must be completely reliable, and are therefore most likely to be recruited from the ranks of the crypto-Communists. There are many other militant revolutionaries who are prepared to do anything to destroy existing society but they are unlikely to be trusted by the GRU. For the same reason those who might betray their country to an enemy for money are unlikely to be regarded as reliable 'on the night', when total dedication to the tasks allotted would be essential.

Two current factors contribute to the ease with which *Spetsnaz* traitors can be recruited in Britain and Europe – rabid anti-Americanism and anti-militarism, which expresses itself most vocally in the 'peace' campaigns against nuclear weapons. There can be little doubt that the quick neutralization of the United Kingdom as an American reinforcement base for NATO's forces in Europe would end the war in the Soviet Union's favour. If this could be achieved by *Spetsnaz* forces using conventional means, a nuclear 'holocaust' might be prevented. Many who have deluded themselves into believing that Britain is already 'occupied' by the Americans, and that if they were to be expelled all military threat would disappear, seem prepared to accept the risk of permanent occupation by the Red Army, with all that would entail.

Defence intelligence departments of Britain and NATO know that the GRU and KGB have penetrated the various 'peace' movements and would have been derelict in their duty had they not done so. *Spetsnaz* auxiliaries posing as 'peace' campaigners are ideally placed to carry out day-to-day reconnaissance-on-foot of the nuclear bases, for which there is continuous need. The regular assaults on perimeter fences and surreptitious entry into nuclear and other defence establishments provide valuable information about weak points for those who might wish to enter with more serious intent.

The difficulty of using Soviet-bloc agents for this purpose was demonstrated in April 1976 when two Hungarian 'diplomats' were caught taking photographs of the perimeter of the Royal Ordnance Factory at Burghfield, near Reading, which is involved in the maintenance of nuclear weapons. Burghfield is now regularly 'picketed' by 'peace' protesters, many of whom are equipped with cameras ostensibly to take photographs of 'police brutality'.[16] A clear indication of the misuse of the 'peace' movement, in a way from which the Soviets gain advantage, was given by Jon Bloomfield when a member of the Communist Party and of the CND Council. 'Direct action and civil disobedience can spotlight key military installations, such as missile sites, and reveal bunkers and plans which the government wants to keep secret,' he stated in *Marxism Today*.[17] Such bunkers would be prime targets for *Spetsnaz* attack.

The mass of the 'peace' campaigners are motivated by straightforward anti-militarism and anti-Americanism, but many of them are committed to interfere with the movement of nuclear weapons, physically and by attempting to saturate the telephone communications system. If they did so during a military emergency these enthusiastic amateurs might well find themselves being treated as traitors by the defending forces.

The threat from *Spetsnaz* troops and their traitorous auxiliaries has been appreciated by the British and other governments for many years; but they have sought until recently to keep it secret, against the advice of some military chiefs, apparently to avoid public disquiet and questions about counter-measures being taken. The first official expression of the danger – in 1985 – was the military exercise Brave Defender, the biggest to be staged in Britain since the war. Designed to test the defence of key targets against clandestine assault by *Spetsnaz* forces and their British assistants, it involved 65,000 personnel, including 1,000 Americans, and police from many areas. The *Spetsnaz* troops and their agents were played by people from the SAS, the Special Boat Service (SBS), and the Parachute Regiment, and included some women.

The size of this first exercise, which will be followed by others (there will be a *Spetsnaz* component in all future military exercises in Britain), not only revealed the extent of the *Spetsnaz* threat but the vulnerability of open societies to it. No nuclear installations were included in the targets being tested because of fear that anti-nuclear campaigners would seriously interfere with the exercise.

Because of legal restrictions no action can be taken about Britons known to have been recruited for *Spetsnaz* operations until they commit an offence and they are required to avoid doing so. Lists of recruits and suspects are kept as up to date as possible, but the forces available for this work are dangerously limited in all the true democracies. In Britain the responsibility rests with MI5, which is a civilian organization, when the threat posed by the *Spetsnaz* auxiliaries is essentially military. It is intended that at a time of extreme military tension the auxiliaries would be rounded up under emergency powers, as happened with Fascists and enemy aliens at the beginning of the Second World War. Defence chiefs fear that *Spetsnaz* forces, however, could be infiltrated weeks, or even months, in advance of Soviet mobilization.

MI5, which is already over-extended because of its involvement in anti-terrorism as well as in general counter-espionage and security, is responsible for penetrating subversion units, as it is with the IRA. It has nevertheless successfully resisted moves by the Defence Ministry to take over a greater share of the responsibility for anti-*Spetsnaz* operations. The SAS, which would be heavily concerned with military action against *Spetsnaz* incursions and with the quick elimination of *Spetsnaz* traitors – who, according to one former SAS commander, 'would have to be shot' – is an Army regiment yet appears to be subservient in this respect to MI5.[18]

Because of the ruthlessness of the methods which *Spetsnaz* forces are trained to use, the defector Suvorov refers to them as 'terrorist troops'. Those other aspects of terrorism which involve treachery and, to some minds, treason will be considered in Chapter 19.

CHAPTER NINETEEN

Terrorists as Traitors

The Italian Red Brigades, who like to think that they speak
for many or most of their kind, have made it plain that
theirs is a war for the destruction of Western democracy.
Claire Sterling, *The Terror Network*

In the early 1980s an MI5 anti-IRA cell operating in Ulster lost four
of its undercover members, who were shot dead by the IRA in a short
period. Inquiries showed that a woman soldier in an Army office had
had access to the names and duties of the men. She disappeared before
she could be questioned and has not been found. There can be little
doubt that she had been deliberately infiltrated into the headquarters,
being one of several known IRA sympathizers who joined the Army
through the normal recruitment channels. Any person betraying Britons to their deaths in such a way is assuredly a traitor by any
reasonable definition of the word, and so, under British law, were the
terrorists who committed the murders.

According to Britain's most senior lawyer, Lord Chancellor Hailsham, terrorism is the use of terror and criminal violence against a
community or individuals, usually innocent people, to attain a political
end from the government responsible for the safety of those people.[1]
Lord Hailsham has pronounced that terrorism committed in Britain
is legally a form of treason because it amounts to an act of war against
the Queen and her realm. It does not matter whether the terrorists
are British subjects or not, because an alien within the realm owes a
local and temporary allegiance to the local sovereign, so long as he is
there.

Under existing British law, terrorism is theoretically a form of
treason, thus a capital crime. However, the government has no intention of invoking it, because Parliament has specifically voted against
the death penalty for terrorist murder.[2] Like spies and other clandestine operators, terrorists need support in the form of safe accommodation, hiding-places for weapons and explosives, and communication

and escape arrangements; auxiliaries who assist them share the guilt for the casualties and damage which terrorists inflict. In so far as terrorists like the IRA are enemies and declare themselves to be at war, those giving aid and comfort to them, as some politicians do, make themselves look like traitors of a kind.

The concept of the terrorist as a traitor is complicated by the general acceptance of terrorism, in what is now called 'hot' war, as morally justified and laudable – the violent exploits of resistance fighters, like the assassination of the vicious Nazi Heydrich, being even heroic. Since most terrorists claim to be at war with society or some section of it they regard themselves as traitors only if they betray their cause or their comrades. Nevertheless, whatever sophistry they may employ to justify their actions, those who use violence against their fellow citizens for political purposes are certainly treacherous. Where terrorists owe allegiance, as the IRA does in Ulster and on the British mainland, their atrocities are legally and morally an expression of treason, with the perpetrators being traitors to Britain.

Terrorists are at one with the kind of traitor already considered in that they are usually attracted to an ideological faction like the IRA or the Spanish ETA, which began as independence movements. Many, however, are Marxists, too impatient to wait for revolution or aware that it is unlikely to happen. IRA supporters like Bernadette Devlin and Michael Farell make no secret of their belief that the 'struggle' in Northern Ireland is 'an integral part of the working-class movement' and that the IRA is also working for the collapse of the governments of Eire and the UK.[3] The evidence studied by Professor John Norton Moore, chairman of the American Bar Association's Standing Committee on Law and National Security, has convinced him that the increase in terrorism is mainly due to the world-wide expansion of the Marxist–Leninist 'religion'.[4]

In the same way as the IRA and Ulster Loyalist atrocities have religious overtones, there is a religious component to the activities of the various Palestinian organizations, though they are mainly concerned with the recovery of territory. Another, more truly religious motive responsible for an increasing number of deaths mainly in the Middle East, is the Islamic Fundamentalist movement inspired from Iran.

Terrorists who are not Marxists or otherwise religious tend to be alienated students and so-called intellectuals. With some, money is a major factor or becomes one. Ilich Ramirez Sanchez, the terrorist known as 'Carlos', for example, has been paid huge sums for his kidnappings and killings.

Adventure and excitement are certainly factors in attracting the young who can be almost assured of dangerous action. Among these are sadists who believe they will enjoy killing for killing's sake and do so, as the activities of the Baader-Meinhof gang clearly showed. The violence essential to terrorism has special appeal, giving a sense of power and of 'doing something' positive. Those who cannot hope to be creative, lacking talent or opportunity, seek satisfaction in destruction, perhaps convincing themselves they are making a contribution to what may be built on the ruins they have brought about.

Those recruiting terrorists would seem to be appealing to the same type of basic mentality as those inducing people to become traitors. Marxist–Leninists have no ideological problems in embracing violence as a political tool because they are taught to regard non-violence as a 'bourgeois luxury'. Boris Ponomarev, for many years in charge of the Kremlin's active-measures offensive, wrote: 'Violence itself is not an evil. It depends on what its purpose is. In the hands of Socialists it is a progressive force.' There is not a great deal of difference in kind between a Marxist–Leninist like 'Carlos' who kills and one like Philby who knowingly sends people to their death.

The connection between Communist revolution and terrorism and treachery was patently demonstrated by a court action in February 1986 when Peter Jordan, a 61-year-old retired schoolmaster, was jailed for fourteen years for serving as intelligence gatherer for an Irish plot to assassinate a former SAS officer. In an operation similar to those required by *Spetsnaz* forces, Jordan, a Marxist and veteran Communist, had carried out detailed reconnaissance over a period of two years to assist hit-men of the Irish National Liberation Army to eliminate, with bombs or bullets, several prime targets he and his friends had selected. They included three senior generals, the heads of MI5 and MI6, and a senior judge. Jordan's motive was revolutionary hatred of the 'ruling class', and he pleaded guilty after the plot was countered following information received from a traitor or a penetration agent within the conspirators' ranks.[5] The Jordan case, like the Brighton bombing, demonstrated that as with other more conventional forms of treachery terrorists plan most carefully and may subject their targets to surveillance over many months.

While blackmail is not widely used in recruitment, the terrorists' controllers make regular use of it through taking hostages and abusing them to secure publicity and political aims. The blackmail threat of violence is widely used to secure money to finance terrorism. Many Ulster and Irish business men, landowners, and racehorse trainers pay regular protection money to avoid IRA violence.[6]

Like espionage and subversion, terrorism is increasing world-wide. In the ten years ending in 1985, more than 6,000 terrorist incidents were recorded, with some 4,700 dead and more than 9,000 injured. In 1985 there were more than 800 international incidents, a 60 per cent increase over the previous two years.[7] In the first half of 1986 there were about 425 incidents, compared with 352 for 1985, and with more than 1,000 casualties, 318 of them fatal.

There were 42 known terrorist groups in 1978, but by 1985 the number had risen to 125.[8] Currently, the main terrorist thrust is aimed at destabilizing the West. Like the efforts of most spies and subversives, it has the backing and support of the Soviet Union, which rarely, if ever, condemns terrorism. While terror as a deliberate national political policy was promoted by the French revolutionaries, the modern movement stems from its use and further refinement by the Bolsheviks and their successors to subjugate the Soviet and satellite peoples and to 'smash' societies of which they disapprove. It has since been taken up and extended by Muslim radicals and others.

Because terrorism used against other nations furthers Soviet hostility to true democracy it has been adopted by the Soviet leadership as one of its weapons of international ideological warfare. The Soviets were exploiting terrorism abroad as far back as the 1930s, as evidenced by the activities of George Mink, a Russian-born taxi-driver in Philadelphia, who operated as a KGB agent. After training in Moscow he returned to the USA on forged papers in 1936, was involved in political kidnappings there, and went to Spain, where he assisted in the killing of left-wing volunteer fighters regarded as 'untrustworthy' by his Moscow masters.

Since then, through the KGB, the GRU, and the International Department, the Soviets have woven terrorism into the tapestry of their clandestine operations against the West. They have forged close links with the Palestine liberation groups, with Muslim fundamentalists such as those who assassinated President Sadat, with the African National Congress in South Africa, with the Libyan terrorists spurred on by Colonel Gadafi, and with many others, including the IRA. There are special training areas for foreign terrorists in the Soviet Union and in the satellite countries such as Czechoslovakia, Bulgaria, and Cuba.[9] As General Jan Sejna has revealed, the Soviet government decided in 1964 to increase spending on terrorism and set up extra camps for terrorist training.[10]

The murderous German Baader-Meinhof terrorists were directly financed by the KGB through East Berlin in their early days, but the Kremlin is careful now to distance itself by making use of surrogates. It provides them with weapons and leaves them to create chaos among the Soviet Union's political adversaries, to break down their social structures, to undermine their police and security forces by making them seem powerless and incompetent, and to eliminate opposing political leaders by proxy. For this purpose young 'progressively minded' people spotted by KGB talent-scouts are enrolled as students at the so-called Patrice Lumumba Friendship University in Moscow for training in the techniques of subversion and violence – 'Carlos' being one of the university's distinguished sons.[11] Libya, Syria, South Yemen, Iraq, North Korea, Cuba, and Bulgaria all sponsor terrorism, and it is no coincidence that they are Soviet client-states or have strong Soviet connections.

Soviet support of terrorism has such direct military value that it has been a sound investment on that score alone. The IRA ties down thousands of troops which should be committed to national and NATO defence and attacks forces and installations inside the United Kingdom. The French terrorist organization called Action Directe, the Red Army Faction in West Germany, and the Fighting Communist cells in Belgium are all giving the Soviets assistance by attacking NATO installations and personnel with bombs and bullets. They also intimidate and attack politicians and business men involved in the defence industries.

It is significant that terrorists do not strike against the tyrannies of the Soviet Union and its satellites or those in Cuba and Africa.

The similarity between terrorists and more conventional traitors is reflected in the fact that counter-intelligence offers the most effective way of combating both of them. The most successful aspect of counter-intelligence in both cases is the penetration of the opposing forces and their support groups by agents. Specific instances are held tightly secret for obvious reasons, but there have been many cases where terrorist operations have been aborted as a result of inside information.

The USA has invested more than a billion dollars in developing an excellent counter-terrorism capability composed of special units from the various armed forces.[12] At the time of writing, a Bill has been introduced in the US Senate to define terrorism as an act of aggression against the USA, the purpose being to legalize the pursuit of terrorists with military force. If it becomes law it would seem to follow that any American subjects assisting terrorists operating against the USA, its citizens, or its interests could be classed as traitors and treated accordingly. No such law is needed in Britain, where the SAS is already used regularly for that purpose.

Terrorists, like spies and other forms of traitor, must be countered much more effectively than they have been to date. All forms of combating terrorism depend on the political will of the governments involved, and there are welcome signs that some, especially those of the USA and Britain, are prepared to exact a higher price from the individuals and states responsible for outrages which are nothing less than barbaric. The mere knowledge that they will be countered and punished by deadly force is a strong deterrent to terrorists in spite of the existence of a few prepared to undertake suicide missions. The resolute SAS response to the terrorist occupation of the Iranian Embassy in 1980, with the killing of almost all the terrorists, had most salutary results with a long period free from hostage-taking. The success of the Israeli raid on Entebbe Airport, with the killing of all the terrorists and rescue of the hostages, halted the hijacking of Israeli or Israel-bound aircraft. When four Soviet diplomats were seized as hostages by Shi'ites in Beirut in 1985, one being murdered in an attempt to force Moscow to exert pressure on Syria, the KGB acted so resolutely and ruthlessly that the remaining three were quickly released.[13]

Until deterrence and offensive action are accomplished more effectively, the balance of terrorism will remain firmly on the side of the Soviet interest, which it serves so well.

CHAPTER TWENTY

Defectors

What exile from his country ever escaped from himself?
Horace, Odes, Book 2

In current parlance a defector is someone who leaves the country to which he owes allegiance in surreptitious circumstances and usually with secret knowledge which makes him of special interest and value to the country in which he chooses to reside. The term is also sometimes used to denote a national who has been working for an alien power and decides to revert to his true loyalty and admit his past treachery.

Some defectors have already been working clandestinely for the country to which they flee, having previously become traitors to their own country for the kind of reason already discussed. In that early stage, before they flee, they are known as *defectors-in-place*, because they appear to be doing their ordinary jobs. This term is also used by professional intelligence people as a synonym for agent-in-place to mean almost any person operating within his own country as a traitor. But in this chapter the word *defector* will be restricted to someone who physically flees his own country to seek asylum in another.

Though most defectors rationalize the reasons for their flight they are likely to be traitors according to the laws of the country to which they owed allegiance. If they submit to intensive debriefing, as they usually do, they become traitors in most people's eyes if they betray their native country's secrets, however welcome these might be to the recipients. Defectors from the USSR are usually tried in their absence on treason charges and often sentenced to death.

Some, like Deriabin, Ilya Dzhirkvelov, Levchenko, and Suvorov, have emphatically denied being traitors, claiming that they simply exerted a human right available in most civilized countries. They rate Stalin and his successors as being the real traitors to the revolution and to the Russian people. As Akhmedov put it: 'The real fighters for the real cause, the cause of freedom, democracy and human dignity, are the Soviet officers who defected to the West, severed all ties with the Communists and revealed the ugly reality of the Soviet police state.[1] Major Aleksei Myagkov, who defected from the KGB in 1974, reasoned: 'I did not betray my country, I betrayed a regime which is oppressing my country. To defend such a regime is treachery, to fight it, no.'[2]

Most defectors realize that they have no hope of changing the Soviet system from within, and the prospect of making some impact through publicity in the West is a powerful motive with some. Nevertheless, however understandable their reasons, the fact that defectors use surreptitious means to leave their countries is evidence enough that they are aware that what they are doing is treacherous and subject to serious legal penalties if they are caught. Some 1,900 years ago the Roman historian Tacitus wrote: 'Betrayers are hated even by those whom they benefit'[3]; as will be seen, that remains true.

Defectors from the Soviet bloc to the West have been called 'the priceless asset'. As far as the United Kingdom is concerned, and I suspect the USA, too, the compliment is thoroughly deserved. One defector who has been well placed for access in the KGB, the GRU, or the Soviet Foreign Office may contribute more to Western security than a whole new weapons system which has taken years to produce and cost billions.

Some defectors bring valuable documents with them. Gouzenko's copies of GRU telegrams and papers changed the whole attitude of the West towards Communism by exposing how the Soviets' had been undermining wartime allies who had given them sacrificial assistance, by subverting politicians, civil servants, scientists, and others, with a possible 'hot' war in mind. It was Lyalin and Suvorov who opened the eyes of the West's military leaders to the *Spetsnaz* threat. Others even bring valuable equipment, as the Red Air Force pilot Viktor Belenko did when he flew the extremely secret Mig 25 ('Foxbat') fighter to Japan in 1976 and sought asylum in the USA.

Time after time when a long-term traitor has been exposed it has been the result of information provided by a defector, as examples given in this chapter show. Without these leads many of the traitors would have continued their betrayals and might never have been caught. The evidence also demonstrates, without doubt, that if leads provided by defectors had been more resolutely pursued, spies such as Maclean, Philby, Blake, Dexter White, Hiss, and (I believe) Hollis, might have been exposed before they inflicted so much damage. When the defector Walter Krivitsky, who had worked for both the KGB and the GRU, was debriefed in London in 1940, he named sixteen British subjects who were active Soviet agents, eight of them in politics and the trade unions, six in the Civil Service, and two in journalism. It is alleged that these people were quietly neutralized but none was prosecuted or publicly exposed.[4] Gordievsky, the KGB officer who had been a defector-in-place for several years before defecting physically to Britain in 1985, named many more who likewise have escaped exposure so far. (He was unable to give any information about Hollis, never having been privy to it. Details of agents are tightly held in the KGB and the GRU, and Gordievsky, who had been very junior when inquiries into Hollis were active, never had 'need to know'.)

Defectors may also yield evidence enabling KGB and GRU officers to be expelled. Lyalin confirmed the identities of so many of his colleagues who were on espionage and subversion work in Britain that 105 of them were expelled in one batch, with the Kremlin being told that in the event of reprisals a further 200 proven subversive officers were earmarked for similar action. Gordievsky's defection led to the expulsion of thirty-one more. As with Lyalin's 105, they were already known to MI5 but the defections confirmed the details of their activities and provided the 'diplomatic' excuse for their expulsion.

Regrettably, defectors have limited value as court witnesses in the prosecution of traitors. First, security agencies are loath to subject them to cross-examination because they might have to make additional admissions damaging to security. Secondly, there are objections to making a defector recognizable because of the danger of assassination. The reality of this danger, which may sound melodramatic, was revealed by the Lyalin case when the drunk-driving charge against him was quashed because he had undergone plastic surgery to change his appearance.[5] Thirdly, unless defectors have provided documents, their evidence is likely to be ruled out as hearsay; this happened with Josef Frolik's in the case against Will Owen and his allegations against the former Labour minister John Stonehouse. Fourthly, a defence counsel can undermine a defector's credibility simply by pointing out that he is a traitor to his own country probably trying to curry favour with his new country and therefore unreliable.

Apart from the information immediately available from defectors, which is sometimes supported by documents, they can be immensely valuable as advisers in using their stored experience – particularly since some intelligence officers, like Anatoly Golitsin, owed their previous positions partly to their powers of memory recall. Shadrin was of value in instructing on Soviet naval tactics, while Suvorov has been a major source of information not only about *Spetsnaz* forces but the GRU in general. Gordievsky briefed Margaret Thatcher before her meeting with Gorbachov and was later flown to Washington to advise President Reagan on Soviet intentions and negotiating ploys in advance of his summit meeting with Gorbachov in Geneva. Both leaders found his advice most valuable.

Philby and Maclean advised the Kremlin on British problems long after their defection and also assisted the Soviet press agency Novosti with the kind of disinformation it might successfully sow in Britain. Maclean and Burgess were of modest use in enabling the Soviets to interpret or foretell British thinking, soon becoming outdated. Philby is believed to have influenced Andropov in improving the image of the KGB and the quality of its recruits, and Yurchenko claimed that both Philby and Blake were still being used as KGB advisers in the 1980s.

Defectors can be of use in disseminating false information. Burgess and Maclean did this at their Moscow press conference in 1956, and the American, Edward Howard, did likewise on Soviet television in 1986 when supporting the Soviet contention that Daniloff, the American journalist, was a CIA agent. They can also be used as disinformation agents through books written to KGB requirements. MI6 believes that Philby's biography, *My Silent War*, was written at the instigation of Andropov when head of the KGB; and according to Philby's wife he ghosted the inaccurate memoirs eventually published under the name of Gordon Lonsdale.[6]

There is always some doubt about the extent to which defectors can be trusted. Philby, Burgess, and Maclean were held away from Moscow for two years, allegedly being 'dried out' of their alcoholic problems, but really being in custody while being debriefed and while inquiries were made to ensure they had not been 'doubled'. Alexander Foote, the Englishman who had served the Soviet Union most loyally in Switzerland where he had been imprisoned after being detected, was treated as a suspect for more than two years when he finally reached Moscow. He was interrogated almost daily and had to write countless reports as a test of his loyalty in case he might have been 'turned'.

The USA also makes good use of defectors through committees of Congress and the Senate which call them to give evidence and then publish reports, which are commented on by the media. That does not happen in Britain because the Parliamentary Select Committees do not bother with them or are prevented from doing so; this is unfortunate, because the questioning of defectors could do a great deal to educate MPs, many of whom seem to be deluded about the Soviet system and its intentions. Select Committee reports could also make MI5 and MI6 less prone to reject or ignore defector evidence for reasons of professional embarrassment.

All defectors take their expertise with them, and this is especially applicable in the case of scientists. Pontecorvo is the type specimen in this regard. He took to Russia not only an outstanding scientific mind but all his knowledge of making certain materials derived from heavy water and essential for the production of hydrogen bombs.

EXAMPLES OF DEFECTORS

Defector	Date	Parent Country	Main agents exposed
August	1968	Czechoslovakia	Prager, Zbytek
Bentley	1945	USA	Silvermaster and Perlo networks Currie, Dexter White
Chambers	1939	USA	Hiss, Ware, Abt, Witt, and others
Frolik	1969	Czechoslovakia	Zbytek, Owen, Driberg, various British journalists
Golitsin	1961	USSR	Vassall, Philby, the French 'Sapphire' ring, Pâques, Hambleton
Goleniewski	1960	Poland	Houghton, Blake, Felfe
Gouzenko	1945	USSR	Nunn May, Hiss, Rose, Carr, Willsher, Hollis(?), and several others
Hayhancn	1957	USSR	Abel
Howard	1985	USA	Tolkachev, and others
Krivitsky	1937	USSR	John King, and at least thirty others
Nosenko	1964	USSR	Johnson, Vassall

NOTE This sample list shows the extent to which defectors have been the major source of the identities of traitors who might otherwise never have been exposed.

Some defectors are also used as lecturers to security and intelligence agencies, while those from the GRU brief British, American, and other NATO forces on Soviet military intelligence and *Spetsnaz* operations. Others from Soviet-bloc diplomatic and civil services can also render ongoing assistance by revealing the truth about the Politburo's intentions and what really happens behind the Iron Curtain. Arkady Shevchenko, who was personal assistant to Gromyko and later an under-secretary general at the United Nations in New York, has not only shed light on secret aspects of Soviet foreign policy but has also provided new evidence of the power of the KGB through which the Politburo maintains its control over the Soviet people – in addition to confirming the extent to which the whole Soviet way of life is based on a gigantic deception.

As would be expected, nearly all defectors have been men. While a few women, like Elizabeth Bentley and Hede Massing have defected from Communism and the Soviet service while living in the West, very few have physically defected from the Soviet bloc to the West, except for wives who have accompanied their defecting husbands, sometimes reluctantly. In a few instances, as with the Pontecorvos, the wife has defected with her spouse to the USSR and has been party to the secret arrangements, which seem to have been made as conspiratorial as possible to secure maximum propaganda value later. Donald Maclean's wife Melinda fled separately with her small children to join her husband, again in surreptitious circumstances organized by the KGB.

Several women of intelligence interest have defected from the West to the Soviet bloc. But in nearly all cases they have been agents recruited by the Soviets in the West or infiltrated there and who have needed to defect because they were about to be exposed. Recent instances of female secretaries in West German government departments who suddenly fled East fall into this category. My type specimen, however, has to be 'Sonia': Ursula Beurton, the professional GRU agent who fled from Britain to East Germany in 1950. She counts as a defector – and a traitor – only because she had married a Briton to secure British citizenship for espionage purposes. For her part, she never considered herself to be anything but a German dedicated to the Soviet cause.

Defectors come in all shapes and sizes but tend to be older than recruited spies, perhaps because it takes many of them years before they become sufficiently disillusioned, or run into insupportable personal problems, and can summon up the resolve to leave their native land and culture. Also, it is the older defectors who have most to offer. Krivitsky, Levchenko, and Maclean were thirty-eight when they defected; Gordievsky was forty-six; Petrov, forty-seven; Shevchenko, forty-eight; Yurchenko, forty-nine; Bokhan, fifty; Philby, fifty-one. There have nevertheless been notable exceptions. Lee Harvey Oswald, the assassin of President Kennedy, was only twenty when he defected to the USSR. Vasily Matuzok, a junior diplomat in the Soviet Embassy in North Korea, was twenty-one when he 'jumped' (to use the CIA term for defecting). Gouzenko was twenty-six when he defected. Martin and Mitchell were twenty-nine and thirty-one respectively; Deriabin, thirty-three; Lyalin and Edward Howard, thirty-four.

Defectors also originate from many different backgrounds. Levchenko was the son of a Red Army major-general, born among the élite and with no expense spared for his education. Viktor Belenko was a highly professional Soviet Air Force pilot. Matuzok's father was a retired Soviet Air Force colonel, while his mother was a doctor. Shevchenko's father was a doctor, Philby's an internationally known Arabist scholar, while Burgess's was a naval officer. Petrov was born a Siberian peasant. Myagkov's parents were peasants from central Russia. Oswald was a Marine of humble origin; Frolik the illegitimate son of a seamstress.

While some defectors are approached by foreign agents and induced to switch allegiance, others take spontaneous action without having previously committed themselves, except in their own minds. They are known in the 'trade' as 'walk-ins'. As former CIA agent William Hood has said: 'It's the walk-in trade that keeps the shop open.'[7] A very few, like the Soviet pilot Belenko, could be more accurately described as 'fly-ins'.

The type specimen of the walk-in will surely always be Igor Gouzenko, a lieutenant in the GRU who had specialized as a cipher clerk and was working for the GRU chief in the Soviet Embassy in Ottawa. His reasons for defecting and the circumstances, which almost led to his being handed back to the Russians when they began to hunt for him, have already been briefly described and are given in greater detail in his own account.[8] During the month before he defected Gouzenko combed secret files to which he had legitimate access for material which would convince the Canadian authorities of the threat they faced. He earmarked cables and other documents with clear leads to the identities of various Canadian and American traitors. Without these documents it is doubtful that he would have been believed, and post-war history might have been different.[9] A similar but less fortunate walk-in was Konstantin Volkov, who literally walked into the British Consulate-General building in Istanbul in August 1945. He could have been even more productive than Gouzenko had he been accepted more eagerly, for he was senior and well placed inside the KGB. He knew about two Soviet agents in the Foreign Office who were providing copies of telegrams, Maclean almost certainly being one of them, and about five agents in the British secret services, Hollis probably being one of these. Instead, the delay, resulting from Foreign Office dislike and distrust of defectors, permitted Philby to send Volkov to his death.

While walk-ins occasionally make their approach in their home country, it is more usually done when they are serving or visiting abroad, because it is so much safer there. The very important defector Anatoly Golitsin made his approach to the CIA in Helsinki. The Soviet film-script writer Yuri Krotkov, who was used by the KGB to set up blackmail sex traps for foreign diplomats, defected to MI5 in 1963 while visiting London with a Russian literary group. More recent Soviet defectors who made the break while abroad include Oleg Bitov, a writer, and Yurchenko, a KGB officer, who both sought asylum, from Britain and the USA respectively, while visiting Italy. Sergei Bokhan, a deputy director of the GRU in Athens, defected to the USA in May 1985.[10] The Romanian Dr Petre Nicolae, who defected in 1981, walked into the American Consulate in Belgrade but was told that it would be safer if he walked in in Vienna, which he duly did.

The most spectacular spontaneous defection was that staged by Vasily Matuzok, who at the age of twenty-two was so disillusioned with Communism that he decided to risk his life to escape it. On a contrived visit to a village which bisects the border between North and South Korea he ran across, surviving a volley of bullets.[11]

On rare occasions a Soviet-bloc citizen may defect from his own country of his own accord and without outside assistance. When Ilya Dzhirkvelov, a KGB officer operating in Geneva, was recalled to Moscow and told he could not return to Switzerland, even to bring back his wife and daughter, he boarded the first plane back to Geneva, using his diplomatic passport and acting on the hunch that the KGB would not have him under surveillance so soon. He quickly crossed the border into France and made contact with British intelligence. Dr Aleksandr Ushakov made a nine-day hike to freedom from the Soviet Union across the Caucasus Mountains to Turkey.

George Blake provides an instance of a British citizen who defected from his own country in a most spectacular manner with no assistance from the country to which he fled. In 1966 he escaped from Wormwood Scrubs Prison in which he had been incarcerated for six years of a forty-two-year sentence. The only professional help he received was from a former fellow prisoner, an Irishman called Sean Bourke who supplied Blake with a two-way radio system so that final plans for the escape could be agreed, threw a rope-ladder over the prison wall, and spirited the traitor away to a flat in his car. A tape-recording which Bourke made during the escape still exists. In it he and Blake can be heard talking to each other in a previously agreed code – one hilarious part being Lovelace's lines: 'Stone walls do not a prison make nor iron bars a cage.'[12] After springing him from jail Bourke arranged for Blake to be taken out of the country in a van with a secret compartment. Money for this was received from a supporter of CND – apparently the closest link with the KGB that has ever been found. It has been suggested that MI5 and MI6 connived at the escape for some devious purpose but the chaos inside the Home Office when senior officials there heard of it explodes that explanation. The late Lord Mountbatten, who carried out an inquiry into the escape, assured me that it had been made possible by appalling laxity in the prison.

Blake's escape is not unique in the traitors' annals if terrorist traitors are included. Many of these have escaped from prison in Northern Ireland, and some have found their way abroad.

All intelligence agencies are on the look-out for likely defectors and are often alerted to them by people who have already defected. They then make the approach. Their prime objective is to induce the target to become a traitor and, if he is in a position giving access to secrets, to remain there as an agent-in-place so long as he feels safe. The offer is backed by a promise of eventual asylum and rescue in case of sudden emergency. Philby lasted for thirty years before he had to defect, but had fallen under such deep suspicion that he was effective 'in place' for only eleven of those years. Gordievsky would seem to hold the record for survival inside the KGB – allegedly twelve years or more, though this may have been a deliberate exaggeration put about by Western intelligence to make the KGB waste time by backtracking excessively in its assessment of the damage inflicted by him.

While a defection, especially of an important penetration agent, is usually hailed as a victory it often represents an intelligence disaster, for it means that an important source has come to the end of his greatest utility. The defection of Philby to the USSR caused great damage to Anglo-American intelligence relations, yet the Soviets would have much preferred to keep him in place, especially in view of his probable promotion in MI6. Similarly, the defection of Oleg Gordievsky from the KGB to MI6 in 1985 ended what may have been the West's most valuable KGB source.

Many who successfully flee to a foreign country have been working as agents-in-place, and contingency plans are always made for such people in case they have to be brought out in a hurry. The Polish defector Michal Goleniewski had become a spontaneous spy for the CIA by sending letters to American embassies in Europe and was helped to escape when he signalled his danger in 1960. Others have been brought out under more exciting circumstances, the most astonishing of recent years being the 'rescue' of Gordievsky from inside the Soviet Union.

Gordievsky was home on summer leave, having no reason to think that he was under any suspicion by his KGB chiefs when he had left London. An authoritative MI6 source has confirmed to me that 'it suddenly became essential that he should escape to save his life'. Either Gordievsky sensed that he was in imminent danger of being interrogated, or MI6 had learned that the KGB was likely to pounce from some other source. A KGB inquiry into the betrayal of its Norwegian agent Arne Treholt may have been pointing too directly at Gordievsky, who had served in Scandinavia.

With remarkable skill, daring, and a substantial element of luck, the MI6 mission in Moscow arranged for his escape. He was smuggled out concealed in a van with secret compartments. This was the way it had been planned to smuggle out Oleg Penkovsky more than twenty years previously when the KGB arrested the driver, Greville Wynne, and stripped his vehicle. The Soviet authorities were furious when they discovered what had happened, but took no retaliatory action until the British expelled thirty-one Soviet agents in 1985. Gorbachov then ensured that those in the British Embassy believed to be responsible for planning the rescue were among the thirty-one Britons expelled from Moscow. Private satisfaction at Gordievsky's rescue was also a factor in Mrs Thatcher's decision to take no further action.

It is almost standard practice for the Soviet authorities to claim that defectors have been kidnapped by the West, but such strong-arm methods on an unwilling subject have been forbidden for many years – thirty years in the case of MI6 and MI5. The Soviet defectors Oleg Bitov and Vitali Yurchenko both claimed to have been kidnapped and drugged once they decided to return home, but the fact that they sought political asylum while visiting Italy is proof enough that their claims were false. Even if kidnapping were permitted, neither Britain nor the USA would attempt it on the sovereign soil of a NATO ally. Yurchenko had, in fact, been ostensibly working for the CIA as an agent-in-place, and signalled that he wanted to defect while visiting Rome.

Like the motives for becoming a conventional traitor, the reasons for physical defection are varied and often complex. In the case of those who have been operating as agents-in-place, flight always becomes urgent when a spy senses that he is under suspicion, or is told that he is, for the common penalty for such gross treachery in the USSR is death. He may detect that certain kinds of document are being withheld from him, or that he is being baited with doctored documents designed to induce him to contact his controller. Myagkov has described how, after some months of working as a British agent-in-place, he simply sensed that all was not well, and used his next official visit to West Berlin to make a run for it.[13]

With agents serving abroad a sudden recall for 'consultations' at home headquarters is often the warning signal. Blake received such a call when he was safe in Beirut, but it was cleverly masked as a hint that he was being promoted. Strangely, the Soviets have been less sophisticated; and a curt telegram recalling an overseas intelligence officer for 'consultations' has often resulted in quick defection. The Russian diplomat and KGB officer Vladimir Sakharov, who had been working for the CIA in the Middle East, received an order to return to Moscow in 1971 and requested asylum in the USA without delay.

The sudden-recall system is such a well-known symbol of fear in the Soviet intelligence services that it has been used by false defectors to provide themselves with an excuse for seeking defection to the West.[14] A well-meaning colleague told Goleniewski that the KGB had information that there was a 'pig', meaning a traitor, in his organization and, realizing that the 'pig' must be himself, he used the emergency telephone number which the CIA had given him. At a face-to-face meeting with an MI6 officer in Beirut in 1963, Philby was told that a witness to his treachery had come forward. He defected with little delay. More recently Edward Howard, the former CIA officer who had been selling secrets to the Russians, managed to quit the USA and reach Moscow when he learned that the FBI was about to arrest him. Conversely, Martin Winkler, an East German diplomat in Argentina defected to West Germany when Tiedge, who probably knew about him, fled to the East.

Often the first information that a defector-in-place is under a dangerous degree of suspicion is secured by the foreign agency running him. If possible, the defector is warned, and arrangements for his departure are put into quick effect. There may be occasions when a foreign agency running an agent-in-place orders him to defect, perhaps for propaganda purposes. Shevchenko realized that the CIA could have forced him to defect, had it wished.[15] It was pressure from the KGB which prompted both Maclean and Burgess to defect and so avoid interrogations dangerous to other agents.

Many dissidents, who might have remained loyal in spite of misgivings, have defected because they suddenly became fearful of disciplinary action or of their professional future. Akhmedov, who had been loyal, received a sudden recall to Moscow after he had criticized the GRU to colleagues, following receipt of a brutally callous cable informing him that his young wife had died. When he could get no satisfactory explanation of the cause of death he assumed that she had been liquidated, since he knew her to be critical of the regime. So he defected. Reino Hayhanen, the KGB assistant to the senior spy Abel in the USA, was recalled to Moscow 'for a vacation' in April 1957, being required to journey there via France. He knew that his drunkenness had been noted and that he was in for serious trouble, so he defected to the American Embassy in Paris. Though Gouzenko defected mainly because he appreciated the quality of life in free Canada, he also feared that he was being recalled to be reprimanded for an error and would never be allowed out of the country again.

The peremptory power of senior officials is so great in the USSR and the satellite states that incurring their displeasure can lead to severe deterioration of life-style for subordinates. Changes of leadership, with consequent shifts in the power of patronage, can also have profound effects on individual careers. The knowledge or belief that such displeasure has been incurred or that a leadership change will be adverse has induced many Soviet citizens to seek a preferable and less hazardous life elsewhere. This seems to have been the prime motivation for the defection of the KGB officer Vladimir Petrov while serving in the cover position of a Soviet diplomat in Australia. Petrov had been appointed by Beria, to whom he had been loyal, and feared that he would be dismissed – or worse, following Beria's summary execution. More recently several KGB and GRU men, like Sergei Bokhan who defected in Athens, are believed to have feared a new-broom purge of the KGB initiated by Mikhail Gorbachov, who needed to ensure complete loyalty from that secret police and intelligence service.

It may well have been mainly fear for his professional future in the West that drove the Harwell atomic scientist Bruno Pontecorvo and his family to defect to the Soviet Union in the summer of 1950. It was widely believed that no reason for his disappearance was known to the security authorities, but it is now clear that the former Italian had become aware that both the FBI and MI5 had belatedly learned of his Communist connections, which he had repeatedly denied during security checks. The FBI reports had been smothered by Philby, but Pontecorvo may have been warned by the Soviets of his predicament, especially as they were in particular need of his services.

Fear of loss of freedom could also be said to apply to defectors from the IRA who become informers and witnesses in court – the so-called 'super-grasses'. They usually hope to secure in this way some reduction of sentence for their own terrorist crimes.

A prime motive for many defections is genuine revulsion against the Communist system: ideology in reverse. Dr Aleksandr Ushakov, a Soviet professor of Marxism–Leninism, became so disillusioned with that theory that he wrote highly critical books for the Russian underground press and others which were about to be smuggled to the West when the KGB arrested him. Knowing that he faced a twelve-year prison sentence, he escaped while on temporary release and defected to the USA in 1984.[16] The GRU defector Akhmedov describes in his memoirs how much he disagreed with Stalin's leadership and with the dominance of the KGB in all areas of Soviet life.[17] A similar explanation for flight from Communism was offered by the KGB officer Peter Deriabin: 'After a long period of working for the State Security I was convinced that the police mechanism exists not because of acts committed by enemies of the people, but because of the system itself, the way that the Soviet state is organized.'[18] His colleague Major Aleksei Myagkov gave similar reasons for his disillusionment:

> I was not able to come to terms with the Soviet system of inherent violence and inhuman oppression, with the repression and persecution of everyone displeasing the regime, with the absence of democratic freedoms, with the unscrupulous exploitation of the workers for the good of those in authority, with the all-pervasive ideological conditioning directed towards completely fooling Soviet citizens and with the many other injustices with which Soviet society abounds.[19]

The dedicated Soviet agent Ignace Reiss was revolted by Stalin's bloody excesses. He was imprudently brave enough to write an open letter stating: 'He who keeps silent at this hour becomes an accomplice of Stalin and a traitor to the cause of the working class and of Socialism' – for which he was hunted down and murdered.

Levchenko has recorded that after his experience of the KGB's use of deception in Japan and against the Soviet people he realized that the Soviet regime was not working for the good of its citizens: 'The Soviets rely on deception because the Communist ideology and the political system structured on it cannot stand on its merits. . . . I could not fight the Kremlin inside the country as an officer of the KGB – I would have ended up in one of the Siberian concentration camps, or in a mental institution, for the rest of my life.'[20] Shevchenko has given his main reason for defecting as 'the monstrous abuses carried out by the KGB' but he was also disturbed by the depth of the Soviet government's deceit in its dealings with the West, and especially by the cynicism of Gromyko, with whom he was closely connected. He had come to detest the corruption and hypocrisy of the élite – the *nomenklatura* – to which he belonged. Having been indoctrinated to believe that the Soviet Union 'is the most progressive society on earth, peaceful, happy and prosperous. . . I discovered that all power is in the hands of a restricted circle of Party élite, top state functionaries and the KGB'.[21]

Associated with this negative factor is the positive lure of a better life, which seems especially attractive to Soviet citizens, as noted in Chapter 8. Dr Petre Nicolae, who had wholeheartedly adopted Communist ideology when young, said he was 'stunned by the reality of life in a democratic country' when he visited Vienna in 1979. The Americans, Martin, Mitchell, and Oswald, apparently believed that they would find life to be more amenable in the Soviet Union.

A few defectors have rebelled against a specific political event. Ladislav Bittman, a major in the Czech intelligence service, had been a committed Communist but defected to the USA in 1968 after the Soviet invasion of his country. But the main effect of such outrages – of which the Nazi–Soviet pact, the invasion of Finland, and the crushing of the Hungarian revolution are further instances – has been to cause defections from the ranks of foreign Communist parties. Two days after the Nazi–Soviet pact was signed, Whittaker Chambers, the Soviet agent who had already quit the Communist Party, travelled to Washington and reported to the FBI how the US government had been infiltrated by Communists. The writer Arthur Koestler, who had been a Comintern agent, turned violently against Communism, in which he had placed such faith, after the pact shattered his illusions.

The imposition of martial law by the Polish government in December 1981 was the final straw for Dr Zdzislaw Rurarz, Poland's Ambassador to Japan, who had also been a military intelligence officer. Feeling that he 'could no longer represent a regime which denies the fundamental rights of the Polish people', he defected to the USA. For young Matuzok the turning point was the invasion of Afghanistan.[22]

Defection has sometimes offered an escape from intolerable domestic problems, and this seems to have been a major motive for the original defection of Yurchenko, whose marriage, according to a CIA document, was seriously strained, his wife being a qualified engineer with a post in a Moscow planning institute.[23] Money trouble has been another inevitable reason for disappearance, the case of Hans Joachim Tiedge being fresh in public memory. He had personal debts of more than $80,000 and was even borrowing from bar-owners when he defected in 1985 to escape from what he called 'a hopeless situation'. However, this might have been something of a cover if, as suspected, he had long been a Soviet-bloc penetration agent and was forced to flee because he had been betrayed by the KGB defector Gordievsky, or someone similar.

There have been undoubted instances where people have defected from the Soviet Union and from the West to escape criminal proceedings, other than for treachery. But the record is clouded by the fact that the Soviets commonly claim that someone who has fled for ideological reasons is a criminal, as they did with Gouzenko.

Some Russians have defected confident that the information they could supply would be worth large sums, especially to the Americans. Golitsin, for instance, entertained grandiose ideas of a special American intelligence unit with himself as the head and did, in fact, receive much money – about £100,000 from Britain alone, according to an MI5 source. Vitaly Yurchenko has claimed publicly that the CIA offered him a down payment of $1 million for all his information, with regular emoluments worth about $180,000 a year in perpetuity. He is not necessarily to be believed.[24]

Major defectors often provide an additional bonus by touching off damaging reorganizations of the departments from which they came with senior staff being dismissed for incompetence. This is believed to have happened in the GRU following the arrest and prosecution of Penkovsky. Such a shake-up is still in train in the KGB following the defection of Gordievsky and its special circumstances.

The mass expulsion of Soviet agents following the defections of intelligence officers like Lyalin and Gordievsky have far-reaching political effects on East–West relations, with the almost inevitable retaliatory measures and cries of lies and unjustified vilification. When Western traitors defect eastwards, the effects on defence alliances are even more serious. The defection of Maclean, Burgess, Pontecorvo, and later of Philby caused such damage to American confidence in British security that it has never been completely restored – though this was due, in part, to the extent to which MI5 and the Foreign Office deliberately misled the FBI on the Maclean case. These defections, and that of Mrs Maclean, seemed to have been stage-managed by the Soviets to produce the maximum eventual publicity and damage to Anglo-American relations, which has long been a KGB target.

The KGB also sets great professional store by blackguarding the intelligence services of its adversaries and making them look ridiculous. The re-defection from Britain of the defector Oleg Bitov may have been a deliberate operation staged for this purpose. Bitov was a Soviet journalist who defected to Britain in 1983 when supposed to be on a visit to Venice for the *Literary Gazette* but was really substituting for a KGB colonel who had been denied a visa. His mission was to find any information from Italian journalists and others which might be used to implicate the CIA in the attempted assassination of the Pope two years previously. After eleven months in Britain, during which he wrote articles censuring the Soviet system and also travelled freely abroad, he disappeared back to Moscow via the Soviet Embassy in London, claiming that he had been drugged and kidnapped in Venice and held in captivity until he had managed to escape. Bitov was an insecure character, and it is possible that he returned willingly and that the KGB then found it more convenient to use him to blacken the West than to punish him. If Bitov had been a 'plant', the only purpose apparent at that time was to provide evidence to Soviet citizens that the West was a jungle full of MI5 thugs and no fit place for them, as he duly pronounced through press conferences and articles.[25] The episode took on a different significance, however, when Vitali Yurchenko re-defected in 1985 in a way which seemed designed to bring maximum discredit and derision to the CIA.

It is a customary axiom of counter-intelligence agencies that any fake defector is unlikely ever to have had deep access to Soviet intelligence secrets because the Russians could never take the chance that he might really defect. Yurchenko, who was a 49-year-old KGB staff officer with twenty-five years' service and claimed the rank of general-designate, had certainly had such access. Nevertheless, while CIA chiefs maintain that he was genuine, there seems to be a growing conviction among others with inside knowledge, in both the USA and Britain, that he was a deliberate plant by the KGB, who always intended that he should re-defect in a way which would inflict the maximum propaganda and political damage on the USA.

Yurchenko sought political asylum through the American Embassy in Rome on 1 August 1985, having almost certainly served as an agent-in-place for some months. He was flown to the USA the next day. During his debriefings by the CIA he confirmed that he had been trained as a submariner in the Red Navy, and after a spell in naval intelligence had transferred to the KGB in 1960. Through steady promotion he worked in departments responsible for the recruitment of foreign agents and their insertion into Western intelligence agencies. He had been security officer in the Soviet Embassy in Washington from 1975 to 1980, which would have given him further insight into Soviet espionage and subversion activities in the USA. He then became a counter-intelligence chief, selecting agents for service abroad, besides having other highly sensitive duties.[26] CIA checks confirmed Yurchenko's account of his career, but during long debriefings he gave leads to only two American traitors, one of whom, Edward Howard, had already been discharged from the CIA and managed to evade arrest and escape to the Soviet Union. The other was Ronald Pelton, a former officer of the National Security Agency. So it would seem that the KGB could have instructed Yurchenko to 'burn' these two as 'chicken-feed' to establish his own credibility. Yurchenko also provided a long list of American agents of influence – what he referred to as 'trusted sources' – but according to the CIA chief William Casey these were all 'those whom you would have expected'.

Yurchenko also seems to have been responsible for the information, which was probably false, that the KGB was spraying doorknobs and steering-wheels with 'spy-dust' – a harmful chemical powder, possibly carcinogenic, to track the movements of Americans in Moscow and so trace their contacts. When the CIA publicized this the Kremlin was able to dismiss it as an absurd CIA invention.

After Yurchenko eluded his lone CIA 'minder' while visiting a restaurant in the Georgetown district of Washington on the evening of 2 November 1985, he apparently made his own way back to the Soviet compound, half an hour's walk away. This was probably by long-term prior arrangement with the KGB, since there is no evidence that the KGB had been able to bring any pressure to bear on him while he was under CIA control. He had bought a hat on the way to the restaurant, and this is now seen to have been an excuse to make a call to the KGB, in which he used a code-word indicating that he would be returning shortly. The FBI monitored the call, as it does with all calls to the Soviet Embassy, but this meant nothing as they did not know what the code-word signified, and the CIA had not told the FBI about the dinner. During the call Yurchenko had not requested any guarantees. Further, after claiming at a press conference in the Soviet Embassy that he had been abducted on the steps of St Peter's Basilica, drugged, held captive, and generally maltreated by the CIA – which was pictured in the world's press as a bunch of thugs – the KGB were so sure of Yurchenko that they allowed him to return to the US State Department without a Soviet escort. There he repeated his claims and his desire to return to the Soviet Union. His whole demeanour indicated that he had nothing to fear though he must have known that genuine defectors from Soviet intelligence are never forgiven and are usually executed once back in Soviet hands, however contrite they may be. I have been assured that there is no foundation for the comforting belief that Yurchenko is a genuine defector whom the CIA has 'played' back to the KGB to work for the CIA as a defector-in-place.

The timing of Yurchenko's return to the Soviet fold and his totally false claims were also far too convenient. They occurred very shortly before the much-publicized summit meeting between President Reagan and Chairman Gorbachov in Geneva, when it was well known that Reagan proposed to tackle the Russian leader on his weakest point: the Soviet failure to implement human rights as required by the Helsinki accord. Gorbachov was presented with a tailor-made, robust response – that no Americans had any right to criticize the Soviet Union on human rights when they abducted Soviet citizens, drugged and abused them. The timing and nature of a long press conference featuring Yurchenko in Moscow, five days before the Summit, seemed deliberately staged to embarrass Reagan and to make the CIA Director look foolish by claiming that when he met Yurchenko his fly-buttons were undone, with the inevitable staged laughter by the assembled Soviet 'journalists'.

Contrary to newspaper reports, Yurchenko has not been executed (he was paraded in front of journalists in March 1986), or apparently even disgraced.[27] Like Bitov, he is to publish his memoirs about the ninety-three days which he claims to have spent in CIA captivity.[28] They will be essentially for Soviet consumption, to convince the Soviet people that life in the West is an appalling jungle where human rights are violated. If Yurchenko was a plant, the defection of Bitov, an expendable 'asset', might have been a trial run, especially if the KGB could not be sure that a defector would be free to return to the USSR if he wished.

Improvements made since in the CIA's treatment of defectors would seem to confirm that the CIA chiefs believe that Yurchenko was originally genuine. The fact that he has not to date been tried as a traitor indicates some sort of accommodation in return for his services. He may not, however, be out of danger from severe disciplinary action once his value as a propagandist has evaporated.

The greatest danger faced by a would-be defector is that once he has made contact with the other side he may be betrayed and apprehended before he can escape. The type specimen is Konstantin Volkov who tried to defect to Britain in Istanbul in August 1945 but was betrayed by Philby, who immediately warned Moscow and delayed his journey to Istanbul to give the KGB time to seize Volkov and take him back to Russia disguised as a sick official, drugged and bound to a stretcher.

A walk-in who has made no previous arrangements runs the risk that he may be returned to his country of origin if the timing of his attempted defection should be considered inimical to diplomatic relations with the country concerned. This almost happened to Gouzenko, because the Canadian Prime Minister, Mackenzie King, was so fearful of upsetting the Soviet government at a so-called 'crucial' moment. This is less likely to happen today, but it might – with horrific consequences for the would-be defector.

The successful defector still faces serious hazards in his new country, including continuing fear of assassination. To deter defections the KGB has always warned that 'its arm is longer than the traitor's leg'. It has substantiated this with many successful revenge murders, believing that a death sentence *in absentia*, like that passed on Golitsin, Levchenko, and many others, justifies an assassination. In 1937 the American Communist activist and Soviet agent Juliet Poyntz, who had become disillusioned and was proposing to write her memoirs, disappeared under such mysterious circumstances that there can be little doubt that she was kidnapped and killed. She took a telephone call while at her club in New York, put on her coat, left the building, and was never seen again.[29] The American Communist and State Department official Laurence Duggan, named as a recruited Soviet agent by Hede Massing, fell to his death from his office window just before he might have testified and named others. The circumstances recalled the KGB adage: 'Any hack can kill a man: it takes an artist to arrange a natural death.'[30]

Assassination also serves to deter others. When Whittaker Chambers

214

learned of the violent death of Walter Krivitsky in Washington in 1941, he abandoned his efforts to expose his former underground associates at that time.[31]

The probable murder of Krivitsky and the assassination of Ignace Reiss are old examples, but a recent revenge killing shows that the ruthless pursuit of Soviet-bloc traitors continues. This was the assassination of the Bulgarian defector Georgi Markov, who had fled his homeland disgusted by the leadership, one of the most repressive and ruthless in the Communist system. Markov, who worked for the BBC Overseas Service and was scathingly critical of the Bulgarian dictator Zhikov, was killed by means of a poison pellet, believed to have been implanted by a weapon disguised as an umbrella while the victim was standing in a London street in 1978. The method had been tried on another dissident, Vladimir Kostov, a former radio and television star in Bulgaria who had worked for the Bulgarian intelligence service until he defected to France in 1977, when he began to attack the Bulgarian leadership on Radio Free Europe. He was assaulted while leaving the Paris Métro, felt a stab in his back and saw a man hurrying away. He was ill for three days but recovered. Ten days later came the fatal attack on Markov in London, perhaps by the same assassin. Kostov did not have his back X-rayed until he heard about the Markov case. An identical pellet was found, but only a small quantity of the poison had escaped from it. The same kind of attack was made on a Polish dissident in a supermarket in Virginia.

The Romanian Ion Pacepa, who is the highest-ranking Soviet-bloc intelligence officer to defect to the West to date, did so because he was ordered to assassinate Emil Georgescu of Radio Free Europe's Romanian Department. The order had come personally from Ceauşescu, the Romanian dictator whom he had been serving as adviser. Georgescu was stabbed twenty-two times in his Munich home in 1981 but survived.[32]

Assassination is a danger which defectors can still never safely ignore. Frolik claims that there have been two attempts on his life. When Frantisek August recently appeared on television he permitted no clear close-up pictures.[33] The same programme presented evidence that the KGB was using Bulgarian intelligence to track down the important defector Kuzichkin, who is believed to be living in Britain, in order to kill him.

Gouzenko, who died in 1982 aged sixty-three, remained so afraid of assassination that his eight children did not know who their father really was until after his death, the eldest being then nearly forty. When MI5 decided to reinterrogate Gouzenko in a hotel in Toronto in 1972, he insisted on having a friend with him because he feared assassination by the interrogator, who might be 'Elli', a Soviet agent whom he knew to be inside MI5 and whom he had not then identified as Hollis, as he did later. When no witness other than his wife was allowed, Gouzenko took the precaution of assuring the friend that if he fell out of the hotel window it would be because he had been pushed, and that he was certainly not contemplating suicide.[34] Whenever he appeared on television Gouzenko insisted on wearing a bag-mask covering the whole of his face save for his eyes. He told me: 'I remain cautious. Even after thirty-six years I do not consider myself safe from assassination.' Evidence provided by a later defector to Canada suggests that one serious effort to kill him was planned by the Soviets in 1965.[35] His widow believes that she and her family remain vulnerable, and they live under pseudonyms at concealed addresses.

The GRU defector Akhmedov was hunted throughout Turkey for eight years, being protected by the Turkish police. Nikolai Khokhlov, a KGB officer who defected in 1954 after being sent on an assassination mission he felt he could not accomplish, insisted on having windows boarded up whenever he lectured in the USA.

Some defectors have even feared assassination at the hands of the Western intelligence service to which they defected. When Goleniewski fled to the USA from Poland he gave details of a spy inside MI6, who turned out to have the code-name 'Diamond'. After the British had failed to identify 'Diamond' (who it later emerged was Blake) an officer was sent to interrogate the defector further, but Goleniewski was so fearful that the officer might be 'Diamond' himself, come to kill him with a poison spray, that he insisted on being in a separate room. The interrogation was conducted with an interpreter running between two rooms!

There would seem to be little opportunity these days for the revenge assassination of Western traitors behind the Iron Curtain. In any event, physical violence of any form has been barred to British officers and agents since 1956 – nobody being 'licensed to kill'. Assassination was formally prohibited in the CIA in 1973, according to its former chief William Colby, and the practice of murder by the CIA before that has been greatly exaggerated for political purposes, if it ever occurred at all. Lyman Kirkpatrick, in his ten years as Inspector General of the CIA, claimed that he never heard of a single case of murder perpetrated by the agency. The best evidence is that tyrants like Idi Amin, Bokassa, Gadafi, Khomeini, and the Sinn Fein backers of the IRA have survived when they could have been assassinated. During Amin's reign the British Ministry of Defence planned a military operation, with advice from MI6, under the command of the late Marshal of the RAF Lord Cameron. The intention was to land on the runway at Entebbe and stage a coup which would topple or kill Amin. But when all was almost complete, the Foreign Office banned it, allowing Amin to go on to kill many more of his fellow Ugandans.

If defectors are spared the attention of assassination squads they may still be the victims of other Soviet activities against them. They are made aware that pressure is being exerted on relatives behind the Iron Curtain and that only their return will relieve it. They may receive emotional telephone calls from their relatives who have been ordered by the KGB to induce them to return. The CIA suspects that Yurchenko gave in to this kind of pressure. While the KGB knows that Levchenko will never return, he has been made aware that his son has been required to write and read out essays at school explaining why his father is a traitor to his country. On occasion, the KGB is able to bring a defector under its control and leave him in his new country as a channel for false information which will undo some of the damage inflicted by him and other defectors.

It might reasonably be expected that Western counter-intelligence services and Foreign Offices would be grateful for the priceless assistance provided by defectors, but in my experience that is not always the case. In fact, defectors tend to be disliked. A defector's exposure of, say, a Western diplomat as a Soviet agent brings discredit on the whole foreign service and is therefore deplored. An important defector usually creates other problems for a diplomatic service which may even be accused of involvement in encouraging foreign nationals to betray their own countries. Unpleasant pressures, some of them public, may be applied to a Western Foreign Office by a country trying to recover its defector under various, usually spurious, pretexts. The type specimen is the recent case in which an American journalist in Moscow, Nicholas Daniloff, was seized as a hostage by the KGB and accused of espionage in an attempt to secure the release of a KGB officer caught spying in New York. The public American outrage was severe enough to threaten the proposed summit meeting between Reagan and Gorbachov.

The situation created by an important defection can be particularly embarrassing for the ambassador and his staff in the country concerned, especially when – as is usually claimed by diplomats – bilateral relations are just in the process of being improved. Since most diplomats prefer a quiet life and disapprove of anything that sours foreign relations, they tend to abhor defectors on principle, and greatly dislike having to house in their embassies intelligence officers, one of whose main functions is to seek out potential defectors.

The attitude of intelligence departments to defectors is strangely ambivalent. CIA veteran F. Mark Wyatt is on record as saying: 'What you have to understand about the CIA is that, despite all the polygraph tests and the interrogations, its people cannot bring themselves to really trust someone who would turn his back on his own country.'

Sir Dick White, who has headed both MI5 and MI6, has expressed his personal distaste at having to deal with defectors.[36] Some defectors, of whom Golitsin is a prime example, have proved to be arrogant and prickly, and profoundly disgusted at the meagre use made of their information. Gouzenko could never understand why so few of his leads were pursued effectively, while Goleniewski was frankly contemptuous of the British attempts to follow the clear lead he had given to George Blake.

Defectors from an alien culture are not easy to deal with, but I suspect there is a more cynical reason for the dislike of them by security and intelligence officers. When a defector pin-points a spy who has been operating for several years inside a secret department, those responsible for the department are in immediate problems of which they might prefer to have remained in ignorance. My inquiries over many years show that there is nothing that any secret service hates more than a scandal or embarrassment which demonstrates its incompetence or, as it claims, impairs its morale. I have heard some secret servicemen argue that the damage done to morale by the exposure of a spy may be worse than allowing him to remain. There is, of course, no doubt that when a defector gives what seems to be a clear lead to a 'mole' inside an intelligence or security agency the efforts to find the culprit can inflict enormous damage, as happened with Golitsin's unproven claim that such a 'mole' existed at high level in the CIA.[37]

Gouzenko does not seem to have been forgiven for providing the Royal Canadian Mounted Police, then responsible for security, with evidence of the existence of twenty Canadian spies of whom ten were convicted. The RCMP's animosity to him, which continued until his death, cannot reasonably be explained by the fact that the defector was a difficult person to deal with. Various anonymous members of the RCMP have vilified him in print and have encouraged journalists to do so, even accusing him of being responsible for the cold war. This unwarranted criticism and ridicule of Gouzenko drew adverse comment from the Commission of Inquiry into the Activities of the Royal Canadian Mounted Police in its report in 1981. Some left-wing journalists, especially in Canada, needed no such encouragement since they deplore the disservice which defectors do to the Soviet Union. Gouzenko, whose contribution to Western awareness of Soviet duplicity was outstanding and remains so, was denigrated so often that he was driven to bring libel actions against his detractors.

Golitsin has likewise been attacked by 'liberal' writers in the USA. Josef Frolik, the Czech defector, suffered a similar fate in Britain, being disparaged in Parliament because of his exposure of treacherous politicians and trade union leaders. Whittaker Chambers, who rendered great service to his country by exposing Soviet agents in high places, suffered the ignominy commonly applied to renegades. It remained to President Reagan, twenty-three years after Chambers died, to 'rehabilitate' him with a posthumous Medal of Freedom.

Similar stigmas apply in the Soviet Union. Though Philby was given Soviet citizenship he was held outside Moscow for a long time while the KGB made extensive checks on his loyalty, in spite of all that he had achieved. When allowed to live in Moscow he was under strict control, being permitted to see very few people; even access to Maclean was barred for many months. Philby was allowed to visit Burgess only briefly when his old friend was dying.[38]

Both Maclean and Burgess were in grave danger of being 'purged' when they arrived in the Soviet Union in 1951, because Stalin was still liquidating former agents he felt he could not trust. They must have suffered severely from what has become known as 'defector blues', which afflicts all adults who switch, suddenly and permanently, from one culture to another. The reasons have been succinctly given by Ladislav Bittman, who defected from Czechoslovakia to the USA in 1968: 'When you defect you give up all that you know – your country, your political beliefs, your family, your relatives, your friends, your entire position in life. You come out like a child. You come to a new place with totally new rules for the game, which you have to learn from the bottom up. It takes a long time.'

The problems facing anyone raised in a true democracy when trying to accommodate to the regimentation of a totalitarian society are obvious; but the reverse – adapting from what has been aptly called the pressure-cooker of a closed Communist society to an open society – is often every bit as traumatic. As Deriabin wrote: 'It is not hard to change your country. It *is* hard to change your customs. The lack of restrictions on a man's thoughts and movements was . . . a bewildering break with everything in my life before.' Matuzok has commented: 'It's a nice feeling to suddenly realize you can do what you want but, at first, it's very confusing.' After a life conditioned simply to waiting for official instructions and to obeying them, accommodating to a system which requires continual choice from a multiplicity of options can be very difficult.

The culture shock can be so severe as to lead to temporary psychological upset, now recognized by the term *post-defection trauma*. Viktor Belenko, the Soviet pilot who defected with his Mig 25 fighter, nearly re-defected to certain death in a fit of irrationality, which is what may have happened to Yurchenko. Feelings of depression, despair, and guilt, with fear of retribution preying on the mind, have often resulted in bizarre behaviour, alcoholism, and even suicide. According to a senior GRU officer, quoted by Suvorov, about 65 per cent of the defectors from the GRU and KGB who reach the West effectively commit suicide by deciding to return to the Soviet Union knowing that they will be executed.[39]

One of the most severe deprivations for Soviet defectors is the lack of opportunity for speaking the native tongue, since so few Westerners speak Russian. They have the benefit of an interpreter during debriefing but, being isolated in 'safe houses' for their own protection as well as for interrogation purposes, they tend to be denied access to other Russians, at least during the critical first few months.

Defectors to the USA have repeatedly complained of the need for support and friendship to combat the inevitable feeling of isolation and often of guilt, especially when they have abandoned their families. Golitsin and his wife suffered from extreme loneliness and near-despair as well as from fear of retribution.[40]

Even when the defector has fled specifically to escape the repressions of Communism he tends to feel guilt. Some, like Akhmedov, seem to be able to slough off their old loyalty to Communism completely. Yet such is the all-pervading influence of the creed that probably very few become complete ex-Communists. There is a saying that 'once a Catholic, always a Catholic', implying that someone born in the faith can never really be free of it and is at least likely to return to it with a death-bed confession. The similar grip of Communism, once it has been instilled over the years, may account for the reluctance of other defectors, like Alexander Orlov, to tell all they know that is damaging to Soviet interests – though loyalty to 'Mother Russia' may be an additional factor. Ideological volatility has played a major role in the saga of treason, but the great majority of ideologues have remained faithful, even if some developed reservations.

Some defectors receive good financial support through generous payments for their information and service as advisers. Even so most need the self-respect of proper employment commensurate with their qualifications; failure to secure this has repeatedly led to disillusionment. Those with readily transferable skills, like musicians and ballerinas, can quickly adjust professionally, as can those with manual skills, such as seamen. Intelligence officers, diplomats, government officials, and some academics and intellectuals are more difficult to place, often being very high-grade people.[41]

Defecting intelligence and military officers whose expertise is properly utilized still tend to be frustrated because they are not completely trusted. The type specimen in this respect is Nikolai Artamonov, better known under his American pseudonym of Nicholas Shadrin. He was an outstanding Soviet naval officer who defected in 1959. While being granted US citizenship and being used as an adviser and lecturer, he was refused CIA security clearance, which limited his prospects. He was eventually sent to Vienna in 1975 on a double-agent mission, when he may have re-defected through frustration or been liquidated.[42] Some defectors have ended up doing menial tasks like dishwashing or driving taxis. Vladimir Sakharov, who worked as a high-level agent-in-place for the CIA in Cairo and Kuwait before defecting in 1971, was earmarked for training in motel management by the CIA bureaucracy; he is on record as saying: 'They squeezed from me all the information they could. They showed no concern about a simple fact: I still had the rest of my life to live.'[43]

A few defectors with a good story and permission to tell it have managed to improve their finances by writing books. Shevchenko's *Breaking with Moscow* was a best-seller, but as a result he has been unjustly criticized as the 'spy who came in for the gold'. Gouzenko, Golitsin, Sejna, and Suvorov are among other successful authors. Dr Rurarz, the former Polish Ambassador, has written his memoirs.

Books by defectors can put much first-hand knowledge in the public domain, but they can also be used as a channel for disinformation – Philby's book, *My Silent War*, being the prime example.[44] Alexander Foote's memoirs, *Handbook for Spies*, was ghosted by an MI5 officer and contains several false statements. The memoirs of Colonel Oleg Penkovsky, the GRU officer who was captured before he could physically defect, were cobbled together by the CIA from various notes and tape-recordings taken during his debriefings and not, as claimed, from his diaries.

Gouzenko conducted a long campaign to induce Western governments to do more to encourage defections through firm promises of financial security and various basic rights, but little was done. Recently, however, this most urgent requirement has been tackled in America by private enterprise in the creation of an organization called the Jamestown Foundation, specifically designed and staffed to assist defectors to adjust to life in the West. It is the result of the individual initiative of the distinguished American lawyer William Geimer, and has already been effective in resettling defectors and dealing with problems which might otherwise induce them to re-defect, a decision which cannot be prevented in a free society. Its able propaganda has alerted the public to the need for the US government to provide a lifetime financial safety-net for valuable defectors, and to make citizenship easier for them to obtain. It assists defectors to take part in public conferences, speaking tours and debates, and sponsors books by them about the Soviet system and its intentions.

In March 1986 President Reagan paid personal tribute to the Jamestown Foundation, stating that the first-hand knowledge and special insights of defectors are 'an invaluable resource for the entire free world'. He also ordered a complete review of the way defectors are handled by the CIA following the Yurchenko débâcle.

There are understandable reasons why any Western government is diffident about accepting certain defectors, especially those who seem too good to be true. Fear that a defector may be a fake sent by the Soviets to sow discord and disinformation or for some more subtle purpose is well substantiated by Western experience. The type specimen of this is the KGB agent code-named 'Fedora' by the FBI, for which he allegedly became a defector-in-place in 1962. This consummate actor, who held a fake post in the Soviet mission to the United Nations in New York, offered his services to the FBI, claiming to be in rebellion against the KGB which had treated him badly. He said his real role in the USA was to obtain technological secrets and that he could supply all manner of information, especially as he would be returning at intervals to Moscow headquarters, where he could consult files. The FBI chief, J. Edgar Hoover, swallowed the bait. For twelve years 'Fedora' fed the FBI with disinformation, much of which Hoover channelled directly to the President. 'Fedora' did much to convince the American administration that the Russians were far behind with nuclear missile technology, which they were not. The duplicity of 'Fedora', who returned safely to the Soviet Union in 1974, and the damaging impact of his activities were held secret until exposed by an investigative writer in 1982.[45]

The truth about the KGB officer Yuri Nosenko, who defected to the USA in 1964, remains unresolved. He was caught out in so many lies that the CIA assumed that he had been sent as a false defector to undermine the true information provided by Golitsin, and to assure the American government that the KGB was not involved in the assassination of President Kennedy. Though Nosenko had provided some true information, it was interpreted as 'chicken-feed', supplied by the KGB to establish his good faith, and he was incarcerated for three and a half years. He never broke, and since his release has shown no inclination to return to the USSR. However, the possibility that Lee Harvey Oswald was a false re-defector sent by the KGB to assassinate Kennedy has never been entirely eliminated.

This fear that a defector may be false operates harshly against those who are genuine and have staked all to leave their own country. They are usually subjected to polygraph tests, which some have found offensive. Vladimir Sakharov, a Soviet diplomat who had worked secretly for the CIA in Cairo and Kuwait and who sought asylum in the USA in 1971 when ordered back to Moscow, expected something of a hero's welcome, but instead was flown to Greece for six weeks' severe interrogation. CIA men insisted that he was really loyal to the GRU. Sakharov's debriefing lasted a year after his removal to Washington, and he complained of being made to feel like a prisoner.[46]

In 1969 a KGB officer stationed in the Consulate in Salzburg offered himself to West German intelligence and he was run as a double for fifteen years. Suddenly in 1984 he insisted that he must defect and did so. Inquiries have since led to the belief that he had been a plant all the time and was ordered to defect to convince Western intelligence that what he had told them must have been accurate, when much of it may have been disinformation.

Whatever the problems faced by defectors in the West, those used to life in the true democracies experience almost insuperable difficulties in trying to adapt to the Soviet way of life. The Macleans were quickly disillusioned by life behind the Iron Curtain. Melinda pined for the luxuries of capitalism and eventually returned to America after her brief marriage to Philby. Philby's previous wife, Eleanor, recorded that she heard Donald and Melinda talking, before their break-up, of the good times they would have in Italy and Paris when 'the revolution comes', indicating not only disillusion but self-deception. Perhaps when the Macleans defected they were naïve enough to believe that world revolution really was round the corner.

Burgess's predicament was even more severe. According to Eleanor Philby, he had no real job and was 'quite obviously bored to death'. He had a permanent minder, and was not allowed out until he had received a telephone call, round about 4 p.m., when most tourists would be back in their hotels. He lived in virtual penury in an enormous old block of flats. 'It was very poor inside his apartment,' said the actress Coral Browne, who visited it. 'His teeth didn't fit. He couldn't eat his lunch.'[47] Several Britons who met him described him as a pathetic figure, wearing his Old Etonian tie. When Burgess met Kenneth Snowman, the Fabergé authority, in Moscow he spent a few moments in ritual abuse of America, saying how much he hated Washington, but then passed to matters of greater interest to him such as news about some hotel in Monte Carlo.

Though Philby was given work to do in Moscow by his KGB case officer, he was almost as pathetic in the way he was so disproportionately delighted by any word of praise from his Russian masters; the KGB clearly appreciated his constant need for reassurance.[48] While there have been rumours of his return to Britain, the KGB would never allow him to venture outside Soviet control. There is no evidence that he has ever visited Cuba, as has been rumoured. The novelist Graham Greene has remained friendly with Philby, and in letters to him has expressed his wish to meet him again, if necessary in an Iron Curtain city like Prague, but Philby has not been permitted to leave the Soviet Union.

Martin and Mitchell, the two American code-breakers who defected to the Soviet Union in 1960 full of such high hopes, quickly became disillusioned. Mitchell, in particular, vainly tried every device to return to the USA. Edward Howard, who was only thirty-four when he fled from the USA to Moscow in 1985, was not an ideologue and must find it far more difficult than most to cope with the deprivation and culture shock. He had some appreciation of his fate, for when forced to abandon his wife and three-year-old son he left a pathetic note saying that he would think of them every day for the rest of his life.

Defectors of no further consequence have occasionally been allowed to leave the Soviet Union, the type specimen being Anthony Wraight, the young RAF officer who defected there in 1956. Disillusioned with an aimless life after three years in an alien culture, and after he had been drained of all information of any value, he was permitted to return to Britain in 1959, knowing that he was likely to face trial as a traitor. Wraight tried to bargain information which he claimed to have learned about KGB methods of interrogation, but the Soviets would never have let him leave had he known anything of value. He was tried and, perhaps because of his youth and instability, given a lenient sentence of three years.

Of twenty-one Americans who elected to remain in North Korea or China at the end of the Korean War, having committed themselves to the Communist cause while in captivity, all but three became disillusioned with the Communist system and drifted back to their homeland. So did the only Briton who took the same course.

As regards numbers of defectors, the balance is hard down in favour of the West. The total, including Red Army and Warsaw Pact soldiers, who make up the bulk, runs into thousands, but the Soviets could have the edge on quality and the number of high-level defectors-in-place.

CHAPTER TWENTY-ONE

What Treachery Does to Traitors

> Though those that are betrayed
> Do feel the treason sharply, yet the traitor
> Stands in worse case of woe.
>
> Shakespeare, *Cymbeline*

The effects which continuing acts of treachery exert on a person's character are closely linked with the moral issues which the traitor faces, if he is not so insensitive as to be unaware of them. In the sense that morality implies the acceptance that some behaviour is right and some wrong, treachery has been considered to be morally justifiable in certain circumstances down the ages. At best, during war or to avert the danger of war, treachery can be an essential, and even heroic, aspect of self-defence; at worst, it is accepted by most cultures as an unfortunate but necessary evil. Exacting faiths, such as Islam and Judaism, from which Christianity is derived, regard treachery as a moral and necessary tool. In the Old Testament God instructed both Moses and Joshua to send out spies to scout the Promised Land. As regards the faith of Communism, Lenin declared that 'morality is subordinate to the class struggle' and urged the use of fraud, deception, and any other immoral or vicious behaviour which would advance the cause, as subsumed in the statement: 'Sink into the mud, embrace the butcher – but change the world; it needs it.'[1]

Since then all the Soviet leaders from Lenin to Gorbachov have consistently taken a totally amoral line concerning what other nations would call treachery, except when they themselves have been on the receiving end. Expediency always takes preference over morality as understood in the true democracies; any action which favours the Soviet Union is permissible and even laudable. The Politburo claims that the Soviet state and the Soviet people, who are its servants, are in a continuous 'struggle' against forces intent on destroying them. So it behaves almost as if it were at war, with morality not being an issue when political survival is alleged to be at stake. As numerous first-hand accounts have testified, the measures taken by Stalin and his successors to keep themselves and their ideology in power have equalled and probably exceeded any recorded horrors in history.[2] It is therefore difficult for an experienced student of the practice of Communist ideology, particularly that of the Soviet Union, to ascribe any moral values to it, and the same applies at the level of the individual Communist. As has been explained in detail in Chapter 7, a committed Communist has usually been subjected to a long period of indoctrination specifically designed to erode and eventually disintegrate normal moral standards of honesty, frankness, integrity, and respect for solemn commitments to employers, originally made in good faith. His character has already been profoundly influenced, and once the justification for treachery in pursuit of the cause has been assimilated, the effects of the acts required are just further stages in the impact on the personality.

Even the most self-deluded traitor must be aware, however, that his integrity is zero and that qualities like rectitude and honesty, which he once believed to be laudable, have been abandoned. This may not be unconnected with the concern which traitors so often show to explain away their treachery. Being called a traitor is shattering, and those who are exposed to the customary condemnation go to great lengths to justify and rationalize their behaviour publicly or to themselves. Baillie Stewart and Tyler Kent undertook legal actions to establish that they had not been traitors, even though they had served sentences for treacherous behaviour. Blunt sought to attribute his behaviour to 'conscience'.

Munir Redfa, the Iraqi Air Force pilot who defected to Israel with a Mig 21, continued to insist that he was not a traitor to his country but a humanist making a protest at the genocidal war being waged by the Iraqi government against its Kurdish minority. After betraying a pro-Canadian Soviet spy to his death for money which he spent on cars, clothes, and fine cigars, James Morrison, the intelligence officer of the Royal Canadian Mounted Police, tried to justify himself, years later, by saying: 'All I did was to sell a God-damned Russian down the drain.'[3] Leo Long was one of the few to admit that his behaviour had been 'frankly treasonable'.

Some degree of self-delusion may be essential for the traitor to be able to live with himself, though this will depend on the extent to which he retains any residue of conscience, meaning the extent to which he is capable of making a reasonable judgement of the moral and social implications of his behaviour. When Fuchs confessed, he claimed that he had begun to have doubts about the Soviet system and had broken off contact with Soviet intelligence early in 1949. This alleged 'crisis of conscience' has been made much of by some writers, who visualized the scientist agonizing over the conflict of his loyalty to the Soviets and his loyalty to his friends and suffering in the process. In fact, the dates suggest that Fuchs had been warned to break contact because the KGB had learned through some other traitor that his activities were being investigated following the decoding of KGB messages.[4] Fuchs's only declared regret was that he had been personally disloyal to his friends, and Bettaney's was similar.

After his defection Philby frequently drank himself senseless when he no longer had any need to hide his treachery and when, in fact, he was praised for it, but this was not the effect of conscience. His wife, who spent much time observing and trying to explain his behaviour, was sure that if he had ever experienced conscience problems he had completely overcome them.[5]

My inquiries have shown that there were official fears that Anthony Blunt might in his old age have a 'fit of conscience' that might induce him to publicize the fact that he had been a traitor and had been granted immunity. It has even been suggested to me, by people well qualified to make such a judgement, that Blunt was appointed adviser for the Queen's pictures and drawings on his retirement from his previous Royal post in 1972 as a sop to make him less likely to talk. My own view, however, is that this rogue who talked a great deal about conscience did not possess any; he may well have hinted at the possibility of 'going public' to retain a Palace connection. Whatever the reason for the appointment it made Blunt the only self-confessed traitor to be rewarded.

A few assassins who became traitors, like Stashinsky and Khoklov, have felt some pangs of conscience about particular murders. But this does not apply to terrorists like those IRA traitors who revel in the deaths they cause, occasionally 'regretting' those of innocent Catholics.

Some traitors who have taken their own lives seem to have been smitten by conscience, though other factors may also have been at work. The reasons for the suicide of Herbert Norman, the Canadian diplomat who jumped to his death from the roof of an apartment block in Cairo in 1957, have been closely studied by Professor James Barros. Norman feared that a US Senate Security Committee was about to produce another witness to his Communist past and suspected treachery. A CIA report from a Cairo source quoted him as saying that if he was called to testify he 'would have to implicate sixty to seventy Americans and Canadians'. Norman claimed that they would be unjustly enmeshed, but his physician said that he was suffering from 'a tremendous sense of guilt', an opinion supported by the tone of his suicide notes. His suicide was particularly determined because he spent some time choosing a building from which his fall was unlikely to hurt anyone else.[6]

The American Army sergeant Jack Dunlap, a Soviet spy inside the National Security Agency, killed himself when he knew that his activities were under investigation following his poor performance in a polygraph test. Larry Wu-Tai Chin, the CIA analyst convicted of spying for the Chinese for thirty years, killed himself in his cell by suffocating himself with a plastic bag tied with shoelaces.[7] The motive could have been a mixture of remorse or despair about his future. Holland's most notorious war traitor, Christiaan Lindemanns, committed suicide in prison by taking poison to escape trial; while Larry Duggan, the KGB agent in the US State Department, fell from a New York hotel window, after being publicly exposed and required to testify to a Senate Security Committee. The British Labour MP Bernard Floud took his life after being interrogated about his KGB connections in 1967. Already deeply depressed after his wife's death, he gassed himself.

There have been too few women traitors for any judgement about the female conscience to be made, but if 'Sonia' was typical she had no problems in that respect.

Many traitors have remained without remorse and seemingly icecold even when their crimes have been publicly exposed. Blunt is the type specimen. According to his elder brother, Wilfrid, he showed no sign of inner tensions when he visited him after the exposure and was able to sleep and eat normally and to continue his guide to the Baroque buildings of Rome and his book on Pietro da Cortona.[8] Like some other traitors, Blunt's only observable regret was the misfortune of having been exposed. This may have been a pose by a consummate actor, however, as it probably was with Wennerstrom, who also took exposure surprisingly calmly. The knowledge that they are publicly branded must burn into the private thoughts of the toughest traitors whatever the pretence they present.

A traitor's only justification for his conduct is the moral value of his cause. This is always claimed to be overridingly high by ideological traitors, but how can the word 'moral' be applied in any meaningful sense to Communists who, as Douglas Hyde confessed, have 'a vested interest in disorder, in economic crisis, social injustice, chaos' and, if necessary, the military defeat of their own country?[9] It can, however, be reasonably applied to the behaviour of former Communists who have defected because they have genuinely come to realize that the Communist system is a corrupt regime of oppression, perpetuating itself by means considered illegal and reprehensible in most other countries which regard themselves as civilized.

It may also apply to defectors from the West, like the Americans Martin and Mitchell, who take offence at certain aspects of capitalist life, such as the inequitable distribution of wealth, which they regard as immoral. Yet such defectors are quickly disillusioned when they discover similar, and less breachable, inequities in the Soviet system.

The case records show that some individual traitors are totally without morality, with the concept of right and wrong, as generally understood, having no bearing on their behaviour. Jerry Whitworth, the American naval analyst in the John Walker spy ring, was described by his trial judge as being completely amoral with no redeeming features, money being his only motive.[10]

Because of blind acceptance of the Marxist–Leninist line, traitors like Philby, Blake, and more recently the American Edward Howard had no conscience difficulties in sending people to their death. It may be that ideological traitors regard themselves as legitimately at war with the society they wish to destroy and can therefore take the same impersonal attitude to inflicting casualties as soldiers do in war, especially when they are acting under orders. Yet, however they may justify their actions to themselves, there can be no morality in being an accessory to murder. What can one make of a character like Blunt who, when asked by a friend if he might have been responsible for the death of British agents, replied blandly: 'Some – not many'?[11]

The same callous attitude is taken by traitors who send others to death or imprisonment purely for money, as did Karel Zbytek, the British-based 'Czech Philby', who sold out 120 of his compatriots for $40,000. Zbytek changed his name to Charles Charles, bought a boarding-house in the pleasant seaside town of Folkestone, and ran it as a genial host until his easy death from a heart attack in 1961, eight years before his treachery was exposed by Czech defectors. Whether he was troubled at all by his conscience only he knew, and this applies to those treacherous senior civil servants and trade union leaders who end up in comfortable retirement as respected citizens, some with honours.

When Philby ensured the execution of the would-be defector Volkov, he might have argued that it was a matter of self-defence, because Volkov would have exposed him as a spy. Such a plea by a traitor pretending to be a loyal servant of his own country would be given short shrift in any court of justice. Philby's amorality, which applied to other aspects of his life, seems to have sprung from his whole-hearted acceptance of the Communist ideology, in which actions are not referred to as right or wrong but as correct or incorrect, depending on whether they have the party's approval or not. His wife, Eleanor, said that her discovery that her husband had been a dedicated Soviet agent for thirty years made her feel the victim of a monstrous confidence trick, which indeed she had been. 'He betrayed many people, me among them,' she wrote.[12]

229

The mind of the ideological traitor may convince itself, subconsciously perhaps, that if the country can justifiably be betrayed, so can anyone in it, including the family. Others seem to be capable of betraying anyone because of their general nature, and perhaps their upbringing. Driberg, for example, who was not ideologically committed, regularly did so. Arthur George Owens, the Welshman who spied for the Abwehr and later for MI5, was described by Ladislav Farago, who had access to the German records about him, as 'totally unscrupulous, unsqueamish, selfish and ruthless. He was cheating so many people that he did not care how many more be betrayed.'[13] The Labour MP Will Owen was described by a parliamentary colleague as prepared to do anything for money. Sir Roger Hollis was hardly taking a moral stance when he declared: 'Every man, without exception, has his price, but mine is a very high one.'[14]

The mercenary traitor, whether he takes small sums or large, is surely devoid of moral argument. He also tends to be devoid of much benefit. Those who spy for money cannot enjoy it safely because undue affluence may raise suspicion. Controllers of long-term traitors therefore tend to keep most of the payment in escrow accounts for use later – a day which often never comes, as happened with Wennerstrom.

When a true double agent is working for both sides for money he is doubly devoid of moral value. He may also be doubly under stress for his pains.

Traitors are not only serious criminals under the laws of their own countries but must constantly remain aware of it because, of all criminals, they are the most habitual. Unlike the burglar, the forger, the confidence trickster, and the murderer, who commit their crimes at intervals, and sometimes only once, the established traitor is required to be active in his masters' interests all day and every day. This knowledge is likely to coarsen the mind as regards its attitude to crime in general, making lesser crimes seem not so reprehensible.

There is, of course, a firm connection between a moral sense and a respect for truth. Traitors, who have to be accomplished and inveterate liars to survive, have automatically deprived themselves of the compass by which most people steer their actions. Their private confusion is likely to be intensified by the incessant masquerade of being permanently on guard against a slip of the tongue, of having to be sure to repeat the same lie to the same people, of having to invent new lies so that the legend can be updated and preserved. Even a traitor's wife has to be constantly deceived unless she happens to be party to the treachery; this creates daily problems for conspiratorial activities which have to be camouflaged. Bossard invented fake intelligence duties to account for the time and journeys spent on his traitorous missions. Even the more case-hardened traitors must undergo some agonizing as to what their wives, parents, children, and friends will think or suffer if they are exposed. Only the toughest can be immune to this anxiety – Philby perhaps being a rare example who really believed his statement to his former MI6 colleague, Nicholas Elliott, that in the service of the Soviet cause family and friends are of little, if any, consequence.

For many traitors whose treachery is exposed the loss of friends, who feel themselves betrayed, is a painful penalty. At first, close friends generally refuse to believe the charge, partly (perhaps mainly) because they cannot bring themselves to accept that they could have been so thoroughly duped. Nicholas Elliott rejected all suspicion against Philby and continued to believe in his innocence until proof was forthcoming, when he became very bitter about the way he had been deceived on both personal and professional grounds. The novelist Graham Greene, on the other hand, still seems to admire Philby, claims to understand what he did for his 'faith', and is on record as believing that 'after thirty years in the underground he had earned his right to a rest'.[15]

Lord Rothschild, who would have 'put his hand in the fire' for Blunt, found his exposure as a traitor 'devastating, crushing and beyond belief'.[16] Many of Blunt's friends felt the same and dropped him, but some preferred to ignore his treachery as being an irrelevancy and concentrated on the virtues of his art career. A few, who tended to be fellow homosexuals, deplored his exposure, shrugged off his treachery, and gave him support.

Almost all MPs declined to believe that Driberg had been a double agent or had ever worked for MI5, when I was given the facts by an MI5 source in 1981, and dismissed the detailed accounts of his activities as 'fairy-tales'. The friends of Charles 'Dick' Ellis behaved similarly when his treachery was revealed at the same time, and I was vilified by some of them in letters to newspapers, though most have finally been convinced by the evidence.[17]

On the part of some friends who are appalled by a traitor's exposure there is a degree of forgiveness. This applies, most peculiarly perhaps, to former colleagues of secret-service traitors. One might imagine that there would be scant sympathy for a man who had undermined a protective organization like MI6 in the interests of an alien adversary, persistently nullifying the work of his loyal colleagues. Nevertheless Sir Maurice Oldfield, the former chief of MI6, forgave Ellis sufficiently to send him a congratulatory cable on his eightieth birthday. Nicholas Elliott, who knew about Ellis's guilt, admonished Oldfield – the latter perhaps appreciating the delicacy of his own secret homosexuality and feeling that there but for the grace of God went he.

After speaking to many other intelligence officers who have nothing personal to hide I have reason to believe that there is sneaking sympathy even for Philby. Perhaps through being party to underhand activities for so long, they appreciate that they have sailed near the wind themselves in line of duty. Those outside the secret world, with its strange influences, are more likely to take the view that no sympathy can ever be warranted for those who worked to overturn hard-won freedoms and to promote the prospects for totalitarian enslavement, especially in Great Britain, the crucible of liberty, or in the USA, now its most effective guardian. This, however, was not the attitude of other prisoners in Wakefield Prison to Klaus Fuchs, who had in a way threatened their lives. They did not despise him, accepting that he had spied for what he believed to be good reasons.[18]

Few traitors have been permitted the luxury of being reasonably open about their dedication and activities, as James Klugmann and Jurgen Kuczynski were, for instance, whose personalities probably suffered less damage as a result. The rest have had to be permanently on stage, presenting a cover personality to the outside world. Klaus Fuchs described in his confession the difficulty of maintaining this, saying that it required the conscious development of a state of 'controlled schizophrenia'. But a few traitors may enjoy this aspect of their lives, as Driberg is believed to have done. His Labour colleague Leo Abse wrote that he 'could have played the part of a spy with superb skill', noting that he would have gained particular pleasure out of fooling and betraying MI5 in the process. For most, however, the constant requirement to act a part must become extremely tedious, as Whittaker Chambers and Elizabeth Bentley have recorded. It must have been especially wearing for traitors like Maclean to continue the acting, without looking furtive, when they knew they were under suspicion.

As already noted, it is a harrowing experience for a Communist traitor when, to facilitate his treachery, he is required to relinquish all connections with the party, thereby depriving himself of the comradeship and other props of party life. For those who have to be publicly disowned the experience seems to be as traumatic as excommunication would be for a devout Roman Catholic. For the good of the British Communist Party's image, Douglas Springhall was ignominiously expelled after his conviction for espionage. The Rosenbergs were likewise ignored by the American Communist Party in their terrible plight, having been declared 'expendable' because they were considered a threat to the party's future in that time of anti-Communist 'witch-hunts'.[19] The KGB cynically preferred the long-term propaganda advantage if the Rosenbergs were executed to any attempt at rescue. The Rosenbergs were expected to go to their death in the interests of Communism and courageously did so, seemingly preferring martyrdom to co-operation with the FBI, which could have saved their lives.[20]

Continuing treachery can exacerbate characteristics which may have been factors in inducing individuals to become traitors in the first place. Blunt's arrogance seems to have been so intensified that he was furious when he was publicly exposed in 1979, taking the attitude of 'How dare anyone expose me!'[21] As long as their treachery remains undetected it puffs up the ego of some traitors, making them feel more important than they would otherwise be and superior to those whom they are betraying or who are failing to detect them. Burgess, while deadly serious in his Communism and espionage, saw treachery as something of a game being played against people for whom he had little intellectual respect. Other traitors have felt enjoyment and pride in their betrayals, especially when praised and rewarded by their masters, as 'Sonia' was, for instance, with two Orders of the Red Banner.

Recruitment to treachery can on occasion bring about a complete change of the persona presented to the world. When Roger Hollis was at Oxford he was highly gregarious with a reputation for undue interest in wine, women, and golf; his interest in drinking was sufficient to earn him the title of 'a good bottle-man'. He remained highly sociable in China, but his character appears then to have altered abruptly to that of someone rather withdrawn and unapproachable, an event which some intelligence officers believe to have been connected with his recruitment to the conspiratorial cause. It is not surprising that, if a traitor is a drinker, continuing treachery will exacerbate the habit and make him drink more heavily. Sensitive spouses are likely to notice other changes in behaviour and attitudes and to wonder about their cause.

Prolonged treachery can even affect a traitor's mode of movement – what might be called, in a pun I cannot resist, the traitor's gait. As a result of their conspiratorial training, traitors are forever looking over their shoulders or taking other precautions, such as staring in shop windows, to ensure that they are not being followed. Klaus Fuchs was able to identify his courier, Harry Gold, only from a film which showed what Fuchs recalled as 'the too-obvious way he has of looking round and looking back'. The Soviet spy Judith Coplon behaved in a similar way, as did Vassall and Graham Mitchell, the MI5 officer who was under deep suspicion.

A traitor's precarious position can rarely be out of his mind. If he tries to ignore it, he is more likely to be caught. So treachery inflicts a penalty of extreme severity in the shape of constant fear of exposure and of what may follow. Anxiety neurosis is an occupational hazard for the traitor; and many, like Burgess – who according to Blunt 'was almost round the bend with worry' – have suffered from it. The longer a traitor continues in treachery the greater the risk he runs of being exposed by a defector or an intercept, however careful he may be, and he knows it. There is a KGB adage that 'You are a bad spy if you don't have ulcers.' Some spies seem to have been one-ulcer men in two-ulcer positions.[22]

Fear and anxiety are suddenly intensified when a traitor is told or senses that he is under suspicion, and the effects can be very severe. Harry Dexter White died of a heart attack after being named by Chambers and Bentley and being publicly grilled by the Un-American Activities Committee. The Canadian diplomat John Watkins suffered the same fate while being interrogated. There was a marked deterioration in Maclean's behaviour when he learned that his code-name, 'Homer', had been deciphered in a KGB intercept. If Roger Hollis was the MI5 spy whom the Russians called 'Elli' his feelings can be appreciated when he learned that Gouzenko had revealed that code-name and a brief description, including the fact that 'Elli' had 'something Russian in his background', as Hollis had, through a family link with Peter the Great. Gouzenko told me that Hollis could not look him in the eye and spent the minimum of time with him.

The announcement of the arrest of a spy or the arrival of a defector must be frightening for other traitors operating in the country concerned, whether they are immediately threatened or not. The arrest of Fuchs terrified all the traitors who had been connected with him. Vassall described the exposure of the Portland spy ring, with which he was not directly associated, as 'a shattering experience'. Philby, who had weathered agonies of anxiety when Burgess and Maclean defected, was in Beirut when he was warned that the KGB defector Golitsin and, later, his English friend Flora Solomon had betrayed him. For months afterwards he lived in fear that attempts would be made to lure him into the British Embassy there so that he could be arrested on British territory. He may have felt confident that he could escape before this happened; but having to defect at short notice, often without family or any possessions, is fearsome in itself. Though given $5,000 provided by the Russians to escape from the USA, the atomic spy David Greenglass could not bring himself to go, preferring imprisonment in the West.

Traitors who have not been exposed continue to live with uncertainty even when they have retired from treachery, never knowing the day when they might be. It is now clear that Blunt, in spite of his hold over MI5, was frequently fearful that some retired civil servant or secret-service officer might publicly expose him. Philby admitted to the same fear when finally cornered. Peter Wright gave me a list of senior civil servants and other notables who had been investigated as Soviet spies or agents of influence and had not been cleared. Most of these are aware of their position and conscious that Wright himself may expose them one day, perhaps through an MP using the privilege of Parliament.

An anxiety which has probably been underestimated in the past is the loss of career which traitors know they risk. According to Maclean's Foreign Office colleagues he was dedicated to his work, with real prospects of high promotion – as were Alger Hiss, Wennerstrom, and possibly Philby. Harry Dexter White was a highly professional government servant, and so was Frank Coe, the American Treasury official who, on his exposure, was dismissed from the International Monetary Fund, where he was secretary, and had to move to Red China. For some, career may be the greatest sacrifice made. One wonders to what extent they appreciate it in advance. Those who are convicted or otherwise exposed find it difficult or impossible to obtain further employment commensurate with their abilities, while the few who manage to defect hardly ever secure comparable work. Much has been made of Philby's value to the KGB in Moscow, but the pathetic picture painted by his wife is likely to be nearer the mark.

Convicted traitors who have completed their sentences tend to go into obscurity like other criminals, often under assumed names. If they are not Soviet citizens they are usually ignored by Moscow, however valuable they may have been. Few show any desire to go behind the Iron Curtain on their release. In his memoirs Vassall relates how he could easily have boarded a Russian ship but did not do so. The scientist Nunn May secured a post in Ghana, and Fuchs, who was deported to East Germany, was exceptional in obtaining a prestigious position. He joined the Central Institute for Nuclear Research at Rossendorf, near Dresden, and became an active member of the Academy of Sciences, being now in pleasant retirement with the recently endowed title of Exceptional Scientist of the People.[23]

The corrosive effects on character of the loneliness imposed by the secret life have been noted by several confessed traitors. Wennerstrom recalled the predicament of having nobody in whom to confide about the secret side of his life and how, as a result, he came to look forward so much to face-to-face contacts with his Soviet case officer that he was 'like an addict needing a fix', his 'swing to the Soviet side' becoming 'complete and definitive'.[24] Professor Hambleton paid similar tribute to his KGB case officers in the loneliness of his long years of espionage. It was as if he were being initiated into the secret rites of a great brotherhood where mighty arms embraced all humanity, he told his friend Leo Heaps. Even John Vassall, whose treachery was the result of ruthlessly cruel Soviet blackmail, developed feelings of friendship and loyalty towards his controllers through being able to be open with them about his treachery.

The distress of mental loneliness has driven some traitors to break the conspiratorial rules in order to secure relief by confiding in another person and, on occasion, has led to exposure. A few others have enjoyed a beneficial mutual confidence from the start, as Blunt did with Burgess and possibly with the Cambridge don A. S. F. Gow, which might help to account for Blunt's extraordinary resilience. It seems that, once he had achieved international fame in the art world and felt secure, Blunt confided in other homosexual friends, even deriving intellectual satisfaction out of having contrived such a perfect cover for his espionage as membership of the staffs of MI5 and Buckingham Palace.[25]

The effect of mental isolation on the behaviour of Elizabeth Bentley is particularly revealing. She remained a dedicated Soviet secret agent as long as she enjoyed the intimate support of her professional KGB case officer and lover, but when he died it was as though scales fell from her eyes. She saw the true nature of the conspiracy and enormity of her treachery against her own country and kinsfolk and then did everything she could to expose others involved in it.[26]

The persistent habit of lying must undermine respect for oaths of allegiance and secrecy and because lying is generally regarded as permissible for intelligence officers in protecting their sources, or anything else to do with their professional work, it might be pertinent to consider if this experience may have been a factor in inducing some of them to become traitors by eroding their moral sense. Since the professional life of intelligence officers sometimes involves activities which in others would be regarded as criminal, this, too, might have some influence on frailer characters in undermining their moral standards. The surreptitious entry of buildings and homes, by methods which are frankly burglarious, so that searches can be made and documents removed or photographed, has been described in detail by the former MI5 officer Peter Wright[27] and in the official report on misdemeanours by the security branch of the Royal Canadian Mounted Police.[28] Eavesdropping by electronic listening devices, often planted during surreptitious entry, and mail-checks are the life-blood of intelligence work; while official permission is granted to those practising it, they know that for anyone else it would be offensive and even criminal.[29] The whole process of security surveillance has such conspiratorial overtones that it would not be surprising if some of those engaged in this kind of activity became hardened as regards their attitude to what is right and wrong. The dissident former MI5 officer Cathy Massiter has claimed that Bettaney, her colleague who became a traitor, was 'a product of the security service itself' and that, though his reactions were extreme, the conflict and dissatisfactions which provoked them are far from rare.[30]

The extent to which secret-service officers face mind-scarring experiences is illustrated by an occasion when Sir Maurice Oldfield, the MI6 chief, received information that an MI6 agent facing torture after capture by the KGB had requested a lethal pill which could, in fact, be surreptitiously supplied. Knowing that the agent could confess a great deal that would be damaging to MI6 and perhaps put other lives at risk, Oldfield put duty before his strong religious objections to suicide; the pill was delivered.

The use of various forms of blackmail to secure agents would be considered criminal if practised by anyone else. Though it is now officially restricted in many Western intelligence agencies, intelligence officers serving abroad are still required to commit the serious offence of sedition, by exerting other forms of pressure on foreign citizens to become traitors to their own country. It is only their diplomatic status which protects them from being prosecuted as criminals when they are caught doing it.[31]

A further peculiar aspect of membership of a secret service is knowledge of the practice of granting immunity to traitors who have committed dreadful crimes because it is believed to serve some intelligence or political purpose. Can the granting of such immunity from prosecution – and usually from publicity – ever be morally justified? Some of the older and staider members of MI5 were deeply offended at the granting of immunity to Blunt, regarding it as an obscenely immoral conspiracy to defeat justice; but others shrugged it off as a routine necessity, or admired it as a professional coup. Following the exposure of the way in which Blunt had been protected, the government took steps to make the granting of immunity unlikely in the future. This was a considerable admission of the immorality of the practice – and of those responsible for it – when draconian punishments had been meted out to others who were not 'establishment' figures.

The moral position of the former intelligence officer who decides to break his oath of secrecy has been highlighted by the activities of Peter Wright, who left MI5 in 1976 and has been trying to publish his memoirs. Wright's original purpose was to expose incompetence and treachery in MI5 in the belief that much needs to be done to prevent penetration by the Soviet bloc and to clear up the effects of previous cases, in particular that of Sir Roger Hollis. More recently, he has extended his 'crusade' to attempting to expose alleged illegal acts which MI5 is required to undertake in line of duty and to which he was party, without objection and believing them to be justified, when

237

a serving officer.[32] While Wright appears to believe that morality is on his side, because enormities are being covered up to spare politicians and officials from embarrassment, the British Security authorities and the government regard his efforts as a reprehensible breach of his solemn undertakings, while many of his former colleagues who could write very saleable memoirs refer to him as a renegade. They also feel that his motives are tainted by the fact that he only provided information for my book *Their Trade Is Treachery* on the understanding that he would receive half the royalties. Whatever the merits of the case, it would appear to be significant that Wright is living in Tasmania and is safe from prosecution under the Official Secrets Act, which provides no power of extradition.

The case histories of traitors indicate a firm connection between lack of moral sense and lack of truly religious belief. Those with no faith or only the Communist faith seem to have no sense of evil, without which any behaviour including sending people to their death can be self-justified. Significantly, several important traitors who fall into this category began their lives in close association with religion and then rebelled against it, filling the gap with Communism, as detailed in Chapter 12. Blunt could be the type specimen, but a detailed study of another Cambridge recruit to the Soviet cause, Herbert Norman, has more recently become available under the very title *No Sense of Evil*. Documents released by the American and Canadian authorities prove that Norman, a missionary's son who lost his religion and was recruited to revolutionary Marxism, was a consummate liar.[33] When interrogated by the Royal Canadian Mounted Police he repeatedly denied ever having been a Communist. What the historian Professor Barros describes as the 'enormity of his falsehoods' was compounded by his persistent complaints that he was being persecuted. Either he was incapable of recognizing the obvious evils of Stalin and his henchmen, including their mass murders, or he was prepared to ignore them.

Like his Cambridge contemporary Klugmann, Norman was of gentle persuasion but was excessively withdrawn and very naïve for such an intelligent person – as he eventually admitted – though cunningly adept at evasive action. In his several suicide notes he wrote about being 'overwhelmed' by his 'consciousness of sin' but maintained his innocence of having conspired against Canada. Admitting that his chief flaw had been naïvety, he wrote that he had lived under illusions too long and that Christianity was the only true road.

A commentary on the morality of the agent of influence, who surreptitiously promotes the objectives of a foreign power and would almost certainly deny doing so, if challenged, has been made by Tomas Schuman, a former operative for the Soviet Novosti propaganda agency. To secure such foreign agents, Novosti 'journalists' are instructed to concentrate on people 'ready to compromise moral principles for personal advantage'. It is surely immoral, by any standard, for agents of influence and others, including the so-called 'militant' revolutionaries, to exploit civil liberties with the long-term purpose of destroying them.

The moral aspects of assassinations, in which various people regarded as either traitors or patriots have been involved, raise controversial questions. Would it have been moral to kill Hitler before his orders killed so many others? Some, like those whose relatives died in the gas chambers, would argue that it would, while others insist that murder can never be justified morally. In law the principle of self-defence is universally recognized. Could it be effectively argued that a man like Count Stauffenberg, who was hanged as a traitor for attempting to kill Hitler, was acting in the long-term self-defence of himself, of millions of his countrymen, and of the fatherland?

At least one professional assassin has become a traitor because his conscience worried him. This was Bogdan Stashinsky, a Ukrainian, who at the age of twenty-five was sent to Munich by the KGB in 1957 to kill a Ukrainian émigré, which he did by means of a cyanide spray designed to make murder look like a heart attack. Later he killed another anti-Soviet émigré by the same method being personally congratulated by the KGB chief Shelepin, who had other targets in mind for him. After marrying an East German girl, however, Stashinsky escaped to West Germany and confessed his crimes, knowing that he would be tried and probably convicted, as he duly was in 1962.[34] That currently common assassin, the terrorist, has no justifiable moral argument beyond his specious claim that because he is at war all military methods are justified.

The worst of the obvious penalties which treachery inflicts on the traitor is to deprive him of his life or of his freedom. Legal penalties for treachery have always been so severe that it is a matter for wonder that recruits prepared to undertake it, or even volunteering to do so, remain so numerous. In the modern world dictators have invariably taken the toughest line; Hitler declared: 'He who comes only in the shadow of treason has forfeited his life.' Those detected by the Gestapo tended to end up strangled by piano-wire, while those designated traitors by Stalin and his henchmen were summarily shot in droves. Men who had deserted from the Soviets to fight with the Germans, in particular General Vlasov and his troops, were handed back at the war's end and executed. As recently as 1975 eighty-four members of the crew of a Soviet destroyer who had seized it in a dash for freedom in Sweden were executed after the ship was intercepted and towed to a Russian port.[35] The Soviet-bloc traitor serving as an agent-in-place in cold war knows that he risks execution, as happened to Colonel Popov and Colonel Penkovsky, to many of those betrayed by Blake and Blunt, and more recently to Tolkachev.

Many Western traitors in war, such as Joyce, Amery, and Quisling, paid the ultimate penalty because they ended up on the losing side, but few traitors caught in the West in peacetime suffer death, the Rosenbergs being exceptions. Even the most vicious terrorists are spared the death penalty. Nevertheless prison sentences for treachery – usually espionage – now tend to be heavy and far more severe than those for murder. In addition heavy fines are being imposed to prevent profit from treachery. A Norwegian court, for example, confiscated £99,000, which it decided had been paid by the Soviets, from the traitor Arne Treholt, as well as sentencing him to twenty years' imprisonment. Jerry Whitworth of the Walker spy ring was fined $410,000 on top of a prison sentence so great that he will not be eligible for parole before he is 107.

Some traitors in the West, however, have been fortunate in having their sentences slashed by early parole. For example, the naval spy David Bingham, though committed for twenty-one years in 1972 for what the judge called 'a monstrous betrayal', was released after serving only seven.[36] After serving only four years in Britain, Hambleton was transferred to Canada to be near his aged mother and to be eligible for early parole under Canadian law. A few others are enjoying large reductions in sentence through the growing practice of exchanging spies which makes a mockery of justice.

The Krogers, two lifelong professional Soviet agents who were American citizens using the name of Cohen but of Polish origin, were exchanged for the young British lecturer Gerald Brooke, who had done nothing more treacherous than distribute leaflets in Moscow. Heinz Felfe, the East German spy inside the BND, was exchanged for three West Germans held in the Soviet Union, after he had served only six of the fourteen years' sentence imposed for appalling damage, including the liquidation of many agents. These are exceptions, however, for the 'spy-swap' trade is mainly restricted to espionage agents who are not traitors – men and women working abroad in the interests of their own countries. In the exchange accomplished in Berlin in February 1986, Anatoly Shcharansky, the Soviet Jewish dissident, was released by the Soviet authorities as a 'CIA agent' who had been convicted of treason. This was totally fraudulent, since Shcharansky's only crime had been to plead openly for human rights in the USSR and in particular for the implementation of the Soviet Union's agreed commitments under the Helsinki accord.

The East–West acceptance of the spy exchange has increased the risk of treachery, because many of those committing it feel assured that, if caught, they will be soon released. Even with or without that reassurance, treachery and those prepared to commit it are here to stay.

CHAPTER TWENTY-TWO

How Traitors Survive

He forc'd his neck into a noose,
To show his play at fast and loose.
And, when he chanc'd t'escape, mistook
For art and subtlety, his luck.

Samuel Butler

Before examining how traitors come to be exposed it will be instructive to consider how some of them manage to survive for so long. Many do so simply by fulfilling the conspiratorial requirements carefully worked out for their safety by their controllers. Frank Bossard, who spied successfully for four years, abstracting documents and copying them, obeyed the KGB's advice scrupulously. He met his contacts very rarely, usually exchanging his material for money through dead letter drops. He knew when to make the drops by listening to Moscow radio when various tunes, which were a form of code, were played. To protect against the possibility that his house might be searched, he kept his photographic equipment and even the gramophone records which reminded him of his codes in a railway left-luggage office, withdrawing them only when needed. He was never asked to secure information he could not obtain easily and so avoided suspicion on that score. Had he not been 'burned' by the false defector 'Fedora', he might never have been caught.

Harry Houghton, the Portland spy, who took every penny he could, avoided the arousal of suspicion through excessive spending and other evidence of a life beyond normal means. In his memoirs Houghton recalled how he followed KGB advice and made it a golden rule 'never to spend on pleasure, clothes or entertainment more than my monthly salary'.[1] He did not come under suspicion until betrayed by a defector.[2] The extraordinary degree of control which the KGB and GRU centres in Moscow insist on exerting on their agents has occasionally led to exposures, as Chapter 23 will show, but the Soviet authorities believe that it usually provides protection because they alone can see the whole tapestry.

While traitors who stick to the conspiratorial rules do not give counter-intelligence departments much chance to detect them, the case records indicate that many have been so careless that they survived for years only because of counter-intelligence ineptitude. This is illustrated by first-hand evidence I have recently acquired, revealing that no less than *nine* Britons were under special surveillance as suspect Soviet agents *before* the defection of Burgess and Maclean, yet not one of them was brought to book. The nine included Burgess and Maclean themselves, Anthony Blunt, Goronwy Rees, who had worked in the War Office and was a close friend of Burgess, Anthony Rumbold, who was a diplomat, David Footman, an officer of MI6, and almost certainly Philby. The other two, including a man who was then an officer of MI6, cannot be safely named for libel reasons. I have been assured that Lord Rothschild was definitely not on this list – a fact giving further support to the Prime Minister's statement in December 1986 that there was no evidence that he had ever been a Soviet agent. The nine were all subjected to physical and telephone surveillance, in which my informant was involved, and this continued for many months after Maclean and Burgess fled. Blunt was referred to by the code-name 'Blunden', Philby as 'Peach', while Footman was called 'Flaxman'.

The List of Nine, as it became known in MI5, appears to have been drawn up after suspicion against Maclean and Burgess began to harden in 1950. My informant recalls that MI5 investigators, headed by their deputy chief Guy Liddell, then took a new look at the brief statement which had been supplied by the would-be KGB defector Volkov in 1945, and which had been filed away after Philby had, unknown to them, ensured the capture of Volkov by the KGB. Volkov had promised to give leads to seven Soviet agents: five in British intelligence and two in the Foreign Office.

Previous first-hand evidence that Burgess was under suspicion and surveillance in 1950, before he left London on Foreign Office posting to Washington, has been presented in my book *Too Secret Too Long*. Briefly, what happened – according to the individual responsible for the surveillance of Burgess in Washington, who gave me the information – is as follows. MI5 wished to keep some watch on Burgess in Washington, after his arrival there in August 1950, without informing the Foreign Office, and had no facilities for doing so. It therefore selected a young Army officer for posting there, under the cover of being an assistant to General Neil Ritchie, head of the British military mission at the Pentagon. This device also enabled Burgess to be watched without the FBI being informed. As the former FBI agent Robert Lamphere has revealed, MI5 was deliberately withholding from the Americans the results of its inquiries concerning Maclean, and those who might be associated with him.[3]

Arrangements were made to ensure that the Army officer attended all parties to which Burgess had been invited, and he was required to make regular reports on the diplomat's behaviour and contacts. Burgess always behaved impeccably in the company of the officer, who is convinced that the traitor had been warned of his situation in advance. As soon as arrangements had been made for Burgess's return to London, the officer was sent home, and his post was abolished. The firm evidence, from two separate sources, that Burgess was under suspicion helps to explain why he defected with Maclean; he was required to do so by the KGB because he, too, was earmarked to be hauled in for interrogation by MI5. The common idea that he went on the spur of the moment is falsely based. The evidence also helps to explain why the papers about Burgess and Maclean are still being held so tightly secret, though both men are dead. Their publication would show that in permitting them to escape without interrogation the security authorities were even more culpable than they are already known to have been.

It is now well established that Maclean was under deep suspicion before he defected and that it was because he had been warned of it that he fled. The early suspicion of Blunt, however, as shown by his presence on the List of Nine, is an important new disclosure because it has generally been assumed that he was not suspect until the defection of Burgess. As a close friend of Burgess, he was an obvious choice for surveillance, once Burgess himself was suspect. My informant states that all that resulted from the surveillance of Blunt was disclosure of 'his unsavoury private life, including the fact that one of his friends acted as a procurer of young men for him'. While sufficient evidence could have been secured to arraign Blunt for sodomy, nothing was done because of his Palace position. Blunt was subjected to repeated interrogations after the Burgess and Maclean defection had given MI5 the excuse to approach him, but they achieved nothing. In spite of suspicions, Blunt was permitted to assist MI5 officers in a search of Burgess's flat in 1951 and in the process managed to find and conceal a letter which would have incriminated Philby. Because of that, an available witness, the London woman Flora Solomon, who was mentioned in the purloined letter and was suspect herself, was not approached until eleven years later, when she then named Philby as a Soviet agent.[4]

While my informant cannot be completely certain from memory that Philby was on the List of Nine before the Burgess and Maclean defection, the odds are that he was. Liddell and the former MI5 chief Sir David Petrie had both been suspicious of him, and re-examination of the Volkov file would surely have aroused concern about his handling of the case. The likely presence of his name on the list would also explain the appalling disclosure, recently made by Robert Lamphere, that MI5 kept him and his department completely in the dark about any aspects of the List of Nine inquiries, though the FBI was feeding everything it found to MI5. It would seem to be significant that when Lamphere was finally given a list of MI5's reasons for suspecting Philby, in June 1951, his mishandling of the Volkov affair was high on it.[5] Lamphere has confirmed to me that he and his colleagues were never even told of the Volkov affair until after the Maclean and Burgess defection.

Clearly, if serious suspicion had fallen on Philby, MI5 did not feel it safe to inform the Americans about the identification of Maclean as a spy, in case the information leaked. Philby was in Washington and in daily contact with officers of both the FBI and the CIA, whom he had cultivated as friends. Further, the FBI chief, J. Edgar Hoover, would have to have been among the first to be told, and his attitude to spies was such that he would have insisted on the immediate removal of Philby from Washington, which would have signalled MI5's suspicions to the Russians.

In fact nobody, outside the few involved in the List of Nine inquiries, could be told about them. That bar included MI5's own man in Washington, Geoffrey Patterson, who was later to be accused of misleading the FBI by keeping it in ignorance. The truth is that he was himself kept in ignorance.

While leaving Philby at his post in Washington may have protected MI5's inquiries, it enabled him to do further damage to both British and American interests. It is also believed in MI5 that he was warned of the suspicions against him by his KGB case officer in Washington, following a leak to the KGB from a source inside MI5.

David Footman, who continued his long career in MI6, was suspected because he had helped Burgess to secure connections with MI6 and to do some work for it. Though nothing of substance emerged from the surveillance of Footman, Sir Maurice Oldfield, the MI6 chief, remained suspicious of him.[6]

There now seems to be little doubt that Goronwy Rees had been recruited by Soviet Intelligence – as witness Maclean's drunken censure of him: 'You used to be one of us but you ratted.'[7] The way Rees protected both Burgess and Blunt when he knew they were traitors is highly suspect. My informant recalled that tapped telephone conversations, particularly after Burgess and Maclean defected, suggested that Blunt and some others were very afraid that Rees might speak out publicly, if only in an attempt to clear himself. This is further evidence that suspicion of Blunt was very strong in the early 1950s, but no warning whisper of it was ever made to officials of Buckingham Palace, where Blunt was employed.

In the result, while Rees eventually told MI5 that Burgess had confessed to being a spy to him, he did not do so until after Burgess was safely in the Soviet Union. He kept his secret about Blunt until he confessed it on his death-bed to the writer Andrew Boyle in 1978.[8] My informant recalled that nothing derogatory about Rees arose out of the surveillance, observing that it was unlikely that anything would if Rees had been warned of the inquiries, as the rest seem to have been.

After his own exposure, Blunt is said to have stated that Rees was a recruited Soviet agent until the Nazi–Soviet pact of August 1939, when he declined to work for the Russians any more.[9] Had Blunt completed his memoirs, however, he intended to state that Rees was 'up to his neck' in the conspiracy.[10]

Another long-term traitor well known to MI5 in 1950 and who survived because no action was taken against him was James Klugmann. He was known then to have been a major recruiter of the Cambridge ring but was not on the List of Nine because he was an overt Communist.

Also contemporary was Klaus Fuchs, who in his confessions to FBI and MI5 agents in Wormwood Scrubs Prison in 1950 revealed that he had been active in underground Communist work while at the universities of Bristol and Edinburgh. Fuchs had been in touch with the openly Communist German exile Jurgen Kuczynski, who was regarded as the head of the underground section of the German Communist Party in Britain.[11] The section of MI5 headed by Roger Hollis was responsible for countering illicit Communist activity, yet Hollis cleared Fuchs repeatedly for secret work on the atomic bomb, though warned of his Communist connections.

Fuchs, who had been interned in Canada and was known to have been a Communist underground revolutionary in Germany, was cleared by MI5 for entry into the atomic bomb project in May 1941. Soon afterwards, MI5 was warned that Fuchs was well known as a Communist among German exiles who were consorting clandestinely to plot for Communism in Germany after the war. As Hollis admitted at a secret conference in Washington, MI5 expedited Fuchs's naturalization to ease his access to the most secret places, which enabled him to pass most valuable American as well as British nuclear technology to the Russians.[12] While Fuchs was handing secrets to 'Sonia', who served as his courier in Britain and perhaps as his case officer, MI5 was told that he was taking active part in underground Communist affairs in Birmingham.

Nevertheless, when Fuchs was transferred to the USA in 1943, to join the Anglo-American 'crash' programme to produce atomic bombs, MI5 vouched for his security clearances to the Americans. MI5 also reassured the British chiefs of the atomic energy project on that score. The warnings that Fuchs was an active Communist were withheld from the Americans.

It is now certain that the repeated clearances of Fuchs were executed by Hollis and Hollis alone, not by an MI5 committee as previously seemed likely. Before each clearance Hollis had a meeting with Sir Michael Perrin, the assistant director of the British atomic bomb project, then code-named Tube Alloys. The two of them discussed the circumstances, but it was Hollis who took the decisions. This has been established by Professor Robert Williams of Washington University, St Louis, who has completed an academic study of Fuchs.[13]

Hollis was again responsible for taking no effective action against Fuchs when he returned from the USA to work at Harwell, Berkshire, in 1946 and after his name had surfaced in connection with the conviction of Alan Nunn May as a Soviet agent. Hollis was also involved in the ineffective attempt to interrogate 'Sonia' and for failing to take any precautions to prevent her eventual defection to East Germany.

The FBI agent responsible for the American end of the Fuchs case, Robert Lamphere, has provided a mass of new first-hand material in his memoirs, particularly about Operation Bride, the breaking of certain KGB coded messages. Lamphere found that the KGB was quickly warned of Bride breaks, which showed that a Soviet spy had been operating inside the atomic bomb project, and that he was almost certainly Klaus Fuchs. In the past Philby has been blamed for this most damaging leakage, but Lamphere has evidence to show that it occurred before Philby had access to it. 'To me there now remains little doubt that it was Hollis who provided the earliest information to the KGB that the FBI was reading their 1944–45 cables,' he wrote in *The FBI–KGB War*. 'Philby probably added to that knowledge after his arrival in the US but the prime culprit in this affair was Hollis.'

Hollis also failed to take any action against Kuczynski, who had eventually put Fuchs in contact with the GRU, which then controlled his espionage work in Britain. Douglas Hyde made a pointed reference to this when he revealed that a certain Tommy Bell ran a group co-ordinating the activities of foreign Communists in Britain, and that had MI5 kept itself sufficiently aware of this the Fuchs case might never have occurred.[14]

Both Kuczysnki and 'Sonia' had behaved traitorously to Britain yet were allowed to return to Germany unscathed, the former being permitted to visit Britain subsequently. In an incident bordering on farce, 'Sonia' was visited by an MI5 officer at her home near Chipping

Norton in 1947; all he achieved was to warn her that she was under suspicion while her husband, a fellow spy, was never questioned at all. The MI5 management then believed that she and her husband had taken the hint and fled to East Germany, but in fact they did not do so until 1950, so certain were they of their safety from prosecution.

The FBI, which unlike MI5 has powers of arrest, was equally incompetent in preventing the escape of Edward Howard to Moscow in 1985. He is said to have placed a dummy of himself in his car to fool the FBI watchers and escaped in another direction at night. Whatever the means, his emergence in Moscow during the Daniloff affair enabled him to inflict further damage on the USA. The British rescue of Gordievsky from inside the Soviet Union, while superbly handled by MI6, probably owed something to a display of incompetence by the KGB.

While counter-espionage officers quickly spotted the suspicious relationship between the RAF officer Anthony Wraight and Soviet military intelligence in London, they were totally surprised by his defection to the Soviet Union via an ordinary commercial flight to Berlin. More recently, West German counter-intelligence had good evidence that Herbert Willner, an East German refugee who had been in Russian hands during the war and whose wife worked in Chancellor Helmut Kohl's office, was a long-term East German agent. He had been reported for peculiar behaviour, such as staying late at his office to copy reports concerning the Free Democratic Party, with which he was connected, but no effective action was taken, and both managed to defect.

When a team of officers from MI5 and MI6 was investigating the possible treachery of Hollis, they were looking for information that would fulfil a clue given by Gouzenko that an MI5 spy, believed to be Hollis, had 'something Russian in his background'. They failed to discover the fact that the Hollis family and some of their relatives believed that they were descended from the Tsar Peter the Great. Had they discerned this they could have been much tougher when interrogating Hollis.

In addition to ineptitude, counter-intelligence departments have displayed a dangerous degree of arrogance. Following the defection of Maclean and Burgess a system of 'positive vetting' for government employees with access to secrets was introduced in 1952. Parliament was assured that it would apply to all candidates for highly sensitive posts and to those already in them. Such was the arrogance of both MI5 and MI6, however, that they did not apply it to themselves until it was forced on them in 1965, as a result of the suspicions concerning Hollis. This meant that proven spies like Blake and Ellis had never been positively vetted. Neither had Hollis himself, and this substantially limited inquiries into his background, because when he was eventually interrogated in 1970 he was able to plead poor memory.

When positive vetting was finally forced on to the secret services their officers vetted each other and were able to choose friends for the purpose. It was no more than a 'You vet me, Joe, and I'll vet you' situation, which some are now prepared to admit was sometimes hilarious. In the Atomic Energy Authority to which two senior MI5 officers, Guy Liddell and Kenneth Morton Evans, had been seconded, they simply vetted each other.

The danger of in-built arrogance showed itself in the conflict between MI5 and MI6 concerning the two proven MI6 traitors Philby and Ellis. The MI6 chiefs were convinced that none of its officers could possibly have been a spy, the very idea being grotesque – a description similarly applied by the MI5 chief Furnival Jones to the suspicions concerning Hollis, his predecessor.

When the would-be defector Volkov declared that the Soviets were able to read British diplomatic ciphers, the Foreign Office took no notice, in the complacent belief that no diplomat or official would betray them, in spite of the wartime case of King, the cipher clerk convicted of doing just that. As a result the treachery of Maclean went unexplored for a further five years.

The Volkov case demonstrated tragically how being a member of a secret service provides a traitor with other survival advantages. It enables a penetration agent to be forewarned of a potentially dangerous defection and for action to be taken. The officer at risk can even arrange to deal with the defector personally, as I am satisfied happened with Hollis when he and Philby arranged that he should be the man to interview Gouzenko, who had reported the existence of a Soviet spy inside MI5. The move enabled Hollis to 'rubbish' the information which threatened him and to induce his superiors to ignore it.

The penetration agent inside a secret agency can also suppress intercepts which might prove dangerous simply by declaring them to be undecipherable or not worth the effort. Known radio operators can be ignored, as happened when coded Soviet radio messages, which could have included some of 'Sonia's', were handed to Hollis by the wartime Radio Security Service.

In the more believable part of his memoirs, Harry Houghton, the Portland traitor, makes it clear that he and his mistress, Ethel Gee, who was convicted with him, were only part of a large spy ring operated by the KGB officer Gordon Lonsdale and for which the Krogers were the radio operators. Lonsdale and the Krogers, who were high-grade professionals, had been in Britain for three and a half years before Houghton and Gee were even recruited. There were leads to some of the others, who managed to escape because of a failure of communication between MI5 and the police, which led to the premature announcement of Lonsdale's arrest.[15]

Lack of co-ordination between counter-intelligence departments which are supposed to assist one another has been a potent reason for the survival of traitors. MI6 declined to make records available to MI5 when it was first investigating the treachery of Charles Ellis, for example, and the rivalry between these two agencies, which are supposed to share the objective of defending the realm, has often been counter-productive. The effects of MI5's failure to liaise honestly with the FBI over Maclean and Philby have already been described. The same professional offence had been committed earlier with respect to Fuchs. According to Robert Lamphere:

> Even after our investigation of Fuchs had begun in 1949, MI5 did not tell the FBI about Fuchs's Communist background though he had, in fact, been classed as a German Communist while interned in Canada, and later, in 1941, had told an Aliens Hearing Board in Britain that he was a Communist in order to convince the board of his anti-Nazi views, so that he could secure a post in war-related research.[16]

When the extremely well-informed Soviet intelligence officer Walter Krivitsky defected in Paris in 1937, he was so thoroughly debriefed by French security officials that his information filled eighty large volumes. Had the French shared it with Britain and other friendly countries it could have led to the early detection of many Soviet agents, perhaps including Philby, Maclean, and others who were equally damaging. Instead they hoarded it and when asked for copies of the documents, years later, they claimed that they had been stored on an old barge on the Seine and that all had been lost when the bottom of the vessel rotted away. MI5 officers who made the request suspect that the many Soviet penetration agents inside French Intelligence and Security at that time had in reality destroyed the documents.[17]

When Krivitsky was interrogated later in Britain in 1940 he was still able to name about sixty Russian agents operating in the UK or against British interests elsewhere. Sixteen of these were British subjects, eight being active in politics and the trade unions, six in the civil service, and two in journalism. About half these names were new to MI5. Krivitsky also identified about twenty 'apparatus workers', ancillaries acting in Britain as couriers, photographers, and so on. Nearly all these were foreigners: Russians, Germans, Austrians, Dutch, and Americans.[18] Apart from the Foreign Office cipher clerk John King, none was prosecuted, though some may have been neutralized and some were never seriously investigated. This could have been the result of sheer incompetence on the part of MI5 or of the existence of an influential and persuasive Soviet agent inside the organization. While the USA had passed on Krivitsky's disclosure which led to the prosecution of King, details of MI5's interrogation of Krivitsky in 1940 were not made available to the Americans until the 1960s.

Official secrecy has been a fount of protection for traitors. Goronwy Rees, in his memoirs, describes the extraordinary reaction of the senior MI5 officers Guy Liddell and Dick White to his first-hand evidence that Burgess had been a spy. They appeared to be more concerned about protecting the good name of the service and concealing its gross incompetence than with taking any action. Similarly the profound treachery of Blunt, Long, and Ellis and the deep suspicions concerning Hollis were hushed up when publicity might have produced important leads. My own experience has proved again and again that publicity breeds information and that secrecy discourages it. It was monstrous that Blunt, Long, and others who were implicated should have been allowed to continue as honourable – and sometimes honoured – citizens in the community whose downfall they had plotted.

Traitor after traitor has had reason to be grateful for the protective hand of someone in an influential position. My informant who was involved in the surveillance of those on the List of Nine is convinced, from their behaviour, that those who were guilty had been surreptitiously warned of their predicament on the initiative of someone who must have been inside MI5. A former MI5 officer, who is also required to be nameless for his own protection, told me with some feeling that in Hollis's day, 'Working in MI5 was like gardening – whatever one did, however hard one tried, there was always something – or somebody – to bugger it up.' That somebody is now believed by many former officers of MI5 and MI6 and by officers of allied services, such as the FBI and the CIA, to have been Hollis himself, who was Director-General for nine years, Deputy for three years before that, and previously held influential positions in the service for another fifteen years.

Evidence of Hollis's protective hand is not restricted to the case of Klaus Fuchs. He repeatedly prevented the investigation or interrogation of important suspects, including a senior Naval officer, the Communist scientist Alister Watson, and his own deputy, Graham Mitchell, for various spurious reasons.

Philby was able to protect Pontecorvo and Ellis by concealing documentary information pointing to their treachery. In turn Philby was protected by colleagues such as Dick Brooman-White, a former MI6 officer who became an MP and championed his innocence. It could be argued that his most effective protector was Harold Macmillan, who declared him to be a loyal subject when Foreign Secretary in 1955. When required to answer a parliamentary question, Macmillan was given a brief from MI5 indicating that, while there was no evidence against Philby of a kind which could be brought into a court, there was intelligence evidence strong enough to make him suspect. For reasons which he was unable to explain when I questioned him about it, Macmillan gave Philby a total clearance which enabled him to operate for the Soviet Union for a further eight years and then to escape justice and inflict further damage by defecting to Moscow. As Robert Lamphere has recalled, Macmillan's statement that 'I have no reason to conclude that Mr Philby has at any time betrayed the interests of this country' staggered the FBI.[19] It also staggered some MI5 officers. My inquiries leave little doubt that agents of influence among Macmillan's Foreign Office advisers were determined to stifle further inquiries into the Philby–Maclean–Burgess scandal, possibly for motives which they regarded as in the Foreign Office's interests.

The so-called 'clearance' of Sir Roger Hollis by the Prime Minister, Mrs Thatcher, in 1981 was also an attempt to stifle further inquiries. It was made on the advice of senior civil servants and intelligence chiefs, anxious to limit criticism of MI5 and using the hoary argument about the danger of 'damage to morale'. Her statement, which had been prepared for her by MI5, contained obvious fallacies, especially the claim that all the evidence pointing to Hollis could be attributed to the proven traitors Philby or Blunt. In fact, as I pointed out on the day the Prime Minister spoke, Blunt had left secret work in 1946 and Philby had followed him in 1951, yet much of the evidence pointing to Hollis arose in the 1950s and 60s. Peter Wright has now confirmed this criticism and has accused Mrs Thatcher of having misled Parliament.

Herbert Norman was persistently protected by Lester Pearson, Canadian Foreign Secretary and later Prime Minister. When Norman became publicly suspect, Pearson issued a less than truthful statement that he had undergone normal security clearance, when he had not. He helped to stifle suspicions about Norman raised by others, including MI5, and showed his confidence by promoting him. When Norman's position was precarious because of American suspicions, Pearson sent him as High Commissioner to New Zealand until the pressure relaxed; then he transferred him to Cairo, as ambassador, where his access to information and influence was considerable.[20]

While Pearson seems to have been suspiciously active in his protection of Norman, other senior politicians have effectively protected traitors through their sheer inability to accept the possibility that those whom they trusted could be traitors. In 1945 Elizabeth Bentley confessed her own treachery to the FBI, and named more than twenty Washington officials who had delivered secret documents to her. She repeated her evidence to a Federal grand jury in 1948 and parts of it publicly at a meeting of a Senate investigating committee. She then appeared before the Un-American Activities Committee, but her information was dismissed by President Truman as false – quite wrongly, as later evidence proved.

The same treatment was accorded to the evidence of Whittaker Chambers when he gave a detailed account of his subversive activities to Adolf Berle, the assistant secretary of state in charge of security on 2 September 1939, naming those associated with him, including Alger Hiss. Berle told President Roosevelt, who laughed it off.[21] When the allegations became public many years later, messages of support for Hiss flooded in from former associates.

Burgess was protected by Hector McNeil, the Minister at the Foreign Office, at least in saving him from dismissal for his generally outrageous behaviour. The Foreign Office declined to believe the evidence against Maclean, and there has been similar blanket unwillingness to face the mass of evidence against Hollis, especially by those who promoted him and those whom he promoted. The more senior the suspect, the less likely is the evidence against him to be believed.

A traitor can even be protected by another who has been exposed. In his book *My Silent War*, which was controlled by the KGB, Philby, who had nothing to lose, took the blame for betraying the Bride intercepts to protect the real culprit.[22] The KGB will go to almost any lengths to protect an agent in a valuable position. There seems to be little doubt that Vassall was deliberately 'burned' so that he would be blamed for the activities of a much more senior traitor, a naval officer then still in place and who has not yet been exposed. On one occasion during the Second World War Soviet intelligence sacrificed a boat-load of soldiers to protect one well-placed agent. The agent had told them that the boat was to be blown up, but the intelligence chiefs decided to let that happen, because otherwise the agent might come under suspicion as the source of the warning.

The KGB and GRU are both adept at warning traitors in time for them to escape if that happens to suit their long-term purposes. As soon as Julius Rosenberg came under suspicion some of his agents were warned and managed to escape from the USA, presumably reaching the Soviet Union.[23] The same happened to the major agents involved with the Soviet spy ring controller Gordon Lonsdale when he was arrested.

The laws and traditional practices of Western societies also tend to be conducive to the traitor's protection. In the USA many have avoided prosecution, or conviction if prosecuted, by refusing to answer questions or pleading the fifth amendment to the constitution, which gives an American citizen the right to decline to answer any question if he or his lawyer believes that it might incriminate him if he did so. Repeated refusals on that ground tend to increase the public's doubts about the suspect's loyalty, but most of them can live with that.

In Britain many traitors have escaped retribution or public censure simply by refusing to be interviewed by MI5, which has no powers of law enforcement. The prime example is Klugmann, whose involvement in the recruitment of Soviet spies was established by some of the traitors themselves. One of his victims, John Cairncross, agreed to approach Klugmann and to threaten him with exposure if he failed to co-operate after he had himself confessed. He did so, met with a stony response, and no further action was ever taken. Several other Soviet agents, about whom MI5 had evidence of a kind which could not be presented in a court of law, successfully took the same tough line and continue to live in honourable retirement.

In Western courts undoubted traitors have frequently been acquitted or been excused serving their sentence because of legal technicalities, deliberately seized on by defence lawyers, some of whom must have known that their clients were guilty. Perhaps the most publicized case was that of the American woman spy Judith Coplon, who had joined the Soviet intelligence service and exploited her position of trust inside the Department of Justice, where she had access to many FBI reports of consuming interest to Moscow. She was caught in the act of handing over a batch of secret papers to her Russian courier in March 1949. Though her defence tried every trick, such as claiming that she and the Russian had been meeting surreptitiously only because they were in love, she was sentenced to fifteen years' imprisonment. On a retrial, however, her sentence was quashed, though not the guilty verdict, on the grounds that the FBI had used illegal methods such as telephone-taps to track her down.[24] While any accused person must have proper legal defence, some lawyers seem to overstep moral and ethical boundaries by their efforts to secure acquittals of people they know to have been guilty of gross treachery. Further, they expect to be congratulated professionally for having done so.

Many who have escaped prosecution remain immune from public censure because of severe laws of libel. Former members of secret services who could testify to the treachery of such people would never be permitted to appear in court for security reasons. Some evidence regarded as clinching by intelligence chiefs – like intercepts giving detailed instructions to a traitor – is inadmissible in court, or cannot be used without revealing the code-breaks. If the Bride evidence against Hiss could have been used he might have been tried for more than perjury; that available against the Rosenbergs would have convinced the public of their guilt. Among the very few disclosures made by the short-term KGB defector Vitaly Yurchenko was the fact that the former CIA officer Edward Howard had betrayed important secrets, including the name of a major Soviet intelligence source in Moscow. As defector evidence is not necessarily admissible, the FBI had to make other inquiries before Howard could be arrested. He heard of them and managed to defect.

There is also a tradition in most countries of suppressing unpleasant developments in various interests. The British Labour Party, for example, suppressed the fact for many years that it had harboured a paid Czech agent, in the form of Arthur Bax, to avoid damage to its political image. Similarly, a national newspaper which is never backward at publicizing spy cases concealed the fact that one of its senior journalists had proved to be one.

Quite unwitting agents of influence can serve an adversary's purpose by suppressing information about its spies and other agents. Igor Gouzenko's widow has disclosed that her husband provided evidence of a well-known Canadian lady who was 'deeply involved in the intrigue of espionage'. As she happened to be a personal friend of Mackenzie King, then the Prime Minister, Gouzenko was 'advised' by the Canadian security authorities not to mention her name to the Royal Commission appointed to examine his evidence about the deep Soviet penetration of Canadian life.[25]

Governments and government departments are unquestionably the most proficient and prolific exponents of the cover-up and the most strenuous in denying that they practise it. Until recently the prosecution or otherwise of known peacetime traitors has depended on the whims of the security chiefs, the law officers acting on their advice often not being consulted at all. Some deeply suspected traitors have even escaped questioning because security officials have prevented it for reasons which seem highly suspicious.

Research by investigative writers has brought to light many cases where traitors have been permitted to remain free, often without penalty of any kind, so that politicians or officials could avoid scandals damaging to them or to their departments. When Elizabeth Bentley confessed all she knew to the FBI in 1945, the FBI director J. Edgar Hoover sent the White House a long list of government officials believed to be Soviet agents. None was arrested, and one of the most damaging, Harry Dexter White, was promoted! Ellis, the MI6 traitor, was not prosecuted, though he confessed to having betrayed his colleagues and his country for money during war. The security and intelligence authorities decided that a court case against a man who had been undetected for so long and was deeply suspected of having continued his treachery for the Soviet Union would damage the reputation of the secret services, especially with the USA and other allies, who were therefore kept in ignorance of it. Ellis was allowed not only to remain free on full pension but to enjoy honour as a patriot, save among the very few of his former MI6 colleagues who knew the truth about him.

Roy Guindon, the Canadian soldier security guard who betrayed his country over many years, was permitted to retire on a pension after confessing in private.[26] Even the appalling treachery inflicted by Maclean and Burgess was covered up by misinformation and bald lies until events which the security services could not conceal forced out the truth. Like the traitors they are supposed to root out, secret services generate their own 'legends'.

Most adventurers and danger-seekers need the factor of luck to survive, and traitors seem to have enjoyed more than their fair share of it. A study of the Cambridge ring, for instance, shows that they all had a truly charmed life. Some of them openly exposed their treachery when drunk or when trying to recruit others but managed to survive. Philby had a particularly fortunate escape when a Soviet defector, Alexander Orlov, failed to reveal a crucial clue when he was debriefed in the USA – that a British journalist working in Spain, and who was a Soviet agent, could never be used to communicate by voice radio in an emergency because he had a speech impediment. Philby was the only one with a pronounced stutter. He was lucky again when Krivitsky revealed to MI5 in 1940 that one of the Soviets' British recruits had been a journalist sent to Spain to spy on Franco. While he must have been terrified to learn of the projected defection of Volkov, his luck held out when he was able to talk his superiors into putting him in charge of the operation. The same applied to Hollis when he managed to get himself selected to go out to Canada to deal with the Gouzenko case. How many other defectors have been 'nobbled' in such ways?

During the Second World War Blunt was stopped by a policeman in the blackout with a briefcase full of secret documents which he should not have removed from the office and was taking to the Russians for photocopying. He managed to avoid having the case searched by providing an MI5 telephone number.

Some new evidence has come my way which strongly suggests that, in addition to luck, the Cambridge ring, like other traitors, had some protective hand inside the security service charged with detecting them. Professor G. M. Wickens has revealed that in 1964 – as part of the inquiries into Blunt – he was questioned in Canada on behalf of MI5 which, he was told, had him listed as a member of the Communist Party. Since his only connection with Communists had been at Cambridge in the 1930s, when he knew several of the Cambridge ring, this implied that MI5 had a list of the Cambridge Communists; and clearly, Blunt and Long in particular, who were well known as Communists, should have been on it. MI5 officers who investigated

256

Blunt have assured me that he and Long were not listed as Communists. So it could be, as Professor Wickens suspects, that their names were removed from the MI5 records. If so, who removed them and why? The circumstances might be explicable on the grounds of incompetence in MI5 – what is now referred to, even by academics, as 'cock-up' rather than conspiracy – but the evidence savours more of treacherous protective hands.

CHAPTER TWENTY-THREE

How Traitors Are Exposed

Truth will ultimately prevail where there is pains taken to
bring it to light.

George Washington, *Maxims*

Traitors on occasion bring about their own downfall by failure to obey
the conspiratorial rules to an extent amounting to crass stupidity.
Lyalin was foolish enough to drive a car in London after drinking too
much; his arrest enforced his defection. Penkovsky was so dangerously
indiscreet that he had walked into the American Embassy in Moscow
to offer his services. Later, when he demanded £1,000 from MI6 to
spend while in London and was warned that the KGB was bound to
wonder where he had got it, his answer was: 'Whose neck will get it,
yours or mine?' He took the money and spent it.

The British Army staff sergeant Percy Allen was imprudent enough
occasionally to use a telephone box near the War Office which happened to be 'bugged', when he tried to sell secrets to the Iraqis.
Ronald Pelton, the former NSA officer, rang the Soviet Embassy in
Washington on a tapped line which was recorded in 1980. He escaped
then because his voice was unrecognizable, but it was identified after
the defector Yurchenko named him five years later. The wife of the
naval sub-lieutenant Bingham, who was keen for him to trade some
information, called at the Soviet Embassy in London, which is regularly watched. The American Andrew Daulton Lee betrayed both
himself and his espionage source, Christopher Boyce, by throwing a
note over the gate of the Soviet Embassy in Mexico City to expedite
a meeting, instead of going through the agreed procedure. Mexican
police, who had seen a Soviet guard pick the paper up, arrested him
and found he was carrying microfilms of top-secret documents. He
was handed over to the FBI.[1] Boyce is far from being the only traitor
to owe his exposure to the stupidity of someone else. Penkovsky's poor
conspiratorial practice betrayed his faithful courier, Greville Wynne.
There are many other cases where the indiscretions of traitors should

have led to their exposure but the implications were simply dismissed as incredible.

It was only Geoffrey Prime's need to masturbate in front of little girls that led to knowledge of his treachery. There have been so many other instances in which traitors have been exposed by such a fluke circumstance that counter-intelligence agencies have a name for them: windfalls.

Prime was exposed through the patriotism of his wife, and other traitors who were denounced by wives whom they had alienated have already been mentioned. Recently the wife of a West German traitor, Franz Roski, denounced her husband because of her religious scruples – she was a Jehovah's Witness – while claiming to be still in love with him. When he was sentenced to five years' jail they left the courtroom arm in arm![2]

I know of no traitor who has been exposed to the security authorities by an investigative writer, but several have been exposed to public censure that way. Andrew Boyle exposed Blunt. The *Sunday Times* exposed Long, and my efforts exposed Ellis, Cairncross, Floud, Watson, and others and initiated the long-running public debate about Hollis.

Just as good luck has enabled some traitors to lead charmed lives, a few have been caught through sheer bad luck. In April 1952 a sharp-eyed watcher, a surveillance officer from MI5, was alighting from a bus while off duty and spotted a Soviet intelligence officer, one Pavel Kuznetsov, in conversation with a young Englishman on a park bench. He followed the young man to his home and, noting the address, found that he was William Marshall, a Foreign Office radio operator who had served in Moscow. Marshall was put under surveillance and eventually arrested and sentenced to five years' imprisonment. Until that chance sighting the security authorities had no knowledge of Marshall's treachery, which had been substantial.

The traitor in a secret department which offers wide and regular access can bring about his downfall by overdoing his treachery. The suspicion against Philby hardened after the defection of Burgess and Maclean, because an analysis of his record showed that almost every operation against the Soviets with which he had been associated had gone sour. The same applied to Hollis when his record was scrutinized.[3] Soviet agents are strongly advised against being excessively nosey, especially in areas outside their own, but once a traitor is established his enthusiasm may override his caution. This may, on occasion, be the fault of excessive requirements by the Moscow centre.

A few traitors have raised initial suspicions by flaunting the money they have earned from their treachery. James Morrison, the former 'Mountie' recently jailed for betraying an agent for money, was one of them. Some, who were more careful, had swollen bank accounts which security authorities were able to examine once suspicions had been aroused.

Routine counter-intelligence is not as successful at uncovering traitors as might be expected in view of the money and effort spent on it, but occasionally it succeeds, though suspicions have usually been aroused first from some other source. Clandestine radio operators are particularly at risk. Once their transmissions have been detected, their radio sets can be located by means of goniometry: securing bearings by several detector vans. The British Soviet agent Alexander Foote was tracked down in that way when operating in Switzerland. On occasion, especially in totalitarian countries, where people's rights can be subordinated, counter-intelligence men have located a transmitter which they knew to be in a certain town simply by turning off the electricity supply area by area and then street by street, until the set fell silent.

Even when moved regularly, a transmitter can be spotted because each radio operator tends to have a particular method of operation: an individual speed, touch, and interval between words. The burst transmitter, which sends out Morse signals previously made on punched tape at very high speed, has greatly reduced the risk of detection, but counter-measures are keeping pace. A radio operator who breaks down on interrogation can identify the spies for whom he is working, and that was how Schulze-Boysen and his anti-Nazi ring were tracked down by the Gestapo. Even if he avoids confessing, the capture of his code-books and records may identify his sources.

The degree to which radio intercepts can lead to the exposure of traitors, provided that the messages can be deciphered, was demonstrated by Operation Bride, which was such an extraordinary success that it merits further description. In late 1947 the FBI officer Robert Lamphere and an Army security cryptanalyst called Gardner Meredith began to work through copies of coded highly secret messages which had been sent from Soviet KGB centres in New York and Washington to Moscow by way of commercial cable companies in 1944 and 1945. With great difficulty they managed to reconstruct messages which not only revealed the extent of Russia's espionage against its wartime allies but gave leads to a number of American and British traitors, who were eventually exposed. The early code-breaks referred to a woman KGB agent, with the date when she was being transferred to the Justice Department. It was easy to identify her as Judith Coplon and to prove her guilt by feeding her what in the counter-intelligence 'trade' are called *barium meals*. These were documents which had been doctored to contain information which the FBI believed she would be tempted to pass to her KGB controller without delay. By keeping her under close surveillance FBI men were able to arrest her with her controller and with a summary of the documents in her handbag. Sometimes counter-intelligence officers have to wait for evidence of the arrival of such information in Moscow before they can be sure that a barium meal has been swallowed.

The first clue to Fuchs's treachery was secured by the FBI from the decipherment of a 1944 KGB message containing much secret information about a method of making uranium 235, plus the fact that the source was British.[4] The deciphered messages which led to Maclean quoted the serial numbers of cables sent from Churchill to Truman. One of the breaks which led to the Rosenbergs referred to 'Ethel', Mrs Rosenberg's first name, in a way which fitted her.

Another Bride break referred to a proposed meeting of two KGB agents in the USA. They were to recognize each other by each producing one half of a cinema ticket; the explanatory message to Moscow seeking agreement for the meeting even gave the number of the ticket, half of which was eventually discovered in the possession of one of the agents.[5] Even the locations of individual hiding-places for messages and money have to be cleared by Moscow.

Occasionally the central control exerted over agents by Soviet-bloc intelligence centres provides opportunity for arrant stupidities. It was in such a way that two of the Soviet bloc's most important agents, the West German traitors Gunther Guillaume and his wife Christl, were unmasked. Guillaume, who worked in Chancellor Willy Brandt's office, had been such a successful spy that the East German intelligence headquarters sent coded birthday greetings to him, his wife, and their son. The messages were decoded by GCHQ, which passed them to West German security, which easily identified the Guillaumes from the dates – an excellent example of how efficient relations between allied counter-intelligence agencies can defeat the traitor.

Other applications of advanced technology have taken their toll of traitors. Electronic devices concealed in secret files, and which bleep if they are taken out of a building, enabled MI5 men to follow Bossard to his studio and catch him in the act of making photocopies for sale to the Russians. The modern polygraph is another technological advance which has exposed some traitors.

As already indicated, easily the commonest cause of a traitor's exposure is information provided by a defector, whether from the East or from the West. Blake is a type specimen, having been exposed by the Polish defector Goleniewski. As Blake was safely in Beirut at the time and could have been spirited out by the KGB, there seems to have been either a failure to communicate on his part or an error of judgement in Moscow. If Blake did consult a KGB contact in Beirut when ordered back to Britain, under the subterfuge of discussing a new job involving promotion, then either the KGB thought the risk worthwhile to get Blake into a new position of access or it could not resist the possibility of the scandal of a new spy trial with the inevitable souring of Anglo-American relations. The KGB is prepared to 'burn' an agent for a substantial political advantage, but in Blake's case it would benefit either way.

All Western traitors working in the Soviet interest continue to be of service to Moscow when publicly exposed, particularly if put on trial. The details of their treachery usually reveal some appalling security deficiency on the part of the country which should have detected them, and this exacerbates the distrust of that country by the USA. Ever since the Fuchs case, followed so closely by the Maclean–Burgess–Philby affair, the American security authorities have never quite trusted their British counterparts, in spite of their own failures. This has eroded the Anglo-American exchange of intelligence and military secrets and, to some extent, weakened the Anglo-American alliance. Indeed, it could be argued that Fuchs and Blake did more damage after they were caught than they had perpetrated before. The weakening and final rupture of the defence and intelligence relationship between the USA and its European allies, and with Britain in particular, have long been a prime Soviet objective. The recent spate of traitor scandals in West Germany has inflicted further damage in that regard.

Even a false defector may expose a traitor if he has been told to do so by his superiors in order to establish his credibility as a true one. A traitor near the end of his usefulness may be selected for 'burning' in this way. Bossard is a type specimen; the lead to him was given to the FBI by the false KGB defector code-named 'Fedora' and was one of the reasons why 'Fedora' was accepted as totally genuine by J. Edgar Hoover for ten years.[6]

As happens with other forms of crime, traitors are commonly exposed by others who decide to make confessions. The type specimen is Blunt's exposure to the FBI by Michael Straight, who decided to make a confession after the chance offer of appointment in the White House, which he knew would require security investigation of his background. It was Elizabeth Bentley who gave the first clues to Julius Rosenberg, including his first name, because he had been marginally in the ring run by Bentley's lover. Fuchs gave the lead to Harry Gold, his American courier, simply by volunteering the clue that he must have known something about chemistry and engineering. Eventually he identified photographs of his former courier, whose arrest led to the Rosenberg spy ring. Chambers fingered Hiss, while Blunt gave leads to Long and Cairncross.

Several would-be traitors have been apprehended recently in the US by the use of *agents provocateurs* – FBI officers posing as Soviet agents in search of new recruits for espionage and subversion. In October 1986, for example, Allen John Davies, a British-born former American Air Force sergeant, was charged with giving secret information about air-reconnaissance equipment to a man whom he believed to be a Russian but who was really from the FBI. He claimed that his motive was resentment – he wanted to 'burn the government' in retaliation for his dismissal from the Air Force for 'poor job performance'.[7] Civil libertarians are highly critical of this form of counter-espionage since it could embroil someone who would otherwise never become involved in treachery. There can be little doubt, however, that publicity about such cases is an effective deterrent.

Further instances of ways in which traitors are exposed will be given in Chapter 24, which is concerned with the reasons why some of them confess.

CHAPTER TWENTY-FOUR

Why Traitors Confess

He's half absolved who has confessed.

Matthew Prior

Most traitors tend to confess once they believe they are cornered. Some of them, who behave almost as though they have been awaiting the opportunity, tend to pour out all that has happened. After a routine initial denial, Colonel Stig Wennerstrom confessed so volubly about his fifteen years' membership of the Soviet intelligence service that his statements covered thousands of typewritten pages.[1] Vassall felt so relieved after his arrest that 'For hours I poured out what had been bottled up in my mind for years.'[2] With some there may even be an inner desire to be caught, for they leave clues to their guilt which a psychologist would regard as subconsciously deliberate. Harry Gold was told that the FBI was to visit him in connection with inquiries into the co-conspirators of Klaus Fuchs; and though he knew that there were incriminating documents in his home, he made no determined effort to remove them all.[3]

Relief at being delivered from further treachery does not necessarily indicate remorse. When Fuchs signed a six-and-a-half-page statement summarizing his espionage activities for the FBI, he claimed that his co-operation was 'in some small way restitution for what he had done'. But fellow prisoners to whom he confided were sure that he had no regrets apart from the misfortune of being caught.

The MI5 and MI6 managements seemed to be convinced that Blake was contrite, as he should have been considering that some of the agents he betrayed were tortured and hanged.[4] Kenneth de Courcy and others who knew him in prison do not agree, and his escape and departure to Moscow, where he was eventually decorated, suggest that their view more accurate. Philby and Blunt certainly showed no remorse when they confessed, even though they had sent people to their death, believing that such crimes were justified in their struggle to change society.

If a spy who has decided to confess still feels that he is in a strong position he may be very selective and limit his admissions to what he believes has already been discovered. This happened with Philby during his brief confession in Beirut, when he knew that he was in no danger of being spirited back to London and had a KGB officer on hand to advise him what to admit and what disinformation to include. The same occurred with Blunt, when he had been guaranteed immunity from both prosecution and publicity. He either lied to questions on which he did not wish to be informative or simply declined to answer; MI5 could do little about it. Fuchs withheld the name of the Kuczynskis – 'Sonia' and her brother Jurgen – until he was sure that both were out of reach, and he delayed the identification of Harry Gold until he appreciated that Gold had confessed anyway. Defectors like Alexander Orlov who realized that they would never be returned to Moscow kept back much information partly out of old loyalty but also to reduce the risk of attention from the KGB assassination squads.

It is commonly believed that a traitor is so burdened by his secret that he is driven to confide in at least one other trusted person, and there is some truth in this. Burgess made a private confession to his friend Goronwy Rees that he was a Comintern agent, though this was part of an attempt to recruit him. Harry Gold confessed to an old Communist friend, saying: 'The FBI is looking for Klaus Fuchs's American contact, and I am that man.'[5] To what extent traitors confess to their wives or mistresses, trusting in their greater loyalty to them rather than to their country, is not really known. Philby's wives almost certainly did not know of his double life. Blunt's live-in man-friend, the former Irish Guardsman John Gaskin, makes the same claim.

Only a few traitors have confessed spontaneously to the security authorities, risking the chance that they might be prosecuted. Some have done so in the hope of minimizing punishment when they sensed that they might be exposed. The American Communist spies Whittaker Chambers and Elizabeth Bentley confessed to the FBI when they become disenchanted with the Soviet system and tired of the conspiratorial life. Such former Communists who turn against the party and realize or claim that they have been duped are usually so embittered that they implicate everyone else, becoming widely disliked in the process, even though they are helping their country. Hede Massing was another disillusioned agent who made a long confession to the FBI of her past subversive activities for the KGB, knowing that she would not be prosecuted.

Alexander Foote's reason for confessing in 1947 was disillusionment about the way he and other loyal Soviet spies were treated on their return to Moscow. His chief, Sandor Rado, had been imprisoned for ten years.[6]

Not many confessions seem to have been the result of any crisis of conscience. One that certainly was was that of the KGB assassin Bogdan Stashinsky, who made himself technically a traitor in the process. He had murdered two leading Ukrainian exiles whose antipathy had offended the Soviet leadership. Using a cyanide-gas gun he had killed Lev Rebet, the editor of an exile Ukrainian newspaper, in Munich in 1957, and two years later used the same method to murder Stepan Bandera in the same city. For these deeds, when in his late twenties, he had been presented with the Order of the Red Banner personally by the KGB chief, Shelepin, with the agreement of the Politburo; but the evidence suggests that his conscience had already begun to trouble him. In 1961 he defected to the Americans in Berlin and volunteered a full confession to the two murders, knowing that the West German authorities would have to prosecute him, as they did. The following year he was sentenced to eight years' imprisonment. The court was lenient because of his confession to two deaths which had been regarded as natural.[7]

The most celebrated spontaneous confession of recent times is that of the American writer Michael Straight, who approached the FBI in 1963 to admit his past connections with the KGB following his recruitment by Blunt in 1937, and to expose that arch-traitor in the process. He had been called to the White House to discuss a possible appointment as Presidential adviser on the arts and, when told that he would be subjected to a security check, decided to reject the post but confess his Communist past. He has since described his FBI experience and soul-searchings in memoirs.[8] In my conversations with Straight he has continued to express regret at his involvement, limited as it was. More usually, however, if there is an element of conscience behind a confession it tends to be slight and fleeting.

Some traitors may secure some vain satisfaction through confessing by demonstrating how they have fooled the security authorities for so long. Blunt told MI5 that the KGB insisted that Maclean must defect because, if subjected to interrogation, he would tell all for that reason. James Morrison, the former Mountie, indulged his vanity by confessing on Canadian television, while disguised by a wig and false moustache and identified only by his code-name, 'Long Knife', that he had sold out an agent for $3,500.

Most traitors have confessed only when under interrogation. The situation which has prevailed in the Soviet Union, even in peacetime, has been described by the KGB defector Peter Deriabin: 'The device of the forced voluntary confession, that awesome combination of the revival meeting, the Inquisition and the third degree, is original with

Soviet Communism and it will stand as one of the basest inventions in human history.'[9] Under Soviet law, acts which would not be considered criminal in a Western society can be deemed to be espionage. This is one of the reasons why those arrested, including Red Army generals, have so readily confessed to that serious crime and signed their own death warrant. Since the Soviet state can never be wrong, and the KGB never arrests anyone who is not automatically guilty, the interrogator, who is in serious trouble if he fails to secure a confession, sets out to establish in the prisoner a sense of guilt and of inevitable doom.

Wartime Germany was equally infamous for reprehensible methods of interrogation, especially by the Gestapo. Savage torture and threats to wives and children were in regular use. Simple fear made some professionals confess all they knew, as happened with Heinrich Koenen, a German national parachuted into East Prussia by the Russians with a radio transmitter in 1942, who was quickly picked up because he had already been betrayed. Koenen soon became an active collaborator but was eventually executed as a traitor. The Gestapo acted similarly with the wife of Schulze-Boysen, who not only confessed but agreed to be a witness against her husband and others of his ring, believing that her own life would be spared, which it was not.

The danger with interrogation which includes physical assault or the threat of it is that it can produce false confessions made out of terror or to secure release from unbearable pain. Several victims have described the methods developed by Russian interrogators, none more vividly than Mrs Aino Kuusinen, whose former husband, Otto, was Deputy Chairman of the Praesidium of the USSR from 1940 to 1957. Mrs Kuusinen was subjected to every kind of pressure and indignity for more than a year to force her into falsely confessing that Otto was a traitor and a British spy. She was made to listen to screams, stated to be made by her husband, who was said to have confessed, when in fact he was not even under arrest. At one point she was made to stare at the corpse of a man who had been thrashed to death. When her interrogators realized that she would never sign any incriminating document she was sent, without trial, to a notorious labour camp in the Arctic Circle, where she remained for eight years.[10]

In the true democracies the degree of coercion permissible to interrogators is severely limited. Even in wartime, British and American interrogators were restricted by conventions, though they could use the threat of execution after trial to secure co-operation, as MI5 did to obtain the assistance of former German agents whom it used in its Double X deception operations. In peacetime, if there are any lamentable lapses on the part of Western interrogators a traitor may be able to use them to his advantage through his lawyer.

A suspect has other rights which, if used skilfully by himself or his lawyer, can save him from retribution. In the first place he can decline to be interviewed at all by MI5, and in the absence of admissions the police may be unable to act. True professionals, of course, should not confess to anyone at any time. Blunt revealed that the KGB's advice is to refuse to be interviewed or, if that is not practicable, to admit nothing but keep talking to see how much the questioners know. The type specimen is James Klugmann, who committed individual treason and assisted others to do so by helping in their recruitment and by other means. He resolutely refused to say anything that might incriminate him, and without a confession there was nothing that the law could do. Since then several other members of the Cambridge and Oxford spy rings, whose names and activities have been made available to me by the thwarted officers of MI5 but cannot yet be exposed because of libel problems, have availed themselves of the same defence and have continued to hold important positions and to be respected by the community. 'Sonia' escaped her deserts with a curt 'I do not wish to co-operate' when MI5 officers called at her home, while her British-born husband was never approached.

The British Communist traitor Douglas Springhall declined to give any help or evidence at his trial. The Rosenbergs did not confess to save their lives. The Krogers admitted nothing. While Philby confessed his general treachery, his admissions were either marginal or untrue. As his wife, Eleanor, observed, he would not have been so welcome in Moscow had he made a full confession.[11]

Before a suspected traitor is formally charged in Britain, the USA or any of the true democracies, where justice has to be seen to be done, there is often pressing need to secure a confession and then a guilty plea to limit the amount of secret information likely to be revealed in court. Without a confession the authorities may prefer to proceed no further, even in camera, to avoid using evidence which might endanger sources, and because uncorroborated statements from secret sources are often inadmissible in court. Confessions made, or alleged to have been made, under duress can also be withdrawn in Western societies – so a softly, softly approach is usually essential.

When the Foreign Office traitor Captain John King had to be interrogated, an MI5 officer and a Foreign Office security official managed to loosen his tongue with nothing more harassing than a few large whiskies in a Mayfair pub. The quiet, unflamboyant William 'Jim' Skardon was chosen for the task of interrogating Fuchs and opened by making an excuse to discuss the security problems presented by Fuchs's father, who had accepted an academic post in East Germany. Skardon's technique was to secure co-operation through engendering a feeling of friendliness and understanding. After several days of such sympathetic and almost deferential treatment, with no note-taking (which can inhibit a suspect), Fuchs's resistance suddenly collapsed. This event demonstrates the importance of having someone else listening in surreptitiously to the interrogation of a suspect, as is usually contrived. In Fuchs's case a perceptive woman officer from MI5, Evelyn Grist, felt 'in her bones' that Fuchs was lying on four points, and urged Skardon to try again, concentrating on them, which he did.

A confession may come easily if a suspect feels that by being able to implicate others he can improve his own position. In confessing their betrayal of atomic bomb secrets both David Greenglass and his wife, Ruth, implicated their relatives, the Rosenbergs, to improve their own predicament.

Details of exactly what has happened during the interrogations of suspected traitors are rarely published. However, some – such as those relating to Blunt and Ellis – have been made available to me, while Robert Lamphere has also recently described some American cases.[12] The FBI reports on the interrogation of Michael Straight are available, too, though much in them which concerns British traitors has been blacked out at MI5's request. They all show that there is little truth in the common notion that such people are subjected to a 'third degree' or even 'grilled'. The process, which usually begins as interviews, was accurately described by Blunt as 'comfortable'. The first interrogation of Philby by Sir Helenus 'Buster' Milmo is said to have been 'tough', but the tape-recordings show otherwise; it was easily resisted by such an experienced liar, who made effective use of his stammer when he needed extra time to answer.

The degree of toughness permissible in security interrogations was considered officially in 1986 in a report of an inquiry by an independent QC on eight young servicemen who had been acquitted of offences under the Official Secrets Act alleged to have been committed while serving on highly secret signals-intercept operations in Cyprus. The men, who had been interrogated separately, had signed individual confessions implying that they were prepared to plead guilty, but later all withdrew them; they claimed that the confessions had been secured from them under duress. None of the eight chose to give evidence to the inquiry. The report concluded that none of them had been subjected to any violence or threats of violence, and it cleared the service interrogators of using 'brainwashing' or any other unlawful techniques. It concluded, however, that the defendants had spent so many days in 'improper custody' that they were likely to give unreliable answers. The main outcome of the case, which lasted four months and cost the taxpayers £4,500,000, is that future suspects will be tried by

269

court martial under Queen's Regulations and not in a civil court under the Official Secrets Act.[13]

There has been at least one death of a suspect under interrogation in the West in recent times: that of John Watkins, the former Canadian Ambassador who was compromised homosexually while serving in the Soviet Union. This event, in 1964, raised questions about the harshness of the interrogation, in which Watkins had freely admitted the compromise but insisted that he had never obliged the KGB as a result. My inquiries with one of the officers concerned has convinced me that Watkins, who had a heart condition, died from entirely natural causes and that, while the fact of being interrogated was inevitably stressful in itself, no undue pressure had been applied.[14]

I have secured very full details of the interrogation in 1966 of Charles Howard Ellis, who had held very high rank in MI6 and other intelligence departments.[15] Because he was seventy-one, he was interviewed for only a few hours a day and was at first taken gently through his career. He was then confronted with the report of a German officer who had named him as a spy; after he insisted that it was a forgery, he was told there were more incriminating documents and sent home to think about it. The interrogation was gradually made more hostile. When Ellis continued to profess his innocence with a stream of lies he was threatened with being faced by the German officer, which was a bluff. On the following day he made a partial confession and then went on to admit his major treachery of betraying to the Germans, for money, the MI6 'order of battle' – charts showing the personnel and the way they were organized. He also admitted betraying the fact that MI6 had been tapping the telephone lines between Von Ribbentrop, the pre-war German Ambassador to Britain, and Hitler, which ended that valuable information source. Ellis resolutely denied having become a spy for the Russians – as MI5 still suspect that he was, probably for almost thirty years – knowing that there was no firm evidence against him, nor were there any witnesses.[16]

A few traitors confess immediately they become aware that their interrogators know a great deal about them, as did the German MP Alfred Frenzel, and John Vassall. Another who did so was a young British Foreign Office official who had allowed himself to be recruited on ideological grounds and was betrayed by a defector. He was required to resign, but because of his co-operation, and to help in covering up the case, a post was found for him in the media.

When George Blake was tricked into returning to Britain from Beirut in April 1961 to be interrogated, mainly on the basis of defector information, the MI6 interrogator Terence Lecky knew that there was no evidence which could be brought into a British court. If Blake was to be prosecuted it could only be through the abstraction of a signed confession. Lecky therefore set the stage with an imposing heap of files to which he made menacing glances, hoping to convince Blake that there was usable evidence there. It is standard practice to lie to a suspect to convince him that his interrogator has all the information needed; when, in fact, the information is really to hand its production often causes a total collapse of resistance, as it did with Gold, Wennerstrom, and Gerhardt. Blake, however, stonewalled all the questions effectively and may well have guessed that, provided he admitted nothing, he would be safe. But when the weary Lecky made what was described to me as 'positively his last throw', Blake broke down and confessed to all the crimes of which he had become suspect and more, knowing that he would be held responsible for the torture and execution of British agents. He appeared to show no remorse, so his behaviour in confessing looked symptomatic of some basic instability.

The Attorney-General who prosecuted Blake, Sir Reginald Manningham Buller, with whom I became friendly when he became Lord Chancellor, told me that right until the moment of Blake's guilty plea in court there were fears that he might withdraw his confession on the grounds that it had been made under duress and that the case would then have collapsed. No steps had been taken to offer Blake immunity if he failed to confess, and presumably he would have gone free.

Brian Linney, the traitorous electronics engineer, was bluffed into confessing by a particularly persuasive MI5 officer, who tape-recorded the statement against possible future claims that it had been made under duress. It is nevertheless doubtful that the tape would have been admissible evidence.

An interrogator may play on a suspect's naïvety by encouraging him to entertain false hopes of not being prosecuted, or of mitigation of sentence if he is. When Fuchs decided to confess he did not think he would be prosecuted, believing that because he had spied for a principle he had not committed a crime. He later told his fellow prisoner, Hume, that he felt cheated. His main concern, when confessing, was not about going to prison but whether he would be free of questioning in time to attend an Anglo-American declassification conference! He later claimed that the only reason he confessed was 'because the atmosphere at Harwell was becoming intolerable with all his friends being interrogated and being regarded with suspicion'.[17] Fuchs's stance was all the more pathetic because without a confession he could not have been prosecuted.

Vassall, too, deluded himself into thinking that after confessing he would just be discreetly moved away from the Admiralty to Canada or some other quiet backwater out of reach of the Russians.[18] He told MI5 that he was a victim of circumstance, more to be pitied than hounded, and argued in his memoirs: 'If one is blackmailed into action of this kind, surely one is not acting freely.'

A defence lawyer will normally advise a client to withdraw a confession which virtually rules out a not-guilty plea. The servicemen in the recent Cyprus case who had all signed confessions all withdrew them after acquiring civil legal representation. Vassall's solicitor did not want him to plead guilty, believing that he 'would not necessarily be held totally responsible for his actions'; but having signed the confession, Vassall declined to withdraw it.

In recent years, when seeking confessions, the US security authorities have made increasing use of the lie-detecting polygraph, which, as already described, is now a standard American tool in the positive-vetting process. While being polygraphed in 1984, Richard Miller, the FBI agent, confessed to having demanded $50,000 in gold from the Russians for documents he delivered. The traitor William Kampiles was also unmasked as a result of a polygraph test. He attempted to deceive the CIA into enabling him to serve as a disinformation agent with the Russians so that he could, in fact, sell them more American secrets. Claiming to have met a GRU agent in Athens by accident and, without giving any secrets away, he said he had been paid $3,000 in the hope that he would provide information in the future. When CIA officials declined to believe him without a polygraph test he agreed to undergo one. On failing it, Kampiles broke down and confessed the truth that he had approached the Soviet Embassy in Athens with an offer of secrets, had been recruited by the GRU, and had sold the KH–11 manual giving most secret details of the surveillance satellite system.[19]

Following the Prime case, members of the British Security Commission visited Washington and were impressed by the 'record of confessions induced by the polygraph in security screening, both of previous criminal activity or other disqualifying defects of character and even, in some cases, of an intention to gain access to secret information for hostile purposes'.[20]

Securing a confession is made much easier when there is a prior promise of immunity. When the MI6 officer Nicholas Elliott interrogated Philby in Beirut in January 1963 he had been instructed to assure the traitor that he would be given immunity from prosecution if he made a full confession and returned to Britain for a long debriefing. Had he accepted the offer, Philby might have remained respectable into old age, protected by the libel laws as he disported himself in his old clubs, like the Athenaeum. Instead, knowing that he was outside British jurisdiction, Philby confessed to having been a Soviet agent since 1934, claimed to have been the 'third man' who had warned Maclean, and admitted various other acts of treachery, including the sabotage of operations against Albania. He insisted that Blunt had not been a spy, which was a lie. He also made so many other misleading statements that MI5 became convinced that the 'confession' had been cobbled together by Philby and a KGB controller who 'happened' to be in Beirut.[21] Parts of it have since been seen as disinformation to take the heat off a high-level Soviet agent in London, who was still functioning, by volunteering responsibility for acts he had not committed.

The British Prime Minister at the time, Harold Macmillan, confused the issue by writing in his diary that Philby had confessed 'in a drunken fit', but Elliott has assured me that he was sober. It is most unlikely that the KGB would have permitted him to attend the meeting in a drunken state. MI5 is in no doubt that Philby had been warned in advance of Elliott's visit and its purpose. The sudden withdrawal of Philby from Beirut by the KGB before Elliott's arrival would have warned MI5 of the leakage and endangered the source of the warning; so a limited confession, containing some disinformation, was in the KGB's best interests. The confession also served the purpose of souring Anglo-American relations still further once the CIA was told of it.

MI5's alleged objective in offering secret immunity to Blunt was to secure the maximum amount of information, but its prime purpose was to prevent a public scandal, embarrassment to the government and MI5 itself, and to cover the treachery of Blunt's associates. The immunity granted to Will Owen, the MP accused of selling secrets, made more security sense because further prosecution would have been extremely difficult after his acquittal in 1970. Owen then did confess to substantial acts of treachery.[22]

While plea-bargaining regularly occurs in American legal cases, there seem to have been few cases where total immunity has been granted to a traitor, any 'rewards' for assistance being usually in the form of reduced sentences. In 1982, however, a US Air Force Second Lieutenant, who confessed to giving the Soviets secrets about the Titan intercontinental missile, was granted immunity by the military authorities in return for a confession.[23] Current FBI policy is to prosecute traitors wherever possible because they deserve to be severely punished, to discourage others, and to show the public the threat it faces from the Soviet bloc. An exception is made of defectors even when they confess to treacherous acts committed as part of their previous duties.

Hugh Hambleton made history by confessing in open court. After being betrayed by a Soviet-bloc defector and branded publicly as a spy by the FBI, he was granted immunity from prosecution and publicity by the Mounties in return for a written confession in 1980. The British Attorney-General did not want to embarrass the Canadian government by arresting Hambleton if he came to Britain, so he was urged to stay away, but the spy was so arrogantly sure of his immunity that he made the journey and was arrested. Though he knew that his prosecutors were aware he had signed a confession in Canada, Hambleton protested his innocence in the witness box and claimed that he had been serving as a double agent. Then, suddenly, he admitted his guilt.

Hambleton later told a friend, Leo Heaps, who talked with him in prison for several hours, that he confessed because he had been caught out in a lie about his fantasized war record and realized that he was beaten. Some inner need to unburden himself may have turned the scale. The act of describing his exploits, including a dinner with the KGB chief, Andropov, may have appealed to his excessive vanity, though Heaps believes his confession was limited to areas where he had been exposed.[24] Hambleton did not explain why he still had so much espionage equipment at a time when he had no access to secrets; MI5 believed that he was running other agents in Canada.

The public exposure of the Blunt case in 1979 brought the whole morality of immunity to public notice. The prosecution of Hambleton was an expression of the British government's decision to end it, except possibly for very special cases. In the public mind immunity may be morally justified in terms of turning Queen's evidence, a traitor being prepared to give evidence against others to secure their conviction, but the immunity granted to Blunt effectively gave immunity to his accomplices and others he named – no attempt was made to prosecute any of them.

Exposure of the background to Blunt's immunity, which had been held tightly secret, convinced MPs and the public that he had been given unjustifiably generous treatment because he was an establishment figure and that less well-placed traitors would have been rigorously subjected to prosecution and public censure.[25] The Tory government's determination to expose Blunt in 1979, in spite of strong MI5 objections, resulted from the reaction by the Attorney-General, Sir Michael Havers, to information that Blunt intended to bring a libel action against Andrew Boyle, author of the book which effectively exposed him, hoping to secure damages of £100,000. When Havers told MI5 chiefs that they would have to give evidence of his guilt they declined to do so and indicated that they would remain silent even if Blunt won his damages. Realizing the political penalty if Blunt was allowed to win the action, and if the deal with such a traitor which had made it possible was exposed later, the government decided to go ahead with the previous Labour administration's plan to make a parliamentary statement about Blunt, to which the Queen had already agreed.[26]

Several traitors have confessed, either in interviews or in their own memoirs, following their public exposure, usually by investigative writers. Blunt made an extremely limited confession to *The Times*, avoiding the more difficult questions by hiding behind the Official Secrets Act. He has since left a 30,000-word document which has been conveniently given to the British Library with the proviso that it is not to be released for thirty years. Though his brother, who has read it, claims that it contains little meat, it was valued for probate at £120,000, showing that a traitor who has been granted immunity could safely publish memoirs admitting to all kinds of treason and earn a great deal of money from them.

My own investigative efforts led to the public exposure of the past activities of Michael Straight and Flora Solomon, who subsequently published their own admissions of their behaviour.[27] 'Sonia' and her brother, Jurgen Kuczynski, have published memoirs admitting their treachery, and so has Philby, but they are larded with disinformation and omit their more serious activities.[28] Vassall has published his own account of his activities, though it is incomplete because of his reluctance to implicate certain MPs and others. Whatever such memoirs offer by way of what their authors' treachery has done to others, they certainly provide insight into what treachery has done to them.

CHAPTER TWENTY-FIVE

Lessons To Be Learned

Some of you may be wondering if the large number of spy arrests in recent weeks means that we are looking harder or whether there are more spies to be found. Well, I think the answer to both questions is 'Yes'.

President Reagan in an address to the nation,
December 1985

The recent spate of espionage and subversion cases is evidence enough that treachery is rife and that the motivations for it, with the possible exception of old-style Communist ideology, remain as strong as ever. The human agent will continue to be an inherent component of intelligence operations, which will always be essential to all governments, especially to those determined to remain major military and political powers with strength enough to ensure their freedom. There can be no doubt, then, that for the foreseeable future all nations will continue to recruit traitors. The only defence against them will be resolute precautions to prevent their recruitment and installation in sensitive positions, with improved methods of detecting those who manage to establish themselves – what is summarized by the terms *counter-espionage* and *counter-intelligence*. Do the known case histories of traitors, as analysed here, provide any reliable guidance to the general recognition of individuals capable of treachery or actually committing it?

When studying human behaviour psychologists and medical researchers often resort to a concept borrowed from mathematics: the presentation of their theories in a form which looks like algebraic equations. They do not suggest that behaviour can be quantified, but their use of what they call *factorial analysis* and mathematical symbols is a convenient form of shorthand enabling them to present their concepts with simplicity and clarity. With the limitations clearly in mind, it may be useful to summarize the relevant information about traitors and treachery in this way. While the data would seem to show that almost anyone, even the unlikeliest candidate – like Burgess, the habitual drunkard; Philby, the affable professional; Blunt, the brilliant aesthete; Maclean, the polished diplomat; or Walker, the former sailor – may turn out to be a traitor, there may be some common factors worthy of note.

For the great majority of traitors it is feasible to write the statement:

$$A \text{ (for Access)} + M \text{ (for Motivation)} \rightarrow T \text{ (for Treachery)}.$$

The significant variable in this equation is M, because, although there are various forms of access, it is only the opportunity of access, whatever form it takes, that matters. Only very rarely, if ever, is M a single factor, like money or ideology. In almost every instance the motivation is more complex. So can M be broken down into subsidiary factors in a way which has any worthwhile meaning? And how many of these subsidiary factors are common to the majority of traitors?

The one factor that is almost invariably present is money, which we can call m. It may be a major factor, as in the case of the essentially mercenary spy, or it may be minor, as in the case of those ideological traitors who were forced into taking money to strengthen the hold of their Soviet controllers.

Another almost universal factor is resentment of some kind against society, an organization, or an individual, which we can call r. As the case records show, r may sometimes be entirely concealed but more usually expresses itself as an observable chip on the shoulder.

The motivations which keep treachery going are as important as those which initiate it and may be more so when it continues over many years. There have been many instances of traitors who would have liked to end their treachery but have not been permitted to do so. The weapon used to encourage or enforce the continuation of the treachery is almost invariably some form of blackmail. So the factor of blackmailability, which we can call b, should also appear in any basic equation.

At this stage, therefore, we can write:

$$A + m + r + b \rightarrow T,$$

where the common factors are A, for access, m for money, r for resentment, and b for blackmailability.

It is trite simply to allege that the character of anyone who betrays his country and his compatriots must automatically be flawed. Yet the case records show that almost all the known traitors had a discernible flaw such as amorality or extreme sexual immorality, including deviations, a propensity for lying, arrogance and boastfulness, or a liability for excessive drinking. We could embrace all these

277

features in one factor, f for flaw, which includes the sex factor which, as the FBI adage says, is rarely absent from the equation. It might even be extended to include resentment, since a capacity for that is regarded by many as a character flaw, but resentment has so often been a prime cause of treachery – as it was, for instance, in the very recent case of the CIA traitor Edward Howard – that it merits separate factor status.

In most case histories the sense of adventure and excitement has played a role, as has a sense of power. These can conveniently be subsumed under a single factor, s for self-satisfaction, which in many instances has been important in keeping a traitor going.

It would therefore seem that for many traitors, possibly most, the basic equation has six common factors and reads:

$$A + m + r + b + f + s \rightarrow T.$$

Only one major factor seems to be missing: that of ideology, i, which for many is the most significant. For primarily mercenary traitors ideology has counted for nothing at any stage of their treachery, but it features so frequently with others that it must figure in the equation, as a seventh factor, with the understanding, common enough in mathematics, that for some traitors its value is zero.

So we can finally write:

$$A + m + r + b + f + s + i \rightarrow T,$$

where A is access, m is money, r is resentment, b is blackmailability, f is flawed character, s is self-satisfaction, and i is ideology.

Even this is an oversimplification but it is possible to develop it with respect to particular traitors. In the case of Blunt, for example, m would be small, with the other factors, especially i, r, f, and s, having high value. With Prime, m was bigger, i and s were smaller. With John Walker, m was the major factor, with i being negligible and the others small. For Vassall, b was the major factor, linked with f, with m becoming increasingly important. Readers may care to consider other examples for themselves.

The relative influence of a traitor's motives may vary during his career of treachery, with i (ideology) receding and m (money) taking precedence – as reported, for example, by the Royal Commission which inquired into the motivations of the Canadian traitors exposed by Gouzenko. In the case of a genuine double agent, the original ideology may be completely swamped by m. Nevertheless, the seven factors often remain, even if some tend towards zero as time passes.

Can such an equation be of any value to counter-intelligence officers either in their search for a suspect or in the positive-vetting process to keep potential traitors away from access? I am advised by professionals that it can. The CIA and the NSA already make use of psychological battery tests and interviews with clinical psychologists to reveal features of the psychological make-up which might affect the reliability of recruits and of some established officers when they are being revetted. In Britain the practicability of such psychological testing is in process of being studied following the Prime case.

Security files on individuals with access to secrets are supposed to be kept up to date as any relevant information about their behaviour accrues. So it should be easy to note when one or more factors in an individual's equation seems to be becoming unduly weighted.

Someone with access who displays the factors of flaw, resentment, and money – through unexplained affluence, excessive indebtedness, or sheer greed – may merit investigation. Drug-taking or heavy drinking, as in the case of Bettaney and Ruby Louise Schuler, is not only a sign of an unstable personality but may indicate a pressing need for extra money. Reports or surveillance, leading to the discovery of a pattern of behaviour, including suspicious meetings and foreign travel to places known to be favoured by Soviet intelligence, might then reveal the factors of ideology or possible blackmail.

These may all seem to be statements of the obvious, but in the history of treachery the obvious has too often been overlooked. When MI6 was finally forced into suspecting Philby, in 1963, his colleagues there found that almost every counter-Soviet case in which he had been involved had 'died'. During Hollis's command of MI5, officers there scorned a suggestion by the FBI that since the war MI5 had failed to produce the initial lead to the exposure of any Soviet traitor, but then found on investigation that all the leads had, in fact, originated in the USA. Surely it should be routine for a running check to be kept on the balance of 'assets' and 'debits' of every counter-intelligence officer, whatever his rank, and for inquiries to follow when the number of case deaths is suspiciously high. This appears to be done, however, only when suspicion has been aroused for some other cause. Had it been done with Hollis, for example, his balance sheet would have been seen to be even more glaringly negative than Philby's, as indeed it was when it was too late to take any preventive action. The routine examination of balance sheets could also point to the existence of protective hands inside secret agencies and other government departments.

Cases investigated by the Security Commission have shown that glaring personality defects and peculiar habits have not been noticed or have been ignored, and the same has happened in the USA. The process of positive vetting has frequently been farcical, with candidates for sensitive posts being able to name character referees guaranteed to know nothing of consequence about them. I have described how officers of MI6 and MI5 vetted each other, sometimes in hilarious fashion.

When Frank Bossard was checked out for an intelligence post in West Germany in 1956 it was known that he had served six months in prison for a cheques fraud, which was ignored as a youthful peccadillo. He was never revetted later when he joined the Aviation Ministry, because his work, which enabled him to sell very important secrets to the KGB, did not require access to 'top-secret' information, only to 'secret' information, and his new masters were therefore not allowed to examine his former PV file to avoid an unnecessary breaching of confidential records. The traitorous MI5 officer Bettaney had a conviction for travelling on British Rail with an invalid ticket as well as a record of drunkenness.

Whatever the civil libertarians may argue, the security authorities should be allowed access to criminal records and other personal information, when being in the dark about the character defects of those with access to secrets can lead to such disastrous consequences. In a true democracy a balance has to be struck between individual freedom and the continuing freedom of society as a whole – but if a sacrifice has to be made it should be made by the individual. Those who feel so strongly about the 'invasion of privacy' should work elsewhere than in the field of secrecy.

It is certainly not enough to react to treachery after it has occurred, as the British Security Commission is required to do now, for example. The folly of such an attitude was demonstrated by the consequences of the official reaction to the publication of my book *Their Trade Is Treachery* in 1981. The Prime Minister set up the first independent inquiry into the security and intelligence services for twenty years, with the purpose of strengthening their defences against foreign penetration. The Security Commission eventually recommended a whole range of improvements, some of them involving the security of computers, word processors, and floppy discs used to store secret information. A further statement by the Prime Minister made it clear that these steps would not have been taken at that stage, if ever, but for the fluke circumstance that I had written a book.[1] Surely if such improvements were necessary – and many were so important that they remain secret – they should have been introduced as a matter of routine and should not have had to wait until someone goaded the government into action.

It should have been blindingly obvious that, because of the ease with which documents can now be photocopied in offices, two people should always be required to be present when documents are being copied, with the numbers made rigorously checked and recorded. But the British authorities were late in introducing this precaution, and the Americans have been equally lax. The case of Koecher, the CIA man who made free with the agency's copying machine when spying for the Czechs, has already been described. When William Kampiles stole the KH–11 photographic satellite manual the authorities found that fourteen copies of it were missing. They had been serially numbered, but their whereabouts had not been regularly checked.

The trial on Official Secrets charges of the eight young servicemen stationed in Cyprus produced another overdue reaction. The Prime Minister asked the Security Commission to undertake a global inquiry into security at all British 'listening-posts'.[2] It might reasonably be asked why such an inquiry could not have been undertaken as a matter of precautionary routine. The government seems to consider it praiseworthy when another disaster enables the Security Commission to discover a possible loophole it can plug. But this should be a matter for regret, if not for censure, that it had not been spotted and remedied before, especially if it is obvious, as so many of the new recommendations prove to be.

Almost unbelievably, there have been moves in the USA and in Britain to reduce the effort and resources invested in counter-intelligence. Following the realization of the Soviet clandestine war against the West, as revealed by the Gouzenko defection and other cases, Presidents Truman and Eisenhower introduced various loyalty criteria for the employment of Americans in secret departments. Since then, year by year, in deference to US civil libertarians, the precautions have been eroded. Obvious character flaws like homosexuality, heavy drinking, the occasional use of drugs, and membership of subversive organizations (the Communist Party, the Trotskyite Socialist Workers' Party, the American Nazi Party, and even the Ku Klux Klan) are no longer a bar to employment, unless it can be established that the defect in question is affecting an individual's ability to perform his task and there is evidence of overt activity. In most cases this places an almost impossible burden of proof on the government.

As a further concession to the civil liberties industry, membership of such organizations alone can no longer even be filed by the protective security authorities.[3] In the late 1970s President Carter, Vice-President Walter Mondale, and some others took the view that covert action, the life-blood of counter-intelligence, was morally wrong and almost evil. As a result more than 800 CIA staff, mostly engaged in counter-intelligence work, were dismissed or prematurely retired, with disastrous effects on the capability of the USA to counter Soviet subversion. It was worse than a replay of the unrealistic behaviour of the overly righteous US Secretary of State Edward Stettinius, who discovered in May 1945 that the FBI had acquired 1,500 pages of Soviet code and cipher material from the Finns, who had captured it in battle. He insisted that it should all be returned as a gesture of goodwill to a gallant ally, which at that time was doing all it could to undermine American democracy through espionage and subversion. Inevitably the Russians immediately changed their codes. No more of their KGB messages to agents operating in the USA could be deciphered. I have little doubt that the main KGB reaction was to regard the Americans as mad.

The Carter ravages have been repaired to some degree under the Reagan administration but with difficulty, because a data-base takes many years to rebuild and those experienced officers who should have trained the new recruits to the CIA were among those dismissed. In Britain the thrust by the civil libertarians for less counter-intelligence has not been as effective, but they would carry much more political clout in the event of the election of a Labour government backed by many extremist MPs.

Civil libertarians are the pacifists of the cold war, and the Soviets are not slow to latch on to their activities and benefit from them. It is one of the many contradictions of Communism that the country with the largest military machine the world has ever seen attracts the support of pacifists and civil libertarians who are reluctant to criticize a system which obliterates civil liberty.

Many civil libertarians are Communists or members of other branches of the hard left, though they make every effort to hide it. This was shown by the obituary notice in *The Times* of 5 April 1986 on Catherine 'Cash' Scorer, described as 'a key figure in civil liberties for more than a decade'. Nothing was said about her membership of the Communist Party or her dedication to the Soviet Union, though this was stressed in the obituary in the *Morning Star*, which rightly described her as 'an outstanding activist in the National Council for Civil Liberties over thirteen years'. It is, of course, the duty of a dedicated Communist to use any such position for Communist – and in her case pro-Soviet – purposes.

Civil libertarians even support terrorists, as happened when Astrid Proll, one of the most wanted members of the Baader-Meinhof gang, was arrested in London, where she had been working under a false name. Together with left-wing extremists, they fought against her extradition to Germany.[4]

Public and political objections to counter-intelligence are exacerbated by the inescapable necessity to apply it to suspect citizens of the home country: what is termed domestic intelligence, which includes regrettable activities like telephone-tapping, mail-checks, 'bugging', surveillance, and on rare occasions the surreptitious entry into private property. Former MI5 officers, like Peter Wright, have recently raised social objections to these practices; but against the ruthless offensive waged by the Soviets to secure traitors, they are essential to a nation's security, especially in the context of those being recruited to assist *Spetsnaz* forces. Demands that the security services must restrict their clandestine activities to those definitely engaged in treachery are unrealistic. Preliminary investigation on suspicion alone must be permitted because this is often the only way that definite evidence can be obtained. To insist that a person has to be guilty of some criminal act before he can be put under surveillance means that the security services can only react to treachery instead of preventing it.

There is urgent need for a change in attitude towards traitors, among not only members of the secret services but the public generally. The history of treachery is littered with examples of individuals who had evidence about the identity of traitors but failed to report it, mainly because of reluctance to do so, particularly when the suspects were friends. In the counter-intelligence conflict when so much is at stake there is no room for such self-indulgence. If it is regarded as anti-social to fail to report a common criminal and a civic duty to assist in his apprehension, then both surely apply to the most serious crime of treachery. The Americans now have a term for watchfulness for treachery inside security agencies: 'corporate alertness'; there is much to recommend it. Jonathan Pollard, the American naval analyst who was spying for Israel, was caught because colleagues reported on the large quantity of documents he was taking home. The unusual behaviour of Geoffrey Prime should have alerted his colleagues, but nobody reported it.

The public needs to be particularly alert to suspicious circumstances which could be relevant to *Spetsnaz* activities and to be prepared to report them. Snooping and sneaking on one's own citizens may be contrary to the British way of life, but most of us have accepted the need to report on possible terrorists. Ordinary people need to be made aware, continuously, that the threat to national security is real and dangerous to the way of life of themselves and their children.

Reports of suspicious behaviour are of scant use, of course, if no notice is taken of them, and there are many instances where this has occurred. Not only were reports on the reliability of Houghton ignored, but he was posted to one of the country's most secret establishments. The history of the secret services is riddled with lost opportunities because officials – some hidebound, some idle, some stupid – did not see fit to follow obvious leads. The former MI5 officer Joan Miller told me how she had interviewed an elderly lady who wanted to denounce a BBC man as a Soviet agent. She recommended further action on the person, whose name was Guy Burgess. Nothing was done, and there was nothing in Burgess's file to this effect when he was eventually investigated after his defection in 1951. Olga Muth, the German nanny to 'Sonia's' children in Switzerland, denounced her and her British husband as spies to the British consular representative in Montreux before they returned to the UK. No notice was taken.

The record clearly shows that career diplomats and ambassadors in particular are generally antipathetic to intelligence. Many of Philby's colleagues in MI6 knew that he was married to a dedicated Comintern agent (his first wife, Lizi) but considered it irrelevant. A former East European in MI5 was known to have close relatives behind the Iron Curtain, increasing his potential vulnerability to KGB pressure, but years passed before he was required to retire.

The British government could greatly assist, as the US government now does, by initiating and encouraging publicity about Soviet clandestine operations instead of stifling it. The Foreign Office is beset with unjustified fear of upsetting the Russians, who seem to have established a psychological ascendancy. This reluctance, which the Soviets inevitably interpret as a weakness to be exploited, has not been confined to Britain. When President Kennedy was assassinated in 1963 there was an overwhelming reluctance on the part of his successor, President Lyndon Johnson, to conduct any sustained investigation into the possibility that the Soviets had been in any way responsible, directly or indirectly. Before examining the evidence, he and his officials took the view that any resulting confrontation with the Soviet government would hold so much potential danger that the murder should be attributed as rapidly as possible to a lone assassin, Lee Harvey Oswald, who had no known motive. In 1972 the Italian counter-intelligence service (SID) recommended the expulsion of twenty Soviet-bloc agents who had been actively involved with Red Brigade terrorists; but the Prime Minister, Giulio Andreotti, vetoed the proposal.[5] In the 1970s MI5 evidence showed that a major British trade union leader was a fully fledged Soviet agent, while another was observed meeting KGB officers in London. Yet successive governments forbade any interviews or interrogation because of political fears that they would be charged with 'union bashing'.

In 1978 the FBI arrested three Soviet agents who tried to suborn a naval officer who played along with them under FBI control. Two of them, who were posing as UN officials, did not have diplomatic immunity, and the FBI wanted to prosecute them. Secretary of State Cyrus Vance opposed this on the grounds that there was more to lose by antagonizing the Soviets. The Soviets should, in fact, be embarrassed to the maximum by official explanations of just what their clandestine operators have been doing when they are expelled, particularly when their activities relate to *Spetsnaz* operations. The public exposure of miscreants through the media is a major weapon available to true democracies that is too little used. The exposure of

Blunt in 1979 demonstrated how much it is dreaded by the individual traitor. While sources must always be protected, disclosure could often be a 'trade-off' preferable to the rigid 'we never discuss such matters' line.

There is currently powerful pressure by civil libertarians to prevent the introduction of the polygraph as an adjunct to the security precautions taken to prevent the entry of potentially dangerous people into British secret establishments and to check on those who may already be there. The polygraph is now much more sophisticated than the old 'lie detector' from which it was developed, as are its professional operators. It has proved its value repeatedly in the experience of American establishments, where its use is being extended to secure clues to the 'trustworthiness, patriotism and integrity' of employees – the horror of the Walker case having induced Congress to drop its objections.[6] Even the liberal CIA chief Admiral Stansfield Turner rated it 'the most important specific tool of counter-intelligence'.[7] While no test can be 100 per cent effective, the polygraph is a better guide than many of the accepted methods of positive vetting such as questioning referees named by the candidate himself. It can reveal dangerous character defects, as occurred with the CIA officer Edward Howard in 1983. Howard was required to leave the service and in the following year was involved in a drunken affray in which he pulled and fired a revolver. Many undergoing the test have confessed to crimes which they would have concealed, including having divulged secret information in the past, trying to gain access for nefarious reasons, and even being involved in terrorist activities. Other have admitted secret membership of the Communist Party.

The polygraph has also acted as a powerful deterrent. According to General Richard D. Stillwell, who was recently responsible for the Pentagon's personnel security programme, the convicted spies Christopher Boyce and William Bell testified that 'they would not even have considered espionage if they had had to undergo a periodic polygraph examination'.[8] Prime told MI5 that he would not have sought employment with GCHQ if he had known that he would be required to undergo a polygraph test, and the Security Commission thought that Bettaney might have been detected if subjected to a routine polygraph test.[9]

The civil libertarians oppose the device on the grounds that it is unreliable and that it might keep innocent people out of secret employment. But when properly used its purpose is simply to provide possible leads for further investigation. The argument that Soviet agents can be trained to resist it, as was probably proved by the success of Vitaly Yurchenko in passing several CIA polygraph tests, is not compelling because professionals can be trained to resist any kind of interrogation, and few would suggest that candidates for secret access should not be interrogated at all. The majority of those subjected to the test will not have had any opportunity for training.

In Britain the unions have used the proposal to introduce the polygraph as evidence of the government's intentions to make further inroads into the personal liberties of their members. However, it is really less intrusive into privacy than background inquiries involving other people, since only the person concerned is questioned. Though the records show how necessary all available precautions are, it seems likely that the unions' view will prevail, because of political objections to giving them further excuse for action.[10]

Union officials and civil libertarians make the same objection to random body searches to check that documents are not being removed from buildings or cameras taken in, yet submit to them, without protest, at airports when their individual safety is at stake. Case records have finally convinced the British and American governments that such searches at security establishments are essential as a deterrent. Kampiles removed the manual of the KH–11 satellite by slipping it under his jacket, knowing that he would not be challenged at the security gate.

One area in which the civil libertarians and government officials are in basic agreement is on the thesis that excessive secrecy encourages treachery. The unnecessary classification of documents which then have to be protected means that resources in manpower and money have to be spread too thinly, when they should be concentrated on the real secrets which matter. As a distinguished American scientist has put it: 'The moment we start guarding our toothbrushes and our diamond rings with equal zeal, we usually lose fewer toothbrushes but more diamond rings.'[11]

Successive British Defence Ministers have assured me that they were determined to reduce classification, but little has happened. This is partly because the task of dealing with the colossal backlog of classified documents seemed so formidable but also because most senior civil servants continue to be in favour of excessive classification – due to both their love of secrecy and to their being unprepared to take any risk for which they might be blamed. The American position is even worse. According to the FBI chief, William H. Webster, more than 4 million Americans now have access to classified information, and statistically it is inevitable that some of these will be potentially capable of treachery. Both in the USA and Britain an immediate and massive improvement could be made simply by abolishing the classification 'confidential', and declassifying all existing documents with that tag.

The mere existence of excessive secrecy may motivate some to breach it, as I have found in my journalistic experience with civil servants at various levels. Some former senior civil servants of high repute are now advocating freedom of information legislation.

Inevitably there has been pressure for the general liberalization of attitudes to homosexuality to be applied to the secret services. In the USA homosexuals may now work for the CIA provided they do not make a secret of their perversion. This relaxation ignores the evidence that homosexuality may be indicative of a nature likely to harbour a dangerous degree of resentment against authority. In Britain homosexuals cannot legitimately belong to the secret services – MI5, MI6, or GCHQ – while homosexual acts remain punishable in the armed forces, but they are no longer barred from work in the home Civil Service, which might bring them into contact with secrets. If there is a further serious case of espionage traceable to a homosexual who has been effectively blackmailed, in either Britain or the USA, the reaction of those responsible for the relaxations will be interesting.

There has also been a general degree of relaxation towards membership of Communist and other revolutionary organizations, with a common feeling that Communist ideology is out of fashion and no longer likely to be a motivation for treachery. This is a consequence of the rapid fall in overt membership of the Communist parties. But in Britain this is due largely to the fact that many have left to infiltrate the Labour Party, which is also attracting young extremists who would otherwise have been Communist Party members. A more reliable measure of the true strength of Communism in Britain is the number of Communists in positions of national and local power in unions.

The discovery of Prime inside GCHQ and Bettaney inside MI5 did something to dispel the dangerous fallacy that Communism has lost its appeal for the traitor. Membership of the Communist Party or any association with it remains a bar to entry to a secret department in Britain, and this has wisely been extended to include other revolutionary organizations with deliberately deceptive names, like the Socialist Workers and Militant. Whether such people are committed to the Soviet cause or not, they are all subversive of true democracy.

Security agencies need to pay more attention to Marxism as a general symptom and what it implies for those seriously 'infected' by it. Former Communists claim that MI5 and MI6 fail to understand Marxist–Leninist philosophy and its implications for treachery.

The dangers of the natural tendency to explain Soviet behaviour by Western standards – what is known as mirror-imaging – are beginning to be understood but not widely enough. When in 1983 the Russians shot down a Korean airliner, killing all aboard, it was the normal response of a Marxist–Leninist regime founded on ruthlessness, yet most people in the West found it easier to explain by assuming that

287

the plane must have been spying, which it was not.[12] The phenomenon of mirror-imaging by the West is so well understood in Moscow that the Soviets exploit it.

A more recent example of the alien attitudes which Marxism–Leninism engenders was the Soviet leadership's behaviour when the Chernobyl nuclear reactor caught fire, showering neighbouring countries and the global sky with radioactive fall-out. In spite of the obvious danger and the urgent need to warn affected foreign communities, the Marxist–Leninist state is so incorrigibly secretive that it was incapable of behaving in what to the true democracies would seem a civilized manner. The Kremlin denied the disaster to its Scandinavian neighbours, who detected that they had been showered with fall-out, and delayed making any announcement for three days. Shortly afterwards the Soviets responded to the arrest of a KGB officer in New York by seizing the American journalist Daniloff as a hostage to secure the officer's release, concocting fraudulent charges. Such occurrences underscore the necessity for Western political, defence, and intelligence leaders and their advisers to try to evaluate events from the peculiar standpoint of the adversary before making judgements, taking decisions, or granting concessions.

Whatever the motivations of individual traitors, the root reason for the great mass of treachery in the second half of the twentieth century is the ideological warfare waged by the Soviet Union in its drive for world Communism in theory and for world domination in practice. While its general appeal in the West may seem to have declined, because of its failures and excesses, it remains the mainspring of the ruling party in the USSR and without it the party would lose most of its purpose and power over the Soviet people. So any internal political change is most unlikely, as is any diminution in the drive to recruit traitors in the West.

Much of the thrust is generated by Soviet military requirements, a fact far too little appreciated in the West, even by political leaders. Whereas the USA could claim superpower status on economic and technological grounds alone, the Soviet Union derives it only from its military might which has to be maintained for that reason alone. Military spending has priority over all else; there is universal male conscription and endless reference in the controlled Soviet media to the need for new arms for 'survival'. Military might must be maintained as the means whereby the Politburo keeps its grip on the Soviet people and the satellites, and as an instrument of political intimidation to generate 'more friendly' attitudes on the part of smaller nations. It is therefore no coincidence that the bulk of the espionage and subversion carried out on the Soviets' behalf is blatantly military, the main thrusts of both the KGB and the GRU being to that purpose.

As Lord Greenhill, a former Head of the Foreign Office, told the House of Lords in 1985: 'The Soviet record of hostile subversive action towards this country is incontrovertible. My own official career has confirmed it again and again. Anyone who attempts to deny it is not living in the real world.'[13] The case histories presented in this book indicate that anyone who doubts the threat is politically blind, deluded, naïve, or part of it. The same applies to anyone who doubts the need for continuing intelligence, including 'domestic intelligence', to counter it.

It is doubtful whether adequate attention is being paid to the programme of traitor recruitment which is the fount of successful espionage and subversion and is being expanded. The universities, technical colleges, and 'high-tech' firms are still being exploited, possibly to a greater degree than ever, with both the KGB and GRU having special 'gathering departments' for the theft or purchase of technological information from the West. Talent-spotting continues as before. In April 1985 Boyce told the US Senate that the KGB asked him for a list of all his co-workers at TRW Inc. 'They wanted me to tell them different things about these people that could be exploited – financial problems, alcohol problems, sex problems, who was going on vacation where and when, to which countries – things that they could use to put hooks into people and exploit them.' KGB and GRU recruiters and the 'residents' in the various embassies are now given quotas of recruits which they must fulfil or be disciplined.[14] This increased pressure from the Moscow centres may explain why so many Soviet intelligence officers are being expelled in so many countries; they are being required to take extra risks.

The Soviets now run their recruiting drive with all the techniques of the best head-hunting firms – looking not only at their targets' immediate needs but at their long-term aspirations. The Soviet scientist Gennadi Zakharov, arrested in August 1986 for recruiting for the KGB in New York while using the UN as cover, promised a young technician that Moscow would pay for him to take an advanced degree to enable him to gain employment with a high-technology firm. The KGB has always been prepared to take such a long-term view, and Zakharov's behaviour shows that it is still looking to the future.[15]

The Zakharov case also demonstrated that the KGB continues to try to subvert young people. Apart from the risk this poses, the case records prove that it is false economy to recruit the very young to secret work. Boyce was only twenty-one when he went to work at TRW as one of only six cleared for access to the ultra-secret 'black vault', his salary being $140 a week. William Kampiles was hired by the CIA when twenty-three and put into one of the most sensitive of all posts: in the 'watch office' of one of the most secret of all the buildings at the Langley headquarters. The British soldier Philip Aldridge was nineteen when he became the youngest offender to be jailed under the Official Secrets Act for abstracting a top-secret document from the Defence Ministry and trying to sell it to the Russians. The document came his way when he was doing the dull chore of destroying surplus copies of secret papers without proper supervision. Michael Walker, the 22-year-old sailor son of the American traitor John Walker, had similar access to surplus secret messages which should have been incinerated. The case of the eight British servicemen in Cyprus, recently acquitted of treachery while on signals duties connected with the work of GCHQ, also highlighted the degree of access to extremely sensitive information experienced by young servicemen. Almost all were in their early twenties.

Britain and the USA have taken some steps to reduce the numbers of KGB and GRU recruiters and spy-masters posing as Soviet 'diplomats', but far too many of them are still allowed to pursue their purposes. The KGB and GRU still work to what I call Stalin's Law: as opportunities for treachery increase, the Soviets will expand their 'assets' to exploit them. About 800 Russians are assigned to the UN as international civil servants, but, according to a US Senate report: 'Approximately one-fourth of the Soviets in the UN Secretariat are intelligence officers and many more are co-opted by the KGB or GRU.' In effect the Politburo is using the UN as an instrument of its foreign policy, with the West paying most of the costs, since 90 per cent of the Soviets' salaries are paid by other member states.[16]

Late in the day the Russians have been told that they must reduce their grossly swollen UN staffs by a third, and twenty-five have already been expelled from the New York headquarters. The Kremlin's usual response is to infiltrate alternative agents into the so-called trade missions and other commercial covers, and to make increased use of satellite intelligence agencies.

The records show that Soviet-bloc personnel employed in British, American, Canadian, and other Western embassies behind the Iron Curtain have been used time and again by the KGB to compromise officials there and to convert them into traitors. About 260 local Russians were employed by the American diplomatic missions in Moscow and Leningrad and they could not be chosen; they were assigned by the Kremlin, and many had been trained by the KGB for specific tasks including seduction, both heterosexual and homosexual. The USA was taking steps to replace some of these penetration agents by Americans, but in October 1986 the problem was resolved, at least temporarily, by the rash response of Mr Gorbachov in withdrawing them all following the US decision to expel a further fifty-five Soviet 'diplomats' from the USA. This long overdue American action was designed to bring the Russian diplomatic representation in the USA down to the same level as that of the USA in the USSR.

The British Foreign Secretary has been urged to follow suit in both respects. Though the number of Soviet diplomats and trade officials in Britain has been substantially reduced from its formerly bloated size, it remains too high in comparison with the number of Britons in the USSR. About eighty Soviet citizens remain employed inside in the British Embassy in Moscow – half the total staff.[17] While admitting the security risks, the Foreign Office argues that the cost of replacing these with British subjects – £660,000 a year – would be prohibitive. However, the cost of only one security disaster, like that of Vassall, can be very much greater.[18]

The Soviets take such an arrogant attitude to Western diplomats that their embassy buildings and staff are subjected to gross surveillance. MI5 has no doubt that the British Embassy in Moscow was deliberately set on fire by the Russians in 1964 to enable KGB officers dressed as firemen to invade it and wreck cipher machines and other equipment. Examination of the security door guarding the GCHQ room showed that the Russians had been entering it surreptitiously at night to read secret ciphers, probably for months. After a fire destroyed part of the American Embassy in 1978 a US security officer was able to see, for the first time, that a chimney on an adjacent Soviet building was hard up against one of the embassy walls. He drilled into the chimney from the American side and spotted an eavesdropping aerial which could be raised and lowered by ropes and pulleys. The officer lowered himself to the base of the chimney by a rope and discovered a small room complete with monitoring equipment and with a tunnel leading into the Russian building next door. Using a torch he began to crawl through the tunnel and encountered a Russian, also with a torch, approaching him. To avoid a confrontation both men scurried away. The Americans issued a press release describing what had happened, and the only response was a protest note from the Kremlin accusing the Americans of violating the lease on their embassy by breaking into the chimney![19]

To combat the thrust of the Soviet secret offensive of espionage, traitor recruitment, subversion, and active measures, there would seem to be a general need for an expansion of the overall resources available in the West. Stinting on protective security and counter-intelligence is a particularly false economy since it can lead to such devastating losses. It is not just specific operations against known or suspected agents which must be financed but the gradual build-up of the records on which any security agency must depend. In the USA these records – the so-called data-base – have become outdated and in some cases completely unavailable following inroads made by well-meaning legislation such as the Privacy Act and the Freedom of Information Act, as well as various court rulings which have followed.[20] Following the public inquiries into the CIA in the 1970s there has been a massive destruction of files on suspects which has been extended to those held by the FBI.

Privacy is an important human right in a true democracy, but over-tight legislation to preserve it can too easily be exploited by those seeking to impose a totalitarian regime under which privacy would be given scant respect if it conflicted with the interests of the secret police. Free societies also have a right to protection, and it is the responsibility of sound government to provide it. Under the Reagan presidency some of the ravages previously inflicted on the CIA are being repaired, but when so much professionalism has been lost recovery is slow.

It is the view of most authorities whom I have consulted that MI5 is not big enough for its responsibilities. With the help of Special Branch it may have the capability to follow a few Soviet seamen on their travels round the UK to check on their possible *Spetsnaz* links, but it cannot cover enough of them. The Soviets easily saturate the resources as they do in the counter-espionage field by putting so many KGB and GRU officers into their embassies and trade missions. Defence Intelligence, which is deeply involved in combating the *Spetsnaz* threat, is inadequately manned because it offers poor salaries for civilians.

More resources would enable the secret services to improve the quality and competence of their officers, who are not well paid. Modest salaries also mean modest pensions, which may make retired officers vulnerable to temptation, which has certainly happened in the USA. The much-publicized experience of Peter Wright, the MI5 officer who retired to Australia on a miserly pension in 1976, should be a lesson to all secret services. In his determination to publish his memoirs he was partly motivated by his belief that Soviet penetration of MI5 and MI6 had not been fully investigated; yet, as I know from personal involvement with him, he was also urgently in need of the royalties which books alone could provide.

The levels of competence in the secret service have also been reflected in the leadership, which has been far from adequate. Several former MI5 officers have remarked to me that their main reason for doubting that Hollis was a Soviet spy is that he was not clever enough. One Attorney-General has described him as 'just a buffoon'. If he was not clever enough to be a spy, he was not clever enough to head Britain's counter-spies. MI5 does not seem to learn from past mistakes. The recent Director-General, Sir John Jones, was another who was regarded by his staff as being too withdrawn, and morale suffered. Morale inside organizations like MI5 will not improve until efficiency there improves; the staffs are only too aware how poorly they have performed.

Sir Maurice Oldfield used to boast that MI6 had not lost a single officer since the war, though it had lost some agents; but there are some who regard this as an indictment, suggesting that MI6 has not been sufficiently aggressive. The recent rescue of Gordievsky out of the Soviet Union indicates a more positive attitude.

The Soviet Union enjoys a major advantage over the West in that the profession of intelligence there is regarded as highly honourable, those who serve in it giving essential service to the party and the nation. Parents there are gratified when their children join the KGB or GRU. In the West the intelligence services have become the focus for abuse and ridicule, with their officers being downgraded as 'spies'. Since the war a long run of incompetence against the Soviet clandestine thrust has undermined their reputation which can be restored only by solid achievement over the years ahead. A period without traitors would be beneficial. People can no longer be hoodwinked by Prime Ministers claiming as triumphs what are in fact disasters in which spies have operated for years under the nose of the security authorities and which have been exposed only through a tip from a chance defector or some other fluke circumstance.

In a previous book I have argued at length the case for some degree of oversight or supervision of the secret services by an independent body with statutory powers.[21] This has often been advocated on the grounds that in a democracy the secret services should be more accountable to the legislature, as they are currently in the USA through oversight committees, mainly to ensure that they do not infringe civil liberties. Oversight is enthusiastically supported by the civil libertarians in the hope that it would diminish the scope of the secret services, but the main reason for my advocacy is my conviction that it would improve their efficiency and reduce the risk that they would be penetrated by long-term traitors. It would also lessen, if not eliminate, the outrageous extent to which Parliament and the public have been misled by official statements on security and intelligence affairs.

Understandably, oversight is opposed not only by those who genuinely fear that it will give still more people access to secrets but by those who see it as a threat to secret preserves which have enabled them to cover their incompetence. Oversight should also help to prevent the dangerous liberties which MI5, in particular, has taken with the American agencies with which it is supposed to interchange information. Security and intelligence experiences since the Second World War have demonstrated Britain's dependence on the American services for leads from defectors and intercepts. Close liaison is more

293

important than ever now that Britain is totally dependent on the USA for all the information originating from reconnaissance satellites, having none of its own. There is, therefore, need for a Parliamentary Select Committee on Security and Intelligence at least to discuss the advisability of oversight, to interest Parliament and the public in the crucial issues of security and intelligence, and to publish reports.

Such a Committee could also address itself to the need for improved legislation covering the security and intelligence fields. On the general issue of secrecy there is widespread agreement that the Official Secrets Act is urgently in need of redrafting. The same applies to the treason legislation. The existing law, the Treason Felony Act of 1848, stems from the Statute of Treasons passed in 1351 to deal with rival claims to the throne and, according to the Attorney-General, Sir Michael Havers, is couched in such archaic language that it would be difficult for a modern jury to come to grips with it.

In my view there is need for some relaxation of the libel laws which enable agents of influence to remain unexposed, though parliamentary privilege could be used on selected occasions to counter them, given the political will, as Margaret Thatcher used it to expose Blunt in 1979.

It would seem to be a dangerous weakness in the law that prevents any action against *Spetsnaz*-linked traitors. Their pro-German counterparts were picked up smartly when the last war was declared, but no declaration is likely to be made by the Russians, who set such store by surprise. In any case, it is the view of the British defence chiefs that *Spetsnaz* operations would be initiated days in advance of any attack in Europe. In view of their intentions, *Spetsnaz* traitors could perhaps be classed as terrorists and dealt with under that legislation.

Defence and intelligence authorities with whom I have recently discussed the implications of treachery are agreed that the most pressing need in Britain, the USA, and the West generally is for a co-ordinated defence against what is without question a superbly co-ordinated assault. The West's security and intelligence counterforces are dangerously fragmented, often with rivalry and conflict between agencies which compete instead of co-operate.

On the public front the immediate need is for greater awareness of the threat through having the mystery and fear taken out of it, with reassurance that something is being done to counter it. This education is needed as much by parliamentarians, many of whom react to the Soviet threat as so many reacted to the threat from Hitler. Those of us who expose what is actually going on and try to spread the message are invariably accused of being 'over the top', not only by those who deplore the exposure but by those complacent enough to believe that their freedom could never be taken away from them. Over the last two or three years general awareness of the threat from within, as well as from without, has substantially increased in the USA, mainly owing to the activities of a few independent organizations like the National Strategy Information Center, the American Bar Association, and the Jamestown Foundation. This healthy trend, which is making sensible inroads into unnecessary secrecy, is being supported by the US government, which provides participants to take part in public debates. American universities are now teaching various facets of intelligence work and its purposes. In Britain public discussion of security and intelligence affairs remains officially taboo and to be discouraged in every way, though exposure of the truth is democracy's most potent weapon in the ideological war.

There is a further American trend which the British people could follow with advantage to their continuing freedom: the resurgence of patriotism and national pride and especially the pride in living in a truly free democracy as opposed to the totalitarian dictatorships calling themselves democracies. While those who would deprive the majority of their freedom call themselves Communists or some variant of that revolutionary creed, the threatened majority do not call themselves anything and perhaps they should. For freedom to be preserved it will not be enough to be anti-Communist. Something more positive will be required. The time has perhaps come, if it is not long overdue, for those who cherish freedom and have no designs on anyone else's to call themselves Freedomists, implying an active loyalty to true democracy as fierce as that lodged in those committed to its destruction.

Biographical Sketches

Akhmedov, Ismail A former GRU agent who defected to Istanbul in 1942. A Moslem, born 1904, he held important field positions and published his memoirs, *In and Out of Stalin's GRU*, when eighty years old and living in the USA.

Bentley, Elizabeth Born in Connecticut, 1908. Died 1963. Graduated from Vassar. Studied in Italy and, revolted by Fascism, joined the American Communist Party in 1935. Became an underground Soviet agent controlled by Jacob Golos (real name Rasin). After his death in 1943 she took over an important espionage network, learning the identities of many other American subversives and reporting to Anatoly Gromov who had been Donald Maclean's KGB controller in London and had been transferred to Washington. Disillusioned by the way the Soviets were exploiting the USA, Bentley quit Communism in 1945 and later volunteered all she knew to the FBI.

Bettaney, Michael Born 1950. Joined MI5 in 1975 being eventually assigned to Soviet counter-espionage. Sentenced to twenty-three years' imprisonment in 1984 for Official Secrets offences on behalf of the KGB.

Beurton, Ursula Born Ursula Kuczynski in Berlin, 1907. Became a committed Communist at seventeen. After her marriage to Rudolf Hamburger moved to China in 1930 where she was recruited by Richard Sorge as a full-time GRU agent and given her code-name 'Sonia'. After service in Poland she was posted to Switzerland in 1938, and recruited Britons for the highly successful 'Lucy' espionage ring. After marrying Len Beurton, a British member of the Lucy ring, to secure British nationality, she was posted to Oxford, arriving there in February 1941. She quickly made contact with the GRU and set up a transmitter. She is known to have serviced Klaus Fuchs and is believed to have serviced Roger Hollis during his wartime sojourn in Oxford. She defected to East Germany in February 1950, followed by her husband, and has since written guarded memoirs and other books under the name of Ruth Werner.

297

Blake, George   Born Behar in Rotterdam, 1922, the son of an Egyptian Jew and a Dutch mother. Worked in Dutch underground from 1940 to 1943 when he moved to Britain, joined the Navy, and worked in intelligence. He transferred to MI6 in 1948 and was captured in Korea while working under diplomatic cover. He returned after thirty-four months under Communist indoctrination, but it is now believed that he had been recruited to the KGB much earlier. Sent to Berlin in April 1955 to run agents for MI6. While there he betrayed many Allied projects and agents, some to their death. Arrested in 1961 after being exposed by the Polish defector Goleniewski, and sentenced to forty-two years' jail. He escaped from Wormwood Scrubs in 1966 and eventually reached Moscow.

Blunt, Anthony   Born 1907. Died 1983. Recruited to Communism in 1934 while a young don at Cambridge, and a year later carried out underground work for the Comintern – in other words the KGB. He recruited others, and in 1940 after brief Army service joined MI5. He was an active KGB 'mole' there for five years. He left to become Director of the Courtauld Institute of Art and Surveyor of the King's Pictures, officially breaking his connection with MI5, but remaining in intimate contact with several of its senior officers. He continued to assist the KGB when he could and was secretly exposed in 1963 by Michael Straight, one of his Cambridge recruits. Granted immunity to prosecution in return for assistance in identifying other 'moles', he was not publicly exposed until 1979.

Bossard, Frank   Born 1912. Convicted of cheque frauds in his twenties. Wartime RAF radar officer, then joined the civil service. Later served with Control Commission in Germany as a technical intelligence officer, returning to London in 1958 to work in a branch of the Joint Intelligence Bureau. In 1960 he was transferred to guided weapons work in the Aviation Ministry. Recruited by Soviet intelligence in 1961 and supplied photocopies of secret Aviation Ministry files in return for money. Sentenced to twenty-one years' jail in 1965.

Boyce, Christopher   Born 1953 in Colorado, son of a former FBI officer. A university drop-out, he secured a junior post in 1974 in a highly secret department of TRW, California, which was operating reconnaissance satellites. Used his friend, Andrew Daulton Lee, to sell the satellite secrets to the KGB. Sentenced to forty years' imprisonment in 1977. Escaped three years later and eventually recaptured.

Britten, Douglas   Born 1931, enlisted in the RAF 1949. Trained as a radio operator, serving in Cyprus where he was involved in work with GCHQ. Recruited by KGB in London in 1962 and provided valuable intelligence for six years for money. Jailed for twenty-one years in 1968.

Burchett, Wilfred   Born 1911 in Melbourne, Australia. Moved to London in 1936, securing a post with the Soviet Intourist organization. Returned to

Australia and became a freelance journalist reporting on the Far East War. Became a committed Stalinist and, in 1956, a paid KGB agent. Reported the Mindszenty trial in Hungary, and the Korean and Vietnam Wars from a pro-Soviet, pro-Chinese, and fiercely anti-American stance. Died 1983.

Burgess, Guy Born 1911 in Devonport. Died 1963 in Moscow. Educated Eton and Cambridge where he was recruited to Communism and the KGB. Worked in the BBC, with MI5 and MI6 connections, and during the Second World War partnered Anthony Blunt in massive wartime pro-Soviet espionage. Joined the Foreign Office permanent staff in 1947. Posted to Washington in 1950. Forced to defect with Donald Maclean in 1951.

Cairncross, John Born 1913 in Scotland. Studied modern languages at Cambridge where he was recruited to Communism and KGB service. Entered the Foreign Office in 1936, and transferred to the Treasury. During the Second World War worked in the Government Code and Cipher School at Bletchley. Later in MI6 he passed all he knew to his KGB controller. Made a partial confession when confronted with evidence in 1952, and has since lived in Italy. The full extent of his treachery was not exposed until 1981.

Casement, Sir Roger Born 1864, in County Antrim, Ireland. Served as British diplomat but identified himself with Irish nationalism. Failed in an attempt to organize a brigade of Irish prisoners-of-war in Germany, but secured German arms for an uprising against British rule and was landed by submarine in County Kerry in 1916. Captured and tried in London for treason, he was executed.

Chambers, Whittaker Born 1901 in Philadelphia. Died 1961. An able journalist who joined the American Communist Party in 1925 and became an underground agent in 1932, acting as a courier and learning the identities of several 'moles' in the US Government service. Disillusioned with Soviet Communism in 1938, he eventually informed to the FBI, naming Alger Hiss as a Soviet agent – information which the FBI already knew from the defector Gouzenko and confirmed from the breaking of KGB codes.

'Cicero' The code-name of Elyesa Bazna, valet to the British Ambassador in Ankara, Sir Hughe Knatchbull-Hugesson, from October 1943 to April 1944. He photographed secret documents and sold them to the Germans. He volunteered his services and was not a double agent, being able to spy only because of blatant security inefficiency by the Ambassador who should have been dismissed. Though well paid by the Germans, 'Cicero' is said to have died in poverty.

Coplon, Judith Born 1922 into an old American-Jewish family. Became a Communist at Barnard College and was recruited by the KGB as a spy. As a political analyst in the Justice Department she was able to warn Soviet espionage groups about the extent to which they were under FBI suspicion.

Exposed as a result of the decipherment of a KGB message, she was sentenced to fifteen years' jail in 1950, but avoided prison on a legal technicality.

Driberg, Tom Born 1905. Died 1976. Educated at Lancing and Oxford. Recruited early by MI5 to become a Communist, and penetrated the Young Communist League and eventually Communist Party Headquarters. A journalist, he was expelled from the Communist Party when his duplicity was discovered in 1941, but continued to work for MI5 when elected as an MP in 1942 and later in 1945. Worked as a double agent with the Czechs and the KGB, always for money, even while Chairman of the Labour Party from 1957 to 1958. Elevated to the peerage as Lord Bradwell in 1975.

Ellis, Charles 'Dick' Born 1895 in Sydney. Died 1975. Served during the First World War with the British Army. A linguist, whose languages included Russian, he joined MI6 in the 1920s, working in Paris and Berlin. Ever short of money he began to sell information to the Nazis, including the entire MI6 'order of battle' – its organization and staff. Served in British Security Co-ordination, the Second World War intelligence agency set up in the USA with American agreement. Later in charge of Far Eastern intelligence. Left MI6 in 1953 to emigrate to Australia apparently on health grounds, and immediately joined the Australian Security Intelligence Service (ASIS) from which he quickly resigned and returned hurriedly to Britain. When interrogated in 1966 he confessed to having spied for Germany but denied that he later spied for the Soviets, although this was and remains deeply suspected.

Felfe, Heinz Born 1918 in Germany. After service with the Wehrmacht in the Second World War, he joined the West German Intelligence Service (BND) under General Gehlen. The East Germans fed him valuable information to establish his position and ensure his rapid promotion. In return he fed back a mass of secrets and betrayed scores of agents, and was well paid for his efforts. Sentenced to fourteen years' jail in 1963, he was handed over to East Germany in a spy exchange after serving only six years, and has since written his memoirs.

Foote, Alexander Born 1905 in Liverpool. Died 1956. Went to Spain to fight for the Communists in 1936. Recruited to GRU by 'Sonia' for service in Germany and later in Switzerland, where he was trained as a clandestine radio operator for the Lucy ring. Imprisoned by the Swiss in 1943. Released and travelled to Moscow posing as a Soviet citizen. The GRU returned him to field operations in 1947, but disillusioned with the Soviet system he defected to Britain.

Fuchs, Klaus Born 1911 in Germany. After underground Communist activities he escaped to Britain, working on theoretical nuclear research at Bristol and Edinburgh universities. Briefly interned as an enemy alien in Canada. Though he had been involved in illicit Communist activities in Britain, he was cleared by MI5 for atomic bomb research at Birmingham

University in 1940. Volunteered his services to GRU in 1941 and continued to spy when seconded to Los Alamos, New Mexico, in 1944, revealing the mechanism of atomic bombs. Transferred to KGB control. Joined the British nuclear weapons project at Harwell, Berkshire, in 1946, continuing to give the Russians information. Confessed to espionage in 1950 following a KGB code-break by the FBI. Sentenced to fourteen years' jail. Released 1959 when he moved to East Germany to work in a nuclear research institute.

Gerhardt, Dieter Born 1935. South African naval officer who offered his services to the GRU for money when on secondment to the Royal Navy in 1962. Married an established GRU agent who served as his courier and assistant. Rose to command the Simonstown dockyard with the rank of commodore and with access to South Africa's intercept station. Sentenced to life imprisonment for high treason in 1983 having spied without suspicion for twenty-two years. His wife received a similar sentence.

Gold, Harry Born 1912 in Switzerland of Russian Jews who emigrated to the USA in 1914. Died 1972. Became a research chemist. Recruited to Communism in 1933, and in 1935 became an industrial spy for the Soviets, later becoming a courier for secrets provided by Fuchs and others. Arrested 1950, sentenced to thirty years' jail. Paroled in 1966.

Goleniewski, Michal A former member of Polish intelligence (UB) who volunteered information to the CIA in 1958 and defected to the USA in 1960. Identified several traitors in Britain, Germany, and elsewhere.

Golitsin, Anatoly Born 1926 in the Ukraine. Joined the KGB in 1946, serving in departments giving him access to many documents which he committed to memory. Defected to the CIA in December 1961. Probably the most informative of all Soviet defectors to the West. His disclosures led to the identification of major spies in Britain, France, and other countries.

Gordievsky, Oleg Born 1939. Joined the KGB in 1962. Served two tours in Copenhagen under the cover of press attaché, 1966–70 and 1972–78. Believed to have volunteered his services to Denmark in 1966. After four years in Moscow was assigned to London in 1982 and succeeded as head of the KGB mission there in 1984. Forced to defect to Britain in the summer of 1985 when KGB suspicions were aroused.

Gouzenko, Igor Born 1919 in USSR. Died 1982 in Canada. Joined GRU as cipher expert in 1942. Defected to Canada from the Soviet Embassy in Ottawa in September 1945 with documents leading to the arrest of Canadian and British spies, and gave leads to Soviet agents in the USA. This was the first proof of Soviet wartime duplicity.

Guillaume, Gunther Born 1927 in Berlin. Was in the Nazi Party for a time and this enabled the East Germans to blackmail him into working for

East German intelligence. Sent to West Germany with his wife, Christl, as 'refugees'. He penetrated the Social Democratic Party and his wife secured secretarial employment in the office of the Chancellor, Willy Brandt. Later Guillaume joined her and became a confidant of Brandt, who resigned when the double espionage was exposed in 1974. Guillaume was sentenced to thirteen years' jail but was handed back to East Germany in a spy exchange in 1981. His wife, Christl, who received an eight-year sentence, had been released in an exchange a few months earlier.

Hambleton, Hugh   Born 1922 in Canada. An economist, he was recruited to Soviet intelligence in about 1952. Served in NATO headquarters 1956–61, providing many documents. Exposed as a long-term Soviet agent in 1979, but granted immunity by the Canadian security authorities. Tried in London in 1982 and sentenced to ten years' jail.

Hiss, Alger   Born 1904 in Baltimore. Lawyer who achieved important positions in the US State Department. Denounced as a Soviet agent by Whittaker Chambers and in deciphered KGB radio traffic. Leads provided by Gouzenko also identified him. Sentenced to five years' jail for perjury in 1950. Released in 1954, still protesting his innocence.

Hollis, Sir Roger   Born 1905. Died 1973. After dropping out of Oxford University went to China in 1927, working first as a journalist then for the British American Tobacco Company. Friendly with leading Communists there. Returned to Britain in 1936 after contracting tuberculosis. Entered MI5 in 1938 and eventually became its Director-General in 1956, continuing until his retirement in 1965. Under suspicion of being a Soviet agent from 1965 onwards and finally interrogated in 1970. Though it was decided that there was no clinching evidence to incriminate Hollis, Britain's closest allies were warned of his possible treachery in 1974, and several MI5 and MI6 officers involved in his investigation are near-certain that he was a spy.

Houghton, Harry   Born 1905. Joined Navy and on retirement became assistant to naval attaché in British Embassy, Warsaw. Posted to the Admiralty Underwater Weapons Establishment in 1952 and recruited to KGB through Polish intermediary. Through his colleague Ethel Gee, who had access to documents, he supplied submarine secrets to a spy ring controlled by the Russian, Konon Molody (alias Gordon Lonsdale). Exposed by a defector, he and Gee were each given fifteen years' jail in 1962 and released after serving ten.

Howard, Edward   Born 1952 in the USA. Worked for the CIA from January 1981 to June 1983 when he was dismissed. He contacted the KGB and told all he knew about CIA activities in Moscow, which enabled the KGB to identify Russians serving as CIA agents and to execute at least one of them. When suspected in 1985 he managed to escape to Russia. In 1986 he appeared on Moscow television, castigating the CIA in connection with the case of Nicholas Daniloff, an American journalist falsely arrested on espionage charges.

Johnson, Robert Lee Born 1920 in the USA. Died 1972. As an Army NCO he contacted the KGB while working in Berlin, and later supplied a mass of most secret material when he had access to a vault near Paris, used by couriers. He was sentenced to twenty-five years' jail in 1965 and died in prison.

Joyce, William Born 1906 in Brooklyn, USA, of Irish parents. Died 1945. His parents came to Britain in 1922. He joined the British Fascist movement and went to Germany, engaging in anti-British radio propaganda. Because of his affected voice he became widely known as 'Lord Haw Haw'. Captured after the Nazi defeat he was tried in September 1945 in London and executed for high treason.

Kampiles, William Born 1954 in the USA. At twenty-three became a Junior Watch Officer at the CIA Operations Centre near Washington. He was fired after only eight months, and stole a manual describing a highly secret reconnaissance satellite system called the KH–11, which he sold to the GRU for $3,000. In 1978 he was sentenced to forty years' jail.

Kent, Tyler Born 1911 in China. Joined the US Foreign Service at twenty-two and was attached to the US Embassy in Moscow in 1934. Transferred to the London Embassy in 1939 as a code clerk. In 1940 he was convicted for passing secret information to German agents, and sentenced to seven years' imprisonment.

Klugmann, James Born 1912. Died 1977. Joined the Communist Party in 1933 while at Cambridge University and remained an overt member until his death. He was an avid recruiter for the Party and for the KGB. Skilled in Balkan languages, he served in SOE during the war surreptitiously doing everything he could in the Soviet interest. After the war became the official historian of the British Communist Party.

Kolbe, Fritz Born 1900 in Germany. Died 1975. Joined the German diplomatic service in 1925. An anti-Nazi he offered his espionage services to the CIA in 1943 and supplied valuable information until the end of the war. He then went to live in the USA, returning to Germany in old age.

Knuth, Maria An attractive German actress, she joined a pro-Soviet spy ring operating against British and American officers stationed in Germany in 1951. Sentenced to four years' imprisonment in 1953 she died two years later.

Krivitsky, Walter Born 1899 in Western Ukraine. Died 1941. Real name Samuel Ginsberg. Joined GRU in 1920. Fluent in many languages, he operated as an illegal agent in Germany and Holland. Transferred under pressure to NKVD (a forerunner of the KGB) in 1934. Broke with Stalin in 1937 and defected to France, moving to the USA in 1938. Debriefed in London in 1940. Found shot dead in Washington. It appeared to be suicide but he might have been assassinated.

Krogers, Peter and Helen Peter Kroger, whose real name was Morris Cohen, was born in New York in 1910, the son of East European immigrants. He became a Communist at university. Married another Communist called Lona Petka and both were soon professional Soviet agents. They disappeared in 1951, following the repercussions of the Fuchs and Rosenberg cases, arriving in London under false names in 1955. Their KGB task was to act as 'housekeepers' and radio operators for a spy ring being run by Konon Molody ('Gordon Lonsdale'). They were sentenced to twenty years' jail in 1961, and sent to Poland in a political exchange in 1969.

Kuczinski, Jurgen Born 1904 in Germany. Economist. Joined Communist Party in 1930 and soon recruited to the GRU. Posted to Britain in 1936, entering as a Jewish refugee. His main task was to politicize German exiles to the left to ensure Communism in post-war Germany. He also served as a GRU agent cultivating British sources. He was interned as a dangerous alien in January 1940 but was released after only three months, and was responsible for putting Fuchs in touch with the GRU. He returned to Germany in November 1945, playing an important role in establishing the Communist state.

Kuczinski, Robert René Born 1876 in Berlin. Died 1947 in London. The father of Jurgen and Ursula ('Sonia') Kuczynski. He emigrated to London in 1933 and joined the staff of the London School of Economics. He had GRU connections and assisted the espionage activities of his children.

Lee, Andrew Daulton Born 1952 in the USA. A drug pedlar, he served as courier for Christopher Boyce in selling satellite secrets to the Soviets. Sentenced to life imprisonment in 1977.

Lindemanns, Christiaan Born 1917 in Holland. Died 1946. Known as 'King Kong' on account of his massive stature. Joined the Dutch resistance in 1941, serving heroically until he turned traitor to save his brother's life. He committed suicide in prison while awaiting trial, as was confirmed by an exhumation in 1986.

Long, Leo Born 1917. Joined Communist Party at Cambridge. Fluent in German. He served in wartime and post-war military intelligence. Recruited as a Soviet spy by Blunt in 1941. Granted effective immunity after being exposed to MI5 in 1964. Not publicly exposed until 1981.

Lyalin, Oleg Born 1937 in the USSR. Joined the KGB. A sabotage specialist, he was posted to London under cover of trade mission. Defected to Britain in 1971, confirming the names and activities of so many Soviet agents that 105 were made *personae non grata*.

Maclean, Donald   Born 1913 in Britain. Died 1983 in Moscow. Recruited to Communism and Soviet intelligence at Cambridge University in 1934. Joined Foreign Office in 1935. Served as productive KGB source at home and abroad until his defection along with Guy Burgess in May 1951.

Massing, Hede   Born Hede Tune 1900 in Austria. Died in the USA in 1981. An actress who married Gerhart Eisler, the Communist agent who converted her to Marxism and espionage. She later married Paul Massing, another dedicated Communist. The Massings operated for the Soviet Union in Germany and the USA until 1946 when she confessed to the FBI.

May, Alan Nunn   Born 1911 in Britain. A Russian sympathizer at an early age. An atomic scientist, he served in the wartime British-Canadian bomb project and was recruited to the service of the GRU, providing information and even uranium samples. Exposed by Gouzenko he was sentenced to ten years' jail in 1946. He was released in 1952 and returned to scientific work in Ghana and elsewhere.

Miller, Richard   Born 1937 in the USA. Joined the FBI in 1966. Sold FBI secrets to a woman Soviet agent in return for money and sex. Received two life terms in 1986.

Norman, Herbert   Born 1909 in Japan of Canadian parents. Died 1957. Recruited to Communism, and probably to the Soviet service, at Cambridge University. Joined Canadian Foreign Service in 1939. Wartime intelligence work then diplomatic service in Japan. Ambassador to Egypt. Committed suicide in Cairo when publicly under suspicion.

Owen, Will   Born 1901. Died 1981. Labour MP for Morpeth from 1954 to 1970. As a member of defence committees he had access to secrets which he sold to the Czechs. Resigned in 1970 when exposed by defectors. He was tried and acquitted on a technicality then, when immune from further prosecution, made a frank confession of treachery to MI5.

Owens, Arthur George   Born 1899 in Wales. Died 1976 in Eire. Electrical engineer whose work took him abroad. Spied for the Germans for money and sex. Also worked for MI6 under the cover name of Snow. His duplicity resulted in his imprisonment by the British.

Pâques, Georges   Born 1914 in France. Contacted the Russians while in Algeria in 1944. Became deputy-head of the French section of NATO's press and information department at headquarters in Paris. Provided a mass of information to KGB. When arrested in 1963 confessed to having been under continuous KGB control for nearly twenty years. Imprisoned for life in 1964, later reduced to twenty years.

Pathé, Pierre-Charles   Born 1908, son of the cinema pioneer. Became an influential journalist. Recruited by KGB in 1959. Functioned mainly as a disinformation propagandist and agent of influence. Jailed for five years in 1979 but released and pardoned because of his age.

Pelton, Ronald   Born 1942 in the USA. Joined the NSA in 1965. Resigned 1979 having spent six years on liaison duties in Britain. Passed secrets to KGB from 1980 to 1985 for money. Given life imprisonment in 1986.

Penkovsky, Oleg   Born 1919 in the USSR. Artillery officer who became a colonel in the GRU. Provided valuable military and political secrets to MI6 and the CIA from April 1961 to August 1962. Sentenced to be shot for treason in 1963 after a show trial, but some former MI5 officers suspect this was part of a deception operation and that Penkovsky had been a plant.

Petrov, Vladimir   Born 1907 in Siberia. Joined KGB. Posted to Canberra under cover of being consul in 1951. Defected to Australia in 1954. His wife, Evdokia, also a KGB officer, defected with him after the KGB tried to airlift her to Moscow by force. Publicly confirmed that Burgess and Maclean had been spies in 1955.

Philby, Harold 'Kim'   Born 1912 in Ambala, India. Entered Trinity College, Cambridge 1929. Committed to Communist cause before leaving in 1933. Recruited to KGB in Vienna. Covered the Spanish Civil War as a journalist, ostensibly reporting on the Franco side but providing intelligence for the Soviets. He recruited others and joined MI6 during the war, securing rapid promotion, and remained on the permanent staff until 1951 when his connection with the Burgess and Maclean defection forced his resignation. He continued to work for the KGB as a journalist in the Middle East and defected to Moscow in 1963.

Popov, Pyotr   Born *c.*1920 in the USSR. Infantry officer transferred to the GRU. Volunteered his services to CIA in 1952. Disclosed many operational secrets. Arrested by the KGB in 1959 and executed.

Prime, Geoffrey   Born 1938. Joined the RAF in 1956. Learned Russian. Posted to Berlin on signals duties in 1964. Volunteered his services to KGB in 1968. Served in GCHQ as a civilian from 1968 to 1977 when he resigned. His treachery was discovered only as a result of his arrest on sex charges. Sentenced to thirty-five years' imprisonment in 1982.

Quisling, Vidkun   Born 1887 in Norway. Died 1945. Joined Army. Studied Russian and served in diplomatic capacity in Leningrad. Was pro-Communist, then switched his support to Nazi Germany and became friendly with Hitler. He became a Nazi puppet during the German occupation of Norway, and was executed after trial.

Reiss, Ignace Born 1899 in Western Ukraine. Died 1937. Real name Ignace Poretsky. Joined the Communist Party in 1919, and in 1922 was recruited to the GRU for illegal work abroad under the cover-name 'Ludwig'. Ran successful agents in Europe and Britain. He broke with Stalin in 1937 and was assassinated by Soviet agents.

Roessler, Rudolf Born 1897 in Germany. Died 1958. Moved to Switzerland as a political refugee in 1933. Began to work for Swiss intelligence in 1939, and then additionally for the GRU under the code-name 'Lucy'. He was thought to have had high-level sources in Germany which gave him continuous updates of military intentions, but the CIA believes that most of this information was given to him by the Swiss as a means of getting it to Moscow in a form which would be believed.

Rosenberg, Julius Born 1918. Died 1953. His parents were Jewish immigrants. Became a Marxist–Leninist and member of the Communist Party. His wife, Ethel, was also a Communist. An electrical engineer, Julius had access to defence projects and became a full-time Soviet agent, recruiting and running a large spy ring. This included his brother-in-law, David Greenglass, who had access to nuclear bomb secrets. The Rosenbergs were sent to the electric chair in 1953.

Schulze-Boysen, Harro Born 1909 in Germany. Died 1942. Outstanding linguist. Became a Communist in 1933. Worked in the Air Ministry in counter-intelligence. Recruited as a Soviet agent and formed an espionage ring which included his wife, Libertas. He and his wife were executed in December 1942.

Sejna, Jan Born 1927 in Czechoslovakia. Became a dedicated Communist after his experience with the Nazi invaders. Appointed to the Czech Parliament and Communist Party with important positions in the Defence Ministry. Became major-general and defected to the USA in 1968.

Shadrin, Nicholas Born 1928 in Leningrad. Real name Nikolai Artamonov. Joined the Red Navy. Defected to the USA via Sweden in 1959. He lectured on Soviet naval affairs, but was never fully trusted by the CIA. He became a double agent for the Defense Intelligence Agency and was induced to visit Vienna in 1975 on a mission from which he never returned. Either he re-defected or lost his life.

'Sonia' see **Beurton, Ursula**

Sorge, Richard Born 1895 in Russia, of German parents. Died 1944. Joined the German Army in 1914 and was wounded. Disillusioned by the German defeat, he joined the Communist Party. Was recruited to the GRU and trained in Moscow. He mastered many languages, including Chinese and Japanese. Sent under journalistic cover to Shanghai in 1930, where among others he recruited 'Sonia', and built up a large espionage ring. After recall to Moscow in 1932 he moved to Tokyo in 1933, establishing a spy ring which penetrated the German Embassy and the Japanese government. Sorge was able to assure Stalin that Japan would not attack the Soviet Union, enabling Army reserves from the Far East to be switched to the defence of Moscow. He was executed by the Japanese.

Springhall, Douglas Born 1901. Died 1953. A seaman who became a leading figure in the British Communist Party. A political commissar to the International Brigade in Spain. Sentenced to seven years' jail in 1943 for suborning a woman clerk in the Air Ministry. Moved to China and died in Moscow where he was receiving medical treatment.

Straight, Michael Born 1916 in the USA of rich parents. Entered the London School of Economics in 1933 where he became interested in left-wing politics. Moved to Trinity College, Cambridge, in 1934 and joined the Communist cell there. Recruited to Soviet service in 1937 by Blunt. Ordered to operate in Moscow's interests in the USA. Contacted by a KGB agent in the USA and wrote reports on the economic situation, but claims he gave no information of consequence. He ended his association in 1942 when about to join the US Air Force. Confessed his past association to the FBI in 1963, naming Blunt and Long.

Tiedge, Hans Joachim Born 1937 in Germany. Joined the Office for the Protection of the Constitution (BfV) in 1966 and became a senior counter-espionage officer. An alcoholic burdened by debt, he defected to East Germany in 1985.

Treholt, Arne Born 1943. Became Head of Information in the Norwegian Foreign Ministry. Recruited by the KGB, probably by sexual blackmail, in 1975, and provided defence and economic information. Sentenced to twenty years' jail in 1985, the money (£60,000) which the Russians paid him being confiscated.

Vassall, John Born 1924 in London. Homosexual from an early age. Joined the civil service and in 1953 posted to Moscow as clerk to the Naval Attaché. Recruited by KGB through homosexual blackmail. Returned to London to work in the office of Naval intelligence, then transferred to work with the Civil Lord of the Admiralty. Two years later he was transferred to the Military Branch of the Admiralty. Under constant KGB control, he supplied masses of secret documents which were photographed and returned. Sentenced to eighteen years' jail in 1962. Released on parole in 1973.

Walker, John Born 1938 in the USA. Former Chief Petty Officer in the

US Navy. Volunteered services to KGB in 1968 for money. Recruited other members of his family and friends to form a highly productive spy ring. Sentenced to two life terms in 1986.

Wennerstrom, Stig   Born 1906 in Sweden. Joined the Swedish Navy then the Air Force. Learned Russian and served in Moscow. Recruited to GRU in 1948 for money. Served in Washington then in Stockholm. Sentenced to life imprisonment in 1964.

White, Harry Dexter   Born 1892 in the USA. Died 1948. Parents were Russian-Jewish immigrants. An economist, he held important government positions. According to fellow Communists, he became a very influential member of a pro-Soviet spy ring.

Yurchenko, Vitaly   Born 1936 in the USSR. Joined Soviet Navy 1958. Transferred to the KGB 1960. Served in Egypt 1968–72, at Moscow headquarters 1972–75, Washington 1975–80, and Moscow headquarters 1980–85. Defected to the CIA in August 1985. Re-defected to Moscow in November 1985. May have been a plant.

Notes and Sources

Introduction (pages ix–xvii)

1 This is made clear by Robert Rhodes James who had access to Eden's personal papers when preparing the official biography (*Anthony Eden*, Weidenfeld and Nicolson), published in 1986.
2 Academic studies of the historical impact of Fuchs, Blunt, and others are in preparation, while a study on Norman has been published. Several general histories of intelligence operations involving traitors have been published in Britain and the USA.
3 See Thomas, Hugh, *Armed Truce*, Hamish Hamilton, 1986.
4 See Pincher, Chapman, *The Secret Offensive*, Sidgwick and Jackson, 1985.
5 For example, the case of the civil servant, Clive Ponting, who leaked information about the Falklands War. The government has also declined to take action against several former officers of secret services who have made public statements clearly in breach of their contractual undertakings.
6 Dame Rebecca West produced a beautifully written book, *The New Meaning of Treason* (Viking Press, 1964), but her knowledge of the subject was limited to what she had learned from attending a few spy trials. The evidence given at such trials is always minimal and often deliberately misleading, and, as Dame Rebecca had little or no access to prime sources of information about intelligence or security, the result was inevitably superficial.
7 *The Times*, 27 April 1986. Report of a speech by Lord Hailsham in Grantham on the previous evening. Also see *The Times*, 16 May 1986.
8 See Sawyer, Roger, *Casement: The Flawed Hero*, Routledge and Kegan Paul, 1985.
9 Sir John Harington (1561–1612).
10 Leon Brittan.

Chapter 1: The Concept of Loyalty (pages 1–14)

1 Baroness Ewart-Biggs and Louis Blom-Cooper, QC.
2 Lindsey, Robert, *The Falcon and the Snowman*, Simon and Schuster, 1979.

3 Hood, William, *Mole*, Weidenfeld and Nicolson, 1982.
4 Gill, William, *The Ordeal of Otto Otepka*, Arlington House, New York, 1969.
5 Introduction to *My Silent War* by Kim Philby, Macgibbon and Kee, 1968.
6 Aleister Crowley.
7 *Humint*, Vol. IV, Issues 16–20. The left-wing phobia for patriotism is exemplified by the reaction of some TV officials to entertainers who have expressed it: they have been barred from the screens. For the experiences of Hughie Green and Michael Bentine, see Pincher, Chapman, *The Secret Offensive*, Sidgwick and Jackson, 1985.
8 *The Lay of the Last Minstrel.*
9 Straight, Whitney, *Daily Mail*, 11 February 1963.
10 Farago, Ladislav, *The Game of Foxes*, Hodder and Stoughton, 1972.
11 Von Papen, Franz, *Memoirs*, André Deutsch, 1952.
12 Hyde, Douglas, *I Believed*, William Heinemann, 1951.
13 *Ibid.*
14 *Out of the Night*, under the pseudonym Jan Valtin, Alliance Book Corp, New York, 1941.
15 Foote, Alexander, *Handbook for Spies*, Museum Press, 1964.
16 CIA, *The Rote Kapelle*, University Publications of America, Inc., 1982.
17 Akhmedov, Ismail, *In and Out of Stalin's GRU*, Arms and Armour Press, 1984. He made a similar statement when debriefed by Peter Wright. As David Dallin observed: 'More officers of Soviet intelligence have been killed in Russia than in operations posts abroad.'
18 Werner, Sonja, *Sonja's Rapport*, Verlag Neues Leben, 1977.
19 Driberg, Tom, *Ruling Passions*, Quartet, 1978.
20 Pincher, Chapman, *Inside Story*, Sidgwick and Jackson, 1978, and *Their Trade Is Treachery*, Sidgwick and Jackson, 1981.
21 Haynes, Joe, *The Politics of Power*, Coronet, 1977, and Pincher, Chapman, *Inside Story*.
22 Pincher, *Ibid.*
23 Braley, Russ, *Bad News*, Regnery Gateway, Chicago, 1984.
24 Gill, *op cit.*
25 Silber, J. C., *Invisible Weapons*, Hutchinson, 1932.
26 Seth, Ronald, *The Spy Who Wasn't Caught*, Robert Hale, 1966.
27 Werner, *op cit.* BBC transcript of Soviet TV *Memories of Richard Sorge*, 9 February 1985.
28 Pincher, Chapman, *Too Secret Too Long*, Sidgwick and Jackson, 1984.
29 *Ibid* and Solomon, Flora, *Baku to Baker Street*, 1984.
30 Massing, Hede, *This Deception*, Duell, Sloan, Pierce, 1952. Lamphere, Robert and Shachtman, Tom, *The FBI–KGB War*, Random House, New York, 1986.
31 Bamford, James, *The Puzzle Palace*, Sidgwick and Jackson, 1983.

Chapter 2: The Minor Loyalties (pages 15–21)

1 Hyde, *op cit.*
2 Sejna, Jan, *We Will Bury You*, Sidgwick and Jackson, 1982.

3   Wickens, G. M., paper presented by the Centre of Religious Studies, University of Toronto, 6 April 1984.
4   Andrew, Christopher, *Secret Service*, William Heinemann, 1985.
5   Lamphere, *op cit.*
6   Chambers, Whittaker, *Witness*, Random House, New York, 1952.
7   Radosh, Ronald and Milton, Joyce, *The Rosenberg File*, Holt, Rinehart and Winston, New York, 1983.
8   Straight, Michael, *After Long Silence*, Collins, 1983.
9   *Daily Telegraph*, 14 May 1986.
10 Radosh and Milton, *op cit.*
11 Werner, *op cit.*
12 Pincher, *Too Secret Too Long*, and Straight, *op cit.*
13 Straight, *op cit.*
14 Bamford, *op cit.*
15 Pincher, *Inside Story*. Radcliffe Committee Report Cmnd 1681, 1962.
16 Philby, Eleanor, *Kim Philby*, Hamish Hamilton, 1968.

Chapter 3: Types of Traitor (pages 22–33)

1   *NOW!*, 7 December 1979.
2   Lamphere, *op cit.* Colepaugh received a long prison sentence.
3   Brown, Anthony Cave, *Bodyguard of Lies*, W. H. Allen, 1976.
4   Bethell, Nicholas, *The Great Betrayal*, Hodder and Stoughton, 1984.
5   Bernikow, Louise, *Abel*, Hodder and Stoughton, 1970. Abel was exchanged for the downed American U2 pilot, Francis Gary Powers, in February 1962.
6   Eisenberg, Dennis *et alii*, *Mossad*, Paddington, 1978.
7   Dulles papers. See *The Times*, 22 March 1986.
8   Jones, R. V., *Most Secret War*, Hamish Hamilton, 1978. Arnold Kramish has named Dr Paul Rosbaud as being the author of the Oslo Report and many other secrets he allegedly passed to the British. (*The Griffin*, Houghton Mifflin, New York, 1986.)
9   Gehlen, Reinhard, *The Gehlen Memoirs*, Collins, 1972.
10 Pincher, *The Secret Offensive*.
11 Masterman, J. C., *The Double Cross System*, Granada, 1979.
12 Hayes, Paul, *Quisling*, David and Charles, 1971.
13 Gehlen, *op cit.*
14 Pincher, *Their Trade Is Treachery*. See Klatt Affair.
15 Martin, David, *Patriot or Traitor*, Hoover Institution, 1978.
16 Tolstoy, Nikolai, *The Minister and the Massacres*, Century Hutchinson, 1986.

Chapter 4: Agents of Influence (pages 34–48)

1   Martin, David, *Screening Federal Employees*, Heritage Foundation, 1983.
2   Weinstein, Allen, *Perjury*, Alfred A. Knopf, New York, 1978.
3   Gouzenko provided evidence that the GRU had a spy among the officials serving Stettinius.

4 Lamphere, *op cit.* 'KGB Connection', CBS TV 8 June 1982, filmed shortly before Hede Massing's death in 1981.
5 Colonel Boris Bykov.
6 A long list sent to the White House by Hoover is given by Dallin in *Soviet Espionage*, Yale University Press, 1955. Also see *Harry Dexter White* by David Rees, Macmillan, 1973, and *The Web of Subversion*, Day, 1959, by James Burnham.
7 Martin, *Patriot or Traitor*, and Lord Clifford of Chudleigh, House of Lords *Hansard*, 12 February 1975, col. 890.
8 Minutes of the Advisory Committee on the Examination Unit dated September 1942.
9 Various documents released under the Canadian Access to Information Act in 1986.
10 Barros, James, *No Sense of Evil*, Deneau, Canada, 1986.
11 Statements made by Lord Gladwyn.
12 Diary at Churchill College.
13 In 1974, at a meeting of security and intelligence chiefs of the CAZAB group (Canada, Australia, New Zealand, America, and Britain), the MI5 Director-General, Sir Michael Hanley, gave the evidence against Hollis so that they could take damage-limitation action if they wished.
14 Akhmedov, *op cit.*
15 Hyde, *op cit.*
16 Wright, Peter, TV programme 'World in Action', 16 July 1984.
17 Document by Pacepa supplied by the Jamestown Foundation.
18 Frolik, Josef, *The Frolik Defection*, Leo Cooper, 1975. August, Frantisek, *Red Star Over Prague*, Sherwood Press, 1984.
19 *Maclean's* (Canada), 30 September 1985.
20 Shevchenko, Arkady, *Breaking with Moscow*, Alfred A. Knopf, New York, 1985.
21 This infiltration has been in progress for many years. A fellow student of mine at the London Institute of Education in 1935 never revealed his Communism until he appeared as a lecturer in Liverpool, appealing for money for the Spanish Civil War. He then told me he had been instructed, among others, to become a secret Communist to secure a teaching job from which he could influence the young.
22 Pincher, *The Secret Offensive*.
23 *Ibid.*
24 *Soviet Active Measures*, US Government Printing Office, 1982. Petersen, *True Blues*, Joe Hill Press, 1980.
25 The statement, published in several national dailies, listed seventy-nine sponsors including Neil Kinnock.
26 See *The Protection of Military Information*, Cmnd 9112, 15 December 1983.
27 Manne, Robert, *Quadrant*, September 1985, and Morrisby, Edwin, *Quadrant*, October 1985.
28 Burchett, Wilfrid, *At the Barricades*, Quartet, 1980.
29 Morris, Stephen J., *A Scandalous Journalistic Career*, *Commentary*, November 1981.

30 The prisoner was Derek Kinne, a Briton.
31 Manne, *op cit.*
32 Deposition of Yuri Krotkov, Supreme Court of New South Wales, 193 of 1973.
33 See Pincher, *The Secret Offensive*, Chapter 1.

Chapter 5: *The Lure of Adventure and Excitement* (pages 49–55)

1   Foote, *op cit.*
2   Lamphere, *op cit.*
3   Hagen, Louis, *The Secret War for Europe*, Macdonald, 1968.
4   Soviet TV, 9 February 1985.
5   Whiteside, Thomas, *Agent in Place*, Viking Press, New York, 1966.
6   Houghton, Harry, *Operation Portland*, Hart-Davis, 1972.
7   Vassall, John, *Vassall*, Sidgwick and Jackson, 1975.
8   Bruce Lockhart, Robin, *Ace of Spies*, Hodder and Stoughton, 1967. Andrew, Christopher, *Secret Service*, William Heinemann, 1985.
9   Abse, Leo, *Spectator*, 20 March 1982. Driberg worked for MI5 for many years.
10 Whiteside, *op cit.*
11 Wickens, *op cit.*
12 Farago, *op cit.*
13 *Situation Report*, Vol. 2, No. 1.
14 Lindsey, *op cit.*
15 See Radosh, *op cit*, and Eleanor Philby, *op cit.*
16 Interview with *The Times*, 21 November 1979.

Chapter 6: *Power-Lust* (pages 56–61)

1   Hayes, *op cit.*
2   *Daily Telegraph*, 25 August 1986. *The Times*, 4 September 1986.
3   Wickens, *op cit.*
4   Rees, *op cit.*
5   Philby, Eleanor, *op cit.*
6   Interview published in *Daily Express*, 17 October 1977.

Chapter 7: *The Pull of Ideology* (pages 62–73)

1   Deriabin, Peter, and Gibney, Frank, *The Secret World*, Arthur Barker, 1960.
2   Hyde, *op cit.*
3   Canadian Royal Commission Report, 27 June 1946.
4   *Ibid.*
5   Foote, *op cit.*
6   Werner, *op cit.*
7   Straight, *op cit.*
8   *Daily Telegraph*, 25 August 1986.
9   Report of Security Commission May 1983, Cmnd 8876.

10   Report of Security Commission, May 1985, Cmnd 9514.
11   Letter from de Courcy, 18 October 1985.
12   *The Times* interview with Blunt, 21 November 1979.
13   See Pincher, *Their Trade Is Treachery*.
14   Obituary of Klugmann, *The Times*, 26 September 1977, Ferns, H. S., *Reading from Left to Right*, Toronto, 1983.
15   Pickersgill, J. W. and Foster, D. F., *The Mackenzie King Record*, Vol. 3, University of Toronto Press.
16   Foote, *op cit*.
17   Straight, *op cit*.
18   Radosh, *op cit*.
19   Kisch, *The Days of the Good Soldiers. Communists in the Armed Forces WWII*, Journeyman Press, 1985.
20   Baruch 'Bert' Ramelson was the 'industrial organizer' of the Communist Party for many years.
21   Radosh, *op cit*.
22   Information from British Army Commanders, past and present.
23   Godson, Roy, *Clandestine Collection*, National Strategy Information Centre, Washington, 1982.

Chapter 8: Money and Other Material Inducements (pages 74–88)

1   Bothwell, Robert and Granatstein, J. L., *The Gouzenko Transcripts*, Deneau, Canada, 1982.
2   Canadian Royal Commission Report, 27 June 1946.
3   Deriabin, *op cit*.
4   Sterling, Claire, *The Terror Network*, Berkley, New York, 1981.
5   *The Times*, 10 February 1986.
6   As many of these are in the North Atlantic the disclosures have, presumably, damaged Nato's anti-submarine defences.
7   In the autumn of 1945 Elizabeth Bentley, then voluntarily under FBI surveillance on a New York street, was seen to receive a package containing $2,000 from Gromov. Also see Bentley, *Out of Bondage*, New York, Devin-Adair, 1951.
8   Information from Donald Hume, the fellow prisoner.
9   Radosh, *op cit*.
10   Philby, Eleanor, *op cit*.
11   Whiteside, *op cit*.
12   The case officer was Theodore Maly.
13   *Soviet Acquisition of Militarily Significant Technology: An Update*, US Government, 1985.
14   Information from Stanislav Levchenko. See Pincher, *The Secret Offensive*.
15   Letter from Anthony Courtney, 4 September 1984.
16   *NOW!*, 7 December 1979, and Home Office files released February 1986, reported in *Daily Telegraph*, 12 February 1986.
17   After public exposure by the Canadian journalist John Sawatsky, Morrison pleaded guilty in January 1986 on being arraigned, following a

confession on Canadian TV. The Soviet traitor, code-named Gideon, was an 'illegal' using photography as a cover.

18 *The Times*, 12 January 1986. 5 June 1986.
19 Von Papen, *op cit*. Schellenberg, *The Schellenberg Memoirs*, Harper and Row, New York, 1956.
20 Suggestions that he was some sort of double cleverly feeding disinformation to the Germans is totally untrue, and may have been encouraged to cover up what was simply a disgraceful breach of Foreign Service security.
21 Andrew, *op cit*.
22 *Ibid*.
23 CIA Handbook, *The Rote Kapelle*. 'Lucy' was derived from Lucerne.
24 *Ibid*. Read, Anthony and Fisher, David, *Operation Lucy*, Coward, McCann and Geoghegan, New York, 1981.
25 Frolik, *op cit* and August, *op cit*.
26 *Daily Telegraph*, 24 August 1985, 3 September 1985, *Observer*, 1 September 1985.
27 Bingham was released on parole after serving eight years, *Daily Mail*, 30 July 1982.
28 *Times-Colonist*, 23 June 1985.
29 *Daily Telegraph*, 21 June 1986. *The Times*, 16 July 1986.
30 The sailors were quietly sentenced to hard labour and then dismissed from the service.
31 See Pincher, *Too Secret Too Long*. The case was confirmed to me and to others by former MI6 officers, including Christopher Phillpotts and Nicholas Elliott.
32 Abse, *op cit* and *The Times*, 26 October 1981.
33 Frolik, *op cit*.
34 This betrayal was the consequence of the duplicity which he claimed successfully at a French court-martial in 1948 had the full approval of British intelligence. It is even possible that the betrayal was part of an Allied deception plan to make the Germans believe that an invasion of Europe was imminent in 1943. James Rusbridger, *Bluff Deceit and Treachery*, Encounter, May 1986.

Chapter 9: *The Hetero-Sex Factor* (pages 89–102)

1 Philby, Eleanor, *op cit*.
2 See Seale, Patrick and McConville, Maureen, *Philby*, Penguin, 1978.
3 Lamphere, *op cit*. Massing, *op cit*.
4 Burnham, *op cit*.
5 Hagen, *op cit*.
6 'KGB Connection', CBS TV programme, 8 June 1982.
7 Sawatsky, John, *For Services Rendered*, Doubleday, 1982. Confirmation from RCMP source.
8 Barron, John, *KGB*, Hodder and Stoughton, 1974.
9 See Pincher, *Too Secret Too Long*.
10 Myagkov, Aleksei, *Inside the KGB*, Foreign Affairs Publishing, 1976.

11 August, *op cit.*
12 Deriabin, *op cit.*
13 Hyde, H. Montgomery, *Cynthia*, Hamish Hamilton, 1966. 'Cynthia' was born in 1910, was seduced at fourteen and married the English diplomat Arthur Pack. Later she married Charles Brousse. She died in 1963.
14 Eisenberg *et alia, op cit.*
15 *Daily Express*, 30 September 1971. Pincher, *Too Secret Too Long*.
16 Hood, *op cit.*
17 Popov, Dusko, *Spy, Counterspy*, Weidenfeld and Nicolson, 1974.
18 *Daily Telegraph*, 14 May 1986.
19 Houghton, *op cit.* The Security Officer dismissed her story as hysterical malice and was eventually retired from his post as a result.
20 Report by the Office for the Protection of the Constitution, Bonn. See *Daily Telegraph*, 11 June 1986.
21 *The Times*, 21 and 22 August 1985, *Observer*, 1 September 1985.
22 Hearing before the Subcommittee to Investigate the Administration of the Internal Security Laws, 18 November 1975. US Government Printing Office.
23 *Daily Mail*, 17 April 1984. Bettaney later consoled himself with occasional affairs – some of which, according to his statement, were with female members of the MI5 staff.
24 Philby, Eleanor, *op cit.*
25 *Ottawa Citizen*, 8 November 1985.

Chapter 10: The Homo-Sex Factor (pages 103–114)

1 Blunt, Wilfrid, *Slow on the Feather*, Russell, 1986.
2 To save embarrassment governments have not been told of what MI5 officers concerned with the case regard as the confession of this former politician who died recently.
3 Weinstein, *op cit.*
4 *The Times*, 6 May 1986, *Daily Mail*, 6 and 7 May 1986.
5 Vassall, *op cit.*
6 Hearing of 18 November 1975. US Government Printing Office, 1975.
7 See Pincher, *Their Trade Is Treachery*.
8 *Ibid.*
9 Golitsin, Anatoly, *New Lies for Old*, Bodley Head, 1984.
10 *Daily Mail*, 23 and 28 July 1982.
11 *Daily Telegraph*, 10 April 1986.
12 Sawyer, *op cit.*
13 Driberg, Tom, *Ruling Passions*, Quartet, 1978. Mervyn Stockwood, the former Bishop of Southwark, told me that he had induced Driberg to remove the most self-damaging material from the book.
14 Wickens paper.
15 Collected by Cherry Hughes.
16 Rees, Goronwy, *Chapter of Accidents*, Chatto and Windus, 1972.
17 Connolly, Cyril, *The Missing Diplomats*, Queen Anne Press, 1952.
18 Mann, Wilfrid, *Was There a Fifth Man?*, Pergamon Press, 1982.

19   This may be one reason why MI6 men searched the Marsham Court flat as soon as Oldfield was dead and removed all documents and books. They also removed all papers and letters from his hospital room.
20   *The Times*, 15 September 1986.
21   Pincher, Chapman, *Sex in our Time*, Weidenfeld and Nicolson, 1973.

Chapter 11: Non-Sexual Blackmail (pages 115–120)

1   See Pincher, *Inside Story*.
2   Conversation with Lord Harris.
3   Sawatsky, John, *Men in the Shadows*, Doubleday, 1980.
4   *The Times*, 12 September 1986. This, however, could have been an excuse, because he had received money from the East Germans for almost thirteen years of espionage assistance.
5   Conversations with Sir Richard Way.
6   Security Commission Report, November 1968, Cmnd 3856.
7   Lamphere, *op cit*.
8   Deriabin, *op cit*.
9   Lamphere, *op cit*.
10   Henkine, Cyrille, *'Les Russes Sont Arrivés*, Scarabée, Paris, 1984.
11   *Daily Express*, 4 September 1959.
12· *The Times*, 22 July 1986.
13   *Daily Telegraph*, 11 June 1986.
14   Golitsin, *op cit*.
15   Not knowing this, MI6 took Hooper back to use as a double against the Germans, which the latter quickly detected. See Farago, *op cit*.

Chapter 12: The Influence of Background (pages 121–132)

1   Hollis, Christopher, *Along the Road to Frome*, Harrap, 1958. Moberly, C. A. E., *Dulce Domum*, John Murray, 1911.
2   Sonia has stated that she became a Communist after reading Lenin's book, *The State and Revolution*, when she was a child. Interview on Soviet TV, 9 February 1985 (BBC transcript).
3   FBI Report Foocase – Espionage (R), 4 June 1950.
4   Bowen, Roger, *E. H. Norman. His Life and Scholarship*, University of Toronto Press, 1984.
5   Philby, Eleanor, *op cit*.
6   Weinstein, *op cit*.
7   Security Commission Report, May 1983, Cmnd 8876.
8   Abse, *op cit*.
9   Blunt, Wilfrid, *op cit*.
10   Bowen, *op cit*.
11   Hollis, Christopher, *The Seven Ages*, William Heinemann, 1974.
12   Cowling, Maurice, *Assaults on the Assailants*, 1986.
13   Security Commission Report, May 1985, Cmnd 9514.
14   Hyde, *op cit*.
15   Bowen, *op cit*.

16 FBI Item 3220.
17 Letter from William Jaeger, an MRA witness.
18 Koestler, Arthur, *Arrow in the Blue*, 1952.
19 Hyde, *op cit*.
20 *Ibid*.
21 Barros, *op cit*.
22 Gill, *op cit*.

Chapter 13: Vulnerable Professions: The Impact of Access (pages 133–144)

1 Various personal contacts. See also *Globe and Mail* (Canada), 14 September 1985.
2 Conversation with Admiral Turner.
3 See Pincher, *Inside Story*.
4 *Secrecy and Foreign Policy*, edited by Thomas Franck and Edward Weisband, Oxford University Press, 1974.
5 Federal Government's Security Clearance Programs, S. Rept 99–230, 1986.
6 For this serious offence Kent was sentenced to seven years' imprisonment.
7 Radosh, *op cit*.
8 See Philby, Kim, *My Silent War*.
9 Mann, *op cit*.
10 *Daily Telegraph*, 29 November 1984.
11 See Pincher, *Too Secret Too Long*.
12 *Sunday Telegraph Magazine*, 11 May 1986.
13 Letter and conversations with Mrs Trevor, who regards this experience as additional evidence that Blake had been recruited by the Soviets long before his alleged 'brain-washing' in Korea.
14 *The Times*, 10 November 1986.

Chapter 14: Vulnerable Professions: Defence, Diplomacy, Politics and Science (pages 145–157)

1 Ind, Allison, *A History of Modern Espionage*, Hodder and Stoughton, 1965.
2 See Pincher, *Too Secret Too Long*.
3 Corson, William and Crowley, Robert, *The New KGB*, William Morrow, New York, 1985.
4 Material supplied by the Jamestown Foundation.
5 Gordon W. Creighton. Letter and conversations.
6 Sir Michael Perrin.
7 Canadian Royal Commission Report, 1946.
8 It has been stated that Fuchs did not give the Russians information about the thermonuclear (hydrogen) bomb. But Donald Hume, his fellow prisoner and friend in Wakefield Prison, who made notes of his conversations with Fuchs and provided them to me, claimed that Fuchs told him that he had begun giving the Russians his limited knowledge

about the hydrogen bomb in 1947, telling them of the initiation of the American project and additional information as it came into his hands. He said that he first gave the Russians some of the theoretical mechanics for triggering the H-bomb in 1948 when they urgently pressed him for more information.

9 Information from Donald Hume.
10 More convincing perhaps is the experience of the USSR, where science has been closely applied to political and economic problems. This has not led to economic or agricultural success, and science has been monstrously misapplied for political purposes as, for example, in the notorious Lysenko episode.
11 Evidence to Franks Committee. Report 1972.
12 Hageb, *op cit.*
13 Romerstein, Herbert in Godson *Counter-Intelligence*, National Strategy Information Center, Washington, 1980.
14 See Pincher, *Inside Story.*
15 See references to Schuman and Dzhirkvelov in Pincher, *The Secret Offensive.*
16 See *Citizen*, Ottawa, 31 July 1986.
17 CBS TV programme, 'The KGB Connection', 8 June 1982.
18 The evidence was superbly analysed by Mr C. Cunningham, a psychologist, in an address to the Medico-Legal Society in London on 11 January 1973.
19 Information from George Brown.
20 E. Gomori. Rejtett Szolgalat, *CIA*, Kozmosz, Budapest, 1979. This could be disinformation.
21 Report of Inquiry by David Calcutt, QC, *The Times*, 23 May 1986.

Chapter 15: Personality Traits (pages 158–165)

1 Popov, Dusko, *op cit.*
2 Description by Lady Llewelyn-Davies.
3 For example, Lord Clifford and Julian Amery.
4 Bowen, *op cit.*
5 Muggeridge, *op cit.*
6 Mann, *op cit.*
7 Information from Nicholas Elliott.
8 Philby, Eleanor, *op cit.*
9 Mann, *op cit.*
10 Connolly, *op cit.*
11 Philby, Eleanor, *op cit.*
12 *The Times*, 16 July 1986.
13 Blunt, Wilfrid, *op cit.*
14 Rothschild, *Random Variables*, Collins, 1984.
15 Akhmedov, *op cit.*
16 Philby, Eleanor, *op cit.*
17 Montgomery Hyde, who was one of them, has gone on record as accepting the evidence.

18   Bourke, Sean, *The Springing of George Blake*, Cassell, 1970.
19   Information from a mutual Canadian friend.
20   Lamphere, *op cit.*
21   See Pincher, *Too Secret Too Long*.

Chapter 16: Defects of Character (pages 166–174)

1   See Pincher, *Their Trade Is Treachery*.
2   Blunt, Wilfrid, *op cit.*
3   Told to me by Robertson who reported the episode to those who should
     have taken note of it. None was taken.
4   See Allen, Peter, *The Crown and the Swastika*, Robert Hale, 1983.
5   Letter from Professor Wickens, 18 October 1985.
6   Wickens, *op cit.* Long's vanity and social climbing has been confirmed
     to me by Professor Harry Ferns, who also knew him at Cambridge.
7   *Sunday Times*, 1 November 1981.
8   Documents supplied by Donald Hume.
9   *Daily Telegraph*, 2 August 1982 and letters between Nicholas Winterton,
     MP, and Lord Hailsham, the Lord Chancellor, September 1982.
10   Eisenberg *et alia*, *op cit.*
11   Wright, Christopher, *The Art of the Forger*, Fraser, 1984.
12   Reply to question in the Canadian Parliament by Tom Cossitt, 14 April
     1980.
13   *Daily Mail*, 23 June 1982.
14   See Pincher, *Inside Story*. Also information from Mackenzie's widow and
     Scotland Yard.
15   Security Commission Report, May 1983, Cmnd 8876.
16   Letter from Noel Currer-Briggs, 12 March 1982.
17   Thwaites, Michael, *Truth Will Out*, Collins, 1980.
18   Whiteside, *op cit.*
19   *The Times*, 15 September 1986.
20   *Daily Telegraph*, 30 August 1985. The chief was Heribert Hellenbroich.
21   Turner, Stansfield, *op cit.*
22   *The Times*, 30 May 1986.

Chapter 17: Drink and Drugs (pages 175–180)

1   Lamphere, *op cit.*
2   Bernikow, *op cit.* Hayhanen is believed to have died from cirrhosis of the
     liver.
3   Rees, Goronwy, *op cit.*
4   Kuusinen, Aino, *Before and After Stalin*, Michael Joseph, 1974.
5   *Asiaweek*, 29 April 1983. Evidence of Sorge's former mistress, Hanako.
6   See Pincher, *Too Secret Too Long*.
7   Hood, *op cit.*
8   Letter from Gordon Creighton, 31 March 1981.
9   Mann, *op cit.*
10   Buck, Jerry, *Savannah Evening Press*, 1 November 1984.

11 Rothschild, Lord, *Random Variables*, Collins, 1984.
12 Radosh, *op cit.*
13 Philby, Eleanor, *op cit.*
14 *Observer*, 1 September 1985.
15 Security Commission Report, Cmnd 9514.
16 *Sunday Times*, 14 December 1986.
17 Lindsey, *op cit.*
18 Intelligence Report American Bar Association, Vol. 7, No. 8, August 1985.
19 Lindsey, *op cit.*
20 *Humint* report on a Soviet textbook on 'Psychopolitics', Vol. IV, Issues 16–20.

Chapter 18: Spetsnaz Traitors (pages 181–190)

1 For *spetsaznacheniya*, i.e. special designation forces.
2 For general information on *Spetsnaz* forces, see Suvorov, Viktor, *Soviet Military Intelligence*, Grafton, 1986. *Inside the Aquarium*, Macmillan, 1986.
3 Canadian Royal Commission Report, 1946.
4 *Daily Mail*. Report from Washington, 9 August 1986.
5 Defence Ministry Briefings. Greenham Common ref *Daily Telegraph*, 23 January 1986.
6 Suvorov, Viktor, *Inside the Aquarium*.
7 International Defence Review, June 1984.
8 No comparable facilities are available to British and West European sailors visiting the Soviet Union.
9 The facilities are Soviet-controlled fuel and timber outlets etc.
10 Sejna, Jan, *op cit.*
11 Hood, *op cit.*
12 Akhmedov, *op cit.*
13 *Soviet Active Measures*, US Government Printing Office, 1982.
14 Information from former Commander Rhine Army.
15 National Committee to Restore Internal Security, Vol. XIII, Hearing of 20 May 1986.
16 See *Daily Express*, 23 April 1976. Written answer by Anthony Crosland, *Hansard* 30 April 1976, col. 198. The incident was played down by the then Labour administration to avoid admitting what the Hungarians had really been doing.
17 John Blomfield, *Marxism Today*, June 1983.
18 Lord Slim.

Chapter 19: Terrorists as Traitors (pages 191–196)

1 Speech in Grantham, *The Times*, 27 April 1986.
2 Under the 1814 Treason Act the death penalty for treason by hanging remains in force. *The Times*, 27 April 1986.
3 Sterling, Claire, *The Terror Network*, Berkley, New York, 1981.
4 *Law and National Security*, Intelligence Report, Vol. 8, No. 7, July 1986.

5 See *Daily Telegraph*, 7 February 1986 and *Observer*, 9 February 1986.
6 The racehorse, Shergar, is understood to have been abducted and killed because the owners declined to pay protection money to the IRA.
7 *Law and National Security*, Intelligence Report, Vol. 8, No. 7, July 1986.
8 Gordon, Colonel Don, *Journal of Defense and Diplomacy*, March 1986.
9 Sterling, *op cit.*
10 Sejna, *op cit.*
11 Schuman, Tomas D., *Novosti Press Agency, KGB Front for Active Measures against the Free Media*. Interview supplied by Sir James Goldsmith.
12 Gordon, *op cit.*
13 *Humint* Network Report, January/February 1986.

Chapter 20: Defectors (pages 197–224)

1 Akhmedov, *op cit.*
2 Myagkov, *op cit.*
3 *Annals*, Bk 1.
4 Brook-Shepherd, Gordon, *The Storm Petrels*, Collins, 1977. I have independent confirmation.
5 Information from Lord Rawlinson.
6 Philby, Eleanor, the Lonsdale book was called *Spy* (Spearman, 1965).
7 Hood, *op cit.*
8 Gouzenko, Igor, *This Was My Choice*, Palm, Montreal, 1968.
9 In a telephone conversation shortly before he died Gouzenko said: 'What my case shows is that unless a defector has genuine Russian documents nobody believes him.'
10 Bokhan named five Greeks as Soviet agents. Greek police later charged a 35-year-old naval officer and two businessmen with passing defence secrets and equipment to the Soviets. The naval officer, Lieutenant Vassilis Serepisios, was acquitted by a Greek court martial for lack of independent corroboration. *The Times*, 17 April 1986.
11 Statement by Matuzok supplied by the Jamestown Foundation.
12 Bourke, *op cit.* Kevin O'Connor has a copy of the tape.
13 Myagkov, *op cit.*
14 The Nosenko case is the best-known example. See Henry Hurt, *Shadrin*, Reader's Digest Press, 1981.
15 Shevchenko, Arkady, *Breaking with Moscow*, Alfred A. Knopf, 1985.
16 Statement by Ushakov supplied by the Jamestown Foundation.
17 Akhmedov, *op cit.*
18 Deriabin, *op cit.*
19 Myagkov, *op cit.*
20 *Soviet Active Measures*, US Government Printing Office, 1982.
21 Statement supplied by the Jamestown Foundation. Similar reasons have been given by defectors from Soviet satellites. The Romanian, Petre Nicolae, for example, described Communism as 'the greatest charade in human history', and questioned the ideology of a system which could have produced Stalin.
22 Statement supplied by the Jamestown Foundation.

23 Unreferenced CIA document on Yurchenko.
24 Statement made by Yurchenko at his press conference in Washington, 4 November 1985.
25 See *Daily Telegraph*, 19 September 1984. Duff Hart-Davis, *Sunday Telegraph*, 23 September 1984 and 22 September 1985.
26 Unreferenced CIA statement on Yurchenko.
27 *Daily Mail*, 25 March 1986.
28 *The Times*, 13 March 1986.
29 Cave Brown and MacDonald, *op cit.*
30 Burnham, *op cit.*
31 Weinstein, *op cit.*
32 Statement by Pacepa supplied by the Jamestown Foundation.
33 '20/20 Vision' programme, 12 April 1986.
34 Letter from the friend, Peter Worthington, 27 July 1985.
35 The defector was Anton Sabotka. See *Toronto Sun*, 24 August 1980. Sabotka appeared on Canadian TV.
36 Letter from Sir Dick White.
37 See Martin, David C., *Wilderness of Mirrors*, Harper and Row, New York, 1980.
38 Philby explained this control to his wife as the KGB's fear that he might be assassinated by the CIA or MI6 but this seemed so remote as to be untrue. See Philby, Eleanor, *op cit.*
39 Suvorov, *Inside the Aquarium*. The figure is an exaggeration.
40 Hurt, *op cit.*
41 Describing Vladimir Kuzichkin to me, an American intelligence officer remarked: 'If there are many more like him in the KGB then we sure have a problem.'
42 Hurt, *op cit.* Yurchenko is said to have told the CIA that Shadrin was kidnapped in Vienna and killed in error, possibly in a struggle.
43 *Newsday*, 18 December 1985.
44 For example, the lie that Eisenhower refused to reprieve Ethel Rosenberg because the Russians would then use only women as spies. This was a KGB fabrication. See Lamphere, *op cit.*
45 Henry Hurt. See *Reader's Digest*, October 1982.
46 *Newsweek*, 18 November 1985.
47 *Savannah Evening Press*, 1 November 1984.
48 Philby, Eleanor, *op cit.*

Chapter 21: What Treachery Does To Traitors (pages 225–241)

1 From Bertold Brecht's Play, *The Measures Taken*.
2 See Tolstoy, Nikolai, *Stalin's Secret War*, Jonathan Cape, 1981. Kuusinen, *op cit.*
3 *Ottawa Citizen*, 27 May 1986.
4 According to Lamphere, *op cit.*, Hollis was the culprit.
5 Philby, Eleanor, *op cit.*
6 Barros, *op cit.*
7 *New York Times*, 22 February 1986.

8   Blunt, Wilfrid, *op cit.*
9   Hyde, *op cit.*
10 *The Times*, 30 August 1986.
11 Blunt, Wilfrid, *op cit.*
12 Philby, Eleanor, *op cit.*
13 Farago, *op cit.*
14 Letter from Anthony Courtney, 4 September 1984.
15 Introduction to Philby, Kim, *My Silent War.*
16 Rothschild, *op cit.*
17 For example, Montgomery Hyde in his review of *Too Secret Too Long* in *Books and Bookmen.*
18 Statements from Donald Hume and two other prisoners.
19 Radosh, *op cit.*
20 Lamphere, *op cit.*, and Fuchs's comments to Hume.
21 See Blunt, Wilfrid, *op cit*: 'It was the rage of a man who had been found out.'
22 Hayhanen quoted in Bernikow, *op cit.*
23 *The Times*, 9 October 1986.
24 Whiteside, *op cit.*
25 Blunt, Wilfrid, *op cit.*
26 Bentley, Elizabeth, *op cit.*
27 The operation was called 'Party Piece'. 'World in Action', Granada TV, 16 July 1984.
28 Commission of Inquiry Concerning Certain Activities of the Royal Canadian Mounted Police 1981.
29 While some illegalities are overlooked in the UK (but far less than previously) the CIA is now required to operate within the law.
30 *New Society*, 14 June 1984.
31 Oddly enough, while treachery has substantial impact on international relations, international law has little to say about it. All espionage operations abroad violate the laws of the target countries, yet all nations acquiesce in permitting spies posing as diplomats etc. to be present.
32 'World in Action', 16 July 1984.
33 Barros, *op cit.*
34 He received a sentence of only eight years because of his contrite confession. Another trained KGB assassin, Nikolai Khokhlov, sent to Frankfurt to assassinate another *émigré*, could not even go ahead with his first murder and defected instead.
35 See Meyer, Cord, in Godson, *Clandestine Collection*, National Strategy Information Center, Inc, 1982.
36 *Daily Telegraph*, 30 July 1982.

Chapter 22: *How Traitors Survive* (pages 242–257)

1   Houghton, *op cit.*
2   The defector was Michal Goleniewski.
3   See Lamphere, *op cit*, and Pincher, *Too Secret Too Long*.

4 See Solomon, Flora and Litvinoff, Barnet, *Baku to Baker Street*. The facts are given more fully in Pincher, *Too Secret Too Long*.

5 Lamphere, *op cit*.

6 Information from Anthony Cavendish, formerly of MI6.

7 Rees, Goronwy, *op cit*.

8 Boyle, Andrew, *The Climate of Treason*, Coronet, 1980.

9 *The Times*, 12 July 1984. Blunt's statement was allegedly made to the former diplomat, Robert Cecil.

10 Penrose, Barry and Freeman, Simon, *Conspiracy of Silence*, 1986.

11 FBI Report of Hugh H. Clegg and Robert J. Lamphere covering interviews with Klaus Fuchs in London, 4 June 1950. Foocase – Espionage (R).

12 US Tripartite Talks document, 19–21 June 1950.

13 To be published in 1987. Professor Williams is now at Davidson College, North Carolina.

14 Hyde, *op cit*.

15 See Wigg, *George Wigg*, Michael Joseph, 1972.

16 Lamphere, *op cit*.

17 Information from Peter Wright.

18 This information is taken from the remarkable book, *The Storm Petrels*, by Gordon Brook-Shepherd. (Collins 1977.) My inquiries have satisfied me that Brook-Shepherd was given access to the contents of the report of the MI5 debriefing of Krivitsky by the MI5 officer Jane Archer.

19 Lamphere, *op cit*.

20 Barros, *op cit*. Also letters from Barros dated 9 May and 3 June 1986. According to Peter Wright, Golitsin provided evidence pointing strongly to Pearson, but the RCMP declined to believe it.

21 Burnham, *op cit*.

22 Lamphere, *op cit*. Lamphere believes the culprit to be Hollis.

23 For example, Joel Barr and Al Sarant.

24 Lamphere, *op cit*.

25 Letter to me from Svetlana Gouzenko, dated 6 March 1983.

26 Sawatsky, John, *For Services Rendered*, Doubleday, 1982. Under British law also a secret service officer or civil servant cannot be deprived of his pension rights unless he is prosecuted and convicted.

Chapter 23: How Traitors Are Exposed (pages 258–263)

1 Lindsey, *op cit*.

2 *The Times*, 12 September 1986.

3 Pincher, *Too Secret Too Long*.

4 *Ibid* and Lamphere, *op cit*.

5 Lamphere, *op cit*.

6 Information from an FBI source.

7 *Daily Telegraph*, 29 October 1986.

Chapter 24: Why Traitors Confess (pages 264–275)

1 Whiteside, *op cit.*
2 Vassall, *op cit.*
3 Radosh, *op cit.*
4 According to the former Deputy-Director of MI6, George Young.
5 The friend was Tom Black. Radosh, *op cit.*
6 Foote, *op cit.*
7 Hagen, Louis, *The Secret War for Europe*, Macdonald, 1968. Golitsin, *op cit*, says that Bandera was killed on Shelepin's orders.
8 Straight, *op cit.*
9 Deriabin, *op cit.*
10 Mrs Kuusinen, who managed to reach the West in total disillusion with Soviet Communism in 1966, put her experiences on record in *Before and After Stalin* (Michael Joseph, 1974). It is an indictment of a barbaric system by a very brave woman.
11 Philby, Eleanor, *op cit.*
12 See Pincher, *Too Secret Too Long*, and Lamphere, *op cit.*
13 Report by David Calcutt, QC. *The Times*, 23 May 1986. *Daily Mail*, 29 October 1985.
14 Letters and conversation with James Bennett.
15 See Pincher, *Too Secret Too Long*. The information was supplied by an MI5 officer involved in it.
16 The Ellis case had been entirely suppressed until *Their Trade Is Treachery* was published in 1981.
17 *Soviet Atomic Espionage*, US Government Printing Office, April 1951.
18 Vassall, *op cit.*
19 *Situation Report*, US Security and Intelligence Fund. Vol. 2, No. 1, July 1979.
20 Report of Security Commission, May 1983, Cmnd 8876.
21 Information from Peter Wright. The controller was Yuri Modin.
22 Abse, *The Times*, 26 October 1981.
23 Martin, David, *Screening Federal Employees*, Heritage Foundation, 1983.
24 Conversations with Heaps.
25 See remarks by James Callaghan in the Blunt debate, 21 November 1979. Desmond J. Trenner, *The Times*, 13 November 1981.
26 Conversations with Merlyn Rees and others.
27 Straight, *op cit.* Solomon, *op cit.*
28 There is clear evidence that Philby's 'memoirs', in which he admitted various acts of treachery with glee, were written in Russian and then translated into English. They made the mistake of referring to the Vauxhall underground station which has never existed, this being a clumsy translation of the Russian word *vokzal* meaning station.

Chapter 25: Lessons To Be Learned (pages 276–295)

1 Cmnd 8540. Statement on the Recommendations of the Security Commission. The Prime Minister stated: 'The Commission makes it clear

that . . . the occasion of this reference to it was publication of a book which dealt with a number of cases of proven or suspected disclosure of sensitive information to Soviet bloc intelligence services. . . .'

2 *The Times*, 13 November 1985.
3 Martin, David, *Screening Federal Employees*, Heritage Foundation, 1983.
4 *The Times*, 16 and 17 September 1978.
5 Sterling, *op cit*.
6 *The Times*, 5 January 1985.
7 Turner, Stansfield, *op cit*.
8 Interview with Stillwell, *Human Events*, 22 March 1986.
9 Security Commission Report, May 1985, Cmnd 9514.
10 *Daily Telegraph*, 25 August 1986.
11 Dean Van Vleck of Harvard.
12 Hersh, Seymour, *The Target is Destroyed*, Faber and Faber, 1986.
13 House of Lords Debate, 23 April 1985.
14 US Senate Hearings, April 1985.
15 For details of the four-year build-up of the case against Zakharov by the FBI, see USIS document, dated 25 September 1986.
16 See *Soviet Presence in the UN Secretariat*. Report of the Senate Select Committee on Intelligence, US Government Printing Office, 1985.
17 In 1985 fifty Russians were employed in the administrative section, five in the commercial section, two in the defence section. Others worked as drivers and domestic staff.
18 *Sunday Telegraph*, 29 December 1985.
19 Turner, Stansfield, *op cit*.
20 *Domestic Security*, National Committee to Restore Internal Security, 20 May 1986.
21 See Pincher, *Too Secret Too Long*.

Select Bibliography

Akhmedov, Ismail, *In and Out of Stalin's GRU*, Arms & Armour Press, 1984.
Andrew, Christopher, *Secret Service*, Heinemann, 1985.
Bamford, James, *The Puzzle Palace*, Sidgwick & Jackson, 1983.
Barron, John, *KGB Today: The Hidden Hand*, Coronet, 1984.
Barros, James, *No Sense of Evil*, Deneau, Canada, 1986.
Bentley, Elizabeth, *Out of Bondage*, Devin-Adair, New York, 1951.
Bernikow, Louise, *Abel*, Hodder & Stoughton, 1970.
Bethell, Nicholas, *The Great Betrayal*, Hodder & Stoughton, 1984.
Bourke, Sean, *The Springing of George Blake*, Cassell, 1970.
Brook-Shepherd, Gordon, *The Storm Petrels*, Collins, 1977.
Brown, J. A. C., *Techniques of Persuasion*, Pelican, 1963.
Bulloch, John, *Akin to Treason*, Arthur Barker, 1966.
Burchett, Wilfred, *At the Barricades*, Quartet, 1980.
Burn, Michael, *The Debatable Land*, Hamish Hamilton, 1970.
Burnham, James, *The Web of Subversion*, John Day, New York, 1959.
Canadian Royal Commission Report, 27 June 1946.
CIA Handbook, *The Rote Kapelle*, University Publications of America Inc., 1982.
Corson, William R. and Crowley, Robert T., *The New KGB*, Morrow, New York, 1985.
Dallin, David J., *Soviet Espionage*, Yale University Press, 1955.
Deriabin, Peter and Gibney, Frank, *The Secret World*, Arthur Barker, 1960.
Driberg, Tom, *Guy Burgess*, Weidenfeld & Nicolson, 1956.
Farago, Ladislav, *The Game of Foxes*, Hodder & Stoughton, 1972.
Fromm, Erich, *The Fear of Freedom*, Routledge & Kegan Paul, 1942.
Gill, William J., *The Ordeal of Otto Otepka*, Arlington House, New York, 1969.
Godson, Roy (ed.), *Intelligence Requirements for the 1980s* (seven volumes), National Strategy Information Center, Inc., New York.
Golitsin, Anatoly, *New Lies for Old*, Bodley Head, 1984.
Hagen, Louis, *The Secret War for Europe*, Macdonald, 1968.
Hamilton, Iain, *Koestler*, Secker & Warburg, 1982.
Hayes, Paul M., *Quisling*, David & Charles, 1971.
Heaps, Leo, *Hugh Hambleton, Spy*, Methuen, 1983.

Hood, William, *Mole*, Weidenfeld & Nicolson, 1982.

Hurt, Henry, *Shadrin*, Reader's Digest Press, 1981.

Hurt, Henry, *Reasonable Doubt*, Sidgwick & Jackson, 1986.

Hyde, Douglas, *I Believed*, Heinemann, 1951.

Krivitsky, W. G., *I Was Stalin's Agent*, Hamish Hamilton, 1939.

Kuusinen, Aino, *Before and After Stalin*, Michael Joseph, 1974.

Lamphere, Robert J. and Shachtman, Tom, *The FBI–KGB War*, Random House, New York, 1986.

Laqueur, Walter, *World of Secrets*, Weidenfeld & Nicolson, 1985.

Lindsey, Robert, *The Falcon and the Snowman*, Simon & Schuster, New York, 1979.

Mann, Wilfrid, *Was There a Fifth Man?*, Pergamon, 1982.

Martin, David, *Patriot or Traitor? The Case of General Mihailovich*, Hoover Institution, Stanford, 1978.

Martin, David, *Screening Federal Employees*, Heritage Foundation, Washington, 1983.

Masterman, Sir John, *The Double Cross System*, Yale University Press, 1972.

Moss, Robert, *Urban Guerrillas*, Temple Smith, 1972.

Philby, Eleanor, *Kim Philby*, Hamish Hamilton, 1968.

Pincher, Chapman, *Inside Story*, Sidgwick & Jackson, 1978.

Pincher, Chapman, *Their Trade Is Treachery*, Sidgwick & Jackson, 1981.

Pincher, Chapman, *Too Secret Too Long*, Sidgwick & Jackson, 1984.

Pincher, Chapman, *The Secret Offensive*, Sidgwick & Jackson, 1985.

Popov, Dusko, *Spy, Counter-Spy*, Weidenfeld & Nicolson, 1974.

Powers, Thomas, *The Man Who Kept the Secrets*, Weidenfeld & Nicolson, 1980.

Radosh, Ronald and Milton, Joyce, *The Rosenberg File*, Holt, Rinehart & Winston, New York, 1983.

Read, Anthony and Fisher, David, *Operation Lucy*, Coward, McCann & Geoghegan, New York, 1981.

Rees, David, *Harry Dexter White*, Macmillan, 1973.

Revel, Jean-François, *How Democracies Perish*, Doubleday, New York, 1983.

Richelson, Jeffrey T. and Ball, Desmond, *The Ties that Bind*, Allen & Unwin, 1985.

Sargant, William, *Battle for the Mind*, Heinemann, 1957.

Sawatsky, John, *Men in the Shadows*, Doubleday, Canada, 1980.

Sawatsky, John, *For Services Rendered*, Doubleday, Canada, 1982.

Sawyer, Roger, *Casement: The Flawed Hero*, Routledge & Kegan Paul, 1985.

Sejna, Jan, *We Will Bury You*, Sidgwick & Jackson, 1982.

Sejna, Jan and Douglass, Joseph D., *Decision-Making in Communist Countries: An Inside View*, Pergamon–Brassey's, 1986.

Seth, Ronald, *The Spy Who Wasn't Caught*, Hale, 1966.

Silber, J. C., *Invisible Weapons*, Hutchinson, 1932.

Sterling, Claire, *The Terror Network*, Berkley, New York, 1982.

Suvorov, Viktor, *Soviet Military Intelligence*, Hamish Hamilton, 1984.

Suvorov, Viktor, *Inside the Aquarium*, Macmillan, New York, 1986.

Thwaites, Michael, *Truth Will Out*, Collins, 1980.

Turner, Stansfield, *Secrecy and Democracy*, Sidgwick & Jackson, 1985.

Vassall, John, *Vassall*, Sidgwick & Jackson, 1975.
Von Papen, Franz, *Memoirs*, Deutsch, 1952.
Weinstein, Allen, *Perjury*, Knopf, New York, 1978.
Werner, Ruth (Ursula Kuczynski), *Sonja's Rapport*, Verlag Neues Leben, Berlin, 1982.
West, Rebecca, *The New Meaning of Treason*, Viking, New York, 1964.

Index

341